EMPOWERMENT AND DISEMPOWERMENT OF THE EUROPEAN CITIZEN

This collection of essays engages with a central theme in scholarship on EU citizenship – the emancipation of certain citizens, the alienation of others – and seeks to expand its horizons to interrogate whether similar debates and trends can be identified in other fields of European integration. The focus of the book is distinctly citizen focused. It delivers the potential for the opening out of analysis of the implications of European citizenship beyond the parameters of Articles 18–25 TFEU and beyond the disciplinary confines of legal analysis alone. The book construes 'EU citizenship' in its broadest sense, and explores the extent to which the European citizen is, or indeed is not, genuinely at the heart of EU law and policy-making. Within the broader theme of empowerment and disempowerment, the contributors reflect on a range of cross-cutting themes: for example, the extent to which channels of citizen participation (can) inform EU policy-making in a 'bottom-up' sense; or whether the EU is a catalyst for the construction of new spaces and new identities.

Volume 35 in the series Modern Studies in European Law

Modern Studies in European Law
Recent titles in this series:

Reflexive Governance: Redefining the Public Interest in a Pluralistic World *Edited by Olivier De Schutter and Jacques Lenoble*

The Impact of EU Law on Minority Rights *Tawhida Ahmed*

Direct Investment, National Champions and EU Treaty Freedoms: From Maastricht to Lisbon *Frank S Benyon*

The Cyprus Issue: The Four Freedoms in a Member State under Siege *Nikos Skoutaris*

The European Union and Global Emergencies: A Law and Policy Analysis
Edited by Antonis Antoniadis, Robert Schütze and Eleanor Spaventa

Public Liability in EU Law: *Brasserie, Bergaderm* and Beyond
Pekka Aalto

Professional Services in the EU Internal Market: Quality Regulation and Self-Regulation
Tinne Heremans

Environmental Integration in the EU's External Relations: Beyond Multilateral Dimensions
Gracia Marín Durán and Elisa Morgera

The Constitutional Dimension of European Criminal Law
Ester Herlin-Karnell

EU Counter-Terrorism Law: Pre-Emption and the Rule of Law
Cian Murphy

Children and the European Union: Rights, Welfare and Accountability
Helen Stalford

Federalism in the European Union
Edited by Elke Cloots, Geert De Baere and Stefan Sottiaux

Toward a Prosecutor for the European Union Volume 1: A Comparative Analysis
Edited by Katalin Ligeti

For the complete list of titles in this series, see 'Modern Studies in European Law' link at www.hartpub.co.uk/books/series.asp

Empowerment and Disempowerment of the European Citizen

Edited by
Michael Dougan
Niamh Nic Shuibhne
and
Eleanor Spaventa

·HART·
PUBLISHING

OXFORD AND PORTLAND, OREGON
2012

Published in the United Kingdom by Hart Publishing Ltd
16C Worcester Place, Oxford, OX1 2JW
Telephone: +44 (0)1865 517530
Fax: +44 (0)1865 510710
E-mail: mail@hartpub.co.uk
Website: http://www.hartpub.co.uk

Published in North America (US and Canada) by
Hart Publishing
c/o International Specialized Book Services
920 NE 58th Avenue, Suite 300
Portland, OR 97213-3786
USA
Tel: +1 503 287 3093 or toll-free: (1) 800 944 6190
Fax: +1 503 280 8832
E-mail: orders@isbs.com
Website: http://www.isbs.com

British Library Cataloguing in Publication Data
Data Available

ISBN: 978-1-84946-235-8

Typeset by Hope Services, Abingdon
Printed and bound in Great Britain by
TJ International Ltd, Padstow, Cornwall

FSC
www.fsc.org
MIX
Paper from responsible sources
FSC® C013056

Acknowledgements

The chapters in this collection derive from four workshops. Three events – held in Durham, Liverpool and Edinburgh during the course of 2010 – were very generously supported by the Europa Institute at the University of Edinburgh. The Institute's generosity even extended to covering the costs associated with reorganising the Liverpool workshop after its last-minute cancellation due to the Icelandic volcano, and with assisting travellers to and from Edinburgh whose plans were seriously disrupted by the UK's unexpectedly bad snow storms later that year. The final event – held in Liverpool in May 2011 – was funded by the European Commisison Representation in the United Kingdom and the University Association for Contemporary European Studies. Although that seminar was not originally planned together with the other events, the complementary nature of its subject matter as regards the previous workshops made a strong case for combining the papers together. We are indebted to our authors for so kindly agreeing to write up their workshop presentations for this edited collection (and in many cases, also acting as chairs and discussants at other workshops in the series).

A key objective underpinning this project was to create an early-career researcher community across our three institutions. Our PhD discussants – Ross Carrick, Tom Flynn, Thomas Horsley (PhD, Edinburgh); Bleddyn Davies, Eleanor Drywood, James Organ, Felix Pause (PhD, Liverpool); Jaclyn Booth, Catherine Taroni, Nadine Zipperle (PhD, Durham) – enriched the project even more than we anticipated. Several of them have now successfully defended their theses and gone on to academic and other careers. We were delighted also to welcome Roderic O'Gorman (PhD, Trinity College Dublin) and Paula Ploscar (PhD, University of Antwerp), who found us via our project website; as well as Silvia Renza (PhD, University of Rome Tor Vergata and Visiting Research Fellow at Liverpool). Thanks also to our other academic colleagues who performed various essential roles such as chairing sessions and acting as discussants (Nina Miller, Andrew Scott, Jo Shaw: Edinburgh; Fiona Beveridge, Samantha Currie: Liverpool). We wish particularly to extend our gratitude to Jens Nymand-Christensen (Director of the Secretariat-General, European Commission) for coming to speak in Liverpool at the 2011 workshop. We also very much appreciate the administrative support that made all three workshop events so successful and enjoyable; thanks to Lorna Gallagher (Edinburgh), Kayte Coyne (Liverpool) and Julie Platten (Durham). And, of course, our deep gratitude goes to all the team at Hart Publishing – whose commitment, support and patience we have come to expect, but never to take for granted.

Contents

Contributors

Fabian Amtenbrink, Professor of European Union Law, Erasmus University Rotterdam

Luis Bouza García, Doctoral Researcher, Robert Gordon University, Aberdeen

Deirdre Curtin, Professor of European Law and Director of the Amsterdam Centre of European Law and Governance at the University of Amsterdam and Professor of European and International Governance at the Utrecht School of Governance

Bruno De Witte, Professor of European Union law, Maastricht University and part-time professor at the Robert Schuman Centre of the European University Institute, Florence

Michael Dougan, Professor of European Law and Jean Monnet Chair in EU Law, University of Liverpool

Michelle Everson, Professor of Law, Birkbeck, University of London

Ester Herlin-Karnell, Assistant Professor in EU law, VU University, Amsterdam

Niamh Nic Shuibhne, Professor of European Union Law, University of Edinburgh

Charlotte O'Brien, Lecturer in Law, University of York

Síofra O'Leary, Référendaire at the Court of Justice of the European Union and Visiting Professor, College of Europe (Bruges)

Anastasia Iliopoulou Penot, Professor of Public Law, University of Orléans

Matt Qvortrup, Senior Lecturer in Comparative Politics, Cranfield University

Joanne Scott, Professor of European Law, University College London

Graham Smith, Professor of Politics, University of Southampton

Eleanor Spaventa, Professor of European Law, Durham University

Helen Stalford, Reader in Law, University of Liverpool

Introduction

MICHAEL DOUGAN, NIAMH NIC SHUIBHNE
AND ELEANOR SPAVENTA

THIS PROJECT SEEKS to analyse how the rhetoric of the 'fundamental status' of Union citizenship has been played in actual fact. In particular, the theme of *Empowerment and Disempowerment of the European Citizen* allows an exploration of the consequences of European citizenship far beyond the parameters of Articles 18–25 TFEU (ex 12–13, 17–22 EC) and, additionally, beyond the disciplinary confines of legal analysis alone. The structure of the book reflects four guiding themes: (1) reconfigurations of space and identity within the EU; (2) expectations, rhetoric and reality in the debate about citizenship and constitutional reform in Europe; (3) the role of citizenship discourse in setting the EU's substantive policy agenda; (4) the extent to which citizens can themselves participate in and thus shape their own Union fate. We thus construe 'EU citizenship' in its broadest sense and explore the extent to which the European citizen is, or indeed is *not*, genuinely at the heart of EU law and policy-making. Given the current economic and political climate – thinking especially of the problematic 2009 Parliamentary elections, the ongoing economic crisis and weak political response, and continuing national protectionism unchecked by the Union institutions – are the concerns of European citizens being adopted as the concerns of national and European politicians and judges? Conversely, are the expectations of citizens misplaced given the competence constraints within which the EU must act? What is the purpose and role of this transnational regional regulator, given that citizen concerns seem focused primarily at either the infra-State or global levels?

Within the broad theme of empowerment/disempowerment, we have invited our contributors to reflect on a range of cross-cutting issues in their specific analyses; for example, the extent to which channels of citizen participation (can) inform EU policy-making in a 'bottom-up' sense; whether the requirement of cross-border movement remains essential or not in order for EU citizenship rights to be relevant; or whether the EU is a catalyst for the construction of new spaces and new identities.

PART I: THE RECONFIGURATION OF SPACE

The three chapters which make up this part of the book all explore the idea of how, and how far, Union citizenship challenges our inherited assumptions about the essentially national scaling of territory, while also contributing to the emergence of new spatial configurations and identities, which not only incorporate, but also condition and indeed even limit, a novel 'European' dimension to our senses of geography, membership and belonging.

Anastasia Iliopoulou's contribution begins the discussion by analysing four main sets of ECJ case law: on the personal identity (and especially the names) of migrant citizens; on family reunification for migrant citizens; on fundamental rights violations as obstacles to movement; and on the treatment of wholly internal situations. On that basis, she argues that Union citizenship is about protecting and encouraging 'multiple membership', ie the right of individuals to belong to two different societies: that of the host State (based on residence) and that of the home State (based on nationality). On the one hand, Union citizenship supports and indeed provides incentives for migrants to integrate into their host society; while on the other hand and at the same time, Union citizenship offers them the possibility of preserving links with their home State. That understanding has various implications: for example, the right to become a full member of the host society implies also a responsibility upon migrants to respect the core values of that Member State which form its national identity (in turn raising interesting questions about judicial review by the ECJ of what constitutes the core of national identity). Iliopoulou's analysis also suggests that there are inherent limits to the degree to which Union citizenship can provide a strong point of European identity or loyalty towards the EU among the wider population: Union citizenship acts essentially as a bridge between two spaces so as to protect the *particular identity of the migrant*.

The chapter by Síofra O'Leary proceeds to focus on one important aspect of the debate on what it means to be, and benefit from one's status as, a Union citizen when the latter is intimately linked to questions of borders and movement: the treatment of wholly internal situations. O'Leary explores the evolution of the case law on wholly internal situations from its origins in the late 1970s, to the introduction of Union citizenship, and the more recent rulings in *Zambrano* and *McCarthy*. She seeks to defend the Court against accusations that its jurisprudence in this field is inconsistent or arbitrary: closer analysis of the case law shows that, in situations where Union law applies so as to scrutinise national rules, the Court will be sure to link the situation to the scope of application of Union law. She also rejects the argument that Union citizenship mandates the Court to abandon the wholly internal situation rule: the latter is positively required by respect for the principle of conferral (attributed powers) contained in Article 5 TEU. However, that is not to say that the scope of application of Union law or the scrutiny of national rules will always be limited to cases involving a cross-border element. In fact, the range of circumstances in which individuals can rely on Union law against their own Member State has broadened with each Treaty amendment since Maastricht. That includes developments under the citizenship provisions proper, such as the rulings in *Zambrano* and *McCarthy* on when national action deprives citizens of the substance of their rights. But it also includes, for example, the right not to be discriminated against on grounds of sex, race, disability etc; and also the protection of fundamental rights whenever Member States act within the scope of the Treaties. Indeed, perhaps the real challenge for the Court (particularly since the introduction of the Charter of Fundamental Rights) is to determine the proper scope of EU law (and therefore of the wholly internal rule which is its necessary corollary).

If O'Leary was concerned with Union citizens who find themselves in a situation wholly internal to their own Member State – or rather, to their own national legal system – Charlotte O'Brien examines a group of Union citizens who are often seen as epitomising the Union's commitment to promoting and protecting cross-border movement: frontier workers and other individuals living in border zones. O'Brien is particularly interested in the 'European Groupings of Territorial Cooperation' (EGTCs) as phenomena which offer special opportunities, and create special problems, for European integration and Union citizenship. She argues that such frontier zones have emerged organically as products of localised cross-border integration; the legal dimension represented by EGTCs has then been grafted on, as if in an attempt to allow public infrastructures to catch up with the way people are already living. Moreover, the legal recognition afforded to EGTCs is both tentative and minimal – perhaps reflecting both Member State concerns about relinquishing sovereignty over frontier regions and Union reservations about supporting entities that (far from stressing their 'European' nature) focus on their own local identities. O'Brien argues that this situation creates various problems. For example, both the legal competences and the legal responsibilities of EGTCs are very unclear (with particular difficulties arising from the involvement of multiple actors at different administrative or legislative levels from different Member States) – giving rise to the danger that individual rights remain territorial, while administrative responsibility becomes diffused. Or again, the experience of living in a socially integrated but legally divided frontier zone raises difficult issues about the failure of EGTCs to coordinate sensitive policy areas: frontier zone workers may be subject to very different welfare regimes, with the potential to impact adversely upon persons at risk of social exclusion. Furthermore, in terms of Union law, the frontier *within* the frontier zone still matters very much: it will usually need to be crossed before the rights associated with Union citizenship itself can be triggered, giving rise to further differences in the degree of protection afforded to individuals living and working within one and the same the border region.

PART II: IN THE NAME OF THE CITIZEN?

This section explores the extent to which the rhetoric of citizenship is actually met in the practice of the European institutions: Deidre Curtin focuses on the (lack of) transparency of administrative and law-making processes; whilst Bruno De Witte and Michelle Everson focus on the Court, albeit from completely different perspectives.

Curtin looks at the principle of openness/transparency and its actual functioning in the context of the European Union. As the author remarks, this is particularly important in a system, like the European Union, where representative democracy is not fully developed. After having traced a historical account of the development of the principle of transparency in the EU legal system, Curtin provides a critical analysis of the actual administrative and law-making processes to assess the extent to which transparency works (or does not work) in practice. In this respect, the author identifies four areas as being particularly problematic: comitology; the working of the Commission; the practice of holding 'trialogue' meetings, ie 'informal' meetings with representatives of the Council and the European Parliament aimed at resolving contentious issues at a very early stage of the legislative process; and the input of Member States in the workings in the Council. The author finds that there is an institutional resistance to proactively making these processes open and transparent; and that the Court's approach is at best ambiguous, if not altogether unhelpful. For instance, the latter has accepted that data protection rules grant a right to civil servants and others to participate in meetings with the Commission and other EU authorities anonymously, hence reducing greatly the power of scrutiny that can be exercised by citizens. It is for these reasons that the author prefers to talk about translucency rather than transparency: at the present stage some light 'is allowed to pass through but . . . the persons carrying out public tasks on the opposite side are not always clearly visible'.

De Witte explores the idea that the Court of Justice might be(come) responsive to the interests of European citizens, whilst at the same time remaining independent and performing its assigned constitutional tasks. The author takes as his starting point the factors that might affect the efficiency of the Court, as identified by the Committee of Ministers of the Council of Europe, namely the 'delivery of quality decisions within a reasonable time following fair consideration of the issues'. He finds that whilst the Court of Justice has made real progress in the 'quantitative' elements, ie in the speed with which it reaches its decisions, the situation is less satisfactory in relation to the qualitative elements, ie quality of decisions and fair consideration of the issues raised in the cases. On both counts the Court does not always deliver: thus there are several rulings, *Ruiz Zambrano, Mangold* and *Kükükdeveci* to name but a few, where a rather dramatic outcome follows from scant (if existing at all) reasoning. Thus, in 'many of the Court of Justice's judgments, there is a sense that the outcome is *inevitable* and the reasoning is, carefully or sometimes not so carefully, built so as to convey that sense of inevitability'. As a result, all too often there is no acknowledgment of the fact that, in some instances, rulings reflect a (policy) choice between two hermeneutically valid alternatives. The lack of articulation of policy alternatives also means that there might not be fair consideration of competing issues. Furthermore, since rulings cannot be easily reversed by the legislature, 'the Court of Justice is . . . rather uniquely immune from political pressure before it decides a case, and from political retaliation afterwards'. One way of solving these issues is to allow dissenting opinions, since this would oblige the Court to articulate the strengths of different hermeneutic alternatives as well as the reasons behind the majority choice. However, conscious of the fact that this change is unlikely to happen, De Witte suggests that the Court could become more responsive to European citizens by improving the quality of its rulings: thus, in those cases that matter most to the citizens (because of their complexity or because of their subject matter) the Court should take extra care in drafting its rulings 'more carefully and discursively, and, above all, in showing respect for careful political deliberations that may have taken place either at the EU level or in a member state, depending on the case'.

Everson also engages in a critical assessment of the case law on citizenship but this time from a more theoretical perspective. Taking as her starting point writers such as Arendt, Dahrendorf and Ehrlich, Everson notes how the lack of a coherent scheme of legitimation for the Court's case law threatens the normative integrity of European law as a whole. In particular, the author takes issue, on the one hand, with the 'sentimentality' of the Court's approach, legally encapsulated in the proportionality review, which is excessively focused on the personal circumstances of the individual; and, on the other hand, with the fact that citizenship becomes a tool in fostering European integration (or a given vision of European integration). Everson then links the discourse on citizenship to the earlier discourse on the market/consumer citizen to conclude that 'the love of the CJEU for the individual European – the desire that all should be given opportunity – coincides happily with the frontier-busting universalism of neoliberal precepts and is transformed into a legal semantic of economic technology, which isolates and atomises the individual as a *homo economicus*'.

PART III: THE CITIZEN'S POLICY AGENDA?

In part III, our contributors explore four substantive policy areas – monetary union; the fight against climate change; the further development of EU criminal law; and cross-border family law – within which Union action is increasingly justified by recourse to citizen needs and demands. Do these institutional claims translate appropriately into substantive Union practice?

Fabian Amtenbrink's chapter seeks to connect macroeconomic and monetary policy issues with discourse on EU citizenship, especially the elements of the latter that address identification with the Union, a sense of belonging, and also whether that connection in turn generates a cross-State, citizen-driven sense of solidarity.

Amtenbrink also investigates whether there is any sense in which EU citizens connect with monetary policy in terms of policy 'ownership'. And, more specifically with respect to the current climate of economic crisis, he asks whether economic and monetary union contributes something positive to answering these questions – or quite the contrary: is the current Eurozone crisis actually *undermining* already fragile notions of citizenship and solidarity? He finds that 'Citizens rarely claim ownership of European policies and decision-making. What is missing is an identification with, commitment to and appreciation of policies and decisions that are supposedly formulated and implemented in the citizen's best interest.' But he notes also an increasing trend from disinterest to criticism. Amtenbrink traces both express and implicit references to solidarity in the EU Treaties, but he also notes that rights developed within the framework of EU law tend to be 'individual rights and privileges, rather than convictions and achievements that all citizens of the EU share among themselves, that tie their fates together and that set them apart from others'. He shifts his analysis instead to the more functional notion of 'common goods', testing the hypothesis that if common goods can contribute to some sense of collective experience and ownership, then that effect should be all the more intensive in times of crisis. His work reveals a complex rather than binary picture: citizens both appreciate the common good aspects of EMU and, at the same time, do not agree that EU policies have a positive impact on their lives. Moreover, Amtenbrink is critical of the weakness of the existing legal framework, which cannot properly 'defend' this common good in any event. Looking at citizenship and solidarity against the backdrop of the current economic crisis, he finds a mood of self-interest; he does observe 'a somewhat involuntary, yet inescapable solidarity between Member States and ultimately the (taxpaying) citizens of the Union. Yet, it would be wrong to conclude that this factual economic and financial connectedness brings the citizens of the Union closer to one another.' He also observes a virulent paradox that shapes political discourse within the EU:

> Citizens are left with the impression – often based on public statements by national politicians – that they have to foot the bill for the extravagant lifestyle of other Europeans. What is seldom explained is that this is the natural outcome of a system of economic governance that has been put in place by elected politicians.

More generally, Amtenbrink has explored a thematic question that resonates across the volume: whether we are or are not seeing 'the emergence of a transnational citizenship beyond the creation and upholding of rights'. Maybe pessimistically but perhaps realistically, he concludes that 'Overall, this cacophony in times of crisis signifies the extent to which (national) differences prevail despite the existence of common goods.'

Joanne Scott's chapter is framed by the twin themes of citizen expectation and citizen evaluation. On the first point, EU citizens want and expect the EU to act strongly in the global fight against climate change; but, recalling the second theme, a majority of EU citizens also perceive that the EU is not acting strongly *enough*. Scott's contribution tests this assertion by tracing recent EU action within the global arena of climate change policy. Specifically, she demonstrates a 'recent shift in EU climate change policy in favour of climate unilateralism' – a position that, ultimately, she finds to be both 'important yet controversial'. Scott shows through empirical analysis that the perception of EU citizens about the EU's performance on substantive climate change targets is in fact substantiated; although she also points pragmatically to the limitations on what the EU can actually achieve given that its territory is subsumed into benchmarks set at the global level). The EU cannot succeed, in other words, just by acting alone. Scott thus goes on to assess the EU against evaluative criteria of leadership on the global stage, arguing that 'the capacity of the EU to shape the direction of climate change mitigation policies beyond its own borders will be key'. Softening charges of unilateralism, especially in the context of the EU's regulatory penalty default scheme (she outlines four examples in this context, showing how the EU 'uses (or contemplates using) trade-related environmental measures to secure compliance with EU law on the part of commercial operators who are situated abroad'), Scott presents a more nuanced picture. She characterises the EU approach as one of 'structural leadership', arguing that 'the EU's ultimate goal is not to enforce compliance with EU rules on the part of operators situated abroad, but it is on the contrary to galvanise or incentivise regulatory engagement elsewhere'. The EU's internal market is its key incentivising device. Mirroring some of the themes addressed by Amtenbrink, she notes that:

> The EU is willing to concede that its climate unilateralism is driven in part by the need to level the competitive playing field for EU businesses which compete with businesses abroad, but a citizenship perspective on climate change reminds us that the EU faces demands for effective climate action not just from the commercial sector but from ordinary citizens as well.

Scott also offers a normative framework that could explain and ground EU unilateral action more appropriately. But she ends on a note of caution, observing that opposition to EU unilateral action is growing, this in itself presenting complex challenges for the EU as it seeks to balance citizen expectations with citizen evaluations.

The EU has explicitly stated that 'serving and protecting the EU citizen' lies at the heart of its criminal law agenda; in fact, this objective is part of the subtitle of the Stockholm Programme. Ester Herlin-Karnell's chapter seeks to evaluate the veracity of that claim. We see here similar themes to those addressed by Stalford – notably, the need to ensure an appropriate balance between policy effectiveness and the protection of fundamental rights. As in the area of family justice, both of these concerns can be attributed to values rooted in the idea of EU citizenship; indeed, as Herlin-Karnell demonstrates, most policy- and law-making initiatives on EU criminal law make express linkages between their rationales and the rights of EU citizens (if not actually the more formal rights attached to citizen-*ship*). The critical question is, however, whether the right balance between the two is actually being struck. Putting this in concrete terms, she argues that 'the focus on speedy prosecutions may undermine the values it seeks to protect: namely the guarantee of due process and procedural safeguards for the individual'. Reflecting the new capacity for both enforcement and judicial review, she also comments that the Lisbon Treaty's extension of CJEU jurisdiction over EU criminal law is 'one of the most important constitutional restructurings under the Lisbon Treaty and one of the most crucial changes for the individual'. Herlin-Karnell first outlines the more obvious linkages between citizenship and criminal law, notably in the application of procedural rights. But she then goes further, exploring a broader notion of EU citizenship and its demands – especially with respect to free movement, and to the principles of non-discrimination and proportionality – and assessing the extent to which an imprint of that understanding can be seen in recent EU criminal case law. More than this, she argues strongly that a more intensive focus on the protection of the individual should be the priority for the development of EU criminal law, as an important next step beyond the foundational policy-need to generate trust between the Member States through the current of mutual recognition. Herlin-Karnell reviews the most recent agenda-setting initiative in the field, the Stockholm Programme, to see whether this objective is properly infused into the EU's plan of action. Her assessment is mixed, mainly because the Programme 'contains so many general wishes and statements that, for the individual, it remains unclear to what extent this programme is genuinely driving citizens' rights'. Drawing on the (somewhat ambiguous) values set out in the EU Treaties, she calls for the construction of 'a European common sense of fairness, which genuinely cares for the individual'. In order to demonstrate the work still to be done, however, Herlin-Karnell presents two case studies – on data protection and joint investigation orders – where she argues that concern for the individual does *not* seem to be driving the EU agenda. Ensuring effectiveness and efficiency can, therefore, work against, as well as in, the interests of EU citizens.

In her chapter on the evolution of EU family law, Helen Stalford locates the origins of this policy field in a movement imperative, driven by the 'increasing prevalence of private relationship formation between individuals of different nationalities, itself a product of the progressive "normalisation" of cross-national migration'); and thematically reinforced by 'the need for an effective supranational legal and administrative response' – the 'free movement of decisions' being critical, in other words, to ensure the free movement of persons. But even though this free movement imperative is shared by both family justice and EU citizenship, Stalford notes that academic and judicial work on both domains has proceeded on essentially two parallel tracks. Moreover, and in contrast to EU citizenship law, EU family law principally effects procedural rather than substantive harmonisation: it is about facilitating cross-border life (or even, making it possible), but leaving substantive choices on regulatory content to the Member States. Bearing these similarities and differences both in mind, the purpose of this chapter is to explore further potential convergence between the two regimes – whether it exists to any extent, whether it should exist to a greater extent, and so on. First, Stalford identifies an emerging shared theme: recognition of the rights of the individual (and especially the right to family life) over and above the internal market rationale attached to free movement. But the Court's concern with establishing the limits of EU protection in this context is also apparent in both strands of case law. Stalford suggests that this concern stems from the Court's awareness of the 'political exigencies of mutual trust'. The emergence of 'export' case law in both spheres also dilutes the formerly central migration condition. The theme of empowerment comes out most strongly with respect to recent changes to the choice of applicable law rules for family disputes, geared towards vesting choice with and thus empowering the individuals involved. Stalford nonetheless links the developments with the notions of autonomy and legal certainty, finding, again, clear parallels here with the values of EU citizenship. Perhaps tellingly, however, only 14 Member States have agreed to be bound by these new rules. Stalford also argues that parties with the best financial resources (and thus the best legal advice) are most likely to benefit – again stirring images of similar charges against the economic conditions attached to the exercise of most citizenship rights and conveying the practical reality of disempowerment. Finally, she raises the question, more broadly, as to whether family justice and citizenship rights should be subsumed within one regime, given that many of the claims, in real terms, do not really fit with the operational dividing line being reinforced in case law at present. She is broadly in favour of greater convergence, principally through 'greater cross-referencing' of essentially the same concepts that are often currently addressed under different judicial formulas, but she points too to relevant limits, including, for example, the still primarily procedure-focused character of EU family justice law, as well as its more horizontal impact on private agreements, compared to the more substantive, vertical profile of EU citizenship.

PART IV: NEW MODES OF CITIZENSHIP PARTICIPATION

The final trio of chapters offers a political science perspective on the Treaty of Lisbon's innovations as regards the possibilities for participatory democracy within a Union whose strong credentials *on paper* as a representative and deliberative democracy have, however, not translated *in practice* into an equally impressive claim to popular legitimacy.

Luis Bouza García considers the participatory democracy provisions now contained in Article 11 TEU: civil dialogue and the new Citizens' Initiative. He argues that Article 11 TEU was not purposely designed to redress democratic legitimacy problems; its contents resulted from the demands of well-established civil society actors converging with the discourse of the Commission on Union governance. However, the changing political context since the European Convention proposals first emerged (not least the negative referenda in France, the Netherlands and Ireland) means that Article 11 TEU now offers a real opportunity for democratisation within the Union – provided that mechanisms designed to improve Union governance (and which thus focus on conflict avoidance) can actually be oriented towards enhancing its democratic participation (which presupposes a greater degree of political contestation). In that regard, although Article 11 TEU has serious drawbacks in terms of its potential to influence Union policy-making, it may nevertheless provide an important opportunity for the inclusion of new actors and (more broadly) to foster the emergence of a genuine 'European public sphere'. Against that background, García argues that the civil dialogue limb (on the one hand) and the new Citizens' Initiative limb (on the other hand) of Article 11 TEU could be mutually complementary and makes concrete suggestions for their interaction and improved performance. For example, it is argued that participants in civil dialogue should be able to demonstrate their ability to represent causes or constituencies; in that regard, the ability to foster democratic debates could be used as an alternative measure of representativeness, operationalised by considering any given organisation's usage of the Citizens' Initiative to promote its causes. Furthermore, the Commission could voluntarily decide to adopt a policy of presenting proposals for Union action based on *all* successful citizens' initiatives, in order to reward organisations that have succeeded in mobilising citizens, and also to foster pan-European debates of a genuinely democratic (contested/politicised) character, which it becomes the responsibility of the Council and the European Parliament to confront and address.

Graham Smith focuses his attention more specifically upon the new Citizens' Initiative. Having described the evolution of the Citizens' Initiative from its origins at the European Convention, and summarised the main provisions of Regulation 211/2011 on implementation of the Citizens' Initiative, Smith argues that the introduction of the Citizens' Initiative offers a new mechanism for placing issues on the Union's political agenda. But he also suggests that, in terms of both its substantive impact on Union decision-making and its influence on citizens' perceptions of engagement/empowerment, the effects of the Citizens' Initiative are likely to be limited. First, it is more a petition than a right of initiative in the usual sense of the term. Secondly, drawing upon experience in other jurisdictions, Smith argues that the Citizens' Initiative may actually disempower particular groups if it is used to pursue anti-minority issues. Thirdly, organised interests rather than individual citizens are most likely to be significantly empowered through the Citizens' Initiative. The Citizens' Initiative therefore embodies the idea of an empowered European or transnational citizenship; but in practice, this will not be realised to the extent that the rhetoric of its supporters would suggest. Smith further argues that the creation of the Citizens' Initiative might have the unhelpful effect of pushing off the Commission's agenda further experimentation with deliberative democracy at the Union level. That would be particularly disappointing because some of the weaknesses of the Citizens' Initiative could be ameliorated through recourse to complementary deliberative democratic structures: for example, the limitations of the Citizens' Initiative in terms of encouraging dialogue and reflection (as opposed to registering existing preferences), and the difficulties facing the Commission in judging the real extent of public support for any given citizens' initiative, could be helped by empowering a representative sample of Union citizens to consider any citizens' initiative which was successfully submitted for consideration; or even creating a citizens' assembly bringing together a transnational 'mini-public' to offer a more considered judgement which better represents the diversity of perspectives from across the Union.

The Citizens' Initiative may be new to the European Union – but of course, citizens' initiatives are far from being new to the world of Western democratic theory and practice. Matt Qvortrup explores the national experience of citizens' initiatives across the EU's Member States, with a view to ascertaining what lessons (if any) can be learned about the likely experience of the Union's own Citizens' Initiative in the future. Qvortrup argues that there is evidence from various countries (such as Austria, Italy and Poland) to suggest that citizens' initiatives, although on paper they may appear weak, have nevertheless had a greater impact on the national law-making process than the apparently much stronger instrument of citizen-initiated referendums (such as those used in Hungary, Latvia and Lithuania). In particular, citizens' initiatives which have proposed realistic and constructive (as well as popular) proposals seem to have more success than more radical provisions. Qvortrup argues that, despite scepticism about its real usefulness, there is nothing to suggest that the Union's new Citizens' Initiative will be ineffectual: although they are not a panacea for problems of legitimacy or participation, citizens' initiatives can work in their own modest way, ie by giving citizens a voice where otherwise they would have had none.

Part I

The Reconfiguration of Space

1

The Transnational Character of Union Citizenship

ANASTASIA ILIOPOULOU PENOT*

I INTRODUCTION

IS IT POSSIBLE for an individual to cease to be a foreigner in the eyes of a State without his or her becoming this State's national? The answer is yes. This was the function of federal citizenship in the early days of American, German and Swiss federalism.[1] This also seems to be the function of Union citizenship as it has developed mainly through case law and legislation inspired by it, namely Directive 2004/38.[2] Indeed, Union citizenship today constitutes an interstate status entailing membership in a transnational community rather than a form of political participation in a supranational polity. Considering the fact that doctrinal analysis had initially (almost entirely) focused on the latter aspect, we have to ask *how* this evolution actually took place.

When Union citizenship was introduced in the Treaties, the European Court of Justice ('the Court') was soon invited by the actors of the European judicial stage to live up to its reputation of 'transforming weakly conceived legal institutions into strong concepts of rights'.[3] After hesitating for a while, the Court finally became the driving force behind the *construction* of a new legal right-conferring status.[4] Since the first and most important right attached to EU citizenship by the

* I am especially grateful to Christoph Krenn for his help concerning the *Sayn-Wittgenstein* case and to Charles Gosme for all useful comments on the chapter. All errors remain of course mine.

[1] See C Schönberger, 'European Citizenship as Federal Citizenship. Some Lessons of Comparative Federalism' (2007) 19 *Revue européenne de droit public* 61. Looking at the broader experience of federalism which has taken place in the historical confederations and early federal States and which has later been obscured by the growing centralisation in many federal States during the twentieth century, the author identifies the function of federal citizenship as the abolition of the distinction between citizens and foreigners among the States of the Union. This is why he qualifies Union citizenship as a federal one.

[2] Directive 2004/38 on the right of citizens of the Union and their family members to move and reside freely within the territory of the Member States [2004] OJ L158/77.

[3] S Kadelbach, 'Union Citizenship' in A Von Bogdandy and J Bast (eds), *Principles of European Constitutional Law* (Oxford, Hart Publishing, 2006) 453.

[4] D Kostakopoulou, 'Ideas, Norms and European Citizenship: Explaining Institutional Change' (2005) 68 *MLR* 233.

Treaties is the right to move and reside freely, the Court turned for inspiration to its own case law on economic movement,[5] which had given birth to the figure of the 'market citizen',[6] the ancestor of the Union citizen.

Thus, next to the quasi-theological, eschatological statement which depicts Union citizenship as 'destined to be the fundamental status of nationals of the Member States',[7] a more functional approach was applied in the case law. In order to cement the edifice of Union citizenship, the Court made use of the building blocks and methods of the internal market case law which had already attained a certain degree of maturity. Thus, concepts designed specifically in relation to economic freedoms were transposed to Union citizenship law. Infringements of the rights of the Union citizen have been conceptualised as notions elaborated in the context of the internal market: discriminations, unjustified or disproportionate restrictions, obstacles.

The Court's choice presented certain advantages. It allowed Union citizenship to develop both at a quick pace and on solid foundations, since the main legal actors involved were already familiar with the concepts and methods used. It also had the potential to ensure the 'narrative coherence' of the case law on free movement while incorporating the new value of citizenship in the jurisprudential chain.

The Court's approach was, however, not devoid of problems. First, by linking the interpretation of Union citizenship with that of the provisions on economic freedoms, the Court has on several occasions affirmed the subsidiary character of Union citizenship in comparison with the status of economic agents. This conception of EU citizenship as a sort of 'spare wheel'[8] sits uneasily with its judicially declared 'telos' of becoming a fundamental status with constitutional significance.[9]

Secondly, the Court's case law on citizenship has imported some of the uncertainties and unresolved dilemmas surrounding the law of the internal market. The exact meaning and scope of the concept of 'obstacle' to free movement is one of these thorny issues.[10]

[5] According to AG Cosmas's Opinion in Case C-378/97 *Wijsenbeek* [1999] ECR I-6207, certain elements anterior to the Treaty of Maastricht are useful for the conceptual comprehension and the application of ex-Art 18 EC (now Art 21 TFEU) to the extent that this provision occupies in the economy of the EC Treaty a position equivalent to that occupied by the provisions on free movement of economic actors in the EEC Treaty.

[6] M Everson, 'The Legacy of the Market Citizen' in J Shaw and G More (eds), *New Legal Dynamics of European Union* (Oxford, Clarendon Press, 1995); T Downes, 'Market Citizenship: Functionalism and Fig-leaves' in R Bellamy and A Warleigh (eds), *Citizenship and Governance in the European Union* (London, Continuum, 2001).

[7] This statement appeared for the first time in Case C-184/99 *Grzelczyk* [2001] ECR I-6193 and has become a leitmotiv of the case law on Union citizenship since.

[8] J-Y Carlier, 'Chronique: La libre circulation des personnes dans l'Union européenne (1er janvier–31 décembre 2003)' [2004] *Journal des Tribunaux – Droit européen* 74.

[9] A Tryfonidou argues that the Court's statement suggests that 'Member State nationals are first and foremost Union citizens and any other status (such as that of "worker"' or "service provider") thereby becomes secondary': 'Further Steps on the Road to Convergence among the Market Freedoms' (2010) 35 *EL Rev* 36.

[10] See A Iliopoulou, 'Entrave et citoyenneté de l'Union' in L Azoulai (ed), *L'entrave dans le droit du marché intérieur* (Brussels, Bruylant, 2011).

Thirdly, the Court left purely internal situations outside the scope of application of Union citizenship and thus missed an important opportunity to condemn reverse discrimination. Therefore Union citizenship mainly becomes relevant and of significance for the individual when there is some kind of interstate movement.[11] This indicates the essentially transnational character of Union citizenship, also highlighted in the 3rd recital of Directive 2004/38, which states that 'Union citizenship should be the fundamental status of nationals of Member States *when* they exercise their right to free movement and residence.'

In parallel with what is borrowed from the internal market edifice, the construction of Union citizenship has gradually developed its own internal logic, inspired by the permanent demand for inclusion found in every account of the notion of citizenship. Such logic is especially reflected in the 'real links' case law.[12] This case law invites national authorities to examine the reality of a migrant's (and even a national's)[13] attachment to the host society when deciding whether he or she is entitled to available benefits. In other words, time spent within, as well as integration into, the host State constitute factors which matter. In a similar vein, the EU legislator has introduced the new status of the permanent resident, acquired after five years of legal and continuous residence in the host State and guaranteeing unrestricted equal treatment with nationals of this State.

Due to its predominantly judicial nature, the actual development of Union citizenship as a transnational status is incremental and not entirely coherent. Even though the case law is still evolving and will further be shaped by the interpretation of Directive 2004/38, its principal traits have nevertheless already been determined. The central theme underpinning the judicial construction of Union citizenship is the will to facilitate movement if migration contributes to the realisation of the individual's personal potential, be it professional or social. The key ideas are those of *enabling* the individual to leave the home State, if he or she decides to do so, and *encouraging* his or her integration into the host State. How are these ends to be achieved? First of all, by guaranteeing the migrant's social status and ensuring his or her access to welfare benefits. Thus, the host State is called upon to accept participation of new members within the national solidaristic community.[14] As for the home State, it cannot automatically sever links

[11] This is so even after the judgment in Case C-34/09 *Zambrano*, judgment of 8 March 2011, examined in section V.

[12] See Case C-209/03 *Bidar* [2005] ECR I-2119 and Case C-158/07 *Förster* [2008] ECR I-8507 regarding migrant students as well as Case C-224/98 *D'Hoop* [2002] ECR I-6191 and Case C-138/02 *Collins* [2004] ECR I-2703 regarding jobseekers. See C O'Brien, 'Real Links, Abstract Rights and False Alarms: The Relationship between the ECJ's 'Real Link' Caselaw and National Solidarity' (2008) 33 *EL Rev* 643 and S O'Leary, 'Developing an Ever Closer Union between the Peoples of Europe? A Reappraisal of the Caselaw of the Court of Justice on the Free Movement of Persons and EU Citizenship' (2008) 27 *Yearbook of European Law* 167.

[13] Case C-224/98 *D'Hoop* [2002] ECR I-6191; Cases C-11/06 & C-12/06 *Morgan and Bucher* [2007] ECR I-9161.

[14] C Barnard, 'EU Citizenship and the Principle of Solidarity' and M Dougan and E Spaventa, '"Wish You Weren't Here…" New Models of Social Solidarity in the European Union' both in M Dougan and E Spaventa (eds), *Social Welfare and EU Law* (Oxford, Hart Publishing, 2005).

between the migrant national and its welfare society.[15] This so far constitutes the backbone of the case law on Union citizenship.

There are, however, other important aspects contained in the case law. These aspects indicate the potential of Union citizenship to protect the individual's choice to migrate and to become a member of a new community against disproportionate interference of State authority, whether this interference originates from the host or the home State. The author is referring to the protection of the individual's identity, illustrated by the name cases (Section II) and the protection of the migrant's family life (Section III). Both these aspects justify the qualification of Union citizenship as 'a status of social integration', suggested by Loïc Azoulai.[16] They also invite us to examine the question of the protection of fundamental rights through the legal tool of Union citizenship (Section IV). So far construed as a status with significance in transnational situations, Union citizenship has recently been the object of a new and potentially far-reaching approach. Indeed the judgment in *Zambrano*[17] indicates a move beyond the transnational character of Union citizenship (Section V).

II UNION CITIZENSHIP AND PROTECTION OF IDENTITY ELEMENTS IN TRANSNATIONAL SITUATIONS

The name cases are of particular interest since the name constitutes one of the main bearings of identity[18] as well as an important aspect of the individual's personal status.

In *Garcia Avello*,[19] the parents of two children with dual Belgian and Spanish nationality, born and residing in Belgium, contested the refusal by Belgian authorities to accept the registration of the surname in the Spanish embassy according to Spanish tradition (Garcia Weber) instead of the name formed in accordance with Belgian law (Garcia Avello). In *Grunkin Paul*,[20] the parents of a young German, born and residing in Denmark, contested the refusal by German authorities to accept the surname formed according to the Danish system. In both cases, the Court found that the national authorities' refusal amounted to a disproportionate restriction of the rights of Union citizens. These authorities were called upon to recognise a situation created in accordance with the legal system of another Member State. The logic followed was that a Member State has to recognise the personal status conferred upon a Union citizen by another Member

[15] M Dougan, 'Expanding the Frontiers of Union Citizenship by Dismantling the Territorial Boundaries of the National Welfare States?' in C Barnard and O Odudu (eds), *The Outer Limits of European Union Law* (Oxford, Hart Publishing, 2009).

[16] L Azoulai, 'La citoyenneté européenne, un statut d'intégration sociale' in *Chemins d'Europe. Mélanges en l'honneur de Jean-Paul Jacqué* (Paris, Dalloz, 2010).

[17] Case C-34/09 *Zambrano*, judgment of 8 March 2011.

[18] U Haltern defines identity as the 'self-perception of an individual resulting from the awareness of belonging to a certain group': 'On Finality' in Von Bogdandy and Bast (n 3).

[19] Case C-148/02 *Garcia Avello* [2003] ECR I-11613.

[20] Case C-353/06 *Grunkin Paul* [2008] ECR I-3561.

State.[21] The principle of mutual recognition, born in the context of the market freedoms, is henceforth now applied in the field of the personal status of the individuals.[22] Once again the law of the internal market provides the necessary tools for the construction of Union citizenship law.

Both judgments have attracted criticism from specialists in private international law who accuse the Court of disregarding the traditional (and natural) function of nationality as a connecting factor in order to determine personal status. From this perspective, individuals were allowed by the Court to escape the constraints of nationhood and impose their preference for the system of another State. It is true that both judgments can be seen as examples of the protection offered by Union citizenship to individuals' *autonomy*, since the parents' *choice* of a name system was defended. There is, however, another plausible reading of the judgments.[23]

The Court safeguarded the children's legitimate interest in having a surname constituted according to the law of a State with which they shared particular links:[24] the State of their second nationality in *Garcia Avello* and the State of residence in *Grunkin Paul*. It is the specificity of the identity of the dual national and the migrant that is, at the end of the day, recognised and protected by the Court. Thus, in *Garcia Avello*, the children could legitimately aspire to maintain their attachment to Spanish custom. The parents' argument before the Court is enlightening: 'the children felt more closely related to Spanish tradition'. Moreover, even though the judgment does not refer to the father who is a Spanish migrant in Belgium, its effect is to also protect his wish to transmit his name according to his national tradition. Finally, in *Grunkin Paul*, the migrant was allowed to acquire a new identity element in accordance with the model of the host State in which he was born, raised and (probably) integrated.

Interestingly, in *Garcia Avello*, the Belgian government argued that its practice could be justified by the objective of promoting *integration* (and equality) into Belgian society of nationals from other Member States. The Court rejects this argument in view of the fact that migration within the Union has already led to the coexistence in Member States of different systems for the attribution of surnames applicable to residents.[25] As a result of this migration, the situation of the children in the *Garcia Avello* case, as well as in the *Grunkin Paul* case, cannot be assessed by reference to the framework of only one national society. Instead, it has to be repositioned within a wider social context, recomposed at the European

[21] T Ackermann, Casenote on *Garcia Avello* (2007) 44 *CML Rev* 141. The question remains whether the same logic applies to *all* elements of the personal status acquired in accordance with the law of another Member State.

[22] Mutual recognition is based upon mutual trust which, in turn, especially when citizenship cases are concerned, presupposes the existence of a certain commonality of basic values. These values are today expressed in the Charter of Fundamental Rights of the EU.

[23] See Azoulai (n 16).

[24] For a similar view, see E Pataut, 'Citoyenneté communautaire et libre circulation des personnes-de la construction d'un marché à l'élaboration d'un statut' in S Bollée, Y-M Laithier and C Pérès (eds), *L'efficacité économique en droit* (Paris, Economica, 2010).

[25] Paras 42 and 43 of the judgment in Case C-148/02 *Garcia Avello* [2003] ECR I-11613.

level.[26] The legal bond of EU citizenship reflects a certain social reality resulting from migration and membership in European society conceived as 'a society of societies'. This status protects against the risk, somehow inherent to migration, that original identity will be changed or even erased against the will of the individual. Therefore, new identity elements can only be chosen by the migrant (as in *Grunkin Paul*); they cannot be imposed on him or her. It is certain that integration into the host society is desirable. But integration does not mean assimilation. Instead, it can sometimes be better achieved by recognition of the migrant's difference. In other words, when in Rome, you do not (necessarily) have to do as the Romans do.

The case law under examination also illustrates the changing conception of the State. Member States can no longer be represented as bounded worlds which correspond to closed and isolated entities. Instead, they belong to a wider area where movement is continuous and where diversity is accepted, preserved and even encouraged as a source of richness.[27] As parts of a larger organism, Member States have to consider the potential impact of their choices on transnational situations. Interests beyond the confines of the national polity have to be taken into account within the policy- and decision-making system.[28] Judicial review on grounds of Union citizenship seeks to ensure precisely this.[29] Therefore, Union citizenship enhances a phenomenon already taking place because of the internal market where Member States are 'forced to confront and to internalise the externalities that they cause for one another'.[30] This phenomenon is now extended as a result of Union citizenship to new areas such as personal and family status.

Our reading of the name cases begs a final question: how far does the host State's obligation to recognise aspects of the migrant's identity stretch? In other words, is there a limit to the migrant's potential claims and to the State's acceptance? Elements of an answer to this question can be identified in recent judgments of national constitutional courts. In a line of cases concerning the implementation of Union directives in national law, the French *Conseil constitutionnel* identifies the ultimate limit of internal acceptance of European integration as lying in the respect of 'rules and principles inherent to the constitutional identity of France'.[31] Such judgments highlight the importance of the national

[26] Azoulai (n 16).

[27] AG Jacobs also speaks of a 'free, and possibly repeated or even continuous, movement within a single area of freedom, security and justice, in which both cultural diversity and freedom from discrimination are ensured' (para 72 of the Opinion in Case C-148/02 *Garcia Avello* [2003] ECR I-11613).

[28] See L Azoulai, 'L'Etat' in J-B Auby (ed), *L'influence du droit européen sur les catégories du droit public* (Paris, Dalloz, 2010) 151.

[29] N Nic Shuibhne, 'The Outer Limits of EU Citizenship: Displacing Economic Free Movement Rights?' in Barnard and Odudu (n 15).

[30] A Somek, 'The Argument from Transnational Effects: Representing Outsiders through Freedom of Movement' (2010) 16 *European Law Journal* 315.

[31] The first case where the term 'constitutional identity' appears is CC, 27 July 2006, *Loi relative au droit d'auteur et aux droits voisins dans la société de l'information*, n° 2006-540 DC. See also CC, 30 November 2006, *Loi relative au secteur de l'énergie*, n° 2006-543 DC; CC, 19 June 2008, *Loi relative aux organismes génétiquement modifiés*, n° 2008-564 DC. Nevertheless, the idea was already present in earlier decisions starting with CC, 10 June 2004, *Loi pour la confiance dans l'économie numérique*, n°

community's capacity of self-determination.[32] They suggest or imply the existence of a core of preserved State values, of a protected national value space. The *Conseil constitutionnel* seems to consider as crucial the need to maintain the distinctive features of the French Republic, what distinguishes it from other States.[33] This obviously begs the question of the content of such identity. In other words: what is Frenchness made up of? There have been many developments on the issue of constitutional identity in French legal literature,[34] but so far no decision of the *Conseil constitutionnel* gives any hint as to what this identity encompasses. There is consensus among most authors about the inclusion of certain values such as *laïcité* (religious neutrality of the public space) and the French conception of equality (excluding the recognition of collective rights to minorities and other groups). Such values are seen as cornerstones of the French *vivre-ensemble.*

Therefore we could argue that the migrant can claim the recognition of his or her different identity as long as this does not clash with certain values considered as fundamental in the host State. In other words, the migrant would have the *duty* to respect certain values considered as essential elements of the social contract, as

2004-496 DC. Of course, the identity review could result in inapplicability of EU law only in exceptional cases.

[32] The terminology of 'constitutional identity' is also to be found in the judgment of the German constitutional court (*BverfG)* of 30 June 2009 on the Treaty of Lisbon (BverfG, 2 BvE 2/08). According to the *BverfG*, the protection of the content of the German constitutional identity demands that a substantial scope of action for key areas remains within the State. After affirming that the Federal Republic has to 'retain sufficient space for the political formation of the economic, cultural and social circumstances of life' (para 249), the *BverfG* provides a relatively detailed list of such core competences (paras 253 ff). Therefore, whereas in the French judgments 'constitutional identity' is more about an inviolable core of national *values* that have to be preserved, in the German judgment the term designates an inviolable core of *powers* that have to stay with the Federal Republic.

[33] See the comments of the former President of the Conseil constitutionnel, Pierre Mazeaud, in the wishes adressed to the President of the Republic on 3 January 2005: '. . . le droit européen, si loin qu'aillent sa primauté et son immédiateté, ne peut remettre en cause ce qui expressément inscrit dans nos textes constitutionnels et *qui nous est propre.* Je veux parler ici de tout ce qui est inhérent à notre identité constitutionnelle *au double sens du terme 'inhérent': crucial et distinctif.* Autrement dit: l'essentiel de la République' (emphasis added). For a similar doctrinal vision, see V Constantinesco, 'La confrontation entre identité constitutionnelle européenne et identités constitutionnelles nationales. Convergence ou contradiction? Contrepoint ou hiérarchie?' in *L'Union européenne: Union de droit, Union des droits. Mélanges en l'honneur de Philippe Manin* (Paris, Pedone, 2010) 79: 'Les nations, ces êtres collectifs, ont aussi, chacune, leur identité propre: ne sont-elles pas dotées de certains caractères stables, permanents et fondamentaux qui les distinguent des autres, leurs semblables, mais non leurs identiques? Montesquieu ne relevait-il pas déjà l'existence d'un *esprit général* de chaque nation, qui expliquait la variété des lois que chacune se donne? Il n'est pas étonnant que ces caractères spécifiques figurent dans les cartes d'identité des Etats que sont leurs constitutions, produit des choix des constituants, produits de la culture et de l'histoire politique nationale.'

[34] See, eg Constantinesco(n 32); A Levade, 'Quelle identité constitutionnelle nationale préserver face à l'UE ?' in *Annuaire de droit européen 2004* (Brussels, Bruylant, 2007); B Mathieu, 'Les règles et les principes inhérents à l'identité constitutionnelle de la France: une catégorie juridique fonctionnelle à définir' in *Mélanges Francis Delpérée* (Brussels, Bruylant-LGDJ, 2007); J-D Mouton, 'Vers la reconnaissance d'un droit au respect de l'identité nationale pour les Etats membres de l'Union' in *La France, l'Europe et le monde. Mélanges en l'honneur de Jean Charpentier* (Paris, Pedone, 2009); M Troper, 'Identité constitutionnelle' in B Mathieu (ed), *1958–2008. Cinquantième anniversaire de la Constitution française* (Paris, Dalloz, 2008).

basic choices of the host society. The recognition of such a duty could put some further flesh on the bare bones of the reference made by Article 20(2) TFEU to citizens' duties.[35]

From this perspective, European citizenship could be linked with the legitimacy of the EU, which implies achieving further integration while preserving national identity (and sovereign authority) of the Member States. National identity forms part of the very political existence of the States, which has to be maintained within the Union of peoples and of States established by the Treaties. It has to be recalled that Article 6 TEU provides that the Union shall respect the national identities of its Member States; this provision, existing since the Treaty of Maastricht, has been considerably reinforced by the Treaty of Lisbon.[36]

How does the Court deal with Member States asserting the respect owed to their constitutional identity? In 1996, in a case concerning the public service exception to free movement of workers, the Court explicitly recognised that the preservation of Member States' national identities was a legitimate aim.[37] More recently, in cases like *Omega* (prohibition of a laser-game considered as contrary to the German conception of human dignity),[38] or *Spain v UK* (the right of Gibraltar residents who were non-EU citizens to participate in elections for the European Parliament),[39] the Court has lent sympathetic ears to arguments invoking national constitutional specificities. Thus, in *Omega*, Germany could rely on its particular conception of human dignity, shaped by its history and political culture and enshrined in its constitution, in order to justify a restriction to the free movement of services, even though this conception was not shared by other Member States. In *Spain v UK*, the UK was allowed to interpret the personal scope of electoral rights associated with Union citizenship in accordance with its 'constitutional traditions' and therefore grant such rights to non-Union citizens who possessed stable ties with its territory.

Furthermore, Advocate General Poiares Maduro, in his opinion in *Michaniki*, after qualifying the Union's obligation to respect the constitutional identity of Member States as 'part of the very essence of the European project', argues that

[35] The duty not to engage in abusive conduct in the host society could be seen as another duty of the EU citizen. See the Opinion of AG Poiares Maduro in Case C-222/07 *Rottmann*, judgment of 2 March 2010.

[36] SC Sieberson also thinks that the Treaty of Lisbon goes beyond former Art 6(3) TEU, stressing 'the continuing importance and vitality of the Member States as sovereign nations whose national identities are manifested in the functions and structures of nationhood': *Dividing Lines between the European Union and its Member States* (Cambridge, Cambridge University Press, 2008) 93.

[37] Case C-473/93 *Commission v Luxembourg* [1996] ECR I-3207. The Luxembourg government argued that school teachers had to be Luxembourg nationals in order to transmit traditional values and that, in view of the specific demographic situation of the country, the nationality requirement was essential for preserving Luxembourg's national identity. The Court answered that the general exclusion of non-nationals was disproportionate and that less restrictive conditions relating to training, experience and knowledge of the language could be imposed in order to satisfy the legitimate aim of preserving national identity.

[38] Case C-36/02 *Omega* [2004] ECR I-9609.

[39] Case C-145/04 *Spain v UK* [2006] ECR I-7917.

protection of such identity can be asserted 'in order to justify a derogation from the application of the fundamental freedoms of movement'.[40]

Governments should, of course, thoroughly demonstrate the particular sensitivity of national value judgements reflected in challenged legislation or practice.[41] And somehow paradoxically, the Court could become the ultimate judge of what national constitutional identity is actually comprised of. Such review, as Niamh Nic Shuibhne points out, 'entrusts the Court of Justice with a deep degree of confidence (an investment that can bear mixed dividends) to be able to distinguish appropriately between commendable preservation of national values and more pliable national standards that should legitimately give way to free movement law. Working out what should and should not be included within the preserved State value core is by no means straightforward.'[42] Another name case, *Sayn-Wittgenstein*,[43] illustrates this difficulty.

The claimant, an Austrian citizen, was adopted, already being of adult age, by a German national, Fürst von Sayn-Wittgenstein (Prince of Sayn-Wittgenstein). She was then allowed under German law to use the name Fürstin von Sayn-Wittgenstein (Princess of Sayn-Wittgenstein). The competent Austrian authorities had been informed of the adoption and had entered the name Fürstin von Sayn-Wittgenstein. Fifteen years later they rectified it deleting the 'Fürstin von' part. This rectification was based on Austrian constitutional law, more specifically on the Adelsaufhebungsgesetz (Law Abolishing Nobility). This law, enacted in 1919 when Austria abolished monarchy and established the First Republic, prohibits the use of nobility titles. The referring tribunal asked whether the prohibition on the use of the 'princess' part of the name was contrary to Article 18 EC (now Article 21 TFEU).

The Austrian government argued that the abolition of the nobility is a constitutional principle of overriding importance in Austria, based on fundamental considerations of public policy such as equality between citizens and the eradication of privilege. Such principle is capable of justifying a prohibition on the use of noble titles, even if that prohibition might cause inconvenience to an Austrian national exercising his or her rights as a citizen of the Union.

Following the position of Advocate General Sharpston, the Court admits that the law of 1919 should be considered as a core element of Austrian constitutional

[40] Paras 31 and 32 of the Opinion in Case C-127/07 *Michaniki* [2009] ECR I-9999.

[41] AG Poiares Maduro also stresses that 'respect owed to the constitutional identity of the Member States cannot be understood as an absolute obligation to defer to all national constitutional rules. Were that the case, national constitutions could become instruments allowing Member States to avoid Community law in given fields. Furthermore, it could lead to discrimination between Member States based on the contents of their respective national constitutions. Just as Community law takes the national constitutional identity of the Member States into consideration, national constitutional law must be adapted to the requirements of the Community legal order': para 33 of the Opinion in Case C-127/07 *Michaniki* [2009] ECR I-9999.

[42] N Nic Shuibhne, 'Margins of Appreciation: National Values, Fundamental Rights and EC Free Movement Law' (2009) 34 *EL Rev* 230.

[43] Case C-208/09 *Sayn-Wittgenstein*, judgment of 22 December 2010; annotation by D Simon, *Europe*, February 2011, 11.

identity, capable of justifying derogations from a Treaty freedom. In other words, the Court does not put into question what the Austrian government presents as being part of Austrian identity. However, it has to be noted that Austrian legal doctrine is not unanimous on the question. On the one hand, Martin Attlmayr gives a positive answer since this Law, which reflects an essential value judgement, is closely linked to the republican and democratic principles that are pillars of the Austrian constitutional order.[44] On the other hand, Thomas Kröll argues that the law is no longer an essential element of the republican principle and, therefore, not crucial to the Austrian constitutional identity;[45] Austria is no longer a young and fragile republic struggling out of the ruins of an empire dominated by privileged classes and thus requiring special guarantees. The Court does not enter into such debate and thus avoids what some might qualify as undue interference with national capacity to decide what constitutional identity should be all about. Instead, it explicitly recognises a margin of discretion benefiting national authorities when relying on public policy grounds,[46] to which the Court seems to attach protection of constitutional identity. Indeed, it has to be noted that in a case whose circumstances were similar to those of the *Sayn-Wittgenstein* case, the Austrian Constitutional Court had ruled, in 2003, that the law of 1919 precluded an Austrian citizen from acquiring, through adoption by a German citizen, a surname composed of a former title of nobility.[47]

The 'hands-off' approach of the Court can also be witnessed in the control of the proportionality of the Austrian measure. The standard of review seems unusually low in the present case since the Court simply states that 'by refusing to recognise the noble elements of a name such as that of the applicant in the main proceedings, the Austrian authorities responsible for civil status matters do not appear to have gone further than is necessary in order to ensure the constitutional objective pursued by them'.[48] The Court refrains from mentioning, at this stage, any of the particular factual circumstances of the case, such as the length of time (15 years) over which the name was used without challenge, legitimate expectation thus created and the personal and professional interest which the applicant had in maintaining the use of the name Fürstin von Sayn-Wittgenstein. All these elements were highlighted in the opinion of Advocate General Sharpston, who suggested leaving the final word on proportionality to the referring judge.

[44] M Attlmayr, 'Adelsaufhebungsgesetz und das Gemeinschaftsrecht' [2010] *Journal für Rechtspolitik* 1. The republican principle can only be changed by a 2/3 majority in the Austrian Parliament in combination with an obligatory referendum.

[45] T Kröll, 'Adelsaufhebungsgesetz und Unionbürgerschaft oder EuGH und Emotionen (C-208/09 *Sayn-Wittgenstein*)' [2010] *Zeitschrift für Verwaltung* 177.

[46] Case C-208/09 *Sayn-Wittgenstein*, judgment of 22 December 2010, para 87.

[47] Verfassungsgerichtshof, 27 November 2003, B 557/03. More recently, the Austrian Constitutional Court stressed the constitutional importance attached to the prohibition of the nobility, by upholding the so-called 'Habsburg law' of 1919, which prohibits members of the Habsburg family from running in the presidential election in Austria. This law was challenged by a descendant of the ancient royal family who was not allowed run for president in the last election in 2010.

[48] Case C-208/09 *Sayn-Wittgenstein*, judgment of 22 December 2010, para 93.

The judgment in *Sayn-Wittgenstein* will certainly be remembered as the first reference made by the Court to Article 4(2) TEU and the obligation of the Union 'to respect the national identities of its Member States, which include the status of the State as a Republic'.[49] This provision, which could previously have been seen as incorporating a political declaration with merely symbolic value, may now become an important source of legal arguments for Member States. Such transformation is, at the same time, carefully framed by the Court. Indeed, the Court places the accent on the fact that the Law on the abolition of the nobility constitutes implementation of the more general principle of equality before the law of all Austrian citizens.[50] The Court is keen on reminding that equality is also a general principle of EU law, furthermore enshrined in Article 20 of the Charter of Fundamental Rights. According to the Court, 'there can therefore be no doubt that the objective of observing the principle of equal treatment is compatible with European Union law'.[51] In other words, the Court signals its intention to control compatibility of constitutional identities with European values. It somehow seeks to incorporate national identities into a wider European identity, based on common values.

Given the novelty and the importance of the solution in *Sayn-Wittgenstein*, one regrets the ambivalence of the Court's reasoning concerning the precise nature of the justification based on the protection of national identity. At first, the Court seems to validate the point of view of the Austrian government and the referring judge considering such justification as a legitimate objective of general interest (ie a jurisprudential derogation).[52] Yet, quite surprisingly, the Court then affirms that 'the justification relied upon by the Austrian government by reference to the Austrian constitutional situation is to be interpreted as reliance on public policy'[53] (ie an express treaty derogation). However, the subsequent judgment in *Vardyn & Wardyn*,[54] another name case, makes no reference to the public policy derogation and solely uses the terms 'legitimate objective' and 'objective considerations'.

Vardyn & Wardyn illustrates the States' readiness to plead respect owed to their national identity. In this case, Mrs Wardyn, a Lithuanian national belonging to the Polish minority of Lithuania, and her Polish husband, both residing in Belgium, were contesting the Lithuanian rules providing that a person's name may be entered on the certificates of civil status only in a form which complies with the rules governing the spelling of Lithuanian, the official national language. In its judgment, the Court reiterates the reference to Article 4(2) TEU and indicates that national identity 'includes protection of a State's official national language'.[55] The Court adds

[49] Ibid, para 92.

[50] Ibid, para 88.

[51] Ibid, para 89.

[52] Such a position is also in line with the judgment in Case C-473/93 *Commission v Luxembourg* [1996] ECR I-3207.

[53] Case C-208/09 *Sayn-Wittgenstein*, judgment of 22 December 2010, para 84.

[54] Case C-391/09 *Vardyn & Wardyn*, judgment of 12 May 2011.

[55] Ibid, para 86. The Lithuanian government stressed, in particular, that 'the Lithuanian language constitutes a constitutional asset which preserves the nation's identity, contributes to the integration of citizens and ensures the expression of national sovereignty, the indivisibility of the State and the proper functioning of the services of the State and the local authorities' (see para 84 of the judgment).

a reference to the Union's duty, enshrined in the Charter of Fundamental Rights, to respect its cultural and linguistic diversity.

Sayn-Wittgenstein and *Vardyn & Wardyn* thus make clear that Member States may argue the protection of their national identities in order to justify restrictions on the exercise of Union citizenship rights. Even though (quite ironically) *Sayn-Wittgenstein* concerns the claim of a national migrant against her home State, in *Vardyn & Wardyn* the argument concerning national identity is used by Lithuania against the claims of both Mrs Wardyn (a Lithuanian national) and her husband (a Polish national). The shield of national identity could then be used against the claims of migrant citizens contesting essential rules and/or practices of the host Member State.

The developments in this section can be summarised as follows. Union citizenship guarantees a double right for the migrant:

- The right to become a full member of the society of the host Member State. The corollary of this right is the duty to respect this Member State's founding values and principles which form its national identity.
- The right to preserve one's ties with the home Member State. Membership of the national community cannot be deemed to be forfeited when an individual decides to leave the State.[56]

Therefore, the migrant, empowered by his or her 'fundamental status' of Union citizenship, becomes a mediator, a bridge between two spaces, the home and the host Member State. European citizenship is thus not about creating a European identity but about protecting the particular identity of the migrant (and the dual national). There lies the essence of the transnational character of European citizenship.

III UNION CITIZENSHIP AND PROTECTION OF FAMILY LIFE IN TRANSNATIONAL SITUATIONS

The right to become a full member of the society of the host Member State implies securing stability of residence not only for the Union citizen but also for his or her family members, irrespective of whether they are Union citizens or third country nationals. Indeed one is likely to establish oneself in a State in which one is able to live with one's family. This is why Directive 2004/38 provides for residency rights for family members of Union citizens who are third country nationals, as Regulation 1612/68 had previously done for workers. Interestingly, these provi-

[56] For a different opinion, see G Davies, '"Any place I hang my hat?" or: residence is the new nationality' (2005) 11 ELJ 43. This author argues that 'Europe does not just require the absorption of foreigners, but also the rejection of expatriates'. According to him, a meaningful notion of equality 'means treating the emigré national like a foreigner, not just treating the foreign resident like a national. This challenges directly the idea that the national enjoys a permanent bond with his home country, wherever he may go.'

sions of the Directive are the ones that have met the most serious problems of implementation in Member States, according to a European Commission report.[57]

In a series of cases, the ECJ gives full effect to the derivative right of residence of family members of the EU citizen, imposing in this way a further limit to the powers of Member States in relation to immigration control. The case that has attracted most attention (and highly negative reactions) from the political class and the media is *Metock*.[58] The Court recognised the existence of a right of residence for third country national spouses of migrant Union citizens, in cases where the wedding had taken place in the host State and even if the spouses had previously been unlawfully present on the Member State's territory.[59] The Court emphasised 'the importance of ensuring the protection of the family life of nationals of the Member States in order to eliminate obstacles to the exercise of the fundamental freedoms guaranteed by the EC Treaty'.[60] 'If Union citizens were not allowed to lead a normal family life in the host Member State, the exercise of the freedoms that are guaranteed by the treaty would be seriously obstructed.'[61]

Metock thus 'represents recognition of the reality of family life in the context of mobility'[62] and reflects the Court's pragmatic and modern vision of such reality. This constitutes a big leap from the traditional model of family relations reflected in Regulation 1612/68 where the male worker moved with his wife and children to the host Member State. This model is still reflected in the wording of Directive 2004/38, which refers to family members who 'accompany or join' the Union citizen in the host State. The Court attaches no significance to a literal reading of the Directive. Its reasoning is inspired by the will to guarantee the effectiveness of the right of residence of Union citizens through the protection of their family life. The migrant is empowered to create family ties in the host society. The host State is no longer considered essentially as a working context where migrants can simply realise their professional potential; it is equally a social area where migrants are invited to develop new social and family relations. If the status of Community worker guaranteed family reunification for the migrant, Union citizenship enables and motivates family formation in the host State.

The '*Metock* ethos' of securing residency rights of EU citizens' family members also informs the *Ibrahim* and *Texeira* rulings,[63] which broaden the potential scope

57 Report from the Commission to the European Parliament and the Council on the application of Directive 2004/38 on the right of citizens of the Union and their family members to move and reside freely within the territory of the Member States, COM (2008) 840.

58 Case C-127/08 *Metock* [2008] ECR I-6241.

59 Overruling in this way Case C-109/01 *Akrich* [2003] ECR I-9607, which imposed the condition of previous legal residence of third country nationals.

60 Case C-127/08 *Metock* [2008] ECR I-6241, para 56.

61 Ibid, para 62.

62 S Currie, 'Accelerated Justice or a Step too Far? Residence Rights of Non-EU Family Members and the Court's Ruling in *Metock*' (2009) 34 *EL Rev* 310.

63 Case C-310/08 *Ibrahim*, judgment of 23 February 2010; Case C-480/08 *Texeira*, judgment of 23 February 2010. See annotations by C O'Brien (2011) 48 *CML Rev* 203; E Starup and H Elsmore (2010) 35 *EL Rev* 571.

of *Baumbast and R*.[64] Children of former EU migrant workers can rely on Article 12 of Regulation 1612/68 in order to claim autonomous educational and residency rights in the host State. Their primary carer, either a Union citizen or a third country national, also derives a right of residence, even if he or she does not satisfy conditions of economic autonomy. Such solutions contribute to the construction of security of residence for Union citizens,[65] including for those whose migration was not chosen but which resulted from their parents' decision. The host society has to allow Union citizens' family members to continue their process of integration, especially through the educational system and the support of their primary carer.

It remains to be seen whether the *Metock* ethos will also prove capable of protecting residency rights of less typical family members, such as partners. Article 2(2)(b) of Directive 2004/38 includes in the notion of 'family members' who are beneficiaries of the right of residence 'the partner with whom the Union citizen has contracted a registered partnership, on the basis of the legislation of a Member State, if the legislation of the host Member State treats registered partnership as equivalent to marriage and in accordance with the conditions laid down in the relevant legislation of the host Member State'. Outside this hypothesis, the Directive provides that the host State should facilitate entry and residence of 'the partner with whom the Union citizen has a durable relation, duly attested',[66] 'in order to maintain the unity of the family in a broader sense'.[67] In case of refusal opposed by national authorities, the citizen's claim could be directly based on primary law, ie Article 21 TFEU. After all, this would not be the first time the Court used this provision in order to read EU secondary legislation in a more favourable light for the migrant at the moment of enforcement by national authorities.[68] Directive 2004/38 simply regulates the right conferred by Article 21 TFEU. Such provision then becomes relevant as (probably more than anything else) the impossibility of living with one's partner is likely to discourage any initiative to exercise the right to free movement.[69]

IV UNION CITIZENSHIP AND PROTECTION OF FUNDAMENTAL RIGHTS IN TRANSNATIONAL SITUATIONS

In the name cases, Union citizenship, combined either with the principle of non-discrimination or with the 'obstacle to free movement' approach, becomes the legal tool for protecting the citizen's right to a name. In *Metock*, Union citizenship

[64] Case C-413/99 *Baumbast and R* [2002] ECR I-7091.

[65] Even though the judgments do not engage with Union citizenship but focus entirely on Art 12 of Reg 1612/68 and initial migrant work as a source of these rights.

[66] Art 3(2) of Dir 2004/38.

[67] Recital 6 of Dir 2004/38.

[68] See Case C-413/99 *Baumbast and R* [2002] ECR I-7091 and the analysis of M Dougan, 'The Constitutional Dimension to the Caselaw on Union Citizenship' (2006) 31 *EL Rev* 613.

[69] H Toner, *Partnership Rights, Free Movement and EU Law* (Oxford, Hart Publishing, 2004) 193 ff.

in alliance with the 'barrier to movement' approach performs the same function regarding the right to respect for family life.[70] In both cases, Union citizenship fulfils a specific role, which was enshrined in ex-Article 2 TEU – that of an instrument designed to 'strengthen the protection of the rights and interests of the nationals of Member States'. This protection offered through the prism of EU law is more extensive than that provided by the European Court of Human Rights on the basis of Article 8 ECHR.[71] This means that a human rights conflict with a transnational dimension is sometimes likely to have a more favourable outcome for the individual than a 'purely internal' conflict of a similar nature. Individuals (their legal advisors actually) will then be tempted to look for transnational elements in their situation for their claim to stand a better chance.

And this once again begs the question: can *any* violation of human rights qualify as an obstacle to free movement? A similar question has been asked outside the EU context, when the Supreme Court of the USA was called upon to interpret the (interstate) commerce clause empowering Congress to enact appropriate legislation. Two judgments delivered in 1964, *Heart of Atlanta Motel Inc v United States*[72] and *Katzenbach v McClung*,[73] are of particular interest in this respect. The Supreme Court considered that the politics of exclusion practised by a motel (in the first case) and a restaurant (in the second case) against black travellers affected interstate commerce, since such 'a moral and social wrong'[74] had 'a direct and highly restrictive effect upon interstate travel'.[75] The Supreme Court stressed 'the overwhelming evidence of the disruptive effect that racial discrimination has had on commercial intercourse'.[76] Its case law over the past thirty years has provided generous interpretations of the commerce clause and the respective powers of Congress. In the 1990s, the Supreme Court decided to place some limits on this approach, considering that only activities (including those related to human rights protection) which *substantially* affect the interstate commerce could become the object of a federal regulation on the basis of the commerce clause.[77]

[70] Also see Case C-274/96 *Bickel and Franz* [1998] ECR I-7637, where the Court protected through the means of Union citizenship the right to due process.

[71] On this point, see (for the name cases) A Iliopoulou, 'What's in a name? Citoyenneté, égalité et droit au nom. A propos de l'arrêt *Garcia Avello*' [2004] *Revue trimestrielle de droit européen* 565; and (for the *Metock* case), C Costello, '*Metock*: Free Movement and "Normal Family Life" in the Union' (2009) 46 *CML Rev* 587.

[72] 379 US 241 (1964).

[73] 379 US 294 (1964).

[74] *Heart of Atlanta Motel*, para 7.

[75] *Katzenbach v McClung*, para 4: 'Moreover there was an impressive array of testimony that discrimination in restaurants had a direct and highly restrictive effect upon interstate travel by Negroes. This resulted, it was said because discriminatory practices prevent Negroes from buying prepared food served on the premises while on a trip, except in isolated and unkempt restaurants and under most unsatisfactory and often unpleasant conditions. This obviously discourages travel and obstructs interstate commerce for one can hardly travel without eating. Likewise, it was said that discrimination deterred professional, as well as skilled, people from moving into areas where such practices occurred and thereby caused industry to be reluctant to establish there.'

[76] *Heart of Atlanta Motel*, para 7.

[77] *United States v Lopez*, 514 US 549 (1995); *United States v Morrison*, 529 US 598 (2000).

In the EU context, fundamental rights protection acquires relevance with reference to the *effectiveness* of freedom to move. The Court has construed effectiveness as a particularly flexible notion through the (now familiar) large definition of an obstacle to movement as anything likely to hinder, deter or simply discourage movement. Given the elasticity of the 'dissuasion effect' notion, human rights issues can easily obtain a transnational dimension in the context of Union citizenship. Let us take an example. French legislation adopted on 15 March 2004 is prohibiting students at school from wearing ostensible symbols of religious membership such as headscarves, crosses or the Sikh turban. A British Muslim moves to France and her daughter cannot wear the headscarf at school. Both mother and daughter could argue that this type of measure renders migration to France less attractive. The French government would then reply that this measure is necessary in order to preserve *laïcité*, which is a founding principle of its national society. Given that the ECtHR has already affirmed the compatibility of the French statute with the ECHR on the ground of France's margin of appreciation,[78] the ECJ would probably consider the French measure to constitute a justified and proportionate restriction to movement. In other cases however, if the ECtHR has not yet ruled on the issue, assessment by the ECJ becomes a more complicated and tricky exercise. In any case, since fundamental rights claims are likely to become more prominent in the context of citizens' movement, opportunities for the ECJ to scrutinise national legislation on human rights grounds will increase.

The impact which broad interpretations of *barriers* to movement may have on human rights issues could thus cause 'what might seem as undue interference with national autonomy in setting the fundamental rights standards in the domestic arena'.[79] This explains why, after the celebrated '*civis europeus sum*' statement of Advocate General Jacobs in *Konstantinidis*, depicting Union citizenship as a shield against *any* violation of the migrant's fundamental rights,[80] Advocate General Poiares Maduro has recently taken a different stand on the matter. In *Centro Europa 7 Srl* he states that 'only serious and persistent violations which highlight a problem of systemic nature in the protection of fundamental rights in the Member State at issue, would qualify as violations of the rules on free movement, by virtue of the direct threat they would pose to the transnational dimension of European citizenship and integrity of the EU legal order'.[81]

[78] ECHR, *Tuba Actas v France*, judgment of 30 June 2009, No 43563/08.

[79] E Spaventa, 'Federalisation Versus Centralization: Tensions in Fundamental Rights Discourse in the EU' in M Dougan and S Currie (eds), *50 years of the European Treaties: Looking Back and Thinking Forward* (Oxford, Hart Publishing, 2009).

[80] Paragraph 46 of the Opinion in Case C-168/91 *Konstantinidis* [1993] ECR I-1191: 'In my opinion, a Community national who goes to another Member State as a worker or self-employed person under Articles 48, 52 or 59 of the Treaty is entitled not just to pursue his trade or profession and to enjoy the same living and working conditions as nationals of the host State; he is in addition entitled to assume that, wherever he goes to earn his living in the European Community, he will be treated in accordance with a common code of fundamental values, in particular those laid down in the European Convention on Human Rights. In other words, *he is entitled to say 'civis europeus sum' and to invoke that status in order to oppose any violation of his fundamental rights*.'

[81] Para 22 of the Opinion in Case C-380/05 *Centro Europa 7 Srl* [2008] ECR I-349.

It has to be noted that the Advocate General uses the wording ('serious and persistent violations') of Article 7 TEU, which provides the possibility of inflicting political sanctions against a State infringing human rights. In light of the disappointing use of this mechanism up until now, the Advocate General's position in *Centro Europa 7* appears to place a rather high threshold for the intervention of the Court in matters relating to free movement and fundamental rights protection. For example: could we qualify as a 'persistent problem of systemic nature' the stigmatisation of the Roma community that took place in France in August 2010 as a result of the large-scale expulsions brought into the limelight by the French government itself?[82] The Commission seemed to think that way in the beginning but later changed its mind and focused on a less politically sensitive aspect: problematic implementation of Directive 2004/38.[83]

The Court has so far provided no clear and unambiguous answer to the question of which human rights violations are to be considered as obstacles to citizens' free movement. This question forms part of the more general uncertainty surrounding the exact scope of the Court's competence regarding fundamental rights protection. This uncertainty has to be dispelled especially at a time when fundamental rights protection is on a path to becoming an autonomous objective of the EU.[84] In the author's view, the Court should openly accept that any violation of human rights may qualify as a barrier to free movement. This is the only way of ensuring a coherent approach to the general definition of *obstacle* in the field of free movement. As for the Member States' regulatory autonomy in setting fundamental rights standards, such autonomy could best be preserved through the Court leaving the 'final word' to national judges on the assessment of a contested measure's proportionality. If the balancing exercise between conflicting interests takes place at national level, national preferences and particular sensitivities relating to certain issues are likely to be more adequately taken into consideration. This approach of 'jurisdictional subsidiarity'[85] is likely to enhance trust and

[82] In its *Comparative Report 2009: The Situation of Roma Citizens Moving to and Settling in other EU Member States* (available at www.fra.eu), the Fundamental Rights Agency convincingly argued that phenomena of racism, hostile behavior and stigmatisation of the Roma community place considerable barriers to the exercise by Union citizens of Roma origin of their right to free movement. It is interesting to see how this new European body in the human rights field uses the language and legal tools of 'free movement of EU citizens' to tackle a human rights issue.

[83] See A Iliopoulou, 'Le temps des gitans: à propos de la libre circulation des Roms dans l'Union', *Europe*, January 2011, 5.

[84] This is also the point of view of AG Sharpston in her Opinion in Case C-34/09 *Zambrano*, judgment of 8 March 2011. According to the AG, 'in the long run, the clearest rule would be one that made the availability of EU fundamental rights protection dependent neither on whether a Treaty provision was directly applicable nor on whether secondary legislation had been enacted, but rather on the existence and scope of a material EU competence. To put the point another way: the rule would be that, provided that the EU had competence (whether exclusive or shared) in a particular area of law, EU fundamental rights should protect the citizen of the EU even if such competence has not yet been exercised' (para 163 of the Opinion). The AG admits that such an evolution would require 'an unequivocal political statement from the constituent powers of the EU (its Member States), pointing at a new role for fundamental rights in the EU' (para 173 of the Opinion).

[85] D Simon, 'La subsidiarité juridictionnelle: notion-gadget ou concept opératoire?' [1998] *Revue des Affaires Européennes* 84.

cooperation between the ECJ and national judges as well as the legitimacy of the ECJ's intervention in the field of fundamental rights protection.

V BEYOND THE TRANSNATIONAL CHARACTER OF UNION CITIZENSHIP?

On 8 March 2011 the Grand Chamber of the Court delivered a decision eagerly expected after the remarkable and largely echoed opinion of Advocate General Sharpston, asserting the importance of bearing the consequences of the establishment of Union citizenship.[86] This ruling might be the starting point of a considerable change regarding the very nature of Union citizenship, even though it could take some time for its full implications to be realised. The Court held that Article 20 TFEU conferred a right of residence and employment upon the parents, third country nationals, of minor Union citizens who were born and had always resided in the Member State of their nationality.

No cross-border element could be found in the present case, yet the Court chose to allow the Zambrano family to rely on EU law. *Zambrano* thus takes a step further the evolution observed in cases such as *Carpenter*, *Garcia Avello*, *Chen* and *Rottmann*,[87] where a tenuous (or even artificial) link was identified in order to trigger application of the Treaty.[88] The Court further develops rather than simply reiterates the finding in *Rottmann*, when it holds that Union citizens must not be deprived of 'the genuine enjoyment of the substance of the rights conferred by virtue of their status as citizens of the Union'.[89] In this way, Article 20 TFEU as such was held capable to grant sedentary citizens, in the particular circumstances of the *Zambrano* case,[90] the same family reunification rights that Directive 2004/38 confers upon migrant citizens. Interestingly, even though Union citizenship is used to guarantee respect for family life, no human rights considerations appear in the judgment.[91] Accent is only placed on the necessary effectiveness of the rights composing the status of Union citizen and on the link between the citizen and the territory of the Union. The legal foundation of the judgment is Article 20 TFEU whereas previous judicial 'fleshing' of Union citizenship was based either on Article 21 TFEU or the combination of Articles 20 and 18 TFEU.[92] *Zambrano* could thus be seen as revealing the potential of Article 20 TFEU to develop to an autonomous source of rights freed from the obligation to move, and as the found-

[86] Case C-34/09 *Zambrano*, judgment of 8 March 2011.

[87] Cases C-60/00 *Carpenter* [2002] ECR I-6279; C-148/02 *Garcia Avello* [2003] ECR I-11613; C-200/02 *Chen* [2004] ECR I-9925; Case C-222/07 *Rottmann*, judgment of 2 March 2010.

[88] Though compare the analysis of Síofra O'Leary in this collection.

[89] Case C-34/09 *Zambrano*, judgment of 8 March 2011, para 42.

[90] The Zambrano children, born in Belgium, had acquired Belgian nationality because they would otherwise have been stateless.

[91] The fundamental rights issues were raised by the referring judge and analysed by AG Sharpston (paras 151–177 of the Opinion).

[92] The only case decided upon ex-Art 17 EC alone is Case C-222/07 *Rottmann*, judgment of 2 March 2010.

ing stone of a new construction of Union citizenship whose value would not only be located in transnational situations.

Yet in *Zambrano* the Court did not address two essential questions regarding the interpretation and scope of Union citizenship, even though these questions were raised by the referring judge and analysed by Advocate General Sharpston. First, the Court gave no answer to the interrogation as to whether Articles 18, 20 and 21 TFEU, read separately or in conjunction, conferred a right of residence in the territory of the Member State of nationality, irrespective of a previous exercise of free movement.[93] Secondly, the Court did not tackle the issue of reverse discrimination mentioned in the second preliminary question.[94] Nor did the Court indicate any intention to overrule previous judgments such as *Metock*, which left the family situation of sedentary citizens outside the realm of EU law. One then had to be cautious as to the conclusions to be drawn from *Zambrano*. The 'sympathetic character' of the case and the rather elliptical motivation of the judgment suggested the need to wait for new rulings providing further clarification of the Court's new reading of Union citizenship provisions.

The judgment in *McCarthy*,[95] a case referred to the Court by the Supreme Court of the United Kingdom, provides such clarification. Ms McCarthy, a dual British and Irish citizen, was born and always resided in the United Kingdom. Following her marriage to a Jamaican national lacking leave to remain under the British Immigration rules, she sought to rely on her Irish nationality and Directive 2004/38 in order to obtain residence rights for her and her husband in their respective qualities as a migrant Union citizen and her spouse. A literal, teleological and contextual interpretation of Directive 2004/38 logically led the Court to conclude that its provisions were not applicable to a citizen in a situation such as that of Ms McCarthy, who, despite her dual nationality, had never exercised her right of free movement. Having provided the interpretation of the secondary law sought by the referring judge, the Court then decided to stretch its answer further and to also address the issue on the basis of primary law. It is this part of the judgment that answers the questions left open by *Zambrano*.

The Court rules that Article 21 TFEU cannot in principle be relied upon by a sedentary Union citizen, even one possessing dual nationality. The Court recognises two exceptions to this rule, corresponding to the solutions given in *Zambrano* and *Garcia Avello*. Article 21 TFEU can be invoked against national measures that have the effect either of depriving the individual of the genuine enjoyment of the substance of the rights conferred by Union citizenship (*Zambrano*), or of impeding the exercise of his or her right of free movement and residence within

[93] AG Sharpston considers that 'Article 21 TFEU contains a separate right to reside that is independent of the right of free movement' and recommends 'that the Court now recognize the existence of that free-standing right of residence' (paras 100 and 101 of the Opinion).

[94] According to AG Sharpston 'Article 18 TFEU should be interpreted as prohibiting reverse discrimination caused by the interaction between Article 21 TFEU and national law that entails a violation of a fundamental right protected under EU law, where at least equivalent protection is not available under national law' (para 144 of the Opinion).

[95] Case C-434/09, *McCarthy*, judgment of 5 May 2011.

the territory of the Member States (*Garcia Avello*). The Court then distinguishes the situation of Ms McCarthy from the factual contexts of these precedents. The refusal of the British authorities to take into account the Irish nationality of Ms McCarthy does not oblige her to leave the territory of the Union. Being a British national and an adult, she enjoys, without the need of any support, an unconditional right of residence in the United Kingdom, whereas the Zambrano children, because of their young age, could not in practice exercise their Union citizenship rights independently of their parents' presence in Belgium. Neither is, according to the Court, Ms McCarthy impeded from exercising her movement rights within the territory of the Member States.

Clearly then the Court in *McCarthy* opts for a narrow reading of *Zambrano* and considerably limits its potential effects.[96] The sedentary citizen will have to demonstrate the risk of being deprived of the very substance of his or her Union citizenship rights in order to avail him- or herself of the protection offered by this status. Recent jurisprudential developments certainly attenuate but do not erase the distinction between 'mobile-cosmopolitan' and 'sedentary-provincial' citizens. At least for the years to come, Union citizenship will represent added value in principle for the former and only exceptionally for the latter. In other words the character of this status will mainly remain transnational.

VI CONCLUSION

If citizenship is ultimately about membership, European citizenship is about protecting and encouraging dual (more generally, multiple) membership, one defined by nationality and the other by residence. The legal bond resulting from European citizenship provides a certain account of the migrant's particular position in two systems and his or her privileged relations with respect to two different spaces: the home State and the host State. It empowers and provides incentives for migrants to integrate into the host society while at the same time offering the possibility of preserving links with the home State. European citizenship thus harbours a particular conception of integration into the host society: the acculturation of new members following from adhesion to the host society's core values should respectfully coexist with their original identities.

Consequently, EU migrants are likely to develop a commitment to the EU as it is EU law which guarantees their rights in transnational situations. The legal bond resulting from Union citizenship would therefore correspond to social reality but only as far as migrants are concerned.[97] This is certainly important but definitely not sufficient for the creation of a stronger common identity of all Union

[96] See, more recently, case C-256/11, *Dereci and others*, judgment of 15 November 2011.

[97] This is criticised by E Spaventa, 'Seeing the Wood Despite the Trees? On the Scope of Union Citizenship and its Constitutional Effects' (2008) 45 *CML Rev* 13, who notes that 'the very idea of citizenship sits uncomfortably with an a priori differentiation between citizens based on the sole ground that a border has been crossed'.

citizens.[98] It nevertheless seems logical for Union citizenship to predominantly deal with the protection of EU migrants since the Union itself is perceived by a significant proportion of Europeans as signifying first and foremost the 'freedom to travel, study and work anywhere in the EU'.[99]

[98] Editorial, 'Two-speed European Citizenship? Can the Lisbon Treaty Help Close the Gap?' (2008) 45 *CML Rev* 1.

[99] This is what 42% of Europeans answered when asked 'What does the EU mean?', according to the September 2009 Eurobarometer report.

2

The Past, Present and Future of the Purely Internal Rule in EU Law

SÍOFRA O'LEARY*

I INTRODUCTION

ACCORDING TO ONE of the orthodox, even sacred, tenets of EU law, developed principally in the context of the rules on the free movement of goods, persons and services, the latter cannot be invoked in respect of activities which have no bearing on any of the situations governed by EU law.[1] Where there is no factor linking a case with any of those situations and all of the elements of the case are purely internal to a single Member State, the Treaty rules governing free movement are deemed not to be applicable. That link or attachment has traditionally taken the form of some cross-border economic activity which brought the applicant's case outside the bounds of national and into the realm of EU law. Thus, in order to rely on EU as distinct from national law to found a right of residence for himself and his non-EU spouse, a Member State national had to move from one Member State to another, thereby activating the rights of residence and related rights to family reunification conferred by EU law. That same national could also rely on EU law as against his own Member State on his return, but prior movement was regarded as a necessary precondition. Purely internal situations were deemed not to come within the scope of application of EU law and, as a result, did not fall within the jurisdiction of the Court.[2]

* The views expressed in this chapter are purely personal to the author. An earlier version of this chapter was published in (2010) *Irish Jurist* 13–46.

[1] The key provisions of the EEC Treaty on the free movement of persons and services are, subject to amendment and renumbering, to be found in Arts 45 (workers), 49 (establishment) and 56 (services) TFEU, which came into force following the ratification of the Treaty of Lisbon. In this chapter, reference will generally be made to EU law and the relevant provisions of the TFEU unless clarity requires otherwise.

[2] Note that the Court has, on occasion, confirmed that a case is wholly internal but nevertheless maintained its jurisdiction to answer the preliminary reference from the national court. It has justified its position with reference to the cooperative nature of its relationship with national courts in the context of the preliminary reference procedure (Art 267 TFEU), the need to provide those courts with answers which they may deem useful and the need to ensure the uniformity of EU law in the event that the provisions of national law require that a Member State's own nationals be granted the same rights

The EU operates on the basis of attributed competences, albeit ones which have been expanded by successive, often far-reaching, Treaty amendments. The principle of conferral in Articles 5(1) and 5(2) TEU provides that the EU shall act only within the limits of the competences conferred upon it by the Member States in the Treaties to attain the objectives set out therein. The purpose of the purely internal rule is essentially to delimit the scope of application of EU law with reference to the objectives or goals the EU seeks to achieve while respecting the delicate and often contested division of competence between it and its Member States. Nevertheless, the much-criticised consequence of the application of this rule is reverse discrimination: a situation which arises when a Member State's own nationals find themselves treated less favourably by their Member State of origin than nationals of other Member States. Absent any cross-border element, their failure to avail of their free movement rights under EU law or their inability to link themselves in some way with one of the situations envisaged or governed by EU law, their case is regarded as purely internal to that Member State and, therefore, governed by its laws. Where the application of national law leads to less favourable treatment than would result from the application of EU rules, reverse discrimination arises.[3] It is, according to the Court's established case law, for Member States to remedy any difference in treatment which may result from the application of two distinct but parallel regulatory regimes, if necessary with reference to their obligations pursuant to the European Convention for the Protection of Human Rights and Fundamental Freedoms (ECHR) signed in Rome on 4 November 1950.[4]

The purpose of this chapter is to reappraise the origins, raison d'être, application and evolution of the purely internal rule. It explores what situations are governed or

as those which other Member States' nationals would derive from EU law. See, eg Cases C-297/88 and C-197/89 *Dzodzi* [1990] ECR I-3763; Case C-448/98 *Guimont* [2000] ECR I-663; more recently, Case C-570/07 *Blanco Perez*, judgment of 1 June 2010. This 'jurisdictional' deviation in the case law on the purely internal rule is not examined in this chapter.

[3] See further D Pickup, 'Reverse Discrimination and Freedom of Movement for Workers' (1986) 23 *CML Rev* 137; M Poiares Maduro, 'The Scope of European Remedies: The Case of Purely Internal Situations and Reverse Discrimination' in C Kilpatrick, T Novitz and P Skidmore (eds), *The Future of European Remedies* (Oxford, Hart Publishing, 2000); F Picod, 'Libre circulation et situation interne' (2003–2004) 1 *Revue des affaires européennes* 47; N Nic Shuibhne, 'Free Movement of Persons and the Wholly Internal Rule: Time to Move On?' (2002) 39 *CML Rev* 763; E Spaventa, 'Seeing the Wood Despite the Trees? On the scope of Union Citizenship and its Constitutional Effects' (2008) 45 *CML Rev* 44; C Dauticourt and S Thomas, 'Reverse Discrimination and Free Movement of Persons under Community law: All for Ulysses, Nothing for Penelope?' (2009) 34 *EL Rev* 433; S Currie, 'The Transformation of Union Citizenship' in M Dougan and S Currie (eds), *50 Years of the European Treaties* (Oxford, Hart Publishing, 2009) 365; A Tryfonidou, 'Reverse Discrimination in Purely Internal Situations: An Incongruity in a Citizens' Europe' (2008) 35 *Legal Issues of Economic Integration* 43; A Tryfonidou, *Reverse Discrimination in EC Law* (Alphen aan den Rijn, Kluwer Law International, 2009).

[4] See Cases C-64/96 and C-65/96 *Uecker and Jacquet* [1997] ECR I-3171, para 23; Case C-127/08 *Metock* [2008] ECR I-6241, paras 78–79; Case C-104/08 *Kurt* [2008] ECR I-97, para 23. On reverse discrimination as a product of two competing regimes see, in particular, E Cannizzaro, '"Producing" Reverse Discrimination through the Exercise of EC Competences' (1997) 17 *Yearbook of European Law* 29.

envisaged by EU law, thereby escaping the exclusionary effects of that rule. It examines whether, in the light of repeated Treaty amendments, notably the introduction of the status of Union citizenship,[5] the exercise of free movement and the existence of a cross-border element still remain central to the protection afforded individual Member State nationals by EU law. All Member State nationals are Union citizens and their right to move and reside freely, albeit subject to conditions and limitations, is now no longer dependent on the performance of an economic activity as a worker, self-employed person or provider of services as it was under the Treaty of Rome. A perceived lack of coherence, even arbitrariness, in the Court's case law since the introduction of that status has led to calls for the abandonment of the purely internal rule. In addition, since the Court acknowledges that Union citizenship incorporates, at its core, an equal treatment rule,[6] it has been argued that it is no longer tenable to differentiate between the rights of mobile and static Union citizens or determine the regulatory regime to which they are subject simply with reference to whether a border has been crossed or some other transnational element can be established.[7]

This chapter will suggest that a clearer understanding of the purely internal rule and its application by the Court can be gleaned by charting the evolving objectives of the EU and how the Court has deployed those objectives at various stages in its teleological interpretation of EU law.[8] The rationale for the purely internal rule when enunciated in early free movement case law was to include within the scope of EU law on the fundamental (economic) freedoms only situations which were sufficiently connected with the (economic) aims underpinning those freedoms. The relegation of those economic aims may have obscured the identification of the aims and objectives to which the Court must now refer in order to delimit the scope of EU law but that does not mean it has rendered the purely internal rule redundant. Concentrating on the evolving objectives of the EU to explain the application of the purely internal rule will not silence the critics of reverse discrimination, but it may go some way to explaining why the introduction of Union citizenship should be regarded as a far less transformative development than is otherwise supposed. It may also provide something of a riposte to those who depict the Court's application of the purely internal rule as entirely lacking in

[5] Union citizenship, introduced by the Treaty of Maastricht in 1992, was conferred on all Member State nationals who, qua Union citizens, enjoy the rights and are subject to the duties provided for in the Treaties (Art 20 TFEU).

[6] See, eg Case C-184/99 *Grzelczyk* [2001] ECR I-6193, para 31 and Case C-391/09 *Runevič-Vardyn*, judgment of 12 May 2011, para 65. The link between the status of citizen and the principle of equality is also made explicit in Art 9 TEU: 'In all its activities, the Union shall observe the principle of the equality of its citizens, who shall receive equal attention from its institutions, bodies, offices and agencies. Every national of a Member State shall be a citizen of the Union.'

[7] See, for a criticism of the Court's case law, the Opinions of Advocate General Sharpston in Case C-212/06 *Government of the French Community and Walloon Government* (hereafter the *Flemish Welfare Aid* case) [2008] ECR I-1683 and in Case C-34/09 *Ruiz Zambrano*, Opinion of 30 September 2010.

[8] The Court often adopts a contextual and/or teleological approach, placing a provision within its context and interpreting it with reference to the other provisions of EU law and examining its purpose, object or 'spirit'. See further, eg LN Brown and T Kennedy, *The Court of Justice of the European Communities*, 4th edn (London, Sweet & Maxwell, 1994) 311–17.

coherence. That being said, the Court has relied on the concept of Union citizenship, often in conjunction with fundamental rights, to justify or explain some of its more innovative decisions. It is suggested that the Treaty of Lisbon – a Treaty in which, ironically, Member States sought to delimit more clearly the division of Member State and EU competence – may, through its recognition of equal legal value for the Charter of Fundamental Rights, represent a far greater challenge to the purely internal rule and that division of competence than the creation of the status of Union citizenship.

II THE ORIGINS AND PAST APPLICATION OF THE PURELY INTERNAL RULE

To understand the purely internal rule it is essential to revisit the early case law of the Court on economic free movement in the common market which engendered it. These early cases divulge why cross-border movement was central to the purely internal rule, a rule which is both defined by and delimits the scope of application of EU rules and, consequently, the jurisdiction of the Court.

A The Origins of the Purely Internal Rule

In contrast to the provisions on establishment and services, the wording of Article 48 EEC on the free movement of workers (now Article 45 TFEU) did not suggest that the existence of a cross-border element was a condition precedent for the enjoyment of the rights conferred by that provision, not least the right not to be discriminated against on grounds of nationality.[9] Nevertheless, the Treaty provisions on the free movement of persons and services were applied in secondary legislation and interpreted by the Court with reference to the objective of precluding national measures which might place EU nationals at a disadvantage when they wished to pursue an economic activity in the territory of another Member State.[10] These rules thus came into play not when Member State nationals remained within the territory of their own Member State but when they moved to the territory of another host Member State for one of the purposes – essentially economic – defined by those freedoms and sought in that context to avail of the protection afforded by EU law. As regards their Member States of origin, EU nationals could rely on EU law on their return subsequent to employment as a migrant worker in another Member State or when seeking to work or establish themselves in their Member State of origin on the basis of qualifications achieved

[9] Article 48 EEC simply provided that freedom of movement for workers shall be secured within the then EEC by the end of the twelve-year transitional period. Article 52 EEC (now Art 49 TFEU) provided, in contrast, that 'restrictions on the freedom of establishment of nationals of a Member State *in the territory of another Member State* shall be abolished' (emphasis added).

[10] See, eg Art 1 Reg 1612/68 on freedom of movement for workers within the Community [1968] OJ L257/2; Art 3 Dir 2004/38/EC on the right of citizens of the Union and their family members to move and reside freely within the territory of the Member States [2004] OJ L229/35.

in another State.[11] However, these instances in which a Member State national relied on the provisions of the Treaty on free movement against his or her own State were supported by the essential objective initially underpinning the free movement rules, namely to facilitate free movement in a single market and guarantee its exercise free from discrimination. This essential objective can be clearly discerned in the discussions leading to the insertion of the free movement provisions in the EEC Treaty and in the 1956 Spaak Report, which contained the basic pattern for the European Atomic Energy Community and the EEC. The proposed inclusion of provisions on free movement was based on the unmistakeable belief that the elimination of obstacles to the free movement of persons would stimulate labour movements from Member States of low productivity to those industrial regions and economic sectors where productivity and demand for labour were highest, improving working and living standards across the region.[12] The principle of non-discrimination on grounds of nationality in Article 18 TFEU, which applies within the scope of application of the Treaties, was, in this context, a tool appropriated to further the economic goals of the EEC and, accordingly, its scope of application was shaped by those goals.[13]

The purely internal rule was first enunciated by the Court in *Knoors*, a case involving a Dutch national seeking to rely against his Member State of origin on an EU directive regulating self-employed activities.[14] Albeit stating clearly that the provisions of the Treaty on establishment and services cannot be applied to situations which are purely internal to a Member State, the Court held that the applicant, with regard to his State of origin, was in a situation which could be assimilated to that of any other person enjoying the rights and liberties guaranteed by the Treaty.[15] Those rights and liberties were provided to facilitate movement of employed and self-employed workers and (at that time) providers of services. Two elements brought the *Knoors* case outwith the purely internal rule. On the one hand, the applicant had resided, qualified and exercised his profession in another Member State. On the other, his trade qualification, acquired in a Member State other than his own, was recognised by EU harmonising legislation.[16]

Expressed as an obiter dictum in *Knoors*, the rule was first applied by the Court in *Saunders*. Ms Saunders, who originated from Northern Ireland but was working in England, was convicted of theft and was bound over by the criminal courts

[11] See Case 115/78 *Knoors* [1979] ECR 399 (effect in Member State of origin of acquisition of qualifications in another Member State) or Case C-370/90 *Singh* [1992] ECR I-4265 (right to family reunification in Member State of origin on return following establishment in another Member State) as discussed further below.

[12] The Spaak Report was produced by the intergovernmental committee established by the Messina conference of June 1956 and presented to the foreign ministries of the six founding Member States on 21 April 1956.

[13] See further G De Búrca, 'The Role of Equality in European Community Law' in A Dashwood and S O'Leary (eds), *The Principle of Equal Treatment in EC Law* (London, Sweet & Maxwell, 1997).

[14] *Knoors*, paras 2–6.

[15] Ibid, para 24.

[16] On the significance of EU harmonising legislation when applying the purely internal rule, see Case 136/78 *Auer* [1979] ECR 399 or Case C-61/89 *Bouchoucha* [1990] ECR I-3551.

in England in return for an undertaking that she remain in Northern Ireland for a period of three years.[17] On her arrest for failure to comply with this order, she claimed that this restriction on her movement within the UK was incompatible with the right to free movement conferred by Article 45 TFEU.[18] The Court in *Saunders* held that that provision seeks to abolish Member State legislation according to which a worker who is a national of another Member State is subject to more severe treatment or is placed in an unfavourable situation in law or in fact as compared with the situation of a national in the same circumstances.[19] It conceded that Article 45 TFEU can confer rights on a Member State national against his or her own Member State but reiterated that the Treaty does not concern situations which are wholly internal to a Member State. It defined such situations loosely as those 'where there is no factor connecting them to any of the situations envisaged by [EU] law' and excluded the application of EU free movement rules in the instant case on that basis.[20] Advocate General Warner was much more circumspect than the Court as regards the scope and application of the purely internal rule. He insisted that the dictum in *Knoors* could not be treated as a sweeping principle to the effect that no provision on free movement could be applied in a wholly internal situation. The true question in *Saunders*, in his view, was not whether the case had any connection with another Member State but whether, and if so, to what extent, EU law conferred rights on a person in the applicant's position. In his view, deportation orders had to be justified with reference to public policy or public security requirements, regardless of the nationality of the subject of deportation, on condition that the person in question possessed the nationality of a Member State. Thus, nationality of a Member State alone, could, in certain circumstances, suffice to bring a case within one of the situations envisaged by EU law. In essence, what was relevant to Advocate General Warner was not the existence of a cross-border element and proof of movement for the purpose of exercising an economic activity, but the effect which the decision being taken would have on the exercise by the individual of rights conferred by EU law.

B Cases Where the Link with EU Free Movement Law is Too Remote

In other cases the Court has rejected application of EU rules on the grounds that the obstacle or restriction of movement of which the applicant was complaining was too uncertain, indirect or remote to be considered capable of hindering free movement. Thus, the merely hypothetical chance that an EU national might

[17] Case 178/78 *Saunders* [1979] ECR 1129. For application of the *Knoors* case in the field of services see, eg Case 292/86 *Gullung* [1988] ECR 111.

[18] Following the introduction of Union citizenship, the question raised in *Saunders* reappeared in Case C-229/94 *Adams* [1994] OJ C275/19, where the Court was asked to examine the compatibility with the right of free movement of Union citizens under Art 21 TFEU of the exclusion order barring the leader of Sinn Féin, Gerry Adams, from entry into England and Wales. The case was withdrawn before judgment was reached.

[19] *Saunders*, para 9.

[20] Ibid, para 11.

move to another Member State and that his employment prospects in that State might be affected constitutes an insufficient or excessively remote connection with one of the situations envisaged by the EU rules on free movement.[21] The applicant in the *Kremzow* case, for example, was an Austrian national convicted of murder in Austria in a judgment later found to violate the ECHR.[22] He argued that, since he was a Union citizen and thus the beneficiary of a right of free movement under Article 21 TFEU, a Member State which violated that fundamental right by executing an unlawful penalty of imprisonment must be held to be liable in damages by virtue of EU law. As in *Saunders*, the applicant was challenging an internal obstacle to free movement which he claimed affected the rights conferred on him by EU law. The Court recognised that fundamental rights form an integral part of EU law and that it has jurisdiction to assess the compatibility with fundamental rights of national legislation which falls within the field of application of EU law. However, the applicant's situation was held not to be connected in any way with any of the situations contemplated by the Treaty provisions on the free movement of persons.[23] Mr Kremzow had been sentenced for murder under provisions of national law which were not designed to secure compliance with the rules of EU law and he was relying in support of his claim on a purely hypothetical exercise of his right to free movement in the EU. As a result, his situation did not fall within the field of application of EU law and the Court had no jurisdiction to examine whether the impugned national legislation was in conformity with fundamental rights, such as those deriving from the ECHR.

C The Purely Internal Rule and Reverse Discrimination in the Context of Family Reunification

Cases on the reunification of EU and non-EU family members highlight in the clearest and indeed rawest form the effects of the purely internal rule and its progeny – reverse discrimination. They also highlight to what extent reverse discrimination is the product of the parallel existence of two (competing) regulatory regimes at EU and national level. EU secondary legislation on free movement, adopted in the late 1960s, provided that a worker's family members, regardless of their nationality, could install themselves with the worker in the territory of the host Member State in which he or she was employed.[24] Both the Treaty and

[21] See Case 180/83 *Moser* [1984] ECR 2539 or Case C-190/98 *Graf* [2000] ECR I-493.

[22] Case C-299/95 *Kremzow* [1997] ECR I-2629.

[23] For circumstances in which the Member States' exercise of their competence in the field of criminal law may fall foul of the free movement rules, see Case C-348/96 *Calfa* [1999] ECR I-11 and Case C-27/96 *Bickel and Franz* [1998] ECR I-7637.

[24] See Art 10 Reg 1612/68; also Art 1 Dir 73/148 on the abolition of restrictions on movement and residence within the Community for nationals of Member States with regard to establishment and the provision of services [1973] OJ L172/14. These provisions were replaced and extended by Arts 2, 3(1), 5–7, 12–14, 16 of Dir 2004/38. The Court's case law on Reg 1612/68 consistently highlighted the human aspects of migration and the need to interpret the regulation in the light of the right to respect for family life set out in Art 8 of the ECHR: see, eg Case 249/86 *Commission* v *Germany* [1989] ECR 1263, paras 10–11.

secondary legislation were silent on the rights of entry and residence of family members on the return of economically active EU nationals to their Member State of origin following the exercise of their free movement rights. In time, the Court held that, for those rights to be fully effective, when such an EU national avails himself of his free movement rights and then returns to his Member State of origin, his spouse and family members must enjoy at least the same rights of entry and residence as would be granted to him under EU law if his spouse chose to enter and reside in another Member State.[25] EU law thus substitutes the national immigration provisions and controls which would otherwise apply with a substantive right to join the EU spouse, father, mother, daughter or son based on that person's Member State nationality and their exercise of their right to free movement in another Member State or on return to their Member State of origin and provides procedural guarantees to ensure that that right is respected.[26] As immigration rules and controls in many Member States have become more restrictive, the advantages of bringing one's case within the relevant EU rules on family reunification have been further enhanced.

When an EU national has not availed of his free movement rights, attempts to have his right to family reunification determined with reference to EU as distinct from national immigration provisions have proved less successful. The Court has resorted to the purely internal rule to dismiss claims by EU nationals who wished to be joined in their Member State of origin by non-EU family members. The applicants in *Morson and Jhanjan*, Dutch nationals of Surinamese origin resident in the Netherlands, argued that they, like nationals of other EU Member States resident or established in the Netherlands pursuant to Articles 45 and 49 TFEU, should have the right to be joined by their non-EU parents pursuant to the relevant provisions of EU secondary legislation. The Court demurred. Since Article 10 of Regulation 1612/68 did not cover the situation of dependent relatives of an EU worker who was a national of the Member State within whose territory he was employed and resided, the Court examined whether it could be inferred from the context of the free movement provisions and the place they occupy in the EU legal system as a whole that the third country national parents could derive a right of entry and residence from EU law.[27] The Court deduced from the wording of

[25] *Singh*, paras 19–23. The *Singh* decision is the subject of particular criticism because it meant a UK national was entitled, pursuant to EU law, to a right to family reunification on his return to the UK from another Member State which he would not have enjoyed, pursuant to national law, if he had remained in his Member State of origin. The Court is said to have concentrated excessively on the existence of cross-border movement without reference to whether denying the right to family reunification would actually have had a deterrent effect on the Member State national in question.

[26] For the extent of the limits on Member States' powers to refuse residence or expel non-EU family members, see Case C-459/99 *MRAX* [2002] ECR I-6591; and for discussion of the impact of EU law on national immigration law, see the Opinion of Advocate General Geelhoed in Case C-109/01 *Akrich* [2003] ECR I-9607.

[27] Joined Cases 35 and 36/82 *Morson and Jhanjan* [1982] ECR 3723, para 13. The form of the Court's inquiry and its willingness to look beyond the terms of secondary EU legislation highlights the teleological or objective orientated basis of its inquiry. See also, for a similar approach, Case C-60/00 *Carpenter* [2002] ECR I-6279, para 36, albeit the outcome of the latter case was dramatically different (see further below).

Article 18 TFEU, which provides that the principle of non-discrimination on grounds of nationality can only be invoked *within the scope of application of the Treaty*, that the Treaty provisions on the free movement of workers and the rules adopted to implement them cannot be applied to cases which have no factor linking them with any of the situations governed by EU law. This, it said, was undoubtedly the case with workers who have never exercised their right to freedom of movement. Thus, the remedies and protection afforded by EU law could be extended to Member State nationals against their Member States of origin, but only to the extent considered necessary to protect the fundamental principles underpinning the economic freedoms in the context of the internal market.

The harsh consequences which may flow from the absence of intra-EU movement were further evident in *Metock*, a case which generated considerable controversy in Ireland and elsewhere in the EU.[28] Irish legislation transposing Directive 2004/38, which regulates the rights of free movement and residence of all economically active and inactive Union citizens, included, for non-EU family members, a condition of prior lawful residence in another EU Member State. No such condition was explicitly provided for in the Directive.[29] Ireland, supported by several Member States, insisted on a distinction between Member State exclusive competence in the field of immigration – which it claimed governed the admission of third country nationals *into* EU Member States – and EU competence – which it submitted was limited to the regulation of the free movement of Union citizens and family members (including third country nationals) *within* the Union. The Court rejected the argument that Member States retain exclusive competence to regulate the first access to EU territory of non-EU family members. Directive 2004/38 confers on all non-EU nationals who are family members of a Union citizen rights of entry and residence in a host Member State such as Ireland, regardless of prior lawful residence of the non-EU family member in

[28] See the *Metock* case; examined in depth by C Costello, '*Metock*: Free Movement and "Normal Family Life" in the Union' (2009) 46 *CML Rev* 587. The controversy stirred by the *Metock* case was evident in the number and tenor of the interventions made by Member States in the case and the discussions in the Justice and Home Affairs Council of July 2008, following the decision of the Court, where concerns were expressed about the consequence of the ruling for the control of illegal immigration, sham marriages and abuse of rights.

[29] Directive 2004/38 replaced a large number of existing regulations and directives on free movement which dated from the 1960s and 1970s and codified key principles established by the Court in its case law. Prior to the adoption of Dir 2004/38, the Court had held in *Akrich* that in order to be able to benefit from the right to family reunification provided for in Art 10 Reg 1612/68, a non-EU national married to a Union citizen must be lawfully resident in a Member State when he or she moves to another Member State to which the Union citizen is migrating to work or has migrated. The applicant in the *Akrich* case was a UK national who had migrated to and worked in Ireland for a short period with the specific objective of ensuring that, on her return to the UK, her right to be joined by her non-EU spouse – who had previously been deported from the UK – would be assessed with reference to EU and not UK immigration law. The prior lawful residence condition at issue in *Metock* was the logical application of the *Akrich* ruling and one which had been incorporated by numerous Member States into legislation adopted to transpose Dir 2004/38 or national administrative guidelines accompanying it. See further 'Commission Report to the European Parliament and the Council on the application of Directive 2004/38 on the right of citizens of the Union and their family members to move and reside freely within the territory of the Member States' COM (2008) 840.

another Member State.[30] The intervening Member States also submitted that such an interpretation of Directive 2004/38 would lead to unjustified reverse discrimination since Irish nationals who had never exercised their right of freedom of movement would not derive, in Ireland, rights of entry and residence from EU law for their third country national family members. The Court's response to this suggestion that the protection of migrant EU nationals and their family members should be levelled down, rather than Member States levelling up the protection of their own 'static' nationals, was terse. Since EU free movement rules cannot be applied to activities which have no factor linking them with any of the situations governed by EU law, any difference in treatment between Union citizens who have and have not exercised their right of free movement, as regards the entry and residence rights of family members, does not fall within the scope of EU law.[31] In other words, the solution to the reverse discrimination suffered by Irish nationals lay with the Member States who could act individually or in a coordinated manner at EU level.[32] The decision of the Court in *Metock* was articulated in terms of EU objectives relating to free movement in the internal market and free movement of Union citizens more generally as well as EU competence to achieve those objectives.[33]

III FACTORS LINKING A CASE WITH ONE OF THE SITUATIONS GOVERNED BY EU LAW

The question which arises of course is what brings a case within the scope of application of EU law and how is the latter defined and delimited? What is the necessary connecting factor or what degree of connection is required to transform a case from being purely internal to being subject to EU law and thus within the jurisdiction of the Court of Justice? Since all Member State nationals are now Union citizens and since the performance of an economic activity is no longer the basis for the enjoyment of the (free movement) rights which have formed a central plank of the Court's case law, the concern is that identification of the relevant connecting factor has become elusive, even arbitrary. Furthermore, insistence on a cross-border element to bring a case within the scope of application of EU law

[30] *Metock*, paras 58–70. In reaching this decision, the Court explicitly overruled its decision in *Akrich.*

[31] Ibid, paras 77–78.

[32] In this regard it is interesting to note that, in its original draft directive on the right to family reunification for lawfully resident third country nationals (COM (1999) 638 final), the Commission had proposed alignment of family reunification of EU nationals not covered by EU law on the free movement of persons (eg the static Irish nationals referred to in *Metock)* with that of EU nationals who had exercised their right to free movement (eg the applicants in *Metock*). This aspect of the proposal was withdrawn in an amended version of the draft directive (COM (2002) 225 final) and was omitted in the version finally adopted (Dir 2003/86 on the right of family reunification [2003] OJ L251/12). It was proposed to re-examine this issue once the recasting of secondary legislation on free movement in the form of Dir 2004/38 was complete.

[33] *Metock*, para 68.

may no longer make sense when the right to free movement and residence is but one of the rights explicitly conferred by the provisions of the TFEU on Union citizens and when the completion of the internal market entailed, in any event, the abolition of internal frontiers.

In order to identify the nature and extent of the link, attachment or connecting factor necessary to bring a case within the scope of EU law and illustrate that the Court's jurisprudence has lost its way, some commentators have sought to anatomise the Court's case law on economic free movement with quasi-mathematical precision. The Court is said to have applied a three-limbed test, requiring (1) cross-border movement, (2) for the purpose of exercising an economic activity, with (3) a demonstrated obstacle or impediment deterring or affecting that cross-border movement.[34] While the right to free movement conferred on Union citizens no longer requires the beneficiary to be economically active, the Court's case law post Union citizenship is criticised generally for its failure to respect the other limbs of a test said to be of the Court's own making. In reality, however, an examination of cases decided before and after the introduction of that status suggests that identification of what constitutes a sufficient connecting factor or when a case escapes the purely internal rule has always been evolutive. Union citizenship has undoubtedly contributed to this evolution, as it permits applicants to deploy this status in contexts increasingly removed from the internal market and the economically motivated free movement at the heart of the EEC and EC Treaties. However, the different limbs of the test outlined above were under considerable pressure for some time before the establishment of Union citizenship.

The definition of migrant worker has, for example, always been broad and inclusive, with the result that the level of income received in return for the services provided by the migrant worker has never been considered determinative.[35] In addition, the motives of EU nationals applying for entry and residence in another Member State have been held to be irrelevant provided they pursue an effective and genuine activity as employed persons. They had to have a job but that did not mean that their movement had to be economically motivated.[36] Decisions of the Court on the entitlement of migrant workers, even frontier workers, and their family members to social and tax advantages on an equal treatment basis further emphasised the relative ease with which a cross-border element could be established and the benefits which resulted for applicants from a generous interpretation of the principle of non-discrimination viewed increasingly as an instrument to facilitate the integration of migrant workers and their families in the host Member State.[37] The *Singh* decision referred to above – which established a right

[34] See, eg A Tryfonidou, 'In Search of the Aim of the EC Free Movement of Persons Provisions: Has the Court of Justice Missed the Point?' (2009) 46 *CML Rev* 1591.

[35] See, eg Case 53/81 *Levin* [1982] ECR 1035; Case 139/85 *Kempf* [1986] ECR 1741; Joined Cases C-22/08 and C-23/08 *Vatsouras* [2009] ECR I-4585; Case C-14/09 *Genc*, judgment of 4 February 2010.

[36] *Levin*, para 22; *Akrich*, para 55.

[37] See, eg the entitlement to Dutch study grants of the children of Belgian nationals resident in Belgium but working in the Netherlands: Case C-337/97 *Meeusen* [1999] ECR I-3289.

for EU nationals to be joined by their non-EU family members in their Member State of origin following the exercise of their free movement rights – demonstrated that mere movement, regardless of any obvious deterrent effect, might suffice to attract the protection afforded by the relevant provisions of EU law.[38] While the Treaty expressly governed the rights of the providers of services, the Court made clear that Article 56 TFEU also covered recipients of services.[39] Fundamental changes in the nature of services and the manner in which they can be provided and received also led the Court to dilute the requirement of physical cross-border movement in that context. The mere existence of cross-border recipients of services suffices to bring a case within the scope of application of Article 56 TFEU.[40]

In the 1980s, two fundamentally important developments – in themselves precursors of, even catalysts for, the development of the status of Union citizenship – could be discerned in the Court's case law on free movement. The cases in question involved cross-border movement and thus did not fall foul of the purely internal rule, but they heralded a significant expansion in the type of situations which could from then on be regarded as governed by EU law and a concomitant loosening of the attachment, specifically the economic component of an applicant's activities, necessary to bring a case within the scope of EU law. They could also be regarded as evidence of the transformation of the principle of equal treatment in Article 18 TFEU from a tool designed to enhance mobility and complete the internal market to a semi-autonomous value forming a central part of the EU's goals.[41]

As pointed out above, in the context of the free provision of services, the Court held that the Treaty provisions covered not only providers but also recipients of services, including within the latter category tourists, students and medical patients.[42] It also held that, by prohibiting any discrimination on grounds of nationality, Article 18 TFEU requires that persons in a situation governed by EU law be placed on a completely equal footing with nationals of the Member State.[43] The applicant in the *Cowan* case was visiting Paris when he was assaulted leaving the Metro. Since, as a tourist and a recipient of services, he came within the personal scope of EU law, the Court deduced from the principle of non-discrimination on grounds of nationality an entitlement not to be discriminated

[38] See *Singh*, paras 21 and 23. For discussion of examples of the EU rules on the free movement of persons being softened up in this way, see further Nic Shuibhne (n 3).

[39] Joined Cases 286/82 and 26/83 *Luisi and Carbone* [1984] ECR 377, para 16.

[40] See Case C-384/93 *Alpine Investments* [1995] ECR I-1141 regarding cold-calling of potential clients in another Member State. Purely hypothetical receipt of services does not suffice: Case C-215/03 *Oulane* [2005] ECR I-1215, paras 45–56.

[41] See further De Búrca (n 13) for an examination of the different functions played by the principle of equal treatment in EU law. She suggests that that principle has played an instrumental role (equal treatment as an instrument for the attainment of specific EU aims), a mediating role (equal treatment as a value mediating or constraining other specific EU measures or goals) and an autonomous role (equal treatment as an independent EU goal).

[42] *Luisi and Carbone*, para 16.

[43] Case 186/87 *Cowan* [1989] ECR 195, para 10.

against as regards a French compensation scheme for victims of crime.[44] There was undoubtedly cross-border movement in *Cowan* but the economic component of or motivation for that movement was minimal and the deterrent effect which the exclusion of a non-resident tourist from the compensation scheme in question would have had was questionable. A tourist was thus able to claim equal treatment with reference to a benefit governed by national rules on criminal procedure, which remained incontestably within the domain of the Member State in question. Those rules, in situations governed by EU law, had to be interpreted and applied so as not to discriminate against those to whom EU law guaranteed a right to equal treatment.[45]

The *Gravier* decision also highlights revision and expansion of the scope of application of EU law and the potency of the principle of non-discrimination on grounds of nationality in Article 18 TFEU. The latter, unlike the specific expressions of that principle in the free movement provisions, was conditional not on the exercise of an economic activity but on the subject matter with reference to which equal treatment was being claimed, or even the individual claiming it,[46] coming *within the scope of application of EU law*. Pre-dating *Cowan*, the *Gravier* case involved a French national seeking access to a vocational training course in Belgium who challenged the higher fees set by the Belgian authorities for non-national students. The Court first made clear that the Belgian legislation on fees was discriminatory and only then examined whether the case came within the scope of application of EU law. It held that access and participation in courses of instruction and apprenticeship are not unconnected with EU law.[47] Not only was access to education the subject of provisions of secondary EU legislation but the then EEC Treaty provided that the Council was to lay down general principles for implementing a common vocational training policy. That fact, combined with the contribution vocational training makes or could make to the free movement of persons, constituted the basis for concluding that the conditions of access to vocational training fell within the scope of the Treaty, thereby triggering Article 18 TFEU. Once again, *Gravier* contained an unmistakeable cross-border element so that the principle of non-discrimination on grounds of nationality was being applied in that case to the treatment of a Member State national in a Member State other than that of his origin. Nevertheless, the Court's identification of the activities and objectives of the EEC Treaty and the use to which it put them appear crucial: '[The common vocational training policy] constitutes . . . an indispensable element of the activities of the Community, *whose objectives include inter alia, the free movement of persons, the mobility of labour and the improvement of the*

[44] Ibid, paras 15 and 17.

[45] The Court's reasoning in this regard is identical to that applied in later cases on Arts 18 and 21 TFEU and the right of Union citizens to equal treatment. See, eg, Case C-209/03 *Bidar* [2005] ECR I-2119; Case C-403/03 *Schempp* [2005] ECR I-6421.

[46] See, for confirmation of this point, Case C-85/96 *Martínez Sala* [1998] ECR I-2691; Case C-224/98 *D'Hoop* [2002] ECR I-6191. See further E Spaventa, 'Seeing the Wood from the Trees? On the Scope of Union Citizenship and its Constitutional Effects' (2008) 45 *CML Rev* 13.

[47] Case 293/83 *Gravier* [1985] ECR 593, para 19.

living standards of workers.'[48] The deployment of these broader objectives transformed the use of Article 18 TFEU and opened up vistas which would previously have been considered impossible given the economic imperatives identified as being at the heart of the Court's original jurisprudence on free movement.[49] The personal and material scope of EC free movement law was in the process of transformation well before the establishment of Union citizenship.

IV UNION CITIZENSHIP AND THE PRESENT APPLICATION OF THE PURELY INTERNAL RULE

A The Potentially Transformative Effect of Union Citizenship

The reasons why the introduction of Union citizenship has further heightened calls for revision, even abandonment, of the purely internal rule are manifold. Firstly, all Member State nationals are Union citizens who come, by virtue simply of their citizenship status, within the personal scope of EU law.[50] Since the possession of Union citizenship alone may constitute a connecting factor or link with one of the situations governed by EU law, the situations in which EU law now applies appear (potentially) limitless. In addition, since the rights which can be brought under the citizenship umbrella are many and varied, it has become increasingly unclear whether triggering EU law and coming within the personal and material scope of the relevant EU law provisions is still dependent on the existence of a cross-border element. Similar criticism of the purely internal rule and the Court's acceptance of reverse discrimination had surfaced with the completion of the internal market, characterised by the abolition of internal frontiers, following the Single European Act, signed in 1986. Commentators proposed abandoning the geographical approach, which they said underpinned the Court's approach to original free movement cases, where the emphasis was on borders and movement and factual circumstances which prevented the development of a methodologically coherent approach, in favour of a juridical approach concentrating on whether EU law conferred rights on the person in the reverse discrimination situation with respect to the purposes and policies of the relevant provisions of EU law in dispute.[51]

[48] Ibid, para 23 (emphasis added).

[49] The spirit of *Gravier* appears to be alive in later cases on the free movement of students decided subsequent to the establishment of Union citizenship, when the Court refers to general EU objectives regarding the promotion of quality education and the mobility of students. See, eg, *D'Hoop*, para 32 or *Bidar*, paras 39–42. In the latter case, the combination of a new title in the EC Treaty on education and the introduction of the provisions on Union citizenship served as the basis for previous decisions excluding student maintenance grants from the scope of application of EU law to be overruled.

[50] See, however, *D'Hoop*, para 27, where the Court held that Member State nationals who enjoy the status of Union citizen come within the personal scope of the Treaty provisions on *Union citizenship*.

[51] See HUJ D'Oliveira, 'Is Reverse Discrimination Still Possible under the SEA?' in *Forty Years On: The Evolution of Postwar Private International Law in Europe* (The Hague, Kluwer, 1990).

Secondly, despite the Court's insistence to the contrary, there is evidence to suggest that Union citizenship can and does have an effect on the material scope of application of EU law.[52] Prior to the introduction of Union citizenship, in the context of the common and, subsequently, the internal market, the rights of residence and movement conferred by EU law were reserved, in the main, to clearly identifiable categories of Member State nationals who worked or were self-employed abroad, who provided or received services and who were, to a greater or lesser extent, involved in the performance of an economic activity. By providing a clear basis to detach the possession and enjoyment of many of the rights which EU law confers on the individual from the exercise of specific economic activities, Union citizenship expands or has the potential to expand the situations governed or envisaged by EU law and therefore falling outwith the purely internal rule. Following the introduction of Union citizenship, it has been argued that the Court has recognised the existence of the necessary attachment to or connection with EU law despite the fact that the basis of the connection appeared tenuous and may have led to a rejection of the case with reference to the purely internal rule in the past. Thus, while EU law is deemed to be applicable in certain cases, other not dissimilar cases have languished in chambers of three judges, more often than not disposed of by way of reasoned order, with the Court reasserting the purely internal rule, the absence in the case in question of any attachment to one of the situations envisaged by EU law and its own consequent lack of jurisdiction.[53]

Thirdly, since the general principle of equality is regarded as one of the core principles underpinning a Citizens' Europe, it is argued that the reverse discrimination to which application of the purely internal rule gives rise constitutes an unjustified violation of Union citizenship and, in particular, the prohibition of discrimination on grounds of nationality in Article 18 TFEU.[54] The Court has, after all, stated that Union citizenship enables those who find themselves in the same situation to enjoy the same treatment in law irrespective of their nationality, subject to such exceptions as are expressly provided for.[55] The entry into force of the Lisbon Treaty, recognition that the Charter of Fundamental Rights has the same legal value as the Treaties, and location of the source of the general principle of equality within that Charter have added further fuel to this particular fire.[56]

[52] As regards the right of both job-seekers and students not to be discriminated against on grounds of nationality in relation to entitlement to certain social benefits, the Court has revised its previous case law limiting the rights of these categories of migrant Member State nationals in the light of the introduction of Union citizenship: see Cases C-138/02 *Collins* [2004] ECR I-2703 and *Bidar*.

[53] See, eg Case C-328/04 *Vajnai* [2005] ECR I-8577, where the Court held that the situation of the applicant, a member of the Hungarian Workers' Party, convicted for use of a 'totalitarian symbol' was said not to be connected in any way with any of the situations contemplated by the provisions of the Treaties. The applicant had been relying on Art 2 TEU (the Union is founded on the values of respect for human dignity, freedom, democracy, equality, the rule of law and respect for human rights), the Charter and provisions of secondary EU legislation applying the prohibition of discrimination on grounds of racial or ethnic origin.

[54] See, eg, Tryfonidou (n 3).

[55] *Grzelczyk*, para 31.

[56] See Art 6(1) TEU and further confirmation of the status and influence of the Charter in Case C-555/07 *Kücükdeveci*, judgment of 19 January 2010, para 22.

The Court has repeatedly stated, however, that Union citizenship 'is not intended to extend the scope *ratione materiae* of the Treaty also to internal situations which have no link with Community law'.[57] In *Uecker and Jacquet*, a family reunification case reminiscent of *Morson and Jhanjan*, it held that both the rules on the free movement of workers and the introduction of Union citizenship could not be relied on by Member State nationals residing and working in their Member State of origin to found a right to family reunification pursuant to EU secondary legislation.[58] The Court clearly identified the objectives pursued by the provisions on the free movement of workers – removal of obstacles to the mobility of workers – and relied on these objectives, as it had done in the past, to justify why recognition on the basis of EU law of a right to reside and work for the non-EU spouses of EU nationals who had never availed of their economic free movement rights was not necessary. Tellingly, no similar identification of the objectives underpinning Union citizenship was attempted or relied upon. There was no analysis of the consequences which might flow from conferring such a status on all Member State nationals or detaching the rights bestowed by it from the obligations incumbent on beneficiaries of the traditional economic freedoms. The Court did not address whether there were circumstances in which the possession alone of the status of Union citizenship could, depending on the provisions of EU law relied upon, suffice to forge the necessary connection with the EU legal order required by the Court's case law.

B The Unsettling of the Purely Internal Rule

Several cases are cited to demonstrate that, since the introduction of Union citizenship, the Court has lost the plot, allowing, in an arbitrary manner, ever more remote or tenuous links to trigger the application of EU law. These decisions have been the subject of considerable criticism both from those who claim that the Court has gone too far, and those who contend that, although some applicants may have successfully brought their claims within the scope of application of EU law, the Court has not, given the introduction and import of Union citizenship, gone far enough.[59]

The *Carpenter* case concerned the illegally resident non-EU spouse of a UK national resident in his own Member State. The non-EU spouse derived a right of residence in the UK from the fact that her spouse's right to freely provide services in other Member States pursuant to Article 56 TFEU would be obstructed were she to be expelled.[60] Since secondary legislation on services did not govern the

[57] *Uecker and Jacquet*, para 23. Recently reiterated by the Grand Chamber in *Flemish Welfare Aid*, paras 38–39; and *Metock*, paras 77–78.

[58] *Uecker and Jacquet*, para 21.

[59] See, for a summary of these opposing views, AP van der Mei, 'Combatting Reverse Discrimination: Who Should Do the Job?' (2009) 16 *Maastricht Journal of European and Comparative Law* 379.

[60] *Carpenter*, para 39.

right of residence of a spouse in Mrs Carpenter's situation, the Court, in terms identical to those used in *Morson and Jhanjan*, examined whether such a right could be inferred from the principles or other rules of EU law. It then proceeded to interpret the Treaty provisions on services in the light of the fundamental right to respect for family life. The Court reiterated the purely internal rule but found that since Mr Carpenter provided services to advertisers established in other Member States, he was a provider of services within the meaning of Article 56 TFEU.[61] A cross-border element was thus established. The decision to deport Mrs Carpenter in the circumstances of this case was deemed to constitute an unjustified restriction of her husband's right to provide services. A proper balance between the right to respect for family life and the public order and safety objectives pursued by the national immigration legislation had not been struck.[62] The criticism of the *Carpenter* case focuses on the very weak economic component and tenuous cross-border element which sufficed to bring the case outwith the purely internal rule. Unlike Mr Carpenter, whose client base extended to other EU Member States, a service provider operating exclusively within the UK would not have succeeded in bringing his situation within the scope of application of EU rules on family reunification.

In *D'Hoop*, a Belgian national who had completed her secondary education in France successfully relied on the provisions on Union citizenship to gain access in her Member State of origin to a tideover allowance previously restricted to those educated in Belgium. The case involved an element of movement but the movement had taken place prior to the introduction of Union citizenship and for the purposes of pursuing a secondary education, something which had not until then appeared to be one of the situations governed by EU law as defined by the Court's case law on the free movement of students dating back to *Gravier*.[63] The Court classified the right of Union citizens to move as a fundamental freedom and indicated that the situations coming within the scope of EU law *include* those involving the exercise of the fundamental freedoms, of which the general right of Union citizens to move and reside freely was one.[64]

In the *Schempp* case, although the applicant – a German national, resident in Germany – failed to establish that the impugned German rules on tax relief were discriminatory and, as such, contrary to Articles 18 and 21 TFEU, he did manage to escape the purely internal rule. The unfavourable tax treatment of which he complained resulted from his former wife having moved to reside in another Member State. In other words, there was movement, albeit not of the applicant in the case.[65]

[61] Ibid, para 37.
[62] Ibid, paras 39–43.
[63] Equal access for EU nationals was restricted to forms of vocational training after the decision in *Gravier*, albeit vocational training was interpreted widely as incorporating most if not all forms of third level education.
[64] *D'Hoop*, para 29.
[65] *Schempp*, para 25.

The *Chen* case is also difficult to fit within the traditional cross-border paradigm. It involved a Chinese national with a temporary right to enter the United Kingdom who, on the basis of legal advice, gave birth to the applicant in Northern Ireland.[66] Despite the fact that the mother and child had never left the United Kingdom, the choice of birthplace bestowed on the applicant the possibility of claiming Irish nationality by birth by virtue of the relevant provisions of Irish nationality law then in force. The Court recognised that the purpose of giving birth in Northern Ireland was to create a situation in which the child would be able to acquire the nationality of another Member State of the EU in order thereafter to secure for the child and her parent a long-term right to reside in the United Kingdom on the basis of EU law. However, according to the Court in *Chen*, the acquisition of Irish nationality and, consequently, Union citizenship, in these circumstances was not unlawful and did not, on the facts of the case, constitute an abuse of rights. It was not permissible for a Member State to restrict the effects of the grant of the nationality of another Member State by imposing an additional condition for recognition of that nationality with a view to the exercise of the fundamental freedoms provided for in the Treaty.[67] Despite the fact that the minor child had never moved, the Court rejected arguments to the effect that her situation was purely internal. The capacity of a national of a Member State to be the holder of rights guaranteed by the Treaty and by secondary law on the free movement of persons could not be made conditional upon the attainment by the person concerned of the age prescribed for the acquisition of legal capacity to exercise those rights personally.[68] In these circumstances, the Court held that Article 21 TFEU conferred on the applicant – a minor child possessing the nationality of another Member State – a right to reside for an indefinite period in the United Kingdom.[69]

While the links in these cases might appear more tenuous than those required by the Court in the past, the fact remains that, bar the requirement of an economic component to their movement, a cross-border element was identified by the Court in one form or another as was the possible deterrent effect of denying the applicant the benefit or protection claimed following the exercise of free movement. In more recent cases, the Court seems to construct the necessary connecting factor and bring a case within the scope of application of EU law by looking not at past movement but at the effect which the impugned national measure or decision could have on the *status* of Union citizen and on the exercise by the applicant of rights conferred by that status.

In the *Garcia Avello* case, the children of a Spanish and Belgian couple resident in Belgium, who themselves had dual nationality but who were born and had

[66] Case C-200/02 *Chen* [2004] ECR I-9925, paras 8–11.

[67] Ibid, para 39, reiterating the finding in Case C-369/90 *Micheletti* [1992] ECR I-4239, paras 11 and 14.

[68] *Chen*, para 20.

[69] Ibid, para 46. Subject, of course, to fulfilment of certain conditions imposed for the exercise of the right of residence conferred on Union citizens by Art 21 TFEU.

always resided in Belgium, successfully relied on Articles 18 and 20 TFEU to prevent Belgium applying national rules on the registration of surnames and forenames which would have resulted in the loss of the Spanish part of their name. Since the children had never exercised their free movement rights, the Court's decision could be regarded as an attempt to protect the prospective exercise by these minor Union citizens of their rights of free movement for the future.[70] The Court held that the necessary link with EU law could be identified on the basis of the fact that the children in question are nationals of one Member State resident in another.[71] However, the only movement to have actually taken place was that of the applicants' father and although the Advocate General examined the case from the perspective of his right to free movement, the Court framed its decision exclusively in terms of the rights of the (for now) static children and based it exclusively on Article 20 TFEU. That provision confers the status of Union citizenship and indicates that citizens are the beneficiaries of the rights conferred by the Treaties, some of which it enumerates. It is arguably distinct from Article 21 TFEU, which specifically regulates the right of free movement and residence. Since the children were Union citizens with dual Member State nationality, the requisite link was established and they could rely on Article 18 TFEU against their Member State of residence which was also (one of) their Member State(s) of nationality.

In *Rottmann*, the Court also shunned the question of past movement and concentrated on the prospective effect on the rights of a Union citizen and the status of Union citizen of a national decision on the loss of nationality.[72] The preliminary reference from a German court involved the application, to a German national, resident in Germany, by the German authorities of German administrative law depriving him of his German nationality. The latter had been acquired by the applicant, who was originally of Austrian nationality, by naturalisation in a procedure vitiated by fraud. By virtue of the provisions of both Austrian and German law in force at the relevant time, on acquiring German nationality the applicant had lost his Austrian nationality of origin. The decision of the German authorities to withdraw his German nationality would thus render him stateless and deprive him of his status as a Union citizen and of the rights attached to that status. A number of intervening Member States and the Commission argued that the case was purely internal. The Advocate General disagreed. The applicant was born Austrian and had only acquired German nationality as a result of availing of his free movement rights and settling in that Member State. In other words, a border had been crossed, movement had occurred, albeit in the past. The Court differed from its Advocate General, ignoring the past exercise by the applicant of his free movement rights. Instead it held that:

> It is clear that the situation of a citizen of the Union who, like the applicant in the main proceedings, is faced with a decision withdrawing his naturalisation, adopted by the

[70] See Case C-148/02 *Garcia Avello* [2003] ECR I-11613, para 36.
[71] Ibid, para 27. See also AG Jacobs at para 52 of his Opinion.
[72] Case C-135/08 *Rottmann*, judgment of 2 March 2010.

> authorities of one Member State, and placing him, after he has lost the nationality of another Member State that he originally possessed, in a position capable of causing him to lose the status conferred by Article [20 TFEU] and the rights attaching thereto falls, by reason of its nature and its consequences, within the ambit of European Union law.[73]

While the Court held that it was not contrary to Article 20 TFEU for a Member State to withdraw from an EU citizen the nationality of that Member State acquired by naturalisation and by deception, it indicated that the decision to withdraw had to observe the principle of proportionality.

What is the upshot of these decisions? *Garcia Avello* could be understood narrowly as proof of the privileged position of EU citizens with dual Member State nationality; the latter constituting, automatically and independently of any other element, a sufficient transnational link to bring the case within the scope of application of EU law.[74] In the alternative, the Court may be putting further flesh on the bones of the oft-repeated mantra about Union citizenship being destined to become the fundamental status of Member State nationals. In *Rottmann*, the Court concentrated on the effects of the naturalisation decision on the possession of the *status* of Union citizenship and the exercise of rights associated with that status. It was the gravity of the consequences which the contested national decisions in these cases would have entailed for the status and the rights of the Union citizens in question which appeared to forge the necessary connecting factor with EU law. In *Rottmann*, although the Court avoided clarifying further the objectives of Union citizenship, or indeed its limits, it did emphasise 'the importance which primary law attaches to the status of citizen of the Union'.[75]

It is also possible to explain the decisions on Union citizenship catalogued above not in terms of a change in the Court's application of the purely internal rule but with reference to the fact that the objectives and aims with respect to which it is now assessing the scope of application of EU law have altered substantially since its early decisions in *Knoors* and *Saunders*. The EU's dynamic quality is incontestable. Its policies, objectives and goals have been in a constant, vibrant process of development and expansion for decades. The change in the EU's focus has brought it into contact and conflict with areas incontestably of Member State competence; competence, nevertheless, which must be exercised with due regard to EU law. This expansion is evident in free movement cases before and after the introduction of Union citizenship, as the examination of *Cowan* and *Gravier* sought to underline. When the *Saunders* case was decided, the idea of the common market having anything to do with a Member State's exercise of its powers in

[73] Ibid, para 42.

[74] In Case C-434/09 *McCarthy*, judgment of 5 May 2011, paras 39–41 (discussed below), the Court has since held that Dir 2004/38 is not applicable to a Union citizen who has never exercised his or her free movement rights by virtue simply of his or her dual nationality. Since such a Union citizen falls within the scope of application of the Treaty by virtue of Art 20 TFEU, it remains to be seen whether, on this point, *McCarthy* disposes completely with the *Garcia Avello* thesis.

[75] *Rottmann*, para 56.

the field of criminal law would no doubt have been shocking.[76] By the time the Court decided the *Cowan* case, its focus in internal market cases was shifting from the prohibition of direct and indirect discrimination to the exclusion of national measures which restricted free movement or which, on a more abstract level, might dissuade Member State nationals from availing of the rights conferred by EU law. Given that the EU now seeks to create an area of freedom, security and justice in the context of which it may and has adopted extensive measures on the residence of third country nationals, family reunification, asylum, immigration and external border controls as well as measures for coordinating cooperation between police and judicial authorities, the scope for intrusion into the spheres of traditionally Member State competence becomes even greater and the possibility of identifying some sort of a link with one of the situations governed by EU law increases accordingly.[77] As regards the issue of family reunification, it is hardly surprising in *Morson and Jhanjan*, decided in 1982, that the Court did not interfere with the concerned Member State's competence in the field of immigration in order to avoid a situation of reverse discrimination, which the Member State itself was competent to remedy if it so wished. As *Carpenter*, *Chen* and *Metock* demonstrate, however, the expansion of EU competence in the field of immigration, an expansion which the Court itself emphasised in the latter case, means that it is now more difficult, in certain circumstances, to deny that a link or attachment with EU law exists. This expansion of EU competence could help to explain what are regarded as the Court's sometimes generous interpretations of what falls within the scope of EU law and the obligations it has imposed on Member States in the sensitive field of immigration to take adequate account, when they seek to derogate from the EU rules on free movement, of the impact of their proposed action on the right to respect for family life as protected by Article 8 of the ECHR.[78] Such an expansion does not explain, however, why the Court should abandon the purely internal rule in a case such as *Metock*, thereby requiring Ireland to confer on all Irish nationals in Ireland the same immigration treatment as EU law confers on those who have availed of their free movement rights. It is one thing to require Member States, in situations coming within the scope of application of EU law, to exercise their competence in, for example, the field of immigration, with due regard for EU law. It is another thing entirely to drive a coach and horses through the Member State's competence in that field.[79]

[76] In other free movement cases touching on issues of criminal law decided around the same time as *Saunders*, the focus was on the procedural guarantees afforded EU nationals by EU law (see, eg, Case 98/79 *Pecastaing* [1980] ECR 691); or on derogations relied on by Member States from the free movement rules on grounds of public policy or public security (see, eg, Case 131/79 *Santillo* [1980] ECR 1585).

[77] See, eg, the decisions of the Court on the European Arrest Warrant in Case C-66/08 *Kozłowski* [2008] ECR I-6041 or Case C-123/08 *Wolzenburg* [2009] ECR I-9621.

[78] See Joined Cases C-482/01 and 493/01 *Orfanopoulos* [2004] ECR I-5257, paras 97–100; *MRAX*, paras 53 and 61–62; Case C-413/99 *Baumbast* [2002] ECR I-7091, paras 72–73; *Carpenter*, paras 40–44; Case C-441/02 *Commission v Germany* [2006] ECR I-3449, paras 108–113.

[79] See also Nic Shuibhne (n 3) 763 ff.

That this expansion and alteration of EU objectives can be used to depict the Court's case law as, by and large, coherent, is further illustrated by the fact that its reasoning in *Rottmann* or *Garcia Avello* harks back to the position adopted by Advocate General Warner in *Saunders*. The Advocate General had urged the Court in that case to focus on the nature, gravity and scope of the decision to which the individual EU national was being subject and the effects of that decision on the panoply of rights conferred on her by EU law. Similarly, by depriving an individual in Mr Rottmann's situation of his Member State nationality, the Member State of naturalisation would be depriving him of his Union citizenship. On the one hand, the Court in *Rottmann* recognises that, in accordance with established principles of international law, Member States remain competent as regards rules on the acquisition and loss of their nationality. On the other, given their obligation to act, even in their own spheres of competence, with due regard to EU law, it held that a decision concerning the loss of nationality in these circumstances had to be reviewed for compliance with the principle of proportionality.[80] One commentator has suggested that *Rottmann* is 'the logical conclusion of a line of case law in which the Court countenanced ever more remote links with the putative exercise of free movement rights as justifying scrutiny and control of national laws and policies'.[81] This misses the point. The Court framed its decision in *Rottmann*, and indeed in *Garcia Avello*, not with reference to the provisions on Union citizenship addressing free movement (Article 21 TFEU) but instead with reference to the provision which establishes the status of Union citizenship, what the Court has referred to as 'the principle of Union citizenship' (Article 20 TFEU).[82] Cross-border movement, even after the establishment of Union citizenship, remains relevant to the application of provisions of the Treaty which presuppose movement but these cases began to demonstrate that the protection afforded Union citizens by EU law cannot be reduced to situations of cross-border movement.

C Protection of the Genuine Enjoyment of the Substance of the Rights Conferred by Union Citizenship

A distinction between the status of Union citizenship and the exercise of certain rights which that status confers appears to be gaining ground. In *Ruiz Zambrano*, the Court had to decide whether minor Union citizens who had never exercised

[80] The facts of *Rottmann* were highly unusual: because of the interaction between German and Austrian law, the acquisition of German nationality and its subsequent withdrawal would render the applicant stateless and therefore deprive him of Union citizenship. It remains to be seen whether that case establishes a principle of wider application. Would, for example, proposals by a Member State to withdraw nationality from a naturalised third country national run contrary to the principle established in *Rottmann* since withdrawal of Member State nationality in those circumstances would result in the loss of Union citizenship but not statelessness? The decision in *Ruiz Zambrano* (discussed below), suggests a finding of incompatibility would be possible.

[81] See J Shaw, 'Citizenship: Contrasting Dynamics at the Interface of Integration and Constitutionalism' in P Craig and G De Búrca (eds), *The Evolution of EU Law*, 2nd edn (Oxford, Oxford University Press, 2011).

[82] See, eg *Flemish Welfare Aid*, para 39.

their free movement rights could be said to enjoy a right to reside in their own Member State on the basis of EU law, with the result that they could confer a derived EU right of residence on their third country national parents. The purely internal rule, as applied in *Uecker and Jacquet* or *Metock*, would seem to have excluded an affirmative answer to this question. However, the facts of the *Ruiz Zambrano* case rendered such an answer problematic when viewed in the context of the Court's case law on Union citizenship as a whole. The Union citizens in question were the legally resident, minor children of non-EU nationals themselves illegally resident in Belgium. The parents, both Colombian nationals, had applied for but were refused asylum. They continued to reside in Belgium for several years – their children, on whom Belgian nationality was conferred, were born there, the father was employed there and he paid social security contributions in accordance with Belgian law. Unlike in *Rottmann*, however, where the impugned national decision would have led to the loss of Union citizenship, the children in this case would have retained the status of Union citizens but would have been unable, in practice, to exercise any of the contingent rights and benefits were their parents to be expelled from Belgium and, consequently, the EU. While the non-EU primary care-givers of the children in *Chen* and *Baumbast* had derived a right to reside from the rights conferred by EU law directly on the children, in both of these cases a transnational element was established, although not, as we saw in *Chen*, the physical crossing of a border.[83] Clearly inspired by the approach in *Rottmann*, the Court in *Ruiz Zambrano* focused not on the absence of movement or of a cross-border element but rather on the effects on the children's status as Union citizens and the rights which they would effectively be able to enjoy on that basis were a decision taken to expel their parents. The Court held that Article 20 TFEU precludes national measures which have the effect of depriving Union citizens of the genuine enjoyment of the substance of the rights conferred by their status as Union citizens.[84] The age of the Union citizens in question and the prospect of their expulsion from the EU were central to the Court's reasoning. It is noteworthy that its extremely concise judgment contained no reference to fundamental rights generally or to the need to ensure respect for the right to family life of EU nationals, a right referred to not only in Article 8 ECHR but also in Article 7 of the Charter.[85] Nevertheless, when reading *Ruiz Zambrano*

[83] In *Baumbast*, para 73 and *Chen*, para 45, the Court derived a right to reside for a non-EU parent from their child's right to reside qua child of a migrant worker or qua Union citizen.

[84] *Ruiz Zambrano*, para 42. For discussion of the case, see K Lenaerts, '*Civis Europaeus Sum*: From the Cross-Border Link to the Status of Citizen of the Union' in P Cardonnel et al (eds), *Constitutionalising the EU Judicial System: Essays in Honour of Pernilla Lindh* (Oxford, Hart Publishing, 2012); M Hailbronner and S Iglesias Sánchez, 'The European Court of Justice and Citizenship of the European Union: New Developments Towards a Truly Fundamental Status' at www.ssrn.com; K Hailbronner and D Thym, annotation of Case C-34/09 *Ruiz Zambrano* (2011) 48 *CML Rev* 1253.

[85] In Case C-291/05 *Eind* [2007] ECR I-10719, para 44, the Court spoke of the objectives of the EU legislature, which recognised the importance of ensuring protection for the family life of nationals of the Member States in order to eliminate obstacles to the exercise of the fundamental freedoms guaranteed by the Treaty. By contrast, in *Akrich*, paras 53–58, the Court recognised the need to ensure protection for family life but it appeared to locate this obligation purely in national law with reference to the ECHR.

it is difficult not to recall the words of Advocate General Jacobs, pronounced in 1993 in the *Konstantinidis* case, in which he argued that a Member State national:

> is . . . entitled to assume that, wherever he goes to earn his living in the European Community, he will be treated in accordance with a common code of fundamental values, in particular those laid down in the European Convention on Human Rights. In other words, he is entitled to say '*civis europeus sum*' and to invoke that status in order to oppose any violation of his fundamental rights.[86]

The decision of the Grand Chamber in *Ruiz Zambrano* has, unsurprisingly, proved not to be the last word on the subject. The *McCarthy* case, handed down some weeks later, involved a UK national, born and resident all her life in the UK, who had acquired Irish nationality by virtue of the fact that her mother had been born in Ireland. She applied and acquired Irish nationality following her marriage to a third country national. The question arose whether such a Union citizen, with dual Member State nationality, could rely, against the Member State in which she had always resided, on Directive 2004/38. Her objective in doing so was again to establish a derived EU right of residence for her third country national spouse. In *McCarthy*, the Court held not only that the applicant was not a 'beneficiary' within the meaning of Directive 2004/38, as she had never exercised her free movement rights, but also that Article 21 TFEU could be of no avail to her. Article 21 TFEU would only be relevant were the Union citizen subject to national measures which would have the effect of depriving her of the genuine enjoyment of the substance of the rights conferred by virtue of her status as Union citizen.[87] While the Court recognised that the mere failure to exercise free movement rights did not imply that a Union citizen was in a purely internal situation, it distinguished the situations in *Ruiz Zambrano* and *McCarthy*.[88] In the latter case, the refusal of an EU right of residence for the applicant on the basis of her Irish nationality and the consequent refusal of a right of residence for her third country national spouse would not have the effect of forcing the applicant to leave her Member State of origin and residence or indeed the EU, her right of residence in the UK being, in accordance with public international law, unconditional.[89] Most importantly of all, the Court framed the preliminary reference and its response in terms of Article 21 TFEU as distinct from Article 20 TFEU, viewing the case as one dependant on movement pursuant to the former provision, rather than one in which the very status of Union citizenship pursuant to the latter provision was at risk.[90]

[86] Case C-168/91 *Konstantinidis* [1993] ECR I-1191, para 46 of the Opinion.

[87] *McCarthy*, paras 43 and 56. In reaching this conclusion, the Court rejected the argument canvassed by Advocate General Sharpston at para 38 of her Opinion in *Ruiz Zambrano* to the effect that Dir 2004/38 (and by implication Art 21 TFEU) provided for a right to move and an independent right to reside.

[88] *McCarthy*, paras 46–47.

[89] Ibid, paras 49–52.

[90] See Lenaerts (n 84) for further discussion of *McCarthy*.

V TIME TO ABANDON OR REVISE THE PURELY INTERNAL RULE?

The key criticism of the Court's application of the purely internal rule has centred, as we have seen, on the fact that insistence on cross-border movement to trigger application of the provisions of the TFEU on free movement contradicts the claims made by the Court relating to that status, ignores the qualitative change in the EU's objectives to which the introduction of that status is testament and creates situations of reverse discrimination for static Union citizens which conflict with the principle of non-discrimination on grounds of nationality in Article 18 TFEU. In her Opinion in the *Flemish Welfare Aid* case, Advocate General Sharpston stated that 'at least potentially, the provisions on citizenship . . . challenge the sustainability in its present form of the doctrine on purely internal situations'.[91] However, while reverse discrimination may be a consequence of the application of EU law, several arguments plead against the Court abandoning the purely internal rule and in favour of a solution to reverse discrimination being sought individually at Member State level or by Member States on a coordinated basis through the adoption of secondary EU legislation to combat it in specific fields.

As regards the charge of incoherence and inconsistency, the examination of decisions pre-dating and post-dating Union citizenship suggests it is overstated. The Court has, fairly consistently, looked to the goals, purpose and 'spirit' of EU rules when determining whether a particular case falls within the scope of application of EU law. The juridical approach to the purely internal rule posited above has, in the main, gone hand in hand with its teleological approach to the interpretation of the provisions of EU law. As the EU's goals have changed, so too has the scope of application of EU law as defined by the Court. Where an applicant relies specifically on the provisions of the Treaty on free movement (whether economic freedom of movement or that attached to Union citizenship and devoid of an economic component), the Court has examined the compatibility of the impugned national measure or decision with EU free movement law. In general, where there is no movement, the possibility of relying on rules whose application presupposes movement of some sort has been denied. This does not appear entirely illogical. In addition, where the Court has established a link it is difficult to contend that the link in question was entirely fictitious or hypothetical. The national court in the *Carpenter* case, for example, found, as a matter of fact, that the applicant was engaged in cross-border services. That fact enabled him to rely on the provisions on freedom to provide services. The applicant in *Chen*, although she had not crossed a border, possessed the nationality of a Member State different to the Member State in which she resided. That fact enabled her to rely on the provisions of Union citizenship in her Member State of residence. In *Schempp*,

[91] *Flemish Welfare Aid*, para 140 of the Opinion. A position reiterated and expanded upon in her Opinion in *Ruiz Zambrano*.

although the applicant tax claimant had not himself moved, his case centred on how the movement of his former spouse affected his tax liability. Where applicants have relied on purely hypothetical or excessively remote links the Court has rejected their claims.[92]

As regards the suggestion that the Court should renounce the purely internal rule, do the provisions on Union citizenship mandate such a development? If reverse discrimination occurs because an individual has not moved, it seems odd to rely solely on Article 21 TFEU – a provision which generally requires movement – in conjunction with Article 18 TFEU – a provision which presupposes that the differential treatment complained of is within the scope of application of EU law – to claim rights for the static Union citizen whose difficulty is precisely that the failure to move may leave him outwith Article 18 TFEU. Reverse discrimination is the result of application of the purely internal rule; a rule which provides that situations which demonstrate no connecting factor with one of the situations envisaged by EU law fall outside its scope. Application of Article 18 TFEU is conditional on the differential treatment at issue coming within the scope of application of the Treaties. Can one seek to remedy differential treatment, which until now has been held to fall outside the scope of application of EU law, by referring solely to a provision whose application presupposes that the subject matter falls within the scope of EU law? It is notable, in this respect, that Article 21 of the Charter, which reiterates the prohibition of discrimination on the grounds listed in Articles 18 and 19 TFEU, separates the two and explicitly refers to the limitation regarding the scope of application of the Treaties only with reference to nationality discrimination. The Member States seemed to be taking no chances when it came to conditioning application of the principle of non-discrimination on grounds of nationality.

That the combined effects of Articles 18 and 21 TFEU may be an imperfect tool with which to challenge reverse discrimination at EU level does not mean that static Union citizens may not, on the basis of EU law, derive rights which the latter confers on mobile Union citizens. *Ruiz Zambrano*, *Rottmann*, *Garcia Avello* and even *McCarthy* have all demonstrated that triggering the protection afforded by the provisions on Union citizenship and/or Article 18 TFEU is not simply dependant on movement. National measures which threaten the very status of Union citizenship or render impossible or excessively difficult the enjoyment by EU nationals of the substance of the rights conferred by that status may fall foul of the Treaty provisions on Union citizenship absent any cross-border movement. Aside from the limitation in Article 18 TFEU regarding the scope of application of EU law, reliance on this non-discrimination principle to abolish situations of reverse discrimination would not, in any event, be without its problems. Reverse discrimination is the consequence of the interaction (or lack of sufficient interaction) between national and EU law governing a particular situation. On the one hand, can the differential treatment which results for static Union citizens from a

[92] See, eg, the *Moser* and *Kremzow* cases.

decision like *Metock* on family reunification be attributed to a single source or is it the result of the interaction between two, distinct regulatory regimes?[93] On the other, given that any alleged discrimination must presumably be indirect, not being directly based on nationality, difficult questions relating to comparability and objective justification could ensue.[94]

Further caution regarding abandonment of the purely internal rule stems from the highly criticised effects which Union citizenship has had in other areas of Member State competence. While many commentators assumed, following the adoption of the Maastricht Treaty, that Union citizenship added little to existing rules on economic free movement,[95] it is now established that Article 21 TFEU creates an autonomous and directly effective right to free movement and residence.[96] Limitations and conditions may be imposed in respect of the *exercise* of the right of free movement and residence but cannot, in essence, call into question the *existence*, in principle, of that right. The limitations and conditions referred to in Article 21(1) TFEU must be applied by Member States in accordance with the general principles of EU law, not least respect for fundamental rights and the principle of proportionality.[97] That provision, in conjunction with the principle of non-discrimination in Article 18 TFEU, has, as a result, formed the basis for numerous claims by economically inactive Union citizens to equal treatment as regards access to a wide variety of costly social benefits in host Member States.[98] This case law is seen as representing a threat to national choices about social protection and as placing a considerable burden on national competent authorities and courts who must engage in a case-by-case assessment of whether refusing a Union citizen a disputed social benefit constitutes an unjustified and disproportionate restriction of the rights conferred by Articles 18 and 21 TFEU.[99] There is something incoherent in demanding that the Court abandon a rule such as the purely internal rule, whose primary purpose is to patrol the division of competence between the EU and its members and delimit the scope of EU law, while

[93] See further Van der Mei (n 59) 380. As regards the impossibility of bringing an equal pay claim where the alleged discrimination does not result from a single source see Case C-256/01 *Allonby* [2004] ECR I-873, para 46.

[94] As case law in the field of gender equality has demonstrated, identifying correct comparators is not without its difficulties and issues of comparability and justification can become entangled: see, eg, Case C-220/02 *Österreichischer Gewerkschaftsbund* [2004] ECR I-5907.

[95] See, eg HUJ d'Oliveira, 'European Citizenship: Its Meaning, its Potential' in J Monar, W Ungerer and W Wessels (eds), *The Maastricht Treaty on the European Union* (Brussels, European Interuniversity Press, 1993). The Court's early reluctance to rely on the provisions on Union citizenship (eg Case C-193/94 *Skanavi* [1996] ECR I-929, para 22; *Calfa*, paras 15 and 30) has been replaced by an enthusiasm for those provisions even when the more established provisions on economic free movement could apply (eg Case C-158/07 *Förster* [2008] ECR I-8507).

[96] See, in particular, *Baumbast*, paras 86, 90 and 93. The Court's reliance on Art 20 TFEU in *Rottmann* and *Ruiz Zambrano* may lead to debate about whether it, like Art 21 TFEU, enjoys direct effect.

[97] *Baumbast*, para 91; and Art 27(2) Dir 2004/38.

[98] See, eg *Grzelczyk* (minimum subsistence allowance); *Collins* (job-seekers' allowance); and *Bidar* (favourable conditions for student loans).

[99] See, eg the essays in M Dougan and E Spaventa (eds), *Social Welfare and EU Law* (Oxford, Hart Publishing, 2005); or K Hailbronner, 'Union Citizenship and Access to Social Benefits' (2005) 42 *CML Rev* 1245.

castigating the Court for the inroads its citizenship case law continues to carve into areas of national competence in fields of, for example, taxation, immigration, social welfare, education, health care or the rules on the acquisition and loss of Member State nationality.

The crux of maintaining the distinction between EU and purely internal cases remains the assertion and identification of which level of authority is competent to regulate an individual EU national's rights. It may indeed be unfair that EU nationals who gain entry to Scottish universities are entitled, with reference to the principle established in *Gravier*, to the same treatment as Scottish residents, with the result that they do not pay university fees, while other UK nationals, because their situation is purely internal to their Member State of origin, fall outside the scope of the *Gravier* non-discrimination rule.[100] Nevertheless, is it for the Court of Justice, or for the appropriate regional and national authorities within the UK, to address this differential treatment? It may also be unfair that Irish nationals with non-EU spouses cannot, unlike the applicants in the *Metock* case, rely on EU law to create a right of residence for their non-EU family members. However, were the Court to interpret Article 21 TFEU as entailing a right to move *and* a right to reside it would, while abolishing reverse discrimination, also be covertly harmonising Member State immigration laws. Such an interpretation would also give rise to the highly questionable proposition that Member State nationals residing in their own Member State do so as a matter of EU law. Most Member State nationals regard their right to reside in their own Member State as a right contingent on their Member State nationality and deriving, therefore, from 'the special relationship of solidarity and good faith between [a Member State] and its nationals and also the reciprocity of rights and duties, which form the bedrock of the bond of nationality'.[101] They do not consider that this right is something derived from their status as a Union citizen and conferred on them as a matter of EU law. Indeed such a proposition would appear to subvert the relationship between Union citizenship and Member State nationality.[102] In this regard, it is folly to dismiss Member States' concern to safeguard their regulatory powers as merely symbolic.[103] Successive referenda on the Constitutional and Lisbon Treaties and the discussions in the intergovernmental conference preceding the Treaty of Lisbon on the principle of conferral and the EU's exclusive and shared competences reveal clearly that that is not the case.

[100] The Scottish system is currently under challenge for violating both EU law and the ECHR: see *The Guardian*, 24 August 2011.

[101] See the definition in *Rottmann*, para 50. See also, on the relationship of Member States with their own nationals, Case 41/74 *Van Duyn* [1974] ECR 1337, para 22: 'it is a principle of international law, which the [then EEC] treaty cannot be assumed to disregard in the relations between Member States, that a state is precluded from refusing its own nationals the right of entry or residence'.

[102] A relationship expressed as follows in Art 20(1) TFEU: 'Citizenship of the Union shall be additional to and not replace national citizenship.' See *McCarthy*, para 29, which refers to the principle of public international law reaffirmed in Art 3 of Protocol No 4 of the ECHR and recognised by the Court, which precludes a Member State from refusing its own nationals the right to enter its territory and remain there for any reason.

[103] See Dauticourt and Thomas (n 3) 436.

VI REFLECTIONS ON THE SCOPE OF EU LAW FOR THE FUTURE

Where the Court's case law on free movement and Union citizenship has fallen down is with reference to the articulation of the expanded or additional objectives and goals which now inform the EU integration project generally and the provisions on Union citizenship in particular.[104] Economic free movement as a means to achieve the internal market was a fairly simple proposition. The idea that the principle of non-discrimination on grounds of nationality had an instrumental role in furthering the primarily economic aims of the original EEC was an equally straightforward axiom. What lies behind the provisions of the Treaties on Union citizenship appears under-defined, complex and somewhat remote. Over time, the Court has become fond of repeating that Union citizenship is destined to become the fundamental status of Member State nationals. However powerful this rhetoric may be, it lacks the certainty and clarity of the defined objectives which informed the early free movement provisions. It is of course somewhat implausible to expect of the Court of Justice, in the context of preliminary reference procedures, a discussion of a political, indeed, philosophical nature from which the Member States themselves have shied away in successive Treaty amendments since Maastricht and when adopting secondary legislation.[105] The Court seems to be grappling with the difficulties which the still under-defined notion of Union citizenship throws up. In *McCarthy*, concluding that the applicant's situation was purely internal, it went to some lengths to distinguish its decision from previous citizenship decisions where the opposite conclusion had been reached. However, in doing so it could be argued that it placed free movement back at the heart of Union citizenship.[106] *McCarthy* risks provoking further charges of inconsistency and incoherence to the extent that the Court identifies the existence of a core of citizenship rights but fails to explain what that core encompasses.[107] Had the third country national for whom a derived right of residence was sought been a minor child, a disabled spouse or an aged

[104] See, in particular, N Nic Shuibhne, 'Seven Questions for Seven Paragraphs' (2011) 36 *EL Rev* 161 and Hailbronner and Thym (n 84), who excoriate the Court for the paucity of its reasoning and for the lack of a methodological or dogmatic basis for its decision.

[105] The extent to which the Union legislator simply codified elements of the Court's case law on the free movement of persons when adopting Dir 2004/38 is particularly noticeable in this respect. See also the refusal, referred to in n 32, when adopting Dir 2003/86, to address the issue of family reunification of EU nationals who had not exercised their free movement rights.

[106] At para 27 of *McCarthy*, the Court even refers to the free movement of *persons* as being one of the fundamental freedoms of the *internal market*. At para 49, it applies the principle established in *Rottmann* and *Ruiz Zambrano* – a national measure must not deprive the Union citizen of the genuine enjoyment of the substance of the rights associated with their status as Union citizens – but combines it with a requirement that their free movement rights, identified as being central to that status, must have been impeded in some way.

[107] The statement at para 49 of *McCarthy* to the effect that 'the failure by the authorities of the United Kingdom to take into account the Irish nationality of Mrs McCarthy for the purposes of granting her a right of residence in the United Kingdom in no way affects her right to move and reside freely within the territory of the Member States' might also be said to sit uncomfortably with previous decisions such as *Micheletti*, *Garcia Avello* and *Chen*.

parent, would the genuine enjoyment of the substance of the rights conferred by the status of Union citizen have been called into question? To what extent does the obligation on a Union citizen, such as the applicant in *McCarthy*, to migrate to another Member State and reside there in order to be able to claim a right of residence on her return to her Member State of origin and previous residence interfere with that genuine enjoyment? While in *Ruiz Zambrano* the focus was on the effects on the Union citizens involved of a refusal of residence to their applicant father, in *McCarthy* the Court emphasised the absence of any effect on the Union citizen applicant of a refusal to frame her rights in EU law terms, with little or no reference to the effects of this approach on her third country national spouse and her right to family reunification. The *McCarthy* decision, while it seeks to chart the evolution of the Court's case law on Union citizenship and the purely internal rule, will no doubt be relied on by those who lament an absence of clarity in that case law as regards which situations fall within or outwith that rule and as regards the objectives underpinning Union citizenship itself. The Court has since been asked to clarify its *Ruiz Zambrano* and *McCarthy* decisions in a series of requests for accelerated preliminary reference proceedings.[108] These cases may determine to what extent *Ruiz Zambrano* is a decision limited to the very specific facts of that case or whether *Rottmann* and *Ruiz Zambrano* represent an aperture, however large or small, in the Court's jurisprudence on the purely internal rule, explained by the evolving objectives of EU law generally as reflected in particular in the status of Union citizen.

Overall, what decisions on Union citizenship from *Carpenter* to *Chen* and even *Ruiz Zambrano* suggest is not that the Court has made a choice between legal certainty and the protection of fundamental rights, opting for the latter at the expense of the former, but that in determining the scope of application of EU law, fundamental rights considerations, even if explicit reference is not made to them, may have an increasingly important role to play. While this development may be accentuated by the introduction of Union citizenship, it is far from the only or principal factor behind such a development. Of course, the idea that the scope of EU law or the existence of the necessary connecting factors with one of the situations envisaged by EU law could be influenced by fundamental rights considerations might appear to be at odds with the provisions of the TEU and the Charter. Both explicitly state that the latter shall not extend in any way the competences of the EU as defined in the Treaties.[109] In *McB*, a case on judicial cooperation in civil matters in the field of child custody, the Court emphasised with reference to Article 51(2) of the Charter the limits of its jurisdiction as regards the latter. It has to interpret EU law in the light of the Charter but within the limits of the powers conferred on the EU.[110] Leaving to one side the provisions on Union citizenship and, specifically, Articles 20 and 21 TFEU, it could be argued that the Court's duty

[108] Case C-256/11 *Dereci* [2011] OJ C219/11 and Cases C-356/11 and C-357/11 *O and S* [2011] OJ C269/36. The accelerated procedure was denied in the latter case by order of 8 September 2011.

[109] See Art 6(1) TEU and Art 51(2) Charter.

[110] Case C-400/10 PPU *McB*, judgment of 5 October 2010, para 51.

to ensure respect for fundamental rights within the scope of application of EU law[111] may have an influence on the manner in which it has defined the latter.

In the case of *P v S*, the applicant, a teacher working for Cornwall County Council, claimed that her dismissal, due to the fact that she was undergoing gender reassignment, was contrary to EU gender equality legislation.[112] The sequence of the Court's reasoning in the case is instructive as regards definition of the scope of application of EU law. It recalled that the Equal Treatment Directive was but the expression, in a particular field, of the principle of equality, which is one of the fundamental principles of EU law, and that the right not to be discriminated against on grounds of gender is one of the fundamental human rights whose observance the Court has a duty to ensure.[113] In answer to the fundamental question raised by the case – whether discrimination on grounds of gender within the meaning of EU law extended to discrimination on grounds of gender reassignment – the Court's answer was brief:

> the scope of the [Equal Treatment Directive] cannot be confined simply to discrimination based on the fact that a person is of one or other sex. In view of its purpose and the nature of the rights which it seeks to safeguard, the scope of the directive is also such as to apply to discrimination arising, as in this case, from the gender reassignment of the person concerned.[114]

In the words of the Court, to tolerate discrimination based on gender assignment would be tantamount to a failure to respect the dignity and freedom to which he or she is entitled, and which the Court has a duty to safeguard. This language, reminiscent of that found in the case law of the Strasbourg Court, was less familiar in the context of the EU, where the extent of the Court's duty to observe fundamental rights had been clearly and somewhat strictly circumscribed in its case law.[115] In *P v S*, the Court appeared to rely on the need to respect fundamental rights when determining the scope of application of EU law, rather than determining as a preliminary the scope of application of EU gender equality law, confirming whether or not the situation of the applicant came within that scope and thereafter verifying whether fundamental rights had, in that context, been respected.[116]

When an attempt was made soon after the decision in *P v S* to apply the same reasoning to further extend the scope of application of EU gender equality law to cover sexual orientation discrimination, the Court reverted to a more traditional and less expansive analysis:

[111] See Case 36/75 *Rutili* [1975] ECR 1219; and Case 5/88 *Wachauf* [1989] ECR 2609.

[112] Article 5 Dir 76/207 on the implementation of the principle of equal treatment for men and women as regards access to employment, vocational training and promotion, and working conditions [1976] OJ L39/40 prohibited direct and indirect discrimination as regards conditions governing dismissal.

[113] Case C-13/94 *P v S* [1996] ECR I-2143, paras 18–19.

[114] Ibid, para 20.

[115] Limits which are reproduced in Art 51(1) of the Charter, where it is made clear that the provisions of the Charter are addressed to the Member States only when implementing EU law. See, eg, Case C-442/00 *Rodríguez Caballero* [2002] ECR I-11915, para 30.

[116] See further C Barnard, '*P. v S.*: Kite-flying or New Constitutional Approach?' in Dashwood and O'Leary (n 13).

> although respect for the fundamental rights which form an integral part of those general principles of law is a condition of the legality of [EU] acts, those rights cannot in themselves have the effect of extending the scope of the Treaty provisions beyond the competences of the EU.[117]

The Court made it clear that it was up to the Council – acting on the basis of a provision which had been recently inserted by the Treaty of Amsterdam which prohibited various forms of enumerated discrimination – to take appropriate action to eliminate discrimination based on sexual orientation.[118]

Despite this reversal, vestiges of *P v S* can still be found in the case law, more often than not in some way connected with the general principle of equality. As one commentator has remarked in relation to the Court's technique:

> A common tactic is to introduce a doctrine gradually: in the first case that comes before it, the Court will establish the doctrine as a general principle . . . if there are not too many protests, it will be reaffirmed in later cases: the qualification can then be whittled away and the full extent of the doctrine revealed.[119]

In the *Mangold* case, a German lawyer who had concluded a fixed term contract with his employer claimed to be the victim of discrimination on grounds of age. German law provided, for a transitional period, that such contracts could be concluded with workers of a certain age without the need to provide objective justifications.[120] Directive 2000/78, which prohibited age discrimination, had not, however, been transposed by the German authorities at the time when the contested contract was concluded.[121] According to the Court, echoing *P v S*, that Directive does not itself lay down the principle of equal treatment in the field of employment and occupation. The source of that principle can be found in various international instruments and in the constitutional traditions common to the Member States. Qualifying the principle of non-discrimination on grounds of age as a general principle of EU law, the Court held that the fact that the period for transposing the Directive had not yet expired could not, where a national rule falls within the scope of EU law, deprive the individual relying on the untransposed

[117] Case C-249/96 *Grant* [1998] ECR I-621, para 45.

[118] Art 19 TFEU provides: 'Without prejudice to the other provisions of the Treaties and within the limits of the powers conferred by them upon the Union, the Council . . . may adopt appropriate action to combat discrimination based on sex, racial or ethnic origin, religion or belief, disability, age or sexual orientation.' Dir 2000/78 establishing a general framework for equal treatment in employment and occupation [2000] OJ L303/16 was adopted on that basis.

[119] See TC Hartley, *The Foundations of European Community Law*, 2nd edn (Oxford, Clarendon Press, 1988) 78–79.

[120] Case C-144/04 *Mangold* [2005] ECR I-9981 concerned not only age discrimination but also compliance with Dir 1999/70 concerning the framework agreement on fixed-term work [1999] OJ L175/43, which established certain conditions for the conclusion of fixed term contracts including, as regards the conclusion of successive fixed term contracts, an obligation to furnish objective reasons justifying the choice of such a contract.

[121] Article 18 Dir 2000/78 had provided Member States with the possibility of an additional period for the implementation of the Directive as regards age and disability discrimination.

Directive of the legal protection they derive from the rules of EU law.[122] *Mangold* and the general principle of non-discrimination on grounds of age – whose origin has since been located squarely in the Charter – has also been invoked, in the *Kücükdeveci* case, in conjunction with the principle of the supremacy of EU law, to overcome the difficulties an applicant encountered in another employment law dispute due to the lack of horizontal direct effect of EU directives.[123] These cases provide excellent examples of the use to which the Court puts the general principles of EU law, using them to fill gaps in the law and as aids to interpretation.[124]

It would be a mistake to confine the effect of the Court's reasoning in *Mangold* and *Kücükdeveci* to the enforcement problems faced by the applicants in those specific cases. From a broader perspective these are examples, par excellence, of the Court engaging fully in the language of rights whose legitimating and integrating force in the context of the EU have been evident since the same jurisdiction established the notion of direct effect in the 1960s or clarified the EU's commitment to fundamental rights in the 1970s.[125] The relevance of case law like *P v S* or *Mangold* for the debate on the purely internal rule lies, on the one hand, in the possibility that Article 18 TFEU will also be recast, like the principle of non-discrimination on grounds of sex or age, as a general principle with, as a result, constitutional status,[126] and, on the other, in the possibility that the relocation of this principle within the Charter will influence the manner in which the proviso relating to the scope of application of EU law is to be interpreted. In an article on the general principles of EU law, Lenaerts and Gutiérrez-Fons describe their gap-filling function which, when grounded in the system of the Treaty, aims to create norms that are intrinsically linked to the nature, objectives and functioning of the EU.[127] Is it not possible that identification of general principles will be influenced

[122] What brought the applicant's single fixed-term contract within the scope of EU law in the *Mangold* case was the fact that the German transitional rules were regarded as measures implementing Dir 1999/70. Compare this finding, however, with para 52 of the decision in *Mangold*, where it is stated that 'reduction of the protection which workers are guaranteed in the sphere of fixed-term contracts is not prohibited as such by the Framework Agreement where it is in no way connected to the implementation of that agreement'.

[123] *Kücükdeveci*, paras 20–27 and 50–53. The Court has consistently held that a directive cannot of itself impose obligations on an individual and cannot therefore be relied on as such against an individual before the national courts: see, eg, Case 152/84 *Marshall* [1986] ECR 723; Case C-91/92 *Faccini Dori* [1994] ECR I-3325. Thus while a directive has vertical direct effect and can be relied on before national courts against a public sector employer to oppose national rules contrary to EU law, it cannot be relied on in identical, albeit horizontal, circumstances against a private sector employer.

[124] See further T Tridimas, *The General Principles of EU Law*, 2nd edn (Oxford, OUP, 2006).

[125] See further G De Búrca, 'The Language of Rights in European Integration' in J Shaw and G More (eds), *New Legal Dynamics of European Union* (Oxford, Clarendon Press, 1999) 43, where she suggests that the use of the idea of common constitutional traditions 'can be seen to have both a descriptive and a prescriptive function: it claims to draw on rights and principles which exist and which are recognized in constitutional traditions and, on the other hand it elevates these into general principles of [EU] law and in so doing aims to forge a "common law" or perhaps a "common bill of rights" for the [EU] and, in turn, for the member states'.

[126] See Case C-101/08 *Audiolux* [2009] ECR I-9823.

[127] K Lenaerts and JA Gutiérrez-Fons, 'The Constitutional Allocation of Powers and General Principles of EU Law' (2010) 47 *CML Rev* 1629, 1632.

by and feed into the identification of the EU's nature and objectives and, as we can see from existing case law, that that nature and those objectives may influence in turn the Court's identification of situations governed by, or which have some sort of link with, EU law? The wording of key passages of the decisions in *P v S* and *Rottmann* are remarkably similar. At paragraph 42 of *Rottmann* the Court could as easily have concluded that, in view of the purpose of Union citizenship and the nature of the rights which it confers, a national decision depriving a Member State national of his nationality and therefore his Union citizenship falls within the scope of application of EU law. These parallels between the debate on the evolving shape of the purely internal rule and the debate on general principles of EU law merit further reflection. As regards general principles, some commentators have called, following the decision in *Kücükdeveci*, for a focused and critical debate about what it means for Member State action to fall within the scope of the Treaties for the purposes of triggering the general principles of EU law.[128] Others, referring to the coming into force of the Charter, argue that there is an inherent risk that general principles might be used or at least give the impression of being used as a means to bypass the limitation provisions of the Charter.[129] Both these discussions on general principles and the present discussion on the purely internal rule ultimately relate to questions of competence and the definition of the scope of, and the limits to the reach of, EU law.

VII CONCLUSION

Is the enjoyment of the status of Union citizenship and the rights conferred on Union citizens by the provisions of the Treaties contingent on free movement and the existence of a cross-border element? The answer to this broad question would, as the Court has now indicated in *Rottmann*, *Ruiz Zambrano* and *McCarthy*, have to be no. The range of circumstances in which individual EU nationals can rely on EU law against their own Member States has broadened with each Treaty amendment since Maastricht. All Member State nationals are Union citizens. Within the scope of application of the Treaties they are entitled not to be discriminated against on grounds of nationality, sex, racial or ethnic origin, religion or belief, disability, age or sexual orientation.[130] In addition, fundamental rights, as guaranteed by the ECHR and as they result from the constitutional traditions common to the Member States, constitute general principles of EU law.[131] The Court will ensure respect for those general principles not only when assessing the legality of EU legislation but also when Member States act within the scope of application of EU law.

[128] See Editorial, 'The Scope of Application of the General Principles of Union Law: An Ever Expanding Union?' (2010) 47 *CML Rev* 1589.

[129] See S Prechal, 'Competence Creep and the General Principles of EU Law' (2010) 3 *Review of European Administrative Law* 5, 21.

[130] Arts 18 and 19 TFEU.

[131] Art 6(3) TEU.

It would be wrong to derive from the reference to the cases on the general principle of equality a conclusion to the effect that the Court's commitment to respect for fundamental rights will radically transform the scope of EU law. The general provisions of the Charter have been constructed in terms which the Court cannot ignore. Furthermore, for every *P v S* there is a *Grant*; for every *Mangold* a *Chacón Navas*, a case on disability rather than age discrimination in which the Court emphasised the effects of the principle of conferral and the limited scope of its review of respect for fundamental rights.[132] What the decisions examined in this chapter could suggest is that the general principles of EU law and the Court's obligation to ensure respect for fundamental rights may have an increasingly important role to play in determining the contours of the scope of application of EU law and assessing the connecting factors which will bring an applicant's case within a situation governed by EU law and therefore outwith the purely internal rule. While fundamental rights did not explicitly feature in the Court's reasoning in *Ruiz Zambrano*, it is difficult to contend that they were entirely absent in spirit. The combination of Union citizenship and the EU's general commitment to fundamental rights has already, in cases like *Carpenter* and *Chen*, proved to be a potent one. If one adds to that combination a general principle of equality, which is proving to have far-reaching substantive and procedural effects, and a comprehensive, loosely framed Charter, which is now recognised as having equal legal value to the Treaties, the difficulties which the Court will face in future in determining the confines of EU law and applying the purely internal rule become patent. It is, in this context, both reductive to think of the status of Union citizenship purely in terms of free movement and excessive to suppose that its introduction mandates the Court abandoning a rule whose raison d'être remains valid, if not essential, in a legal order based on attributed competences. Union citizenship has undoubtedly helped to transform the legal landscape within which the Court now has to apply the purely internal rule, but it represents part of a continuum in a larger and much more complex whole.

[132] Case C-13/05 *Chacón Navas* [2006] ECR I-6467, para 56: 'It is true that fundamental rights which form an integral part of the general principles of Community law include the general principle of non-discrimination. That principle is therefore binding on Member States where the national situation at issue in the main proceedings falls within the scope of Community law . . .. However, it does not follow from this that the scope of [Dir] 2000/78 should be extended by analogy beyond the discrimination based on the grounds listed exhaustively in Art 1 thereof.'

3

A Stage, a Spotlight and an Unwritten Script: Frontier Zones and Intersectional Citizens

CHARLOTTE O'BRIEN

I INTRODUCTION

FRONTIER WORKERS HAVE typically been treated as indicators of European integration,[1] but they are also drivers of integration, creating new territories in the form of frontier zones – areas between EU Member States. The tentative nature of the legal responses to these zones suggests concerns about whether it is appropriate for individual migrants to lead the assault on the limits of national and Union law, and highlights the continued importance of borders. But frontier zones challenge the border rationale, and so challenge the limits of Union law. Where exact border delineation is decreasingly visible or culturally relevant, it might be incongruous to apply the border-dependent taxonomy of rights of different Union citizens, a taxonomy further complicated by a swathe of recent ECJ cases.[2]

This chapter analyses the status of intersectional citizens living and/or working in frontier zones between Member States, in particular examining the impact of 'cross border regional authorities',[3] European Groupings of Territorial Cooperation[4] (EGTCs). These are new legal entities composed of regional and local authorities

[1] European Commission, Directorate General for Research, Working Paper Social Affairs Series W 16A, 'Frontier Workers in the European Union', Summary (May 1997) Section 2.2.

[2] Case C-310/08 *London Borough of Harrow v Nimco Hassan Ibrahim and Secretary of State for the Home Department* [2010] ECR I-01065; Case C-480/08 *Maria Teixeira v London Borough of Lambeth and Secretary of State for the Home Department* [2010] ECR I-01107; Case C-135/08 *Janko Rottman v Freistaat Bayern* [2010] ECR I-01449; Case C-434/09 *Shirley McCarthy v Secretary of State for the Home Department* judgment 5 May 2011, nyr; Case C-34/09 *Gerardo Ruiz Zambrano v Office national de l'emploi* judgment 8 March 2011, nyr.

[3] Third Report on Economic and Social Cohesion – A New Partnership for Cohesion, Convergence, Competitiveness, Cooperation (Luxembourg, Office for Official Publications of the European Communities, 2004) 77.

[4] As provided for by Regulation 1082/2006 on the European Grouping of Territorial Cooperation [2006] OJ L210/19.

from different Member States (and potentially from non-Member States) brought together to deal with shared administrative issues.[5] This chapter argues that frontier zones are not merely recent legal fabrications; EGTCs represent the law catching up with social reality. Such projects are not 'simply' about administrative simplification but are bound up with questions of identity, evident in attempts to elide local cross-border regionalism with supranationalism. The degree to which the interaction of legal frameworks has been able to 'catch up' with frontier lives is necessarily limited. National concerns about sovereignty and about the implications of individual-driven Europeanisation, Union concerns about devolved control, and the tenuousness of the link between subnational and supranational, mean that cross-border local governance has to be restricted. Resulting projects are too fraught with internal inconsistency and potential for conflict to be capable of smoothing out the frictions of frontier work. EGTCs thus manage to be ambitious, unpredictable, and insipid.

In adopting a (politically necessarily) minimalist approach to policy harmonisation, EGTCs cannot prevent the continued carving up of different rights for those living in frontier zones. Union institutions have long been clear that crossing borders can legitimately result in disadvantage,[6] assuming that once in the new Member State equilibrium will be achieved through settlement and equal rights with nationals.[7] However, frontier workers, instead of passing through the difficult border-crossing stage continue to occupy, and exist on, that brink. Member States are poised between European openness and national closure, making borders partially permeable. Although nationality is of decreasing significance for EU nationals,[8] territoriality still governs welfare borders; certain benefits are as a general rule[9] not exportable,[10] while residence criteria play a significant part in determining initial eligibility.

As the new groupings do not address core frictional disadvantage, they reveal the bluntness of borders as rights-allocating tools. The rights of frontier zone workers are left contingent upon circumstance, feeling the vicissitudes of ECJ case law more profoundly than static workers. A number of variables (stemming partly from case law) all feed into the calculation of the status of each frontier citizen.

[5] See the definition provided by the European Commission at 'Regional Policy: European Grouping of Territorial Co-operation' www.ec.europa.eu/regional_policy/archive/funds/gect/index_en.htm.

[6] There is no guarantee that such movement will be financially neutral: Joined Cases C-393/99 and C-394/99 *Hervein II* [2002] ECR I-2829, para 51.

[7] According to the preamble, Regulation 1612/68 on freedom of movement for workers within the Community [1968] OJ L257/2 aimed at facilitating 'integration' of workers' families in the new Member State.

[8] Though of primary significance when dividing EU from third country nationals. See, eg D Kostakopoulou, 'Thick, Thin and Thinner Patriotisms: Is This All There Is?' (2006) 26 *OJLS* 73.

[9] Though not an immutable rule – see the part that specific circumstances played to render the exportation of a special non-contributory benefit potentially 'fair' in Case C-287/05 *D P W Hendrix v Raad van Bestuur van het Uitvoeringsinstituut Werknemersverzekeringen* [2007] ECR I-06909; see also C O'Brien 'Case C-212/05 *Hartmann*, Case C-213/05 *Geven*, Case C-287/05 *Hendrix*' (2008) 45 *CML Rev* 499.

[10] Special non-contributory benefits under Art 70(3)–(4) of Regulation 883/2004 on the coordination of social security systems [2004] OJ L166/1, and listed in Annex X of the Regulation.

These complexities are inevitably more pronounced, and more likely to feel incongruous, when slicing through areas that have been encouraged to shift their conceptual borders and proclaim a more 'post-national' identity.

II FRONTIER ZONE CITIZENS AS DRIVERS OF LEGAL INTEGRATION: NATIONAL AND UNION CONCERNS

In some ways the EGTC is simply the latest incarnation of an old idea: territorial cohesion has long been on the Union agenda, and the Commission's 2008 Green Paper on territorial cohesion[11] lists the actions taken since the mid-1990s – including the European Spatial Development Perspective adopted in 1999,[12] the establishing of inter-regional programmes of transnational projects[13] and the creation of the European Spatial Planning Observatory Network.[14] The EGTC is nevertheless a new development – a recognition of the distinct nature (and potential legal personality) of frontier zones. Working and residing in different nations is still a minority pursuit,[15] but spaces are forming around blurred borders in which non-mobile cultures are intermingled, giving rise to distinct local social conditions and creating the need for distinct and coherent administrative support. Whether cooperating regions are charged with fundamental border dismantling and building up a concrete policy competence architecture, or instead provide only light-duty infrastructure, a scaffolding of transport and tourism,[16] through and around which the Member States and EU can proceed as normal, they nevertheless require us to reconceptualise the frontier not as something to be crossed, but as a zone, or as the Committee of the Regions (CoR) describes EGTCs, '"laboratories" for multi-level Governance'.[17]

[11] European Commission, 'Green Paper on Territorial Cohesion: Turning Territorial Diversity into Strength' COM (2008) 616, 10.

[12] European Commission, Committee on Spatial Development, 'European Spatial Development Perspective: Towards Balanced and Sustainable Development of the Territory of the European Union' (Potsdam, 10–11 May 1999).

[13] European Commission, 'Communication from the Commission to the Member States of 7 May 2001 "Interregional cooperation" Strand C of the Interreg III Community initiative' COM (2001) 1188 final.

[14] European Commission, Regional Policy, Inforegio 'Operational programme: ESPON' available at www.ec.europa.eu/regional_policy/country/prordn/details_new.cfm?gv_PAY=EU&gv_reg=ALL&gv_PGM=1257&LAN=7&gv_per=2&gv_defL=7.

[15] A study commissioned by DG Employment and Social Affairs found that 'about 780,000 people in the EU (including EEA/EFTA) were cross-border commuters in the year 2006/2007. Commuting streams are clearly condensed in the area of Central-Western Europe.' European Commission & MKW Wirtschaftsforschung GmbH, Munich, 'Scientific Report on the Mobility of Cross-Border Workers within the EU-27/EEA/EFTA Countries – final report' (January 2009) 7.

[16] Five priorities for cross-border cooperation facilitated by EGTCs are laid down by Art 6 Reg 1080/2006 on the European Regional Development Fund [2006] OJ L210/1. Tourism features twice, while transport and urban–rural links each feature separately.

[17] CoR, 'Own Initiative Opinion on New Perspectives for the Revision of the EGTC Regulation' 88th plenary session (27–28 January 2011) CdR 100/2010.

The promotional work on EGTCs relies to some degree on disavowing the notion of anything new and intrusive, emphasising the legal response to the already special nature of the frontier zones, which have organically emerged through individual mobility and resulting social change. An EGTC monitoring report identifies hot spots for EGTC development on the basis of 'remarkable . . . long-standing history of cooperation'[18] on the Spain-France-Portugal borders, and 'a continuous process of economic and civic integration' observed 'since the 1950s' between Belgium, Luxembourg, France and Germany.[19] Shared history and experience are among the prime sources of EGTC inspiration, and go some way to lending credibility to claims of regional identity. It is Union institutions that have latched upon the lived border/frontier zone experience and clad it with 'European' meaning – casting cross-border regionalism as 'European integration'.[20]

Cross-border groupings are thus responses to social reality – driven by those in the frontier zone, making them 'truly grassroots projects'.[21] This 'bottom-up' approach to integration ignites questions for nation states about the problem of balancing harmonising pressures exerted by individuals with a community-based need to allocate resources, and for the Union about the tenuous link between local identity and pan-European integration.

A National Reservations and Sovereignty Concerns

The cultivation of localised/regionalised autonomous areas may result in creating distance from other polities, such as nation states. United Kingdom scepticism sees EU-fostered legal entities as miniature 'poolings' of sovereignty. If we consider an example difficult region, the 'France (Channel/Manche) England cross border cooperation programme 2007–2013'[22] does not provide for a body such as an EGTC – the programme clearly lists objectives and strategies separately as divided between the nations. The priority to which the largest section of the programme budget is allocated is to 'reinforce the sense of belonging to a common space of citizenship and raise awareness of common interests'[23] – which courts the criticism of Eurosceptic commentators. The related 'Arc Manche' grouping has

[18] J Pucher and A Radzyner, *EGTC Monitoring Report 2010* 'Executive Summary' (European Union, 2011) 6.

[19] Ibid.

[20] Thus EGTCs should, regardless of Union financing, 'secure maximum administrative efficiency in management, economic efficiency and territorially-based European cohesion and integration': CoR CdR 100/2010 (n 17) para 44.

[21] CoR President Mercedes Bresso, 'EGTC Institutional Video 2011. A New Concept in Regional Cooperation': www.portal.cor.europa.eu/egtc/en-US/Pages/welcome.aspx.

[22] The Franco-British programme was created in 1990 but is now covered by Interreg IV – see Interreg France (Manche/Channel) England 'Le programme France (Manche) – Angleterre' available at www.interreg4a-manche.eu/index.php?lang=en.

[23] Europa Press Room, 'France and United Kingdom – Operational Programme 2007–2013: France (Channel)–England Cross-border Co-operation Programme' MEMO/09/197 (Brussels, 24 April 2009).

been defended precisely because 'it has no authority whatsoever'[24] (as though authority itself would be a threat) and because it is a simple mouthpiece – it 'merely serves to articulate the concerns'[25] of its members. On being accused of undermining national authority the Arc Manche website made a virtue out of the fact that it is 'not even a legal entity'.[26] The implication is that a grouping with legal personality may acquire the substance, initiative and autonomy to at some point pose a challenge to national and different local autonomies.

The gist of this perceived threat is not new – EU-sponsored 'local' policies have long been suspected of attempting to 'bypass' State supervision,[27] especially in the context of Structural Funds,[28] which were found to be 'softening' national boundaries and 'domesticating what would previously have been described as international relations'.[29] As with Structural Funds, the incentive for regions to embrace a 'European' stamp is, perhaps inevitably, financial. The second sentence of the CoR's two-sentence summary of what an EGTC is headlines the direct application for and management of European funds,[30] a theme heavily pushed in the guidance.[31] In return, EGTCs must be formed according to a Union instrument, within Union-defined conditions, within a broad cohesion policy framework that has explicitly pro-Union motives.[32] The EGTC thus financially steers bodies to adopt a lexicon – which in itself could be characterised as part of cultural surrender.[33] Interestingly, however, the EGTC concept may be a Union response to *dampen down* the perceived threat of EU regional programmes. The fact that Member States themselves can be members might be an attempt to placate concerns and imply national oversight.[34] But it remains to be seen whether

[24] This was stated in the Arc Manche 'Frequently Asked Questions' in response to the FAQ 'It is obviously a ploy to undermine national authority, or can you give me any reason why this is not the case?' which was recently on the site; the FAQ page has since been redesigned: www.arcmanche.com/en/faq/> (as on 22 October 2010).

[25] Ibid.

[26] Ibid.

[27] R Balme and B Jouve, 'Building the Regional State: Europe and Territorial Organization in France' in L Hooghe (ed), *Cohesion Policy and European Integration: Building Multi-level Governance* (Oxford, Clarendon, 1996).

[28] L Hooghe and G Marks, *Multi-level Governance and European Integration* (Boulder CO, Rowman & Littlefield, 2001).

[29] Ibid, 89.

[30] CoR, 'European Grouping of Territorial Cooperation (EGTC)' available at http://cor.europa.eu/en/activities/networks/Pages/egtc.aspx.

[31] Elsewhere the CoR notes: 'Specifically, the EGTC is dedicated to the management and implementation of territorial cooperation programmes or projects co-financed by the Community': CoR, 'What is the EGTC?' available at www.portal.cor.europa.eu/egtc/en-US/whatis/Pages/welcome.aspx.

[32] The 'exclusive aim' of EGTCs is 'strengthening economic and social cohesion' according to Reg 1082/2006 (Art 1(2)), while the preamble refers to the objective of 'harmonious development of the entire Community territory and greater economic, social and territorial cohesion' (1).

[33] P Bourdieu, *Language and Symbolic Power* (Cambridge, Polity Press, 1992); see also M Foucault on dominance and discourse: *The History of Sexuality I: The Will to Knowledge* (London, Penguin, 1998); and A Gramsci on cultural hegemony: *Prison Notebooks, Vol 3* (New York, Columbia University Press, 2011).

[34] An argument outlined by D Strazzari, 'Harmonizing Trends vs Domestic Regulatory Frameworks: Looking for the European Law on Cross-border Cooperation' (2011) 4 *European Journal of Legal Studies* 151.

the EGTC is in fact treated as *more* of a threat since it not only sets up direct links between subnational and supranational levels of governance, but also grants some independence through legal personality.

Of course, it is not only UK hackles that rise when sovereignty infringements are detected. The Commission in its Green Paper on territorial cohesion acknowledged that the territorial cooperation agenda has been hindered by national concerns about EU interference, noting that the cooperation project had 'not progressed as far as it might have until recently. This is perhaps partly because of *a perception in the Member States* that *national – or regional – competence*[*s* . . . were] open for discussion'.[35] National resistance to a supranational agenda can be discerned in the ways different Member States have personalised 'territorial cohesion' in responses[36] to the Commission's consultation on territorial cohesion.[37] The Belgian position stated that 'cross-fertilisation between territories' is essential,[38] the UK position stressed improving institutional capacity and reducing economic disparity;[39] Italy appeared to suggest that territorial cohesion was a national means for furthering European ends[40] while the UK position reads as though it is the other way round; Malta made a plea that the concept be understood not purely with regard to economic statistics, but taking into account permanent geographic disadvantages.[41] Regional responses are also resistant to uniformity – with one UK county council declaring that the EGTC as a tool for territorial cohesion has 'not worked', due to the absence of take-up in the UK,[42] and a Scottish county council stating that territorial cohesion ought to be considered with regard to, inter alia, quality of life, health and wages.[43] The Welsh Assembly presented territorial cohesion as largely a matter for Member States (and their subsidiaries) to organise, invoking the principle of subsidiarity, stating that the EU should only get involved where it can add value,[44] and rather implying that such cohesion is not necessarily a 'European' phenomenon at all.

Emphasis on local/national agendas, and concerns about State-bypass are tied up with concerns about resource distribution, provoked by the ECJ's rulings on protecting frontier workers from excessive frictional disadvantage. In *Mattern &*

[35] European Commission, (n 11) 10. (emphasis added)

[36] All responses are listed at: European Commission 'Contributions to the Consultation on the Green Paper on Territorial Cohesion – Turning Territorial Diversity into Strength', available at http://ec.europa.eu/regional_policy/archive/consultation/terco/contrib_en.htm.

[37] European Commission, (n 11).

[38] Belgian Position 'Green Paper on Territorial Cohesion Turning Territorial Diversity into Strength' at European Commission (n 36) 3 and section 11, 9.

[39] UK Government's Response, DCLG 10 March 2009, at European Commission (n 36) 4–5.

[40] Italian Contribution at European Commission (n 36) definition at 1–2.

[41] Malta contribution, EU Secretariat, Office of the Prime Minister, 3 March 2009 at European Commission (n 36) 1, 2 and 3.

[42] North Yorkshire County Council response 'towards a consolidated EU programmes and devolved governance' February 2009 at European Commission (n 36) 1.

[43] Aberdeenshire County Council Response, Transportation and Infrastructure, 4 December 2008, at European Commission (n 36) 10.

[44] Welsh Assembly Government Response, 'Territorial Cohesion: The View from Wales', February 2009, at European Commission (n 36) 3, 7, 8, 10, 14.

Cikotic,[45] Advocate General Kokott emphasised the special nature of certain border regions, and the need to smooth the way for cross-border life and work – or creating a common European job market – noting that for many living in border regions the nearest big employment centres lay across borders; 'indeed', it was 'in the area around the borders between Belgium, Luxembourg, France and Germany that frontier workers have become a widespread phenomenon'.[46] Easing the process of cross border work would reduce commuting times, and so have the knock-on effect of promoting 'the integration of Ms Mattern's and Mr Cikotic's joint family life in Belgium'.[47] Advocate General Stix-Hackl has attributed to the Union legislature, in the complicated Regulation 1408/71[48] provisions on unemployed frontier workers, a desire to 'make it easier for wholly unemployed frontier workers to find employment',[49] so recognising the special situation of frontier workers. Conscious that coordination is imperfect, Advocate General Alber described the exclusion of a former frontier worker, who had worked in Luxembourg but was living in Germany, from the Luxembourg benefit system as 'typical of the kind of unfair situation that is regularly to be encountered in relation to frontier workers'.[50] It was a particular concern for the fair treatment of frontier workers that led to close judicial scrutiny, and tightening, of the rules to prevent Member States from liberally using the 'special contributory benefit' label to attach residence restrictions to benefits.[51]

This protection of those commuting across borders to work in a Member State different to that of their nationality has to some degree transcended its origins, to protect all those commuting across EU borders even if it is to work in the Member State of origin and *live* elsewhere (a phenomenon I have described elsewhere as 'reverse frontier work').[52] Once the initial transfer of residence has occurred, which would not be sufficient in itself to grant the status of migrant worker and attendant protections, subsequent cross-border movements back to the State of origin are now, following *Hartmann*,[53] to be treated as making 'full use of . . . [the] right to freedom of movement for workers'.[54] This actually creates a hybrid sort of right – possibly most appropriate within frontier zones – whereby exercise of an Article 21 TFEU right can give rise to Article 45 TFEU-related protections, including those for frontier workers, which were once reserved for those exercising

[45] Case C-10/05 *Cynthia Mattern and Hajrudin Cikotic v Ministre du Travail et de l'Emploi* [2006] ECR I-3145.

[46] Ibid, Opinion of AG Kokott, para 38.

[47] Ibid.

[48] On the application of social security schemes to employed persons and their families moving within the Community [1971] OJ L149/2.

[49] Case C-311/01 *Commission of the European Communities v Kingdom of the Netherlands* [2003] ECR I-13103, Opinion of AG Alber at para 63, referring to Art 71(1)(a)(ii).

[50] Case C-189/00 *Urszula Ruhr v Bundesanstalt für Arbeit* [2001] ECR I-8225.

[51] Case C-215/99 *Friedrich Jauch v Pensionsversicherungsanstalt der Arbeiter* [2001] ECR I-01901, (especially see Opinion of AG Alber, 107); Case C-43/99 *Ghislain Leclere and Alina Deaconescu v Caisse nationale des prestations familiales* [2001] ECR I-04265.

[52] O'Brien (n 9).

[53] Case C-212/05 *Hartmann* [2007] ECR I-6303.

[54] Ibid, para 18.

'labour migration'.[55] This more expansive approach was put forward in connection with the dismantling of internal borders by Advocate General Kokott in *Hendrix*[56] – who argued that in

> an area without internal frontiers, a person who travels from his State of residence in order to work in the State of which he is a national may be no more subject to impediment than a person who commutes from his State of nationality in order to work in another Member State.[57]

A vision of territorial semi-fusion is thus borne out in the Court's desire to capture all cross-border work within Union law, and in the Commission's desire to 'make it easier for citizens to take advantage of the benefits of European integration and the European Single Market'.[58] EGTCs might represent in this vision integration hot spots, where border crossing is increasingly pushed as a simple fact of life 'in a booming and politically stable Europe'.[59] In 2008, the CoR described one of the six elements of the 'mission' of the EGTC construction to be to provide 'Support to cross-border networks of citizens'.[60]

It seems that individual migrants/litigants are capable of exerting surprising, if not disproportionate, harmonising pressure. This in itself must lead Member States to question whether individual and community interests are sufficiently balanced, or whether individual 'rights' of freedom of movement are used to make solidarity concerns – which may determine the territorial conditions of benefit uptake etc – 'appear both ugly and unkind',[61] and, to adopt Newdick's critique of individual-led integration of health care systems, to divert social resources in favour of the '(articulate) consumer and those who compete most effectively for market share'[62] by invoking an appropriate fundamental freedom. While Member States may be concerned about the use of Union law to achieve anti-solidaristic and individualistic objectives, so might the Union be concerned about the outward adoption of Union objectives in order to further regional/local ends.

[55] ie, those who 'take up an activity as an employed person, and . . . pursue such activity, within the territory of another Member State': Art 1 Reg 1612/68.

[56] Above n 9.

[57] Ibid, Opinion of AG Kokott, para 42.

[58] European Commission 'Mobility in Europe' at goo.gl/v2mx6.

[59] CoR, 'The European Grouping of Territorial Co-operation – EGTC –' CdR 117/2007 (Study), 17: 'local players on either side of certain European borders, dependent on different systems but sharing common problems and interests (*border workers*, cross-border pollution, land-use planning or security issues, etc)'. (emphasis added)

[60] INTERACT, *Interact Handbook*, 'The European Grouping of Territorial Cooperation (EGTC): What Use for European Territorial Cooperation Programmes and Projects?' (Austria, December 2008) 76.

[61] A Somek, 'Solidarity Decomposed: Being and Time in European Citizenship' (2007) 32 *EL Rev* 787, 816.

[62] C Newdick, 'Preserving Social Citizenship in Health Care Markets: There May be Trouble Ahead' (2008) 2 *McGill Journal of Law and Health* 93, 108.

B Union Reservations and the Tenuous Link between Local and European Integration

Not only could the creation of cross-border entities excite suspicion that they will act as subsidiaries of the Union, but also Union institutions may doubt the capacity, or the integrity of the motives, of bidding groupings to dispense with funds 'appropriately'. Comments were reported in debate in the European Parliament Committee on Regional Development in 2008 that 'the suggestion to leave the local authorities to manage freely the EU funds met opposition. MEPs reacted that EU funds are not meant for redistributing money from the common EU budget but are allocated for the realisation of specific EU objectives'.[63] The approach that the primary function of such entities is to bid effectively for Union funds may on the one hand sound relatively mercenary and liable to appeal to the more atavistic Member State interests, but on the other it suggests inculcating a conformity with Union norms as to funding awards and rules. In this way, although the *issues* on which cooperation has been found appropriate are supposedly distinctively 'local', the *type of cooperation* established must to some degree embrace European premises and be developed according to a European agenda. The Amphictyony EGTC, with partners from Greece, Cyprus, Italy and France, although stipulating respect for local 'particularity', has cautioned against its being used to undermine territorial cohesion, and outlined amongst other objectives the creation of local European Affairs Officers.[64] Part of its 'local level' mission is the promotion and enhancement of the 'link and coordination between areas-regions and the European Union'.[65]

This objective is an attempt to anticipate and challenge subnational pressures, as Union institutions must know that the Regulation's premise that the 'harmonious development of the entire Community territory and greater economic, social and territorial cohesion imply the strengthening of territorial cooperation'[66] does not make the reverse true. In responses to the Commission's Green Paper on Territorial Cohesion, one UK county council emphasised the principle of *subsidiarity* as an inevitable corollary of territorial cohesion, advocating 'the delegation and devolution of policy development and programme delivery to appropriate dynamic regions'.[67] Just as 'a policy of promoting citizen self-interest will not

[63] European Parliament's Committee on Regional Development (REGI) and the Committee of the Regions' Territorial Cohesion Commission (COTER), 'The Future of the Cohesion Policy after 2013', Debate 7 October 2008, in *Regions and Cities in a Challenging World*, report of the proceedings of the European Week of Regions and Cities, October 2008, Committee of the Regions and Commission DG Regional Policy, 162, at European Commission 'Open Days' available at www.ec.europa.eu/regional_policy/conferences/od2008/report.cfm?nmenu=3&sub=2&smenu=27.

[64] Amphictyony, 'Negotiating text on the "multi-level governance"' available at www.amphictyony.gr/en/article.php?id=81, 5.

[65] Ibid, 3.

[66] Regulation 1082/2006, preamble (1).

[67] Cornwall County Council Territorial Cohesion Green Paper Consultation response, 1–2, at European Commission (n 36).

necessarily generate a sense of allegiance'[68] it seems regional self-interest does not translate automatically into European allegiance, although the CoR insists that local authorities could 'become driving forces in drawing up and implementing EU policy'.[69]

In theory, endowing regions with concrete identities and some autonomy helps 'to make European governance more open, participatory, democratic, accountable and transparent'[70] – or brings Europe closer to its citizens.[71] Indicating a determination to link the EGTC to the broader European integration project, a CoR memo in January 2011 set the objective of 'EGTC community building and networking'[72] – a *network* would have greater potential to displace existing governance structures. However, this identity-building through EGTCs may be little more than rhetoric taken a bit too far, since it relies on exercises such as creating a 'web site, logo, and labelling . . . [and] Eurometropolitan events'.[73]

Cross-border regionalism could in theory exemplify European integration,[74] such as the most well-established 'Euro-metropole' in Lille, Europe's 'first cross-border conurbation',[75] (actually and rhetorically) positioned at the 'heart of north west Europe',[76] and the 'centre of the Paris, London and Brussels triangle'.[77] However, the degree of 'European' flavour imparted to EGTCs will obviously depend on geopolitical location. The hot spots identified by Advocate General Kokott, where cross-border life and work is a 'widespread phenomenon',[78] are clustered around the administrative centres of the Union, where cross-border workers may not only be conscious of the EU rights they are exercising, (or at least know a lawyer conscious of those rights)[79] but be in some way affiliated to an EU

[68] Newdick (n 62) 108.

[69] CoR 'What is the EGTC?' available at www.portal.cor.europa.eu/egtc/en-US/whatis/Pages/welcome.aspx.

[70] Ibid.

[71] An objective advanced by the European Council in the Laeken Declaration on the Future of Europe (14–15 December 2001).

[72] CoR, 127th Meeting of the Committee of the Regions Bureau (26 January 2011), 'Constitution of the Platform of European Groupings of Territorial Cooperation (EGTC) R/CdR 397/2010 item 6, 4.

[73] Marie Vannouque-Digne, the International Relations Director of the Lille Metropolitan Urban Community, in the Mission Operationnelle Transfontailere Guide to European Groupings of Territorial Co-operation (May 2008).

[74] Note the CoR's position in 2007 that giving EGTCs legal identity 'should eventually have major implications . . . for the probable role of territorial authorities in a process of horizontal integration in Europe': CoR (n 59) 112.

[75] Espaces Transfrontaliers, 'Eurometropole Lille-Kortrijk-Tournai' available atwww.espaces-transfrontaliers.org/en/conurbations/terri_doc_ag_eurometropole_lille_en.html.

[76] Ibid.

[77] Lille Metropole.fr: 'At the centre of the Paris, London and Brussels triangle' available at www.lillemetropole.fr:8080/index.php?p=833&art_id=.

[78] Case C-10/05 *Cynthia Mattern and Hajrudin Cikotic v Ministre du Travail et de l'Emploi* [2006] ECR I-3145.

[79] Accounting for the high proportion of ECJ references from those 'central' States' national courts; the latest statistical report published by the ECJ shows that in 2009 the Member States that made the highest numbers of new references for preliminary rulings were Germany, Belgium, Italy, France, the UK and the Netherlands: ECJ Annual Report 2009, 103.

body – an institution,[80] quango or NGO. But even the Lille narrative centres on a highly particularised, distinctive experience of living and working within a 'polycentric, tri-cultural and bi-national urban area',[81] stressing local distinctiveness, which may have little to do with the overarching European integration project. Other cross-border groupings may be much less amenable than others to the 'European integration' label. An emphasis on cross-national regional identity may serve to distance people within those communities from other communities *within their home Member State*, let alone from other parts of Europe.

The emphasis on local, cross-border identity may therefore conflict with pan-Europeanism. The Istergranum grouping across part of the Hungarian and Slovakian border – which began with reconstruction of a bridge across the Danube – has been described in the EGTC baseline study as an example of bridge symbolism, or the 'rebuilding of bridges as a first physical and symbolic link' between recently divided areas,[82] with the explicit long-term objective (and challenge) of the development of a regional identity.[83] This suggests at once a challenge to national borders, and at the same time the paradoxical promotion of a new nationalism, based on the local imagination of 'true' nationality – the use of cross-border regions 'to overcome unnatural barriers between regions and ethnic groups which "naturally" belonged together'.[84]

This reunification theme could pose awkward questions about using links between diaspora to redraw sensitive borders – to exert influence over areas over which the nation has historically asserted a right of control. Zabalo and Imaz note that European cooperation instruments such as the EGTC are 'designed to help resolve problems among adjacent communities across borders that are deemed "neutral"',[85] which may be supported by the fact that Member States have a veto over the creation of EGTCs. Moreover, many EGTCs cover areas of ethnic diversity,[86] making a project of ethnically directed unification difficult. However, it is not clear what would happen should an EGTC, once approved at State level, be 'hijacked' by a particular group interest. Any strong cross-border reunified identity would raise further questions for the Union as to the status of those who

[80] Leading to situations whereby EU institutions are challenged in the ECJ for not sufficiently protecting EU employees' EU rights (as the rules of a Member State might be challenged in a reference); eg, Case C-227/04P *Lindorfer v Council of the European Union* [2007] ECR I-6767.

[81] Espaces Transfrontaliers, 'Presentation, The Eurometropole: a territory with many assets', 1, available at www.espaces-transfrontaliers.org/en/conurbations/Eurometropole_Lille_en.pdf.

[82] EGTC URBACT Project (2008) 'Expertising Governments for Transfrontier Conurbations' Baseline Study, <http://www.espaces-transfrontaliers.org/document/EGTC_BASELINE_STUDY_FINAL.pdf> 86, para 2.3.1.

[83] István Ferencsik, then director of the Istergranum EGTC, presentation, 'Understanding the European Grouping of Territorial Cooperation', Královéhradeck'y (28 February–1 March 2011).

[84] K Lepik, 'Euroregions as Mechanisms for Strengthening Cross-Border Co-operation in the Baltic Sea Region' (2009) 13 *Trames: A Journal of the Humanities and Social Sciences* 265, 267.

[85] J Zabalo and O Imaz, 'The EU and the Basque Conflict: Opportunities for Engagement?' (2011) 22 *Accord: Paix sans frontières: building peace across borders* S2.

[86] See, eg, 'Operational Programme: Cross-border Cooperation Slovenia-Hungary 2007–2013', CCI NUMBER: 2007CB163PO053 March 2010 – Version 02 (as revised by a Commission decision No C (2010) 1732) 2.3.1.

claim to dually 'belong' ethnically in one nationality and legally within another nationality. The ECJ might have to continue the recent 'playing down' of the presumed *García Avello*[87] principle that dual nationality constitutes a sufficient cross-border element for Union law to be invoked. In *McCarthy* the ECJ stated that *Grunkin Paul*[88] had established that dual nationality was not decisive, that what mattered for the purposes of bringing the case within the scope of Union law was the obstacle to free movement.[89] While it may not be sufficient in itself to assert coverage of Union law, the assertion of a second, ethnic nationality might significantly compound the effect of cross-border mobility within the EGTC.

The combination of Union concerns about a centripetal subnational concentration of power with national concerns about a centrifugal outsourcing of power serves to weaken commitment to cross-border cooperation, resulting in a weakly defined instrument, which could be too dogged with conflict to effect significant legal change.

III THE EFFECTS OF CONCERNS AND COMPROMISE: SUPERFICIAL CROSS-BORDER INTEGRATION

Possibly to assuage Member States' concerns about supranational and subnational forces, there is a *national* dimension to the legal construction of EGTCs. Each EGTC must be registered in a single State[90] (despite its multinational nature), which the CoR has identified as likely to cause problems and create imbalances – or 'significant disparities' between EGTC partners. The Regulation does not provide for transferring the State of registration, for example on a rotation basis, but the CoR maintains that, even if it did, such transfer would not be recommended 'under any circumstances' because of the tethering of the EGTC at several points to 'national law'. Movement would effectively 'dissolve' the existing EGTC. This last point could be highly significant, as the Regulation only loosely describes the nature of the EGTC, so that, as the CoR admits in its draft conclusions on the consultation on EGTCs, 'in two neighbouring States the regime may be radically different'.[91] The CoR points to Slovenian EGTCs as wholly private law entities, Italian ones as public law entities;[92] and the fact that the 'Czech Republic does not allow EGTCs with limited liability, but Poland rejects unlimited liability'.[93] Meanwhile other Member States have particular EGTC quirks – 'in practice all the EGTCs set up with French partners must be established in France'

[87] Case 148/02 *Carlos García Avello v Belgian State* [2003] ECR I-11613, para 27.

[88] Case C-353/06 *Stefan Grunkin and Dorothee Regina Paul* [2008] ECR I-7639, para 24.

[89] Case C-434/09 *Shirley McCarthy v Secretary of State for the Home Department,* judgment of 5 May 2011, para 52.

[90] Art 8(2)(a) Reg 1082/2006.

[91] CoR, 'Draft Conclusions of the Committee of the Regions about the Joint Consultation on EGTCs', *The Review of Regulation (EC) 1082/2006 on the European Grouping of Territorial Cooperation* (2010) 9.

[92] Ibid.

[93] Ibid.

and in Italy 'EGTCs do not last indefinitely'.[94] EGTCs are thus local creations. Different regions and Member States will harbour different perceptions and adopt different approaches to EGTCs – some of which may be members of the same grouping. EGTCs could prove to be sites of considerable conflict, in terms of competence and accountability.

A Competence and Inter-institutional Conflict

There are significant competence limitations to EGTCs – competences cannot, unsurprisingly, be awarded by members themselves unequipped with such competences, but less predictably (and maybe more problematically) such tasks must fall within the competences of 'every member' of the EGTC. The EGTC is thus only as powerful as its least competent member. The mutual suspicions of EGTC members and Union funders mean that probably the biggest competence limitation is logistical/financial. The first EGTC set up under the regulations, the Lille-Kortrijk-Tournai Eurometropole, also touted as an exceptionally strong and successful grouping – partly down to a shared history, and to a position at the 'heart' of Europe – is nevertheless a relatively low-budget operation, receiving less than €1 million in its first year of existence, and with a continued projected annual budget of approximately €1.5 million.[95]

Its competences along with its ambitions must be scaled accordingly. It has not taken up the opportunity to co-develop solidaristic public services such as health,[96] as its stated cooperation themes are transport, urban ecology and highways. Expectations regarding future interventions in controversial areas of 'employment' and 'culture' are highly specific and circumscribed so that the 'employment' agenda becomes a collection of one-off, niche projects (as opposed to anything systemic), such as creating discussions about 'business park quality';[97] culture in its turn becomes a conglomeration of bit-projects such as cooperation between two named museums, with the only service programme aim being to develop a cross-border cremation service.[98]

While the initial competence agenda for the first few EGTCs may appear limited, it is nevertheless possible that as territorial 'pooling' of resources between agents of different Member States becomes more commonplace, a deeper form of regional financial social integration – represented by the rhetoric of the Lille Eurometropole[99]

[94] Ibid.

[95] G Pargneaux, Vice-President of Eurometropole LKT, 'Eurometropole Lille-Kortrijk-Tournai', presented at « *EGTC* » *Project Launch Conference* (Strasbourg, 19 November 2008) 7.

[96] Noting the lack of clear rules on access to cross-border health care; though a Directive has been proposed on that subject – European Commission, 'Proposal for a Directive on the application of patients' rights in cross-border healthcare' COM (2008) 414.

[97] Espaces Transfrontaliers (n 81) 4.

[98] Ibid.

[99] eg, that citizens should together be able to 'reap the fruits' of trans-frontier cooperation – Lille metropole.fr, 'Les projets transfrontaliers' (my translation) available at www.lillemetropole.fr/index.php?p=987&art_id=.

– may become more palatable. Such depth might include substantive policies on employment and social security. Marie Vannouque-Digne, the International Relations Director of the Lille Metropolitan Urban Community, has stated the aim of 'ramping up' the EGTC, 'the setting-up of the political organs and the formation of the cross-border agency'.[100]

There is a clear intention to make some tentative foray into contentious policy areas, with Vannouque-Digne referring to a search for 'initial answers' with regard to 'major sectoral cross-border issues (transport, employment, spatial planning, training, health, etc)'.[101] Another EGTC occupied with relatively innocuous (albeit essential) matters of cooperation, but displaying ambitious tendencies, is the Strasbourg-Ortenau EGTC. Measures taken so far – and before the EGTC was established – include giving German emergency vehicles the same driving priorities as French ambulances in the French area of the EGTC;[102] allowing French residents of the German area to collect their identity papers from the town hall in the French area,[103] and establishing a project on epilepsy and 'border seizures'.[104] Projects under discussion include harmonised radio frequencies, mutual recognition of emergency worker diplomas,[105] and potentially rather more challengingly, closer cross-border collaboration with regard to teaching and schools.[106]

Apart from the challenge of reaching acceptable agreements in certain policy areas, there could well be problems interpreting those agreements (or agreeing what the agreement says . . .). This may be exacerbated by issues of translation or deliberately open wording. The ZASNET EGTC between partners from Portugal and Spain, for instance, lists among other broad areas for cooperation the rather eccentrically worded aim to promote 'the territory outside and generate synergies to invert the negative demographic tendencies of the area'.'[107] Similar provisions planted in EGTC instruments adopted between less linguistically similar countries could grow into rather thorny sources of disagreement. Many of the EGTCs 'under preparation' state objectives vague in the extreme – if not simply tautological: 'The partners involved in the existing structure "Alpen-Adria" (Italy, Austria, Slovenia, Hungary and Croatia) decided to establish an EGTC so that

[100] Mission Opérationelle Transfrontalière Guide 7, 'The European Grouping of Territorial Cooperation' (May 2008) 15.

[101] Ibid.

[102] Euro district Strasbourg-Ortenau, 'Autorisation de circuler de manière prioritaire pour les véhicules d'urgence allemands' available at www.eurodistrict.eu/fr/Sante-18.html.

[103] Strasbourg.eu Ville et Communauté urbaine, 'At the Centre of Franco-German Friendship' available at www.strasbourg.eu/en/friendship.html.

[104] SEEK Strasbourg Epileptologie Eurodistrict Kork, 'Projet de cooperation transfrontalière en matière d'épilepsie' available at www.eurodistrict.eu/medias/fichiers/plaquette_seek1.pdf.

[105] Euro district Strasbourg-Ortenau, 'Cooperation des services de secours' available at www.eurodistrict.eu/fr/Sante-18.html.

[106] Eurodistrict Strasbourg-Ortenau, 'Education et bilinguisme' available at www.eurodistrict.eu/fr/Education_et_bilinguisme-20.html.

[107] CoR, 'EGTC Portal: ZASNET' available at http://portal.cor.europa.eu/egtc/en-US/Projects/already/Pages/ZASNET.aspx.

they can benefit from its legal personality and can have a deeper cooperation',[108] and 'North Portugal and Galicia plan to set up an EGTC [Eurocidade Chaves-Verin] in order to implement their common strategy, including the development of a "free social area"'.[109]

Limiting competence to areas where all members have competence clearly does not inoculate it against internal strife, given the different interests at stake. Clashes between Member States and other bodies seem inevitable – and likely to be compounded when the Union wanders into the affray. A rough example may illustrate this tension; an EGTC comprising two Member States and several regional and local authorities may implement a concessionary cross-border travel fare for persons seeking work. However, if the concession were to apply throughout the EGTC region, one Member State may come to realise that it was effectively subsidising transport costs of persons in the frontier zone but from another State to whom it would not have given a 'right to reside' in the first place, its residence rules differing from those of the partner State. This could be because the person is a third country national, or falls into an economically inactive category in which he or she would be ineligible for other concessions in the first Member State.[110] Although the EGTC rules seem to be clear about creating a Member State 'veto' on EGTC formation[111] and action,[112] it is not clear to what extent that veto should always overrule other partner Member States, or create an automatic 'reversal' or amendment right. The Union, in turn, may take issue with the eligibility requirements for, for example, a transport concession, if it is not available to persons in similar situations but who happen to be crossing a different intra-EU border outside of the EGTC – remembering that residence-based preferential treatment is typically treated with suspicion given the tendency to be indirectly discriminatory on the grounds of nationality.[113]

When it comes to conflict resolution, EGTC partners may claim equal weight, but differences in institutional levels speak otherwise. Even those partners institutionally of a kind may exhibit other differences – in geographical size, population, etc which lead them to imply an order of priority. EGTCs clearly stoke up 'unprecedented legal issues when implementing certain activities'.[114] The EGTC Regulation provides for one type of internal argument – if an EGTC acts in contravention of a

[108] CoR, 'EGTC Portal: EGTC setups under preparation' available at http://portal.cor.europa.eu/egtc/en-US/Projects/preparation/Pages/welcome.aspx.

[109] Ibid.

[110] Notwithstanding supposed equal treatment of Union citizens: see C O'Brien, 'Real Links, Abstract Rights and False Alarms: The Relationship between the ECJ's 'Real Link' Case Law and National Solidarity' (2008) 33 *EL Rev* 643.

[111] Article 4(3) Reg 1082/2006.

[112] Art 7(4) Reg 1082/2006.

[113] Hence problems with creating 'localised' solidarity networks – on the complications regarding proportionality and territoriality, see M Dougan, 'Cross-border Educational Mobility and the Exportation of Student Financial Assistance' (2008) 33 *EL Rev* 723; also G Davies, 'Any Place I Hang my Hat?: Or Residence is the New Nationality' (2005) 11 *European Law Journal* 43.

[114] *EGTC Monitoring Report 2010* 'Executive Summary' (n 18) 2.

Member State's public interests.[115] In such a case, the Member State may prohibit the activity on the Member State's territory, or may require the acting partner in question – if it is a partner formed under its own law – to be withdrawn from the EGTC. This is largely a negative right of authority – Member States can prohibit activity on national parts of the EGTC, but cannot positively enforce activities within non-national parts of the EGTC. This would essentially resurrect the border and subdivide the EGTC. The provision does not deal with the issue of one Member State demanding the withdrawal of a partner which was based in the territory of another partner Member State. Nor does the provision define public interests, or deal with actions against the interests of a non-partner Member State,[116] remembering possible 'knock-on' effects of 'common' policies upon other nearby borders. These knock-on effects feed into the next definitional weakness of the EGTC – the problem with locating accountability for EGTC action.

B Searching for Accountability – A New Medievalism?

Along with competence, we should consider responsibilities. Nested governance levels that cross borders challenge accepted lines of responsibility and hierarchy. The EGTC in some ways strongly echoes the description Gamble has made about regional governance in general as a 'new medievalism', ie 'a world in which there is no single source of legitimacy, but a complex set of levels and networks and jurisdictions shaping governance and identities'.[117]

In short, it could be difficult pinning blame for the effects of EGTC action – or inaction – on anyone/thing. Third parties who 'consider themselves wronged by the acts or omissions of an EGTC shall be entitled to pursue their claims by judicial process',[118] according to Union law, or where there is no Union provision of jurisdiction, within the courts of the Member State where the EGTC is registered.[119] The rather weak formulation of those 'who consider themselves wronged' may indicate a reluctance to outline any stringent code of conduct or duties owed by EGTCs to third parties. Locating the source of judicial relief in the State of the EGTC[120] may prove problematic if the wrong is some geographic and cultural distance from that State. Moreover, it is not clear by what standard of judicial review[121] EGTC actions (or Member States' actions against EGTCs) should be measured; could proportionality be a possible defence for a perceived intrusion

[115] Article 13 Reg 1082/2006.

[116] Which are presumably dealt with in subjective, reactive fashion under the banner of third parties considering themselves wronged: Art 15 Reg 1082/2006.

[117] A Gamble, Regional Blocs, World Order and the New Medievalism in M Telò (ed), *European Union and New Regionalism*, 2nd edn (Aldershot, Ashgate, 2007) 21.

[118] Art 15(1) Reg 1082/2006.

[119] Article 15(2) Reg 1082/2006.

[120] Ibid.

[121] On the significance of the tools and standards of judicial review employed, see M Dougan, 'The Constitutional Dimension to the Case Law on Union Citizenship' (2006) 31 *EL Rev* 613, 633.

onto issues of national public interest or an argument against Member State prohibition of EGTC activity? Disputes are also possible over whether an EGTC is abiding by the 'general principles of Union law' with regard to general infringements, or 'knock-on' effects experienced by regions in the same Member States but not in the EGTC, or by other border Member States.

Leaving third parties aside, how would the equivalent of a 'State liability' claim against an EGTC work? Member States are liable to compensate individuals for breaches of Union law 'for which the State can be held responsible'.[122] It is not clear to what extent Member States may be considered responsible for EGTC actions; Member States can incur liability for acts of local authorities and for acts of autonomous bodies governed by public law.[123] However, EGTCs, as cross-border entities, might not be easily categorised as *single State* actors. An EGTC itself 'shall be liable for the acts of its organs as regards third parties, even where such acts do not fall within the tasks of the EGTC'[124] and shall also 'be liable for its debts whatever their nature'[125] which should then be met by the members of the EGTC if the EGTC funds are insufficient. But members may have limited liability – so where does the applicant then go to seek remedy? Member States can prohibit limited liability EGTCs, presumably to avoid liability redounding onto the State – an invitation that the UK, for instance, has taken up.[126] This does not clarify the responsibilities of the partner Member States for compensating EGTC infringements of Union law. In order to avoid reaching questions of liability, Member States may want to tackle the question of enforcement action. It is not clear whether and how a Member State should be responsible for EGTC compliance with Union law, and whether the Commission should take enforcement proceedings against that Member State. The EGTC is a cross-border entity with a potentially rather more diffuse responsibility structure than the State of registration would suggest. If the infringement takes place in another Member State party to the EGTC then the scene is set for some complex fault wrangling with regard to enforcement.

The tensions between, and ambivalence of, nations and the Union with regard to regionalism have produced a weak and highly contestable entity, potentially subject to serious confusion in terms of competence, compliance and blame. The stress upon national oversight, and the curbed range of activities and responsibilities of EGTCs serve to highlight the continued role of borders in defining the scope of nationally defined social policies and the scope of the protection afforded by Union law. This border-dependence is tied to the central EU paradox of how to create a meaningful notion of 'supranational' when drawing explicitly upon nationality (hence only Member State nationals are EU citizens)[127] and upon

[122] Joined Cases C-6/90 and C-9/90 *Andrea Francovich and Danila Bonifaci and others v Italian Republic* [1991] ECR I-5357, para 35.

[123] Case C-424/97 *Haim* [2000] ECR I-5123; Case C-118/00 *Larsy* [2001] ECR I-7681.

[124] Art 10(3) Reg 1082/2006.

[125] Art 13(2) Reg 1082/2006.

[126] UK European Grouping of Territorial Cooperation Regulations 2007, Reg 8.

[127] Art 20 TFEU.

national permission ('It should be made clear that [territorial cooperation] is in no way intended to call into question national and regional competences in these areas').[128] As miscible as frontier zones may seem, the EU and the scope of EU law are still defined by borders and economic agency.

IV EFFECTS OF SUPERFICIAL CROSS-BORDER COOPERATION: INTERSECTIONAL CITIZEN RIGHTS ARE STILL BORDER DEPENDENT

The border dependence of status in national and EU law clashes with the characterisation of EGTCs as European entities. While formalised frontier zones such as EGTCs may contribute to a redrawing of maps, diminish the administrative significance of borders, and normalise governance by multinational regional authorities, the resilience of borders and territoriality is evident in the complex categories of rights and worker statuses. The resulting partial cross-border programmes are unlikely to help those dependent on particular social resources – keeping mobility, and thus the scope of Union law, as something of a right of the privileged.

A National Territorial Social Resources

Frontier work presents a challenging testing ground for European integration. The risk of welfare disadvantages incurred on migration[129] is for frontier (and reverse frontier) workers reignited on a daily basis. Frontier workers represent an ultimate ideal of border permeability, one in general to be facilitated, evident in the description of the Istergranum EGTC as having 'spectacular and immediate' results because of the increase in cross-border commuters.[130] But they do not represent reality – borders are not totally permeable and national territory still counts, so frontier workers are less practically ideal than traditional migrant workers as their loyalties and locations of integration are unclear.

Member States are permitted to subject frontier workers to conditions not applied to other migrant workers, to test their attachment to territory. In both ECJ cases *Geven*[131] and *Hartmann*,[132] a German child-raising allowance was at issue. It was available to *residents* regardless of how much work they did, but non-resident workers – frontier workers crossing borders – could only be eligible if they performed 'more than minor' work in Germany.[133] The division between major and minor work only applied to frontier workers. As the benefit could only be awarded to child-carers not working full time, this 'major work' condition had the potentially sexually discriminatory effect of excluding lone-parent, part-time

[128] European Commission, 'Green Paper on Territorial Cohesion' (n 11) 10.
[129] Joined Cases C-393/99 and C-394/99 *Hervein II* [2002] ECR I-2829.
[130] M Bresso, video (n 21).
[131] Case C-213/05 *Wendy Geven v Land Nordrhein-Westfalen* [2007] ECR I-6347.
[132] Case C-212/05 *Hartmann* [2007] ECR I-6303.
[133] Ibid, para 5.

frontier workers who could not work full time due to child care needs, and rewarding nuclear families with one full-time working parent and one full-time caring parent.[134] Even so, the distinction was allowed, as a proportionate means of not excluding all frontier workers from eligibility. It is clear that the heart of this division was the territory of residence.

The significance of territory when it comes to welfare suggests that policy areas have been carved up, into a few innocuous topics suitable for cross border cooperation, and many more politically salient areas in which borders are still paramount. This distinction is an awkward one. If, for example, child care facilities were subject to a cross-border project, it may become unfeasible and incoherent to have child care *funds* operate in disjuncture across the vector of the national border. Two families may live within a cooperating region, such as the Strasbourg-Ortenau EGTC, but with a border between them, may find themselves in considerably different situations with regard to social advantages; even if both spend most of their time on the German side of the border, with children attending the same German nursery and/or school, and both parents working part time or volunteering in Germany. Only the family living on the German side of the border, even without working at all, would qualify for the German child-raising allowance.

In general, where there is some public service link-up there will be corresponding benefits that cry out for coordination – for example, where there are nurseries there are child care benefits; where there are transport services there are transport concessions; where there are educational projects there are pupil allowances. Such schemes are not simply about age-based reductions, but feed into the complex and intricate web of disability benefit entitlement. Linking up road-way resources, streamlining traffic rules etc would further require attention to be paid to this entitlement. For example, eligibility in the UK for a motability vehicle,[135] or for a blue badge[136] (affecting parking rights) is woven into entitlement for the (non-exportable)[137] mobility component of Disability Living Allowance. Cross-border cooperation on cultural issues would equally need to pay attention to concessionary entitlements. Trans-border educational cooperation, even if limited to 'trips' and exchanges would equally require some way of coordinating on issues of paying for children of low-income families, and for providing, for example, free school meals. The compartmentalisation of minimal common policy aims is artificial. Different 'working time' conditions echoing minor/major work distinctions for non-residents and the non-coordination of attendant social inclusion measures could jeopardise equal opportunities for persons with disabilities, gender equality, and reduction of socio-economic disparity.

[134] See O'Brien (n 9).

[135] Direct Gov, 'Motability Scheme' available at www.direct.gov.uk/en/DisabledPeople/MotoringAndTransport/Yourvehicleandlicence/DG_10028000.

[136] Direct Gov, 'Getting a Blue Badge' available at www.direct.gov.uk/en/DisabledPeople/MotoringAndTransport/Bluebadgescheme/DG_181208.

[137] Case C-537/09 *Ralph James Bartlett and Others v Secretary of State for Work and Pensions*, judgment of 5 May 2011, confirming the exclusion in Case C-299/05 *Commission of the European Communities v European Parliament and Council of the European Union* [2007] ECR I-8695.

As regards work-related benefits, the CoR has recognised the inconsistencies faced by, for instance, the staff of an EGTC whose living and working patterns may be similar but for the location within the zone of residence or work, and so have begun discussing the creation of an EGTC staff status, or of streamlined rules to apply to EGTC staff.[138] Respondents to the CoR consultation highlighted 'the risk of differences in retirement provision, salary, social protection, fiscal system for staff from different countries compared with their national laws'[139] and also the problem outlining the rights of persons seconded from different partners to the EGTC body. It is obviously problematic for people doing similar jobs for the same body to be subject to different conditions. However, the focus on EGTC staff underplays the fact that is not just the persons working *for* the EGTC who may be thus affected, but persons crossing the same border, working for other companies operating *within* the EGTC. In some cases there may be a risk not only of different conditions applied to similar workers on the basis of the circumstance of location of residence, but also of different employment conditions faced by similar employees, for example, where each works for the same company, which has registered head offices either side of the border.

Loss of work is another thorny issue in a frontier zone. The rules within Regulation 883/2004 on former frontier workers[140] are relatively complicated (and require a distinction between the partly and wholly unemployed).[141] If worker A lives and works within a frontier zone, living and working on opposite sides of the border, and becomes unemployed, that worker will be subjected to a different set of rules for jobseeking, as compared to worker B in the same zone who happens to not cross the border; worker A should make herself available for work in the State of residence, but can also look for work as a supplementary step in the State of former employment.[142] The administrative authorities will also need to comply with the complex rules on benefit recoupment, as the State of residence should provide jobseeking benefits but can reclaim three months' worth from the 'competent' Member State.[143] These differences seem a little incongruous, and cumbersome, so arguments may be made for a more harmonised system to respond to unemployment in areas of common cross-border work.

The eminently national, so border-dependent, allocation of social resources is problematic because of the inconsistencies to which it gives rise – and because it perpetuates a model of affluent migration, and particularly of affluent frontier workers, potentially at odds with a citizenship-based enjoyment of free movement rights. It is however explicable, given concerns about inappropriate diversion of collectively designated resources. Less rational, in the EGTC context, is the

[138] CoR, 'Towards the Revision of the EGTC Regulation: Discussion at EUROCITIES' available at http://portal.cor.europa.eu/egtc/en-US/news/Pages/Eurocitiesdiscussion.aspx.

[139] CoR, 'Draft Conclusions' (n 91).

[140] Art 65 on 'unemployed persons who resided in a Member State other than the competent State'.

[141] Arts 65(1) and 65(2).

[142] Art 65(3).

[143] Art 65(6). 3 months extends to 5 months in certain circumstances: Art 65(7).

continued free-movement basis for the enjoyment of Union citizenship. The use of borders to define the scope of Union law may be most susceptible to challenge in the context of frontier zones, where citizens claim to pursue quintessentially 'European' existences.

B The Scope of Union Law: Unchanged but Challengeable?

The requirement of border crossing means that not all citizens within an EGTC will fall within the scope of Union law. The question of reverse discrimination is more intelligently explored in other contributions to this volume than could be captured in this chapter.[144] It is, however, worth reflecting on what may be a more pronounced effect of reverse discrimination within frontier zones, where comparators will always be in easy reach. For some people, living outside but working inside the frontier zone, albeit within the territory of the same State, they may feel strongly as though they are crossing a border, from a distinctly national, maybe monolingual area to a bicultural area, perhaps even more so than someone living and working on either side of a border but within the frontier, bicultural zone. This may be especially so if internal regional borders are involved – an issue raised in *Wallon v Flamand*,[145] a case described by Advocate General Sharpston as coming 'as close to a classic cross-border situation as a supposedly internal situation can'.[146] Only residents of the Walloon region, residents of other Member States working in the region, or nationals of other Member States resident in Belgium but working in the region, were eligible for a care benefit – to exclude Belgian residents of other regions of Belgium (but working in the Walloon region). This was found to highlight 'the arbitrariness of attaching so much importance to crossing a national border'[147] for the purposes of invoking Union law, since it was argued that the excluded Belgians could not rely on Union law, falling instead into a 'wholly internal' situation. The case also underlined the problem of dismantling external borders and allowing Member States to erect internal ones. The Court found that of the Belgians resident in non-Walloon regions of Belgium, only those who had in the past exercised freedom of movement to other Member States could rely on Union law to claim equal access to the care benefit in question.

The choice to circumscribe Union law by placing 'wholly internal' situations without its scope may be rational, and preferable to other 'arbitrary' limitations, but does invite Advocate General Sharpston's criticism of the 'self-contradictory character of aiming at or completing an internal market while continuing to

[144] See, in particular, the contributions by Anastasia Iliopoulou and Síofra O'Leary.

[145] Case C-212/06 *Government of Communauté franaçaise and Gouvernement wallon v Gouvernement flamand* [2008] ECR I-1683.

[146] Ibid, Opinion of AG Sharpston, para 141.

[147] Ibid.

attach importance to the crossing of national borders'.[148] This will feel less appropriate in the context of frontier zones, in which the differences between 'static' and 'mobile' workers may seem little more than technical, and so static workers might resent the extra EU citizenship rights accorded to their mobile neighbours – for example, in terms of family reconciliation measures. Nationals relying on national law can face greater barriers than those able to access Union law. This situation, whereby rights must be activated by cross-border movement,[149] is not considered to be at odds with the construct of a universal (to EU nationals) status of citizenship, as we have seen in *McCarthy*.[150] Instead it is a fact to circumscribe the appropriate scope of Union law and protect sensitive areas of national policy from competence incursion.[151]

It is possible that *Ruiz Zambrano*[152] changes the points of access to citizenship rights, in a way that would help non-migrant frontier zone workers, since some elements of Union citizenship are not dependent on crossing an EU border. In this case it was found that the right to reside in the EU was an autonomous right enjoyed by EU citizens, which in the case of EU national children could only be meaningful if joined by a primary carer. But the contrast with *McCarthy* suggests that *Ruiz Zambrano* might have been a relatively narrow concession, made where the 'right to reside' in question attached to right to reside in the EU at all, not in a specific country, and only extended to others when that very right was threatened (since a child cannot live on its own) – not just when it might be made more difficult (by not having your spouse with you). The *Zambrano* effect might not help nationals able to reside in their Member State of origin but seeking supra-national rights, ie it might not do much to challenge standard reverse discrimination.

Since most Union citizenship-based rights remain contingent upon complete border crossing, rather than living in an area of cultural co-mingling, awkward contrasts may arise as between neighbours in frontier zones with similar 'European worker' credentials. To use the geography of one area of an EGTC – the intersection between Croatia, Hungary and Slovenia within the Alpen-Adria EGTC (listed as 'under preparation')[153] – as a hypothetical example, a number of potential tensions emerge. People working in the Slovenian municipality of Lendava could live in Slovenia or over either border – the Croatian city of Mursko is approximately

[148] Ibid, fn 91, referring for support to HUJ d'Oliveira, 'Is Reverse Discrimination Still Possible under the Single European Act?' in *Forty Years On: The Evolution of Postwar Private International Law in Europe: Symposium in Celebration of the 40th Anniversary of the Centre of Foreign Law and Private International Law*, University of Amsterdam, on 27 October 1989 (Deventer, Kluwer, 1990) 84.

[149] Thus arguably rendering EU citizenship a movement-contingent status: see E Spaventa, 'Seeing the Wood Despite the Trees? On the Scope of Union Citizenship and its Constitutional Effects' (2008) 45 *CML Rev* 13 and S Currie, 'The Transformation of Union Citizenship' in M Dougan and S Currie (eds), *50 years of the European Treaties: Looking Back and Thinking Forward* (Oxford, Hart Publishing, 2009) 387.

[150] Case C-434/09 *Shirley McCarthy v Secretary of State for the Home Department*, judgment of 5 May 2011.

[151] Family reconciliation as in *McCarthy* touching upon sensitive immigration laws – five Member States made representations in the case.

[152] Case C-34/09 *Gerardo Ruiz Zambrano v Office national de l'emploi*, judgment of 8 March 2011.

[153] CoR, EGTC Portal (n 108).

7 km from Lendava, while the Hungarian town of Lenti is about 13 km away. Lendava is in fact twinned with Lenti, and it has an explicitly Hungarian dimension, with a strong ethnic Hungarian presence and Hungarian as a second official language.[154] The municipality website emphasises the specificity of the local multinational identity, referring to the 'diversity of cultural-historical and natural attractions . . . and the closeness of Hungary and Croatia'.[155] Yet different workers will be subject to very different rules according to nationality and where in the 'region' or frontier zone the workers (working in the same company in Slovenia) live.

A Hungarian working in Lendava is clearly an EU migrant worker whether or not he or she moves residence across the border. However, as noted earlier, frontier workers are on a different footing in some situations, such as job loss, to 'complete' migrant workers. A Slovenian worker, though he or she may live in a more dominantly 'Slovenian' area and commute into an extremely mixed, or even predominantly Hungarian area, would still have to move residence across the border, away from his or her place of work to qualify as a migrant worker while still working in Lendava. (This echoes the situation of the Belgians resident in non-Walloon regions of Belgium but working in Wallonia in *Wallon v Flamand*). The Croatian is (at the time of writing at least) a third country national, and whether he or she acquires any EU rights may depend on his or her having EU national children.

The question of third country national rights might also be more pronounced in frontier zones. For static EU citizens, the basic right of residing within the Union is not in jeopardy. However, it may be in the case of third country national workers, with EU children and/or third country national partners or former partners of migrant workers (or former migrant workers) who are also primary carers of EU citizen children. A TCN (third country national) worker who lives in the Member State of work, and whose children have EU citizenship, who loses his or her job and so loses a right of residence, might rely on *Ruiz Zambrano* to assert the right of his or her children to live within the Union, and be joined by their primary carer to prevent the basic right to reside within the Union from being rendered nugatory. However, this may be a right of last resort; it is possible that it cannot be used to challenge national conditions, requirements or restrictions – for instance, not being an EU national or related to a migrant worker it is not clear what rights (if any) of equal treatment the TCN might expect beyond a simple right of residence. The *Zambrano* avenue may not be open to persons in the same situation, but whose children have not been awarded the nationality of the Member State of residence – if they have another Member State's nationality it might be proportionate to refuse a right of residence in the instant State since such refusal would not amount to expulsion from the Union – but to the State of the child's nationality.

[154] Lendava Vabi, 'History' available at www.lendava.si/si/obcina-lendava/zgodovina/.

[155] Lendava Vabi, 'Tourism' available at www.lendava.si/si/turizem/.

Third country national partners or former partners of former EU national migrant workers caring for the children of the (former) EU national worker could have a stronger package of rights on which to rely to enable those children to continue their education 'under the best possible conditions' – ie, residence plus equal treatment. This means relying on *Ibrahim*[156] or *Teixeira*[157] if they have a child who was installed in the Member State in question during the EU national's period of work. But here of course we have the cross-border requirement. The child need not have EU nationality, but needs to be the child of a migrant worker. Thus within frontier zones these rights will only be available to those TCNs looking after children whose parent lived and worked on different sides of the border, setting up differences between similarly situated families. Those rights will also not be available where the border in question was with a third country, setting up substantial differences in areas where a number of borders intersect. Third country nationals working in the EU but living with their children within a frontier zone but outside of the Union will not have recourse to either an *Ibrahim* or *Ruiz Zambrano* remedy – meaning they are subject to the laws of the third country of residence, which is unsurprising, but does emphasise the continued significance of borders and the territorial nature of work-seeking (and suspicions attached to work-seekers such that they are best 'monitored' by their own State of origin),[158] which is perhaps a little in tension with the idea of an EU job market.

Just as the border dependence of national social resources implies socio-economic exclusions from free movement rights, so the border dependence of the scope of Union law effectively entrenches existing patterns of social exclusion, through restricting EU rights to those capable of physical border crossing. This pattern is made all the more clear in the EGTC context. Although members of EGTCs need not necessarily 'border' one another, they almost all do; territorial continuity is only interrupted in two existing EGTCs[159] and one planned EGTC.[160] As a result the emerging picture of territorial cooperation is slightly retrograde – not quite encompassing overlaps between more distant but well-connected territories, for example, through 'air corridors' or via 'virtual' connections. This emphasis on facilitating physical movement across borders implies a presumed necessity of physical presence in a designated 'place of work', whereas common Union policies of equal opportunities for persons with disabilities, and gender equality, and reconciling work and family life, might be better furthered by

[156] Case C-480/08 *London Borough of Harrow v Nimco Hassan Ibrahim and Secretary of State for the Home Department*, judgment of 23 February 2010.

[157] Case C-480/08 *Maria Teixeira v London Borough of Lambeth and Secretary of State for the Home Department*, judgment of 23 February 2010.

[158] Note the emphasis on 'monitoring' in, eg, Case C-406/04 *Gérald De Cuyper v Office national de l'emploi* [2006] ECR I-6947: in the body of the judgment, which deals with an unemployment benefit, excluding the questions from the referring court, monitoring is referred to 11 times.

[159] 'Archimed' (grouping islands), CoR portal, 'Archimed' available at www.portal.cor.europa.eu/egtc/en-US/Projects/already/Pages/ARCHIMED.aspx; and 'Amphictiony' (32 municipalities on the Mediterranean coast) Amphictiony, 'Network of Twinned Cities and Areas on the Mediterranean' available at www.amphictyony.gr/en/index.php.

[160] 'European Urban Knowledge Network' – CoR Portal (n 108).

including some emphasis instead on facilitating the *provision of work* (rather than physical presence) across borders.

While the EGTC itself changes little, it could well be that it provides an appropriate spotlight on the issue, and a stage upon which to promote a more progressive approach to cross-border social inclusion, and so to challenge the existing rules governing the scope of Union law.

V CONCLUSIONS

Frontier zones are not quite *espaces sans frontiers*; Europeans are still territorial creatures. But territory is dynamic, and cross-border conurbations speak to the malleability of the cultural and social environment. The legal environment is necessarily a bit more plastic, so it should be no surprise that the codification of such changes – through the creation of EGTCs – is tentative and minimal. Frontier zones, though they may be represented as the vanguard of true 'Europeanism' have emerged rather organically – as products of local, cross-border integration, with the EGTC element 'added on' to allow the infrastructure to catch up with the way people are already living.[161]

The bottom-up, migrant-driven nature of frontier zones exacerbates national reservations about relinquishing community resources, and about the effects on sovereignty of Union-driven projects, and/or to entities in which other Member States' interests are at play. At the same time, Union institutions are wary of relinquishing much by way of funds to entities that may prove too autonomous and spend it how they like, given that (despite the supposed supranational 'European' identity of these zones), they emphasise each zone's distinct character and needs, and speak of devolving initiatives down to the region.

So EGTCs are conceived as relatively low-budget projects with curbed political ambitions and contained competences, making them unpredictable and potentially volatile. 'Competences' are notoriously difficult to pin down in such a way as to prevent future disputes, and there is little reason to suspect the competences of EGTCs will prove any different, with the added frisson of multiple actors of different administrative/legislative levels. The *processes* of dispute resolution – and the weighing of different bodies' interests – have yet to be tested, never mind the *principles* by which such disputes will be resolved. Along with competences, the question of responsibility, or liability, lurks murkily ahead, along with the locus of enforcement, and the practical hurdles for third parties who may have been indirectly disadvantaged by EGTC action. There is thus the danger that individual rights remain territorial, while administrative responsibility becomes diffused.

The location of competence and liability goes to the heart of what it means to be a legal actor, and the tensions here explored reflect the problems endowing

[161] This point was eloquently made by Síofra O'Leary during the Liverpool conference on 'Empowerment and Disempowerment of the European Citizen' (Liverpool, 22 October 2010).

something that challenges the national imagination with a legal personality, in order to further ends which depend upon the support of nation states – ie, Union objectives. Borders between Member States still count – not only to define the scope of national laws, but to define the scope of Union laws. Nationally, the non-coordination of sensitive policy areas means that frontier zone workers may be subject to very different benefit and health care regimes, even where benefits are closely linked to 'coordinated' services. Such differences may impact upon persons at risk of social exclusion – whether persons with disabilities, carers, or women trying to balance work and family life; persons for whom linked-up transport is no good without linked-up transport concession measures, or linked-up education is no good without linked-up child care and means-tested provisions (such as free school meals).

In terms of Union law, borders are important because they really need to be crossed in most situations for EU citizenship rights to be triggered. As such, those borders describe very different degrees of protection afforded to the same status – EU citizenship – according to a number of potential 'technical' differences between EU, and TCN, citizens and workers in very similar situations. The continued emphasis on a physical crossing of borders embodies a rather 'traditional' image of frontier work (if frontier work is 'traditional'), echoes the social narrowness of the weak degree of benefit coordination, and may also work against more socially inclusive approaches, such as facilitating alternative means of being employed across borders.

As frontier zones become more legally embedded the various enmeshed threads of worker and ex-worker statuses are likely to get knottier, given the close proximity of frontier workers, reverse frontier workers, and EGTC staff who may be frontier workers, static migrant workers, or static home State workers. As a result, although the stark role of borders may serve a helpful jurisdictional purpose, it may come to seem under-nuanced to appropriately serve the lives within overlapping 'zones' between Member States – the lives of intersectional citizens.

Part II

In the Name of the Citizen?

4

The Role of Judge-made Law and EU Supranational Government: A Bumpy Road from Secrecy to Translucence

DEIRDRE CURTIN*

I INTRODUCTION

THE EUROPEAN UNION has come a long way since the principle of transparency was first introduced as such in a declaration to the Maastricht Treaty almost twenty years ago. What started life as an internal discretionary power of three institutions has over the course of time become part of the fundamental constitutional right of 'openness' that is now included in Article 1 of the Lisbon Treaty. This raises a question of definition. In the literature openness and transparency are often used interchangeably and without a great deal of conceptual precision, also in the context of the EU.[1] Weinberg, however, stresses that transparency is one component of openness and participation the other.[2] Transparency is often defined as being able to observe decision-making processes whereas participation refers to the opportunity to participate in these decision-making processes. Transparency can include access to documents only,[3] the actual

* I am grateful to the participants at the original workshop in Durham on 10 September 2010 as well as those at the First Global Conference on Transparency in Newark, 19–20 May 2011 where earlier versions of this chapter were presented. In addition, I am grateful to Dariusz Adamski, Gijs Jan Brandsma, Onne Brouwer, Bettina Leufgen, Joana Mendes and Anne Elizabeth Stie for their helpful comments. All responsibility for remaining imperfections is my own.

[1] See, eg, M O'Neill, 'The Rights of Access to Community-held Documentation as a General Principle of EC Law' (1998) 4 *European Public Law* 403; P Settembri, 'Transparency and the EU Legislator: "Let He Who is Without Sin Cast the First Stone"' (2005) 43 *Journal of Common Market Studies* 637.

[2] J Weinberg, Presentation at the two-day workshop 'Open Government: Defining, Designing, and Sustaining Transparency' (1 January 2010), Princeton (NY): Princeton University, on file with author.

[3] See further U Öberg, 'Public Access to Documents after the Entry into Force of the Amsterdam Treaty: Much Ado About Nothing?' (1998) 2 *European Integration online Papers* 8 (http://eiop.or.at/eiop/pdf/1998-008.pdf).

availability of documents,[4] or even information in a more general sense that reveals the thinking behind a decision or the way in which a decision is made.[5] But openness is the broader concept, which is defined for our purposes as the extent to which citizens can monitor and influence decision-making processes through access to information *and* access to decision-making arenas.[6] Citizens need information to see what is going on inside government and participation to voice their opinions about this. Participants can voice their opinions on the basis of knowledge about decision-making processes. [7]

Transparency concerns the degree to which information, of any kind, about a given entity is made available to the general public.[8] Definitions and models tend not to define the form in which information is disseminated. What matters is that the actor or institution 'knows' or 'does' things about which members of the general public can be made aware. Although remedying information asymmetries in a general sense is the crucial issue from a representative democratic perspective,[9] it does raise legal, political and practical issues as to the specific form in which information is made available, and by what means.[10] The major sub-themes in the debate on transparency in the EU are on the legal regulation of access to information and the proactive release of information, or more specifically access to documents of a limited number of institutions.

This legal approach has given a key role to the supranational courts in Luxembourg in interpreting the legal provisions but also in holding the institutions to account for the manner in which they apply the general provisions to their daily practices and in particular the manner in which they give citizens access or refuse it. The judgments by the courts in individual cases influence the practice of the institutions to a greater or lesser extent if they choose to link proactively the availability of categories of information to the public (for example, the systematic provision of the minutes of meetings, of the internal legal advice given, of court observations when the procedure is finished, and so on and so forth). Little empirical work has to date been carried out in this regard so it is difficult to draw

[4] See, eg, GJ Brandsma, D Curtin and A Meijer, 'How Transparent are EU "Comitology" Committees in Practice?' (2008) 14 *European Law Journal* 819.

[5] See D Stasavage, 'Open-door or Closed-door? Transparency in Domestic and International Bargaining' (2004) 58 *International Organization* 667.

[6] See further A Meijer, D Curtin and M Hillebrandt, 'Open Government: Connecting Vision and Voice' (2012) 78:1 *International Review of Administrative Sciences* (introductory article in edited special issue 'Government Transparency: Creating Clarity in a Confusing Conceptual Debate').

[7] These components of openness or open government can be referred to as vision and voice. See D Curtin and J Mendes, 'Transparence et participation: des principes démocratiques pour l'administration de L'Union Européenne" (2011) 137–138 *Revue française d'administration publique* 101.

[8] A Etzioni, 'Is Transparency the Best Disinfectant?' (2010) 18 *Journal of Political Philosophy* 389.

[9] K Strøm, 'Parliamentary Democracy and Delegation' in K Strøm, W Müller and T Bergman (eds), *Delegation and Accountability in Parliamentary Democracies* (Oxford, Oxford University Press, 2006) 55–106; A Lupia, 'Delegation and its Perils' in K Strøm, W Müller and T Bergman (eds), ibid, 33.

[10] M Pasquier and J-P Villeneuve, 'Organizational Barriers to Transparency: A Typology and Analysis of Organizational Behaviour Tending to Prevent or Restrict Access to Information' (2007) 73 *International Review of Administrative Sciences* 147.

hard and fast conclusions on the links between the passive right to have access to documents (established largely through case law) and the extent to which the institutions subsequently make whole categories of information proactively available via their registers of documents, specialised data bases or otherwise.[11]

The considerable reinforcement of the autonomy and power of the EU-level actors in recent years makes the role of the Courts in Luxembourg more acute as accountability forums with (often) a real sanctioning power. At the same time the role of the Courts is essentially a reactive one dependent on the timing and nature of the actual cases brought before it and its own vision of the nature and effects of the political process. The supranational judicial role must also be viewed in the context of the political power to change the rules of the game through treaty reform processes or legislative amendment. In the meantime, the institutions and actors develop in their day-to-day legal and institutional practices their coping mechanisms and practical application. These in turn may prompt more legal challenges and recourse to the Courts by civil society organisations or, increasingly, by disgruntled parliamentarians as they instrumentally use the various legal provisions to try and change the secrecy culture in a strategic fashion and also to ensure that the right of citizens to claim access to documents is applied horizontally more and more across the board to all policy areas and decision-making forums. All the separate strands contribute to the 'living' constitution of the supranational polity, the European Union.

The purpose of this chapter is to focus on the specificity of the EU as a complex system of supranational government and to explore in that perspective 'transparency' in the sense of access to documents of a number of selected arenas of both legislative and executive processes. On the legislative side the focus will be on the role of certain early-stage trialogue committees composed of representatives of both the European Parliament and the Council, as well as – separately – the input of the representatives of the Member States into the working parties of the Council. On the executive side the focus is on the Commission as well as on the so-called comitology committees that are active in the field of implementation of legislation. These four examples serve as the backdrop for an analysis that explores the extent to which such processes can be said to justify the qualification of 'transparency' and the manner in which the parameters are being interpreted in practice both by the courts and by the actors themselves. Or is the conclusion on the basis of these (limited) case studies rather the dial is more at an in-between stage, between secrecy and transparency, namely 'transluscence'? Translucence implies that some light is allowed to pass through but that the persons carrying out public tasks on the opposite side are not always clearly visible.

The structure of this chapter is as follows. Section II will set out the legal background to transparency regulation in the EU and in particular the manner in which this has been given an explicit constitutional foundation in the Treaty of Lisbon. Section III will look specifically at the interpretation and practice of transparency

[11] But see with regard to 'comitology' practices, Brandsma et al (n 4).

with regard to (aspects of) the legislative process of the EU. Section IV will focus on the interpretation and practice of (aspects of) the executive process of the EU. Finally, section V will draw the threads together and attempt an overall assessment of the state of play with regard to transparency in the EU political and legal systems.

II EU GOVERNMENT IN LAW AND PRACTICE

A Evolving Supranational Government: From Diplomacy to Democracy

The EU has evolved over time into a political system in its own right with legislative, executive and judicial powers. In the political system of the EU the centrality of the Commission as the core public administration at the European level has been established from the early years. Its decision-making processes were for a long time shrouded in secrecy with little possibility for public input or deliberation. At the same time, while the Commission has actively fostered participation of interest groups in the shaping of EU policy since the outset of integration, there were only limited procedural possibilities for interested and affected parties to participate outside the informal lobbying channels. Over time the Council emerged not only as the core legislative power but also as a 'shadow' executive power especially in the newer policy fields that initially sidestepped the Commission.[12] Both as a legislative power and as a nascent executive power its practices were secretive and very largely behind closed doors as it sought to protect the input of the Member States as what it still perceived to be 'diplomatic negotiation' rather than open legislative processes. Even when the European Parliament emerged as a fully-fledged legislative partner with the Council of Ministers in the 'normal' legislative procedure this did not immediately introduce more openness in the legislative process as such.

Change was 'kick-started' in the EU political system by a number of exogenous events.[13] An early one was the very first rejection of an EU Treaty by a national electorate – the Danes – in 1992. In an attempt to persuade the Danish electorate when they voted second time around on the Treaty of Maastricht the adoption of a code of conduct by both the Commission and the Council 'concerning public access to Council and Commission documents'[14] marked a step forward. This gave substance to Declaration no 17 of the Maastricht Treaty that '. . . transparency of the decision-making process strengthens the democratic nature of the institutions and the public's confidence in the administration'. In the long run,

[12] See further, D Curtin, *Executive Power of the EU. Law, Practices and the Living Constitution* (Oxford, Oxford University Press, 2009), in particular ch 4.

[13] For an overview of the emergence of the EU transparency agenda see, S Peers, 'From Maastricht to Laeken: The Political Agenda of Openness and Transparency in the European Union' in V Deckmyn (ed), *Increasing Transparency in the European Union?* (Maastricht, European Institute of Public Administration, 2002) 7.

[14] Code of conduct concerning public access to Council and Commission documents (93/730/EC) [1993] OJ L340/41.

this has had far-reaching consequences with regard to the transparency of the EU institutions.[15]

The second exogenous event was the resignation of the Santer Commission in the aftermath of the publication of the First Report of the Committee of Independent Experts in March 1999. The boils of secrecy and of lack of (collective) responsibility of the Commission were rather publicly lanced as a result. This forced the Commission more particularly to address the issue of openness in relation to its own administration. This was in part addressed in its White Paper on Governance (2001), where the Commission also put visible emphasis on its relations with 'civil society' by seeking to provide new forms of access to civil society actors.[16] Better involvement and more openness was one of the White Paper's leitmotivs. Nevertheless, the overall emphasis was still very much placed on confidence in the EU institutions and on the achievement of better policy delivery, despite cursory references to democracy.[17]

Transparency-related measures were initially viewed as a matter for the three main decision-making institutions (the Council, the Commission and the European Parliament) to do with their internal functioning and falling under their internal rules of procedure. Gradually the principle of transparency 'hardened', first in the Treaty of Amsterdam (1997) and later in legislation (Regulation 1049/2001) although the question whether it enjoyed a fundamental constitutional status was only fully resolved with the provisions of the Treaty of Lisbon (2010). The expanded right of access to documents ('of the Union institutions, bodies, offices and agencies', Article 15(3) TFEU, ex-Article 255 TEC which reiterates Article 42 of the Charter of Fundamental Rights) must be read in the light of its fundamental objective, namely to further the taking of decisions in the EU 'as openly as possible' (Article 1 TEU and Article 10(3)) and that this openness is a defining feature of 'an ever closer union among the peoples of Europe' (Preamble TEU).

These general words must now be read in the light of a deeper democratic meaning *why* openness, transparency and participation are important, namely that, 'increased openness enables citizens to participate more closely in the decision-making process and guarantees that *the administration* enjoys greater legitimacy and is more effective and more accountable to the citizen in a democratic system' (emphasis added).[18] This authoritative statement by the Court of Justice in Luxembourg clearly marks the 'democratic inspiration'[19] behind the concepts

[15] See for a critical perspective, D Curtin and A Meijer, 'Does Transparency Strengthen Legitimacy? A Critical Analysis of European Union Policy Documents' (2006) 11 *Information Polity* 109.

[16] Commission, 'White Paper on Governance' COM (2001) 428 final, p 14, available at www.ec.europa.eu/governance/white_paper/en.pdf.

[17] Ibid, pp 11–18.

[18] Joined Cases C-39/05P and C-52/05P *Turco v Council of Ministers* [2008] ECR I-4723, para 45, reiterating the preamble of Regulation 1049/2001.

[19] J Rivero, 'À propos des métamorphoses de l'administration d'aujourd'hui: démocratie et administration' in E Alfandari and P Ardant (eds), *Mélanges offerts à René Savatier* (Paris, Dalloz, 1965) 821, at 822 and 828.

of openness, transparency and participation in the political system of the EU. It is normally assumed that legislative processes are largely open and that in any event it is not necessary to use transparency regulations to prise open legislative meetings or give access to legislative documents. The fact that this is not the case with regard to the EU has to do with its origin as an international organisation and the fact that its decisions were traditionally neither overtly legislative nor open. Decision-making processes were rather conceived as amounting to diplomatic negotiations among Member States. Such 'international relations' processes often require secrecy in the national context too. It was only later when it became clear that the decisions being adopted at the European level were legislative in nature that this perception became highly problematic and was challenged. Transparency, and more specifically access to documents in the EU, has from the early days been recognised as covering *both* legislative and administrative processes. The right of open decision-making can thus be understood as a general democratic and collective right belonging to all citizens and enjoying in this perspective a more fundamental status than a merely administrative right of individuals to due process in administrative proceedings.

Article 10 TEU makes it clear that openness as a democratic principle goes to the very foundations of the Union on representative democracy. That system of representative democracy in the EU (both European and national) requires open decision-making both of the legislative process itself and of the administrative process (controlled by the legislature). At the European level the system of representative democracy is not only parliamentary in nature (the European Parliament) but also executive (national Ministers in the Council). The Lisbon Treaty signals that early legislative decision-making within the Council can no longer be understood as diplomatic negotiations among Member States but as part of an open and democratic legislative process. The General Court's judgment in *Access Info Europe* of 22 March 2011 also makes this clear.[20] Moreover, Article 15 TFEU clearly includes *both* legislation and administration under the scope of openness.

The fact that the system of representative democracy is not fully developed yet in the political system of the EU as compared to the constituent Member States makes the role that the principle of openness has to play even more crucial. Openness strengthens representative democracy by enabling citizens to find out the considerations underpinning legislative and administrative action in a legal and political context where there is no full political accountability (at the European or national level). This can be the case, for example, with regard to comitology committees, agencies etc. Openness of the administration as a matter of principle for the benefit of all citizens as a collective civil and political right does not replace a system of representative democracy but rather reinforces it. It embraces a notion of 'administrative democracy' that goes far beyond a due process conception of administrative procedure but rather as a way of approximating

[20] Case T-233/09 *Access Info Europe v Council*, judgment of 22 March 2011, nyr.

the citizens to the exercise of power. The Treaty of Lisbon explicitly embraces this vision of the role of the citizen as part of an overall system of representative democracy applied in the multi-level context of the European Union. As stressed by the General Court, 'the principle of transparency is intended to secure a more significant role for citizens in the decision-making process and to ensure that the administration acts with greater propriety, efficiency and responsibility vis-à-vis the citizens in a democratic system'.[21] Transparency 'helps to strengthen the principle of democracy and respect for fundamental rights'.[22]

The right of access to documents is a concrete expression of the principle of open decision-making in the EU. The Treaty of Lisbon for the first time makes it clear that open decision-making in the EU incorporates two aspects that go to make up the whole: access to documents and *participation* by citizens in decision-making. Moreover – and this is novel – it explicitly includes both the right of citizens to participate in the democratic life of the Union and the taking of *open decisions* as part of the 'democratic principles' on which the Union is founded (Title III and Article 10(3)TEU). The manner in which these twin aspects are interrelated is presented in Article 11, which contains a number of more precise obligations on the institutions in terms both of participation and of transparency (Article 11(1) to (3) TEU) and which is supplemented by Article 15 TFEU. In other words the fundamental law of the EU links both participation and transparency as the twin foundations of openness in the context of the EU.

B The Province of Transparency: Legal and Non-Legal Avenues

Prior to the Treaty of Amsterdam (1997), transparency-related measures were viewed as a matter for the affected institutions themselves, to do with their *internal* functioning and hence falling under their respective rules of procedure. This essentially self-regulatory approach meant that initially the tendency was to view the principle of public access to documents as at most a voluntarily assumed specific principle of administrative law that has gradually, through the medium of case law, acquired some *procedural* flesh and substance.[23] The focus in the early period (1992–97) was on gradually constructing a right of access by the public to certain categories of documents held by the three decision-making institutions (the Commission, the Council and the European Parliament). The General Court and the Court of Justice effectively built a body of case law that on the whole kept pressure on the institutions to behave fairly and to devise adequate systems of scrutiny. They tended in the early case law to interpret the scope of the legal provisions (decisions by the institutions based on their internal rules of procedure) rather broadly so that, for example, specific institutional arrangements did not operate to reduce the reach of the access

[21] Case T-211/00 *Kuijer v Council* [2002] ECR II-485, para 52.
[22] Ibid.
[23] On this case law see further, D Curtin, 'Citizens' Fundamental Right of Access to Information: An Evolving Digital Passepartout?' (2000) 37 *CML Rev* 7.

to documents provisions.[24] The technique of legal interpretation used by the Courts during this foundational period involved a type of teleological reasoning which placed the initial Code of Conduct adopted by two decision-making institutions in the context of its broader democratic purpose.[25] The Courts tended to emphasise the underlying purpose of access to documents as resting on general notions of public control of the activities of public institutions. Thus, the Courts developed what can be termed a constitutional perspective on access to documents provisions *avant la lettre.* Only later were these 'rights' given an explicitly constitutional foundation, first in the Treaty of Amsterdam, then in the Charter on Fundamental Rights and later in the Lisbon Treaty (Article 15 TFEU).

The specifically 'legal' approach culminated with the adoption of a new and binding legal instrument, Regulation 1049/2001, which entered into force on 3 December 2001.[26] Although, in accordance with then Article 255 EC, EU-level legislation granted a public right of access to the documents of only the three main law-making institutions (the Commission, the Council of Ministers and the European Parliament), the access to documents legislation was applied voluntarily by a wide variety of other institutions and (quasi-)autonomous actors.[27] The Treaty of Lisbon in Article 15(3) TFEU consolidates this position in practice with the explicit treaty-level provision of the right of access to documents of the 'Union institutions, bodies, offices and agencies, whatever their medium', very much in line with Article 42 of the Charter on Fundamental Rights of the European Union.

The legal-constitutional approach is thus relatively solidly anchored in legal texts, including at the most fundamental level of the Treaty on European Union in its Lisbon version. The provisions on public access to documents clearly have caused changes by giving citizens a tool to obtain the documents they wish to obtain, albeit with a considerable and significant time lag.[28] Access to documents has acquired the status of a rather fundamental norm in the EU legal and constitutional system. At the same time it has, however, also in recent years become highly 'legalised' with many of the most crucial issues as to the meaning of the exceptions, the relationship with national legal provisions and the relationship with other legal rights that also enjoy a fundamental status (eg privacy and data

[24] See further, eg, Case T-194/94 *Carvel and Guardian Newspapers v Council* [1995] ECR II-2765; Case T-174/95 *Svenska Journalistforbundet (Swedish Union of Journalists) v Council* [1998] ECR II-2289.

[25] See further, D Curtin, 'Betwixt and Between: Democracy and Transparency in the Governance of the EU' in JA Winter, D Curtin, AE Kellerman and B de Witte (eds), *Reforming the Treaty on European Union* (The Hague, Kluwer Law International, 1996) 95.

[26] See Reg (EC) No 1049/2001 regarding public access to European Parliament, Council and Commission documents, [2001] OJ L145/43. See further, Commission, 'Green Paper: Public Access to Documents Held by the Institutions of the European Community. A Review' COM (2007) 185 final. See also, Commission, 'Report on the Outcome of the Public Consultation on the Review of Regulation (EC) No 1049/2001 Regarding Public Access to European Parliament, Council and Commission Documents' Staff working document, SEC (2008) 29/2.

[27] See further J Helikoski and P Leino, 'Darkness at the Break of Noon: The Case Law on Regulation No. 1049/2001 on Access to Documents' (2006) 43 *CML Rev* 735.

[28] See further, L Cotino, 'Theory and Reality of Public Access to EU Information' in D Curtin, AE Kellermann and S Blockmans (eds), *The EU Constitution: The Best Way Forward?* (The Hague, Kluwer Law International, 2005) 233.

protection). The Court(s) in Luxembourg, which were once seen as the 'unsung hero' of those seeking to open up the inner institutional workings of the EU, have come under fire at times for what is perceived to be an unnecessarily generous interpretation of the scope and meaning of several key exceptions to the legal right.[29] This is more particularly the case when it considers its own documents and the 'administration of justice'[30] as well as the scope of certain exceptions on the internal space to think for an administration (the Commission) or the exemption for so-called 'sensitive documents'.

The Court's approach is underpinned by the complementary work of the *Ombudsman* (EO) who in the early years also adopted a rather legal approach in his work, although the emphasis was more on the structural aspects of the manner in which certain institutions, mainly the Council and the Commission, made information available or not.[31] As arbiter of maladministration, the Ombudsman has an interest in transparency as good governance and the Code of good administrative behaviour helps to promote transparency through the formulation of policies as rules and guidelines.[32] The Code provides guidance to public servants on requests for access to information. Indeed, the work of the Ombudsman helps to move the understanding of transparency in the EU context away from an individual and passive focus on the legal right of every citizen to have access to certain documents to a much broader and proactive duty of the EU administration to ensure that information about its policies and actions is made genuinely accessible. The EO's inquisitorial procedures allow him to access administrative files and also to make files public during the proceedings and are perhaps the most potent machinery for opening windows on public information yet devised. They can also provide an alternative route for members of the public to access documents – and one that does not entail the costs involved in the more formal 'legal' route. Thus the Ombudsman can act as an important catalyst for openness and transparency.[33] Yet in practice this may not always have been the case where in recent years the Ombudsman (like the Court) has not taken fully into account the manner in which the case law on freedom of expression has been progressively developed by the European Court of Human Rights in the Strasbourg system in a manner that impacts on the interpretation of the EU rules.[34]

[29] See also P Leino, 'Just a Little Sunshine in the Rain: The 2010 Case Law of the European Court of Justice on Access to Documents' (2010) 48 *CML Rev* 1215, and D Adamski, 'Approximating a Workable Compromise on Access to Official Documents: The 2011 Developments in the European Court of Justice' (2012) 49 *CML Rev* 521.

[30] See, Case C-514/07P *Sweden v API and Commission*, judgment of 21 September 2010, nyr, para 85.

[31] For an overview of the activities of the Ombudsman in this respect, see I Harden, 'The European Ombudsman's Efforts to Increase Openness in the Union' in Deckmyn (ed) (n 13) 130 ff.

[32] European Ombudsman, 'European Code of Good Administrative Behaviour', available at www.ombudsman.europa.eu/resources/code.faces.

[33] See also C Harlow, 'Transparency in the European Union: Weighing the Public and Private Interest' in J Wouters, L Verhey and P Kiiver (eds), *European Constitutionalism Beyond Lisbon* (Antwerp, Intersentia, 2009) 209.

[34] See further Adamski (n 29).

C What Do the Institutions Do Proactively?

The best way of understanding overall the legal contribution to the transparency discourse is that it has made some of the institutions more aware of how they can proactively make their own information widely available to the public using information and communication technologies. The Internet played a limited role in the early period since the EU did not for a long time actively create transparency. Just as critical as the formal legal road – and in practice what it is all about – is the quality and scope and completeness of the information and documents that the institutions make available on the Internet, via either specific registers on their respective websites or via specific databases placed by them on the Internet. This is as far as most users get: either they get a 'hit' in terms of the document or information they are looking for or they do not. These 'passive' users, as they might be termed, will, however, benefit greatly from the front-running 'active' – and often highly critical – users who monitor the various registers and at times rather systematically request the institutions to put on the Internet those documents registered but not available. It is sometimes argued that the legal regulations on access to documents are not significant from the perspective of how comparatively little use is made by the public of the legal 'rights' and moreover how limited the range of 'users' is: largely students and researchers (42. 3 per cent) and lawyers (11.5 per cent).[35] However, it can also be noted from the figures for the Council for 2010 that applications from civil society increased from 15.6 per cent in 2009 to 23.1 per cent in 2010.[36]

It is increasingly considered an obligation on the part of all institutions and organs within the EU to put on the Internet extensive information about their tasks, their organisation structure, their activities, and the agendas for their meetings as well as information on the most important documents under discussion in that context. The information placed on the web pages of the various institutions may relate to documents already placed in the public domain. In this case the initial function of putting information on the Internet is simply to make such information more speedily available and more readily accessible to a wide range of users. However, with the advent of *registers of documents* in recent years, in particular that of the Council and of the Commission, more documents are being placed on the Internet at an earlier stage of the decision-making process and including documents that are not necessarily published elsewhere. The combined result of these two developments has, among other results, given researchers the tools to build up a picture of the inner workings of various (sub)-institutions based on a range of empirical data that is immediately accessible via the Internet.[37]

[35] Regarding the Council see European Council, 'Council Annual Report on Access to Documents 2010', May 2011, 12, available at www.consilium.europa.eu/uedocs/cms_data/librairie/PDF/EN_ACC_web-2011.pdf and for the Commission see European Commission, 'Report from the Commission on the Application in 2010 of Regulation (EC) No 1049/2001', 12 August 2011, para 4.4, available at www.eurlex.europa.eu/LexUriServ/LexUriServ.do?uri=COM:2011:0492:FIN:EN:PDF.

[36] European Council (n 35).

[37] See further, D Naurin and HS Wallace (eds), *Unveiling the Council of the European Union: Games Governments Play in Brussels* (Basingstoke, Palgrave Macmillan, 2008).

Overall, it is difficult to assess the effect of these practices in the specific realm of the EU administration, as distinguished from the EU legislator. However, in recent years the Commission in particular has set up several different *specific document registers*. These include a very detailed 'comitology' register[38] and other specific websites by the various Directorate Generals as well as a specific register on expert groups. All of these specific registers and websites relate more generally to the province of the administration in a general sense and may include some documents of a more internal nature (for example minutes of committee meetings, meeting documents and minutes of meetings as well as draft decisions). They are particularly relevant to understanding decision-making processes supporting the enactment of implementing – administrative – rule-making. But the existing registers also provide information on the administrative activity entailed in the preparation of legislative proposals and policy initiatives. This is the case of the 'Register on Expert Groups',[39] which lists formal and informal advisory bodies established either by Commission decisions or created informally by the Commission services, and provides key information on those groups. Also the Commission's register of interest representatives is a voluntary register intended to contribute to the transparency of the administrative activity in the ascendant phase of the legislative procedure.[40] At the same time the Commission and the European Parliament are working towards establishing a common code of conduct and common register of interest representatives in the near future.[41]

Although these proactive efforts have clearly provided the public with more information on EU decision-making than before, it does not necessarily provide it with all the tools to reconstruct a decision-making process. The increased transparency of the comitology committees is a case in point. Major steps have been taken to make more transparent the workings of these committees of Member State civil servants, which discuss and vote on Commission implementing measures. In sum, there are about 250 comitology committees and their involvement is huge: about 40 per cent of *all* Community directives, decisions and regulations are first subjected to a vote in a comitology committee.[42] But although there is now neatly organised information available on it, which is accessible online, it is still impossible to reconstruct discussions in a meeting. The composition of the comitology committees, as well as that of many more informal advisory groups that contribute to the Commission's policy-making, is also made publicly available on the Internet, but most of the minutes that are available on the comitology document register are only annotated agendas and lack substance.[43] The extensive versions of the minutes are only distributed among the actual participants.

[38] See www.ec.europa.eu/transparency/regcomitology/index.cfm.

[39] See, www.ec.europa.eu/transparency/regexpert/index.cfm.

[40] See http://europa.eu/transparency-register/index_en.htm

[41] See press release of 6 May 2010, available at www.europa.eu/rapid/pressReleasesAction.do?reference=IP/10/544&format=HTML&aged=0&language=EN&guiLanguage=en.

[42] Brandsma et al (n 4).

[43] Ibid.

The Commission has not been the only one to take another stance towards transparency. The Council too has already for some years maintained an extensive and on the whole accessible Register on the Internet. For those with the expertise, time and courage to wade through the masses of documents placed on the Internet, it is possible to engage in a process of some scrutiny and deliberation on the multifarious activities of the Council in its diverse configurations. The Council has however been less forthcoming in ordering its information in a user-friendly fashion, perhaps because it has more difficulty in being terribly up-front about the scope of its expanded executive-type tasks in recent years.[44] But the very fact that institutions' document-based registers are made available via the Internet facilitates passive access to documents when interested parties know of the existence of certain documents or meetings that have taken place and can then, via the Access to Documents Regulation, request to receive the full document if it has not been made available in whole or in part on the register of documents.

The practice is that once a document is made available to an applicant it will be made available in a more structured and accessible fashion via the Internet to the public. The main areas where access will not be proactively provided, and also where access will be refused further to a specific request, tend to relate to the exceptions specifically formulated in the EU access law from 2001. This may relate either to the legislative process or the administrative process. The most important ones relate to the preparatory nature of decision-making, in particular of policy-making and of the administrations' space to think and to protection of the institutions' decision-making procedure. Some have thought of this space in terms of a right of privacy for government actors and in substance this is an argument that is being made at the EU level although it is not always qualified in these terms. The right to privacy for those third parties performing tasks of a public nature has been recognised to some extent by the ECJ in recent case law. Four issues have arisen either in recent practice or in case law and will now be separately considered with regard to the legislative process (section III) and the administrative process (section IV).

III PUBLIC ACCESS TO THE (EARLY) LEGISLATIVE PROCESS IN LAW AND PRACTICE: DEMOCRACY NOT DIPLOMACY?

A Transparency of Council Input on EU Legislation

The *Council of Ministers* is the body conceived originally as the principal legislative body for European integration. The Council of Ministers was from the very beginning designed as the *political* decision-making centre among the institutions

[44] See further, D Curtin, 'European Union Executives Evolving in the Shade?' in JW de Zwaan et al (eds), *The European Union: An Ongoing Process of European Integration: Liber Amicorum A.E. Kellermann* (The Hague, TMC Asser Instituut, 2004) 97.

of the Union and its predecessors.[45] In the national political systems government ministers (in some systems) and members of national parliaments will tend to be directly elected. At the level of the political system of the EU the situation is more varied: the 'politicians' are either the ministers participating in the Council of Ministers or the (prime ministers/(French) President – and Commission President – in the European Council), all of whom will have been either directly elected in the national system or appointed by those who have been directly elected. The Council of Ministers continues to be perceived as mainly a political organ, consisting of national ministers, *ipso facto* executive politicians with both formal and substantive *legislative power* that is either autonomous (specific) or shared with the European Parliament (normal case) depending on the policy area.

In order to prepare the decisions at the ministerial level, a great number of committees and working parties have been established in which all Member States and the Commission are represented. At the apex of this hierarchy is Coreper, the committee for the permanent representatives or the EU ambassadors of the Member States, which was established in 1958. Empirical research had shown some time ago that a very large proportion indeed of decisions pass through the upper ministerial and sectoral levels as 'A' points on the agenda.[46] An 'A' point implies that the issue has been settled at a lower level, and it will usually be passed as a matter of course at the higher level with no further discussion required. Ministers when meeting in the Council will therefore concentrate on the B points of the agenda, indicating the – much smaller – number of items on which officials or permanent representatives have not been able to reach agreement in their preparatory meetings. This means that the decisions (taken by the lower echelons in the hierarchy) are approved as such without any substantive negotiation or even discussion. In effect it follows that a large proportion of Council decisions are being taken by either the lower-level civil servants sitting in working parties or the higher-level national civil servants sitting in committees. The high number of legal acts passed in the so-called 'A-point' procedure thus shows the importance of Coreper as well as the whole committee system behind it for the ability of the Council to actually take decisions.[47]

According to the latest figures there are a total of 158 'Council Working Parties'.[48] In the working party meetings, Commission proposals for legislation are discussed, often also including the latest point of view from the European Parliament, and reformulations are sought that are acceptable both to the Member States and to the Commission. The Council's Rules of Procedure only specify that

[45] See W Wessels, 'The EC Council: The Community's Decision-Making Centre' in RO Keohane and S Hoffmann (eds), *The New European Community: Decision-Making and Institutional Change* (Boulder, CO, Westview, 1991) 133; see in general terms, F Hayes-Renshaw and H Wallace, *The Council of Ministers*, 2nd edn (Basingstoke, Palgrave Macmillan, 2011).

[46] See, MPCM van Schendelen, 'The Council Decides': Does the Council Decide?' (1996) 34 *Journal of Common Market Studies* 531.

[47] See further, J Lempp and J Altenschmidt, 'The Prevention of Deadlock through Informal Processes of Supranationalization: The Case of Coreper' (2008) 30 *Journal of European Integration* 511.

[48] See Council of Ministers, 'List of Council Preparatory Bodies' (2011) Ref No 5688/1/11 REV 1.

documents submitted by other institutions and relating to legislative procedures are to be made public, as well as the minutes of *Council* meetings relating to those legislative matters. Although most of the work is done at working party level, the rules of procedure do not mention the disclosure of working party documents. Further, these rules provide that the Council General Secretariat *may* make provisional agendas of working parties and other documents available provided that they do not reflect the individual positions of Member States, and provided that the exceptions in Article 4 of Regulation 1049/2001 do not apply.

A key issue has been to determine the access that the public will be granted to the minutes of working party meetings containing in particular the named contributions by various Member States. The Council has consistently argued that identification of the Member States' delegations which made various legislative proposals at working party level (but also at Council level) fell within the exception contained in Article 4(3) of Regulation 1049/2001 where disclosure 'would seriously undermine the institution's decision-making process, unless there is an overriding public interest in disclosure'. In a case involving a request for access to working minutes involving an ongoing legislative procedure (revision of the Access to Documents Regulation itself!), a public association called *Access Info Europe* challenged the Council's refusal to disclose fully the names of the Member States who put forward suggested changes to the legislative proposal as part of the process of establishing the Council viewpoint on the content of this legislation and prior to negotiation with the other legislative arm, the European Parliament. This refusal continued the long-standing practice of the Council of systematically refusing disclosure of Member States' involvement in legislation further to a request and also of not revealing it proactively. This attitude has to do with the history of the Council as the forum where traditionally a form of diplomatic negotiation takes place among the various Member States in order to reach a common view. Allowing access to the legislative kitchen at an early stage, the Council argues, in effect could destroy the ability to pre-cook decisions at the Council level or even to reach boiling point and thus would impede significantly the decision-making process, an explicit exception from the Access Regulation.

The General Court in a judgment of 22 March 2011 held that the disclosure sought, including information relating to the identity of those who made proposals at working party level, *should* be granted. The General Court insisted that, given the wording of the exception to a fundamental principle, the Council had to prove that disclosure of the information sought would *seriously undermine* the ongoing legislative process relating to the proposal for amending Regulation 1049/2001. Giving the widest possible right of access entails that the exceptions provided in the Access Regulation had to be strictly interpreted. Transparency is regarded as particularly important in the context of the EU legislative process. In the words of the Court: 'Openness contributes to strengthening democracy by enabling citizens to scrutinize all the information which has formed the basis for a legislative act.' The practice developed by the Council of only making information making it possible to identify the input of specific Member States available to the public *after* adoption of the legislative act in question was not upheld by the Court, on the grounds that the Council had not proved that this information would seriously undermine the ongoing legislative process. This ruling by the General Court (which has been appealed to the Court of Justice[49]) means in principle that the Council can no longer continue this practice of blacking out the names of the delegations in the minutes of working parties.

The case of *Info Access Europe* is illustrative of the evolving relationship between law and practice in the quest to make EU decision-making processes more transparent. The laws are contained both in treaty provisions and in legislation on access to documents. Both sets of legal provisions are framed in a general and abstract manner and much depends on how they are actually applied in practice. The Court of Justice has already made clear that it attaches particular importance to the principle of transparency in the context of the EU legislative process. The fact that the legislative process is problematic in terms of transparency has to do with the fact that legislation was originally adopted in the context of the EU (and its predecessor) by a process of diplomatic negotiations among the Member States in the Council. Over time this changed into a more 'normal' legislative process involving a parliament (the European Parliament). The Council has, however, always remained ambiguous about its legislative preparation and in particular the preparation of its standpoint so that the respective Member States could 'negotiate' freely. That ambiguity translated into various 'closed' practices and a reluctance to make initial preparatory work available in working parties either passively or actively. The courts, in their role as accountability forums, are able to scrutinise practices in appropriate cases brought before them and 'sanction' the inadequate practices of the Council and in effect require the Council to make the information requested available. By interpreting the exemptions strictly the courts ensure that the urge to unnecessary secrecy does not trump the widest possible transparency.

The next case study illustrates a later stage in the legislative process, after the Council had formed its viewpoint as one part of the legislative arm and when it attempts to influence the European Parliament before the European Parliament has had its first reading of the legislative proposal in question. This too concerns transparency of the legislative process as such and raises the issue of the legality of certain informal inter-institutional practices not required by the legal texts in question. In this case study the role of the European Parliament is central and in particular the manner in which it fulfils its general agora function in an open and public preparatory process. There has not (yet) been a court case brought by a member of the public refused access to documents discussed at the trilogue meetings but, given the pervasiveness of the practice, this may only be a question of time. For now there is no Court of Justice ruling so the issue must be approached from general principles and in particular the constitutional and fundamental imperatives for an open (legislative) decision-making process 'as far as possible'.

[49] See Case C-280/11 P *Council v Access Info Europe*, appeal of 6 June 2011, OJ C 238/6, available at www.eurlex.europa.eu/LexUriServ/LexUriServ.do?uri=OJ:C:2011:238:0006:0007:EN:PDF.

B Transparency of Co-Legislature Negotiations (Trilogues)

The *European Parliament* has been a very successful constitutional agenda-setter in incrementally increasing its legislative powers through various treaty reform negotiations. The assumption is that the Parliament, directly elected and 'representative' of the citizens of the Member States, ensures a more open and more deliberative element in a legislative procedure, characterised hitherto by behind-closed-doors diplomatic negotiations by representatives of the executive powers of the Member States in the Council. Ever more equal involvement in the EU legislative procedure by the Parliament ensures a more politicised and more open process in which interested stakeholders, citizens and national parliaments can look in and even participate to varying degrees, both formally and informally, at the various decision-making stages. The intensification and expansion of co-decision that has taken place over almost two decades in a whole series of treaty reforms is presented by many policy-makers, academics and some citizens as a panacea for the perceived democratic deficit in the EU political system.

The downside of the dominant legitimating strategy of building a *European* parliamentary democracy has been the manner in which the Council seems to have successfully influenced the Parliament to shift a not insignificant part of its deliberations and even decision-taking to *behind-closed-doors* 'negotiations'. This has to do with the development of so-called 'trilogue meetings'. Trilogue meetings are an informal but structured means of bringing together a reduced number of participants from both sides in order to attempt to resolve contentious issues so that overall agreement can be brokered by the Commission.

The point is that the evolving partnership between the Council and the Parliament is shaped not only by formal treaty-level reforms but also by the formal and informal arrangements made by both institutions to adapt to the altered inter-institutional circumstances. The problem is *not* that informal practices evolve in order to enable effective and timely decision-making to take place. This is quite normal and usual. It is part of the evolving living institution, as formal legal rules come to be applied in practice. The problem is rather that these informal practices lack transparency and visibility, and to a certain extent, bypass political debate and democratic controls.

Weighty new evidence indicates that the Council and the Parliament are working systematically together and attempting to closely network and take into account each other's preferences even in the *very* early stages. The most recent 'activity report' by (three Vice-Presidents of) the European Parliament reveals some startling statistics. Over the five-year period in question, the sixth parliamentary term (1 May 2004–31 May 2009), 'around 80% of the files were concluded at first reading or early second reading with the trend being a constant increase in early agreements'.[50] This means that the vast majority of co-decision

[50] European Parliament, 'Activity Report: I May 2004 to 31 May 2009' (6th parliamentary term) presented by the three Vice-Presidents of the Parliament. See further, T Bunyan, 'Abolish 1st [and 2nd] reading secret deals – bring back democracy "warts and all"' (2009) 19 *Statewatch Journal* 2.

files are negotiated in a *fast track* behind closed doors between representatives of the Parliament and the Council, with input by the Commission. What is new and unprecedented is that they have moved in such overwhelming numbers to a very early stage in the procedure before any political debate has taken place.

The very fact that institutions meet largely behind closed doors to agree legislative rules is surely problematic from a democratic point of view. It can give rise to a growing 'cocoon' of power – negotiations behind closed doors – even with a directly elected parliament. One result is that the co-decision procedure as a whole is made less intelligible for citizens. It is harder for them – and their respective national parliaments – to know in a timely fashion what exactly is being decided. But even more important it denies the opportunity for public debate and input either by citizens or their representatives (also at national level).

With the increase in the numbers of areas subject to co-decision the number of informal meetings going on at any one time on a de-central basis in the European Parliament leads to 'an absolute maze'. With the Lisbon Treaty, co-decision is expanded into new areas, notably agriculture, fisheries and justice and home affairs. The trilogue meetings do not seem to be centrally coordinated, and even central figures in the Parliament might not know about all meetings. In addition there is – according to insiders – little informal control of the work of the key negotiators internally within the Parliament. A code of conduct recently adopted in order to streamline procedures and highlight best practices will apparently be included in the Parliament's rules of procedure. This includes a 'cooling off' period of one month between negotiation of a deal and its submission to a plenary but still uses 'soft' language (the hortatory 'could' and 'should' as opposed to the mandatory 'shall').

Evidence suggests moreover that the Parliament is engaged in a strategy of sorts. The fact is that the Parliament forces the Council to come before it and explain its views publicly, the Council thereby accepting that it owes some accountability to the Parliament. The problem is that as one of the co-legislators it may well be difficult for the Parliament to objectively hold the Council to account in some seriously substantive manner. A wiser strategy may be for the Parliament, now that in the Lisbon Treaty it has finally acquired the status of an equal partner in the general legislative procedure, to ensure that law-making is, as far as possible, taking place in a *public* forum and subject to transparent rules. The alternative – and this is the paradox – is that the promise of more democracy becomes in reality the very opposite. Diplomacy and what are essentially the methods of diplomatic negotiations pre-empt open democratic and inclusive public debate on the adoption of legislation. That would seem to go against the grain of what the Treaty of Lisbon ordains. The only way to break the deadlock may indeed be to claim and then challenge a refusal to disclose trilogue documents especially those of the European Parliament itself. At the same time, from the perspective of the institutions the trilogues are very beneficial to them from the point of view of efficiency of the decision-making procedure since first reading agreements need smaller majorities in the Parliament than second reading agreements, and are thus easier to be adopted. This explains why the practice of early first reading trilogies has become so widespread and also why change is resisted by the institutions themselves as well as efforts to further 'open' up these meetings.

IV PUBLIC ACCESS TO THE EU EXECUTIVE PROCESS IN LAW AND PRACTICE: TRANSPARENCY NOT DATA PROTECTION?

A Transparency of Commission Committees and Working Groups

The Commission starts the legislative process by preparing a legislative proposal that is sent to both branches of the legislative power (the Council and the European Parliament). However, it is also a very important part of the executive power of the EU and for a long time was the only supranational executive power in the EU political system. As an executive power it performs a number of tasks including policy-making, implementation of rules and enforcement of Union law. In this context the Commission grants access to its documents both proactively (via special registers such as for comitology) and also passively pursuant to specific requests by private parties. The line between what is made public and what remains 'secret', or at least is only available to insiders, is determined in large part by the formulation of the exceptions to the Access to Documents Regulation, as interpreted in case of dispute by the courts in Luxembourg. Two of these exceptions can be said to relate in a broad sense to the demarcation of the line between a right to privacy (for individuals and for those performing public tasks) and the right to public access (for citizens).

A number of professional and private confidentiality rules existed prior to the adoption of the access to documents law by the EU with regard to its own institutions. The relationship is not determined in a precise manner but arises *ad hoc* depending on challenges brought by individuals or companies to Commission refusals to disclose certain types of information and the extent to which the courts rule they fall within allowed exceptions to the access rules. Thus, special rules on the confidentiality of information exchanged in the context of customs administrative investigations do not trump the access rules.[51] No specific provisions could conflict with the legislation on access to documents, in the words of the court, 'whose fundamental objective is to give citizens the opportunity to monitor more effectively the lawfulness of the exercise of public powers'.[52] The situation is however different with regard to the data protection exemption (Article 1.4.b) and the more general pre-existing rules on data protection, although here again there is not (yet) a very consistent line of case law.

The Bavarian Lager Company challenged the Commission's refusal to grant it full access to the minutes of a meeting in Brussels with national and European civil servants as well as representatives of the European Beer Brewing Federation, including

[51] Case T-123/99 *JT Corporation v Commission* [2000] ECR II-3269.

[52] Ibid, para 50. See also Case T-3/00 and T-337/04 *Pitsiorlas v Council and ECB* [2007] ECR II-4779, where the Court did not allow an internal rule of the ECB to pre-empt the access law.

the names of all those who attended.[53] The Court of Justice overturned on appeal the earlier decision of the General Court upholding the right to access to the document in question by Bavarian Lager on the grounds that the right to privacy prevailed in the circumstances over the right of access to the document in question.[54]

The appeal in the *Bavarian Lager* case brought into sharp focus the relationship between public access to documents and the underlying principle of transparency with the protection of data and the underlying right to individual privacy and integrity. Is there an essential, operational conflict between the provisions of the two sets of secondary legislation adopted by the EU in the form of the regulations concerning, respectively, access to documents and the protection of personal data[55]? Or are the regulations capable of being harmoniously reconciled and if so how precisely is this to be achieved? It appears that there are – at least – *three* different ways of interpreting the manner of 'harmonious reconciliation' which itself reveals that the exercise is neither self-evident nor arguably 'harmonious'! It is striking that the judgment of the General Court under appeal, the opinion of the Advocate General and the judgment of the Court of Justice itself all adopt what can only be qualified as radically different approaches and perhaps led more by the ultimate solution they wished to achieve rather that any necessary imperative in the structure and wording of the two sets of legislation.[56]

A democratic society governed by the rule of law has, in the words of Advocate General Sharpston, a fundamental interest both in wide public access to documents and in ensuring the protection of individual privacy and integrity and both are fundamental rights recognised under EU law. The legal framework for dealing with the possible conflict of transparency and data protection rules should be based on a balance of the underlying objectives of both rights. The right of access to documents is designed to ensure that access is actually granted to the greatest extent possible as well as to promote good administrative practices. The underlying objective is the improvement of the democratic legitimacy of acts of government and enabling control of the administration. The right to data protection is designed to ensure the protection of the freedoms and fundamental rights of individuals, particularly in their private life, in the handling of personal data. The underlying interest of the data subject is to be able to determine whether personal information is made public or not. This may depend on the context in which the data is to be revealed. Is it purely general and function-related data in a public context or does it relate to more sensitive and specifically private data?

The judgment of the General Court was in line with the earlier view of the European Ombudsman in his Special Report on the subject: there is no right to

[53] Case T-194/04 *Bavarian Lager v Commission* [2007] ECR II-4523.

[54] Case C-28/08 P *Commission v Bavarian Lager* [2010] ECR I-6055.

[55] See Reg (EC) No 45/2001 on the protection of individuals with regard to the processing of personal data by the Community institutions and bodies and on the free movement of such data [2001] OJ L8/1.

[56] See, however, the judgment of the General Court in case T-121/05 *Borax Europe v Commission* [2009] ECR II-27, the logic of which congrues with the General Court's decision in *Bavarian Lager* (and has not been appealed). Also, another interesting and essentially similar case is pending before the General Court: T-190/10 *Egan and Hackett v European Parliament*, judgment of 28 March 2012, nyr.

participate in *public* activities anonymously. In order to control the government, and hold persons who are actively involved in the decision-making process accountable, the citizens simply need to know who is doing what. Anonymity should only be allowed in special circumstances, for instance, if someone is threatened or anonymity is essential for the proper functioning of an official. The mere participation of a representative of a collective body in a meeting held with a Community institution did not in the view of the General Court fall within the sphere of that person's private life, so that the disclosure of minutes revealing his presence at that meeting could not constitute an interference with his private life.

The Court of Justice rejected this view on appeal and basically located its reasoning within the second scenario outlined above: the disclosure of personal data fell within the scope both of privacy protection *and* within the scope of the Data Protection Regulation. It implies acceptance of the argument that respect for private life must be interpreted broadly so as to encompass professional relations. The particular balance of interest was struck in the context of the facts of the specific case, including the actual assessment made by the Commission at the time. In the circumstances of this case partial blanking out of the personal data and providing access to the remainder of the document was a satisfactory solution and sufficient compliance with its duty of openness. The Court explicitly put the burden of proof on the applicant (in accordance with the provisions of the data protection regulation) despite the fact that under the Access Regulation no reason needs to be given when requesting information. It concluded in this regard that, 'as Bavarian Lager has not provided any express and legitimate justification or any convincing argument in order to demonstrate the necessity for these personal data to be transferred, the Commission has not been able to weigh up the various interests of the parties concerned'.[57] It followed that given that no necessity had been shown the Commission was right to reject the application for access to the full minutes of the meeting in question.

The Court interpreted the privacy exception in Article 4(1) of the Access Regulation broadly and in a manner that gave the institution in question considerable discretion as to how it dealt with the request and irrespective of the nature of the type of documents being requested and the type of personal data contained in the document. The reasoning of the Court was that disclosure of information such as that at issue in this case (who participated in meetings and full minutes) had to be read in the light of the specific data protection regulation (rather than simply as 'undermining' or otherwise privacy as required by Article 4(1)(b) of the Access Regulation). The concept of data protection involves a (much wider) set of rules and principles which apply whenever 'personal data' is processed, regardless of whether this is within the scope of privacy or not. In other words the Court's approach was to limit the scope of the access regulation not only through its own exceptions (including specifically privacy) but through a much wider – and separate – reliance on data protection rules more generally.

[57] Case C-28/08 P *Commission v Bavarian Lager* [2010] ECR I-6055, para 78.

The relevance of the Court's judgment in *Bavarian Lager* is that it basically gives the institutions carte blanche not to include the names of participants in meetings and to do so in a systematic fashion but also to deny disclosure of personal data (names etc) of public actors more widely (eg members of the European Parliament).[58] Rather than putting the institutions under an obligation in the interests of greater transparency to examine the nature of the personal data and its relationship to the type of document as a whole as suggested by the Advocate General and to devise a system that proactively takes due account of the need to protect personal data in certain circumstances only, the Court has achieved exactly the opposite. The risk is that the Court's judgment will be interpreted by the Commission and the institutions more generally as giving all civil servants (national and European) participating in EU decision-making at whatever level the right to participate in EU decision-making anonymously as well as giving the same right to trade and other 'representatives'. As such this risks driving a coach and horses through the fundamental objective of the Access Regulation, namely to increase the democratic legitimacy of EU decision-making.

The result of the manner in which the Court interpreted the data protection rules (as opposed to the access to documents rules) is that henceforth civil servants and others would have a right to participate anonymously in meetings with the Commission and other EU public authorities, irrespective of the existence of the specific wording of the Access to Documents Regulation. In this context it is interesting that both the European Data Protection Supervisor (EDPS)[59] and the European Parliament[60] proposed already in the context of the legislative revision process that in considering the question of access to documents no reference should be made to the data protection rules as such, which is a very different approach to that adopted by the Court of Justice in its *Bavarian Lager* judgment.[61] Rather the access regulation should apply, meaning that it is only the scope of the

[58] See, for example, Case T-82/09 *Dennekamp v European Parliament*, judgment of 23 November 2011, nyr, where the General Court upheld the Parliament's refusal to disclose the names of certain MEPs affiliated to an additional pension scheme to a journalist and arguably misinterpreted the Court's judgment in *Bavarian Lager*. Bavarian Lager lost its case because it did not even attempt to establish – as required by Art 8(b) Reg 45/2001 – 'the necessity of having the data transferred and if there is no reason to assume that the data subject's legitimate interests might be prejudiced'. *Dennekamp* was arguably different since the data requested by the journalist was necessary for him to pursue his goal as specified in the request. If a journalist cannot make a case concerning MEPs then this would imply that no one is in effect capable of obtaining a public document containing personal data.

[59] European Data Protection Supervisor, 'Comments on the Current Discussions in Parliament about the Revision of Regulation (EC) No 1049/2001 Relating to Public Access', February 2009, available at www.edps.europa.eu/EDPSWEB/webdav/site/mySite/shared/Documents/Consultation/Comments/2009/09-02-16_Comments_public_access_EN.pdf.

[60] European Parliament, Committee on Civil Liberties, Justice and Home Affairs, 'Draft Report of 12 May 2010 on the proposal for a regulation of the European Parliament and of the Council regarding public access to European Parliament, Council and Commission documents' COM (2008) 0229 – C6-0184/2008 – 2008/0090 (COD), available at www.europarl.europa.eu/sides/getDoc.do?type=COMPARL&mode=XML&language=EN&reference=PE439.989

[61] For a more nuanced and general approach, see further H Kranenborg, 'Access to Documents and Data Protection in the European Union: On the Public Nature of Personal Data' (2008) 45 *CML Rev* 1079, at 1111.

exception in Article 4(1)(b) on 'privacy' that is relevant. Moreover, both the EDPS and the Committee on Civil Liberties of the European Parliament propose an overriding public interest clause. In other words, data falling within the prima facie privacy exemption should nonetheless be disclosed where 'an overriding public interest requires disclosure. In those cases the institution or body shall have to specify the public interest. It shall give reasons why in the specific case the public interest outweighs the interests of the person concerned.'[62] The result would be that access to personal data which falls within the scope of Article 10 Regulation 45/2001 shall be granted in accordance with that provision, unless there is an overriding public interest in non-disclosure. In my view this is the right approach and the one that does not subvert the principle of openness nor undermine the data protection regime.

If people participate in public activities (including national and European civil servants as well as scientific experts) they may normally not expect that their participation is as such kept confidential. Because they cannot have such a legitimate expectation data protection principles are not violated. The EU legislator now has the opportunity to set the record straight on this important issue. Access to a document containing personal data shall then, except for exceptional circumstances and other exceptions in the Access Regulation, be granted if it concerns the name, title, function, contact details or information concerning activities carried out in the course of the function of a person who is actively involved in government activities. In this way justice can be done to the balance between the two public interests at stake and the underlying objectives of both regimes. In the meantime the EDPS argues that the institutions need in any event to take a more proactive approach to ensuring that before, or at least at the moment they collect data from data subjects, they are informed of the extent to which the processing of such data includes or might include its public disclosure.[63] A proactive approach would reduce the number of complicated situations in which the institutions have to be *reactive* and would contribute to reducing time-consuming litigation.

B Transparency of Internal Commission Documents: A 'Space to Deliberate'?

The administrative rationale for control over secrecy extrapolates from the individual's claims to such control in order to protect plans in the making, their implementation and confidential relationships.[64] *Max Weber* already commented

[62] See Opinion of the EDPS on the proposal for a regulation of the European Parliament and of the Council regarding public access to European Parliament, Council and Commission documents [2009] OJ C2/13, available at www.edps.europa.eu/EDPSWEB/webdav/site/mySite/shared/Documents/Consultation/Opinions/2008/08-06-30_access_documents_EN.pdf.

[63] See, EDPS, 'Public access to documents containing personal data after the *Bavarian Lager* ruling' (March 2011), available at www.edps.europa.eu:80/EDPSWEB/webdav/site/mySite/shared/Documents/EDPS/Publications/Papers/BackgroundP/11-03-24_Bavarian_Lager_EN.pdf

[64] S Bok, *Secrets: On the Ethics of Concealment and Revelation* (New York, Vintage Books, 1989).

on the inherent nature of bureaucracies to be secret.[65] Concealment in fact insulates administrators from criticism and interference; it allows them to correct mistakes and to reverse direction without costly, often embarrassing explanations; and it permits them to cut corners with no questions being asked. A key argument in this regard is that rationality and efficiency of decision-making are served by a measure of secrecy in administration. As the British *Francks Committee* wrote in 1972, ministers and administrators must, in order to present clear issues to Parliament and to the electorate, be able in some instances and at some stages to 'argue out all the possibilities with complete frankness and free from the temptation to strike public attitudes'.[66]

We can refer to this as the *space to deliberate* for ministers, civil servants and even (scientific) experts. The argument is that the existence of this secretive space will lead to the enhanced quality of deliberations and decision-making. If this 'private' space exists then policy-makers are said to have more freedom to consider and debate different options, to take risks, to change their minds, to rely on experts. *Privacy* in this sense enables government actors to protect their own domain from unwanted access by outsiders. The issue of some 'privacy' protection in the 'staging processes'[67] of policy formulation is controversial and in the context of the EU depends on the interpretation given to the protection for the decision-making process (Article 4.3 the Access Regulation). This is a key exemption to the right of public access and it is the one relied on to a significant extent by both the Commission and the Council of Ministers in order to deny public access to *internal documents* (preparatory documents, legal advice etc). In the 2010 Annual Report on the application of the Access Regulation it appears that the Commission used Article 4.3 of the Regulation to refuse partial access to documents in over 25 per cent of initial applications and for the Council the figure was 51.7 per cent.[68] Such documents are either not included in public registers of documents or are available in pdf form but blanked out in whole or in part. What is often not realised is that the institutions use this exemption in order to close off the early stages of the *legislative* process and not only the administrative process.

Access to documents on the outcomes of the trilogue legislative meetings described above in section IIIb are routinely denied on the grounds that disclosure would 'seriously undermine the decision-making process'. These joint meetings of the two arms of the legislative power in the EU thus meet in early-stage secret 'negotiations' and deny public access on the grounds that they need

[65] See M Weber, *Economy and Society: An Outline of Interpretive Sociology* (Berkeley, University of California Press, 1978) 992.

[66] Home Office, Departmental Committee on Section 2 of the Official Secrets Act 1911 (Cmd 5104, 1972) para 11.

[67] See A Westin, *Privacy and Freedom* (New York, Atheneum, 1967) 45.

[68] See European Commission, 'Report from the Commission on the Application in 2010 of Regulation (EC) No 1049/2001', 12 August 2011, para 5.3, available at www.eurlex.europa.eu/LexUriServ/LexUriServ.do?uri=COM:2011:0492:FIN:EN:PDF and European Council, 'Council Annual Report on Access to Documents 2010', May 2011, p 14 available at www.consilium.europa.eu/uedocs/cms_data/librairie/PDF/EN_ACC_web-2011.pdf.

effectively a private space to negotiate on the content of legislation (with the outcome effectively rubber-stamped by the Parliament's plenary). In fact the institutional view of the Council is that:

> During ongoing legislative procedures there is not a general right for the public to access documents if the fact of giving access would undermine the institutional decision-making process. That is the protection of ongoing procedures, which means that once the procedure is completed the document is no longer limited in access.[69]

This means that in the EU citizens have no right to know what is being discussed in early-stage legislative procedures; it is only when an agreement has been reached and laws of general application have been adopted that the citizens obtain the right to know what was agreed in their name at a stage too late for them to intervene or participate.

The only way for such crucial issues to be determined is by means of applicants seeking access to such documents and then actively challenging the Commission's refusal to disclose. Article 4(3) of the Access Regulation insists on the 'serious undermining' of the institutions' decision-making process, unless there is 'an overriding public interest in disclosure'. The specific wording, compared to the other derogations, suggests that the legislature wanted to protect the 'space to deliberate' less strongly than other interests (eg privacy). This is the line that is being taken by the Courts in Luxembourg to date where the Commission's arguments in particular have not been accepted. With regard to scientific opinions obtained for the purpose of preparation of legislation, the 'space to think' free of disclosure did not include scientific experts despite the fact that 'public debate born of the disclosure of their opinions may deter experts from taking further part in its decision-making process'.[70] In other words, the experts and their interactions with part of the Union legislature are not 'private' nor will their disclosure seriously undermine the institutions' decision-making process.

More recently, in the *My Travel* case the applicant challenged the refusal to supply it with internal documents of a preparatory nature drawn up by the working group of DG Competition within the Commission.[71] The Court of Justice overruled the judgment of the General Court that the public interest in disclosure had not been established in the context of purely administrative proceedings (even those that had ended). Advocate General Kokott insisted in her Opinion upon the fact that there must be real serious undermining of the administrative decision-making in question and that this must be proven by the institution in question and not just be hypothetical in nature.[72] Nevertheless ongoing administrative procedures merit greater protection than administrative procedures that have run their course, which was the case here. Where the procedure (merger

[69] See, Mr H Legal giving evidence to the UK House of Lords Select Committee, *Codecision and National Parliamentary Scrutiny* (2009) 2 June 2009, Question 208.

[70] See case T-121/05 *Borax Europe v Commission* [2009] ECR II-27, para 67.

[71] Case C-506/08P *Kingdom of Sweden v European Commission*, judgment of 21 July 2011, nyr, paras 55–56.

[72] Ibid, see Opinion of Advocate General Kokott, delivered on 3 March 2011.

control) has run its course, internal opinions as part of the Commission's administrative tasks must in principle be disclosed, unless a serious undermining of the decision-making procedure has been proven by the institution in question. In the words of the Advocate General, 'the risks of self-censorship and a shift to informal forms of deliberation cannot constitute a reasonably foreseeable serious undermining of deliberation processes, but are merely hypothetical. Purely hypothetical undermining cannot justify reliance on an exception.' The Court of Justice stressed the fact that openness 'contributes to the conferring greater legitimacy on the institutions in the eyes of European citizens and increasing their confidence in them by allowing divergences between various points of view to be openly debated'.[73] In this way the Court has yet again stressed the democratic underpinnings of the principle of openness and the reasons why the principle can be considered to be of a fundamental nature and exceptions subject to strict interpretation and non-hypothetical proof.

V THE ROAD FROM SECRECY TO TRANSLUCENCE AND BEYOND

The Treaty of Lisbon explicitly embraces the vision of the role of the citizen as part of an overall system of representative democracy applied in the multi-level context of the European Union. As stressed by the General Court, 'the principle of transparency is intended to secure a more significant role for citizens in the decision-making process and to ensure that the administration acts with greater propriety, efficiency and responsibility vis-à-vis the citizens in a democratic system'.[74] Transparency 'helps to strengthen the principle of democracy and respect for fundamental rights'.[75] It also increases the legitimacy of the decision-making processes of the institutions in the eyes of the citizens, in the view of the Court of Justice. At the end of the day, however, achieving the greatest possible openness in decision-making in the EU, both in legislative and administrative processes, depends on the willingness of the institutions, agencies and bodies of the EU to proactively ensure that their activities are transparent and to cultivate a culture of more openness.

At the same time the role of constitutional law in protecting constitutional and democratic rights seems particularly important. In the ongoing attempt to amend the existing legislation on access to documents, the affected institutions themselves attempt to in some respects turn the clock back and introduce less transparency rather than more[76] – an attempt that is challenged by the European

[73] Ibid, para 91.

[74] Case T-211/00 *Kuijer v Council* [2002] ECR II-485, para 52.

[75] Ibid.

[76] See further F Maiani, J-P Villeneuve and M Pasquier, 'Less is More? The Commission Proposal on access to EU documents and the proper limits of transparency' (2010) IDHEAP Working Paper (Emergence of Administrative Democracy conference, Strasbourg, March 2010). See also 'Proposal for a Regulation of the European Parliament and of the Council amending Regulation (EC) No 1049/2001 regarding public access to European Parliament, Council and Commission Documents' COM (2011)137 final COD 2008/0090 (March 2011).

Parliament but remains blocked. In such circumstances the role of the Courts in Luxembourg is particularly crucial to ensure that the principles of the Lisbon Treaty are correctly interpreted and applied in practice. The four 'cases' discussed in this chapter reveal just how blurred the refracted light can be – both in the legislative process and in the administrative process. The challenge is to move from this state of translucence to a more full-blown system of transparency of legislative and administrative processes and one that is in line with democratic principles confirmed in the Lisbon Treaty.

This will not be easy at all in the current climate. A number of trends indicate that translucence at best, and secrecy at worst, are here to stay. First, if institutions resist openness and impose de facto secrecy even in the (early) legislative process, with full compliance by the European Parliament, then only court cases (or the Ombudsman) can bring about change to entrenched practices and even then only with great difficulty, case after case (as is the case with regard to the disclosure of the legal opinions of the institutions after the *Turco* case). If institutions resist change there is unlikely to be legislative agreement on complex and controversial issues, which is why the revision process of the Access Regulation still seems to be stuck in no-man's-land, almost four years after the Commission proposal.

Secondly, a purely court-based strategy is, from the perspective of the citizen's right to the greatest possible level of openness, at best uncertain. This has to do with the fact that the Courts' lines remain unpredictable in a number of respects and that the advent of 'more sunshine' in the rain is uncertain and often depends on which Court is ruling. Moreover there are clear discrepancies between the two Courts involved – the General Court and the Court of Justice – as to the accurate level of transparency in the Union, so it is very difficult to draw a line and say definitely which Court is more favourable to transparency or even what this precisely means. It varies per case and per subject matter. But there is an extremely favourable appeal rate so far – close to 90 per cent of appeals from the General Court to the Court of Justice have been successful, but going in both directions of transparency and secrecy.[77]

Thirdly, the Courts have readily accepted the need in principle for legislative transparency and its fundamental nature. They have struggled more with the need for administrative transparency and appear to have accepted a lower threshold in this regard. This can be regarded as very problematic given the original rationale for adopting access regulation in the first place. The fact that the Court was so explicit in *Turco* with regard to the legislative process by no means implies that the principle of openness does not apply to the administrative process or indeed at another stage of the decision-making process. The Treaty of Lisbon makes no distinction whatsoever between the institutions and actors depending on the nature of their roles or tasks and their qualification as either legislative or administrative; rather the mandate of open decisions applies across the board to the institutions and wider actors as such and irrespective of the nature of their func-

[77] See Adamski (n 29).

tions or their area of activity. The consistency of the Court(s) in this regard in recent years is troubled and it has been suggested that the Court of Justice in particular may be introducing more restrictions than required in either primary or secondary law.[78]

The underlying rationale for openness in the first place in terms of the citizens may bear repeating, namely that an open public debate including divergences between various points of view (including those of legal services etc) reinforces the legitimacy of the decision-making process as a whole in the eyes of the European citizens. The public interest is open public debate in which the citizens can be informed and also in some circumstances participate. There is a tendency nowadays in Brussels to emphasise the fact that the actual users of the Access Regulation are so limited and specific (representing special interests, law firms etc) and are allowed to – without adequate (any) reasons – disrupt the efficient working of the decision-making processes (both legislative and administrative).[79] Yet this approach arguably loses sight of the fundamental nature of the principle of openness from the perspective of the citizens precisely in a political system with a structurally underdeveloped system of representative democracy. What is needed is for a reappraisal of the nature of the legitimate public interest when disclosure is refused as well as the issue of potential harm.[80] If there is no proven harm in releasing a document (or the names of participants of meetings, experts or advisers) then it should not be regarded as acceptable to limit access either.

Harm and the citizen's 'public' interest are and should be the guiding interpretative leitmotivs in this area and not administrative convenience or the institution's own interest in the efficiency of its own decision-making processes. This seems appropriate with the vista of legislative action on an 'open, efficient and independent' EU administration under Article 298 TFEU drawing closer. In these extraordinary times with bailouts, Eurobonds and economic government (even by a 'limited' number of Member States and potentially outside the framework of the existing Treaty on European Union) the order of the day, this remains a politically salient – and even crucial – question for the future of both the legal and the political systems in Europe.

[78] See also Leino and Adamski (n 29).

[79] It has in particular been argued that *optimal* transparency not maximal transparency can in this perspective provide a solution: see T Heremans, 'Public Access to Documents: Jurisprudence between Principle and Practice' *Egmont Papers* 50, September 2011, available at www.egmontinstitute.be/paperegm/ep50.pdf.

[80] See too Leino and Adamski (n 29).

5

Democratic Adjudication in Europe – How Can the European Court of Justice Be Responsive to the Citizens?

BRUNO DE WITTE

I INTRODUCTION: A DUTY UNDER THE EU TREATY

THE STARTING POINT of this chapter is Article 13(1) EU Treaty which now states, after the Lisbon Treaty revision, that 'The Union shall have an institutional framework which shall aim to promote its values, advance its objectives, serve its interests, those of its citizens and those of the Member States, and ensure the consistency, effectiveness and continuity of its policies and actions.' The Court of Justice of the European Union is not mentioned in so many words in this Treaty provision, and its drafters may not have had the Court in mind, but nevertheless the Court is part of the 'institutional framework', and it is therefore required not only to advance the objectives of the Union (which it is used to doing) but also to *serve the interests of its citizens*, which is a more unusual and uncharted duty. In this chapter I will propose some general reflections on the significance of the statement that the Court should serve the interests of Europe's citizens, and on whether those words have any distinctive meaning at all which could be reflected in the organisation and functioning of the Court. The idea that the Court should serve the interests of the citizens of Europe can also be expressed by the notion of *democratic adjudication*.[1] That controversial notion should not be understood as meaning that the Court should seek to reflect the preferences of the citizens in the same way as representative institutions must do. The Court of Justice, indeed, is expected to *counterbalance* the legislative and executive powers by reviewing their legal acts rather than itself *reflecting* the opinions of the citizens. It is possible, however, to conceive of the Court of Justice as a democratic institution in a different, perhaps more diluted sense, namely that the Court should seek to be *responsive* to the citizens of Europe. The following pages seek to explore this

[1] This term is used, and the notion defended, by KD Ewing, 'A Theory of Democratic Adjudication: Towards a Representative, Accountable and Independent Judiciary' (2000) 38 *Alberta Law Review* 708.

idea of a responsive Court of Justice: how can that Court, whilst remaining independent from the political branches of the EU and from the Member States, and whilst performing its other constitutional tasks, seek to be responsive to the interests of the European citizens and correspond more closely to the ideal laid down in Article 13 TEU?

This chapter does not examine the Court's case law on EU citizenship, which deals essentially with the rights of *supranational citizens*, namely those who make use, or have made use, or are likely to make use, of their right to free movement to go and live in another Member State than their own.[2] This area of the Court's judicial activity has been extensively analysed, often praised and occasionally criticised by legal writers, also in this volume, and therefore it seems appropriate – in the light of Article 13(1) TEU – to put the spotlight for once on the relation between the Court and the European citizens at large, including the vast mass of stay-at-homes who use their free movement rights only, and unknowingly, when receiving the odd touristic service abroad. In fact, the specialised theme of EU citizenship rights is not unconnected with the broader theme of the Court's relation with the citizens of Europe. One strand of the EU citizenship rights literature has highlighted the potentially negative implications for social solidarity and for the interests of the non-mobile citizens of the Court's often generous definition of the rights of the supranational citizens. Bringing the supranational citizen closer to the EU, so it is argued, may lead to the erosion of the legitimacy of European and national public authority from the perspective of the ordinary citizen.[3] This discussion about the European Court's role in the area of citizenship rights has an ideological dimension; but underneath the ideological preferences of the authors, there is also an institutional question about the proper role of the Court of Justice: is it sufficiently responsive to the interests and needs of the ordinary citizens of Europe, in this as in other areas of European law? This is not a question which is part of the standard repertoire of academic writing about the Court of Justice, and it might indeed seem slightly odd to ask such a broad and unfocused question and to try to find meaningful answers to it.

[2] I use the term supranational citizens as a shorthand for this category of persons, following AJ Menéndez, 'European Citizenship after Martínez Sala and Baumbast – Has European Law Become More Human but Less Social?', *RECON Online Working Paper* 2009/05, 15.

[3] M Dougan and E Spaventa, 'Wish You Weren't Here . . . New Models of Social Solidarity in the European Union', in E Spaventa and M Dougan (eds), *Social Welfare and EU Law* (Oxford, Hart Publishing, 2005) 181, 217: 'we have argued that Union citizenship should not seek to deconstruct altogether the thresholds of belonging and exclusion underpinning the domestic/national welfare settlement. Otherwise, one would risk substituting a sense of popular acceptance (however tacit) with a sense of widespread alienation for a legal construct which is still perceived as far removed from any individual's core cultural and emotional ties.' Menéndez (n 2) 2: 'European law may have become more human . . . although only at the expense of it becoming less social'; and 27: the Court's citizenship and free movement case law 'has resulted in problematic distributive outcomes, strengthening the structural power of mobile (and better off) workers to the detriment of immobile (and generally worse off) ones'. See also, in the same sense, G Davies, 'The Process and Side-Effects of Harmonisation of European Welfare States', *Jean Monnet Working Paper* 2/06; and G Davies, 'The Humiliation of the State as a Constitutional Tactic' in F Amtenbrink and PAJ van den Berg (eds), *The Constitutional Integrity of the European Union* (The Hague, TMC Asser Press, 2010) 147.

II 'GIVING COMMUNITY LAW TO THE PEOPLE'?

One useful starting point for the reflection is to recall the widespread perception that the Court of Justice is a traditional and long-standing friend of the average European citizen. Indeed, the *Van Gend en Loos* and *Costa v ENEL* judgments on direct effect and primacy, and their progeny, are often presented, not least by members and former members of the Court themselves, as having opened up the European integration project to the citizens. Those Court-made doctrines have given citizens the means to claim their new European rights in court against their own States which, in turn, has made the concrete benefits of European integration more tangible also for all the others, the non-litigant citizens. The former ECJ judge Mancini glowingly described the effect of those seminal judgments as being to 'take Community law out of the hands of the politicians and bureaucrats and to give it to the people'[4] and to 'enable ordinary men and women to savor the fruits of integration'.[5] This empowering role of the direct effect doctrine can be seen at work, for example, in the *Defrenne* judgment of 1976 in which the Court of Justice, rather surprisingly at the time, decided that the equal pay principle of the EEC Treaty had direct effect.[6] Through this judgment, as Rachel Cichowski notes:

> the Court transformed this treaty provision in an enforceable right, granting women throughout the EU a new legal basis to seek protection from discriminatory practices . . . Litigants activated the ECJ's judicial rulemaking capacity and over time these decisions altered the balance of power and *empowered ordinary citizens.*[7]

In addition to this general contribution made by the Court by means of its primacy and direct effect doctrines, it has also been pointed out that the Court of Justice, in certain areas of EU law, has adopted a more progressive attitude than national courts or than the European legislator, and has offered 'an arena for marginalized interests to escape the hegemony and capture of domestic institutions by regressive majorities or elites'. These interests 'have been able to use the Court to express arguments that were otherwise pushed aside'.[8] The Court has, thus, played an emancipatory role, for example in the area of gender equality and in

[4] F Mancini and D Keeling, 'Democracy and the European Court of Justice' (1994) 57 *MLR* 175, 183.

[5] F Mancini and D Keeling, 'Language, Culture and Politics in the Life of the European Court of Justice' (1995) 1 *Columbia Journal of European Law* 397, 413. I owe this and the preceding quote to H Schepel and E Blankenburg, 'Mobilizing the European Court of Justice', in G de Búrca and JHH Weiler (eds), *The European Court of Justice* (Oxford, Oxford Uuniversity Press, 2001) 9, 11.

[6] Case 43/75 *Defrenne v SABENA* [1976] ECR 455.

[7] R Cichowski, *The European Court and Civil Society: Litigation, Mobilization and Governance* (Cambridge, Cambridge University Press, 2007) 260 (emphasis added). For a variety of recent reflections on the historical significance of the *Defrenne* judgment, see the contributions by Sharpston, Simon, O'Leary and Muir Watt in M Poiares Maduro and L Azoulai (eds), *The Past and Future of EU Law – The Classics of EU Law Revisited on the 50th Anniversary of the Rome Treaty* (Oxford, Hart Publishing, 2010) 249.

[8] D Chalmers, 'Gauging the Cumbersomeness of EU Law (2009) 62 *Current Legal Problems* 405, 428.

developing the equal treatment and residence rights of Turkish nationals under the EEC–Turkey agreement.[9]

Other authors have pointed out, however, that from an overall perspective the Court has principally been mobilised, over the years, by the Member States, by the EU institutions and by economic actors affected by State protectionism or the Community's regulatory machine, and much less often by average citizens or public interest groups.[10] The data shows that, for reasons that may be related both to the restrictive standing rules before the European Courts and to the cost of litigation, few *private individuals* (as opposed to legal persons) bring direct actions for annulment or damages against the EU institutions, and among those few only a small percentage succeed in their challenge.[11] Whereas cases brought by ordinary citizens can more easily reach the Court of Justice through the preliminary reference procedure, provided that the national courts are prepared to 'play the game', that procedure is not very conducive to the development of public debate on issues of European law because it is practically closed off to third party interventions.[12] This makes the Court of Justice rather less open to interventions by civil society organisations than, say, the European Court of Human Rights. So, to present the Court of Justice as a kind of natural ally of the ordinary European citizen seems not altogether right. One of the Court's historical achievements has been to enable ordinary citizens to claim their EU law rights directly before national courts, and it has strengthened the legal rights of particular groups of vulnerable persons, but in other respects the Court of Justice may seem a rather distant body, to which ordinary citizens can only seldom take their claims, and which does not encourage broad debate on issues of public interest arising in the course of the application of EU law.

[9] For an examination of the role of the Court in those two areas, and the efforts made by certain Member States to mitigate the implications of the Court's innovative case law, see respectively Cichowski (n 7), and L Conant, *Justice Contained: Law and Politics in the European Union* (Ithaca, Cornell University Press, 2002).

[10] Schepel and Blankenburg (eds) (n 5) 13.

[11] See T Tridimas and G Gari, 'Winners and Losers in Luxembourg: A Statistical Analysis of Judicial Review before the European Court of Justice and the Court of First Instance 2001–2005' (2010) 35 *ELR* 131.

[12] K Lenaerts, D Arts and I Maselis, *Procedural Law of the European Union*, 2nd edn (London, Sweet & Maxwell, 2006) 569. The President of the Court also refused to allow the European Data Protection Supervisor to intervene in a preliminary reference case dealing with data protection: Order of the President of the Court of 12 September 2007 in Case C-73/07 *Tietosuojavaltuutettu v Satakunnan Markkinapörssi Oy and Satamedia Oy* [2007] ECR I-7075. Only if third parties are considered, under the national law of the referring court, as parties to the domestic proceedings, then they will also be entitled to intervene in the Court of Justice's proceedings in that same case; for example, Amnesty International, the AIRE Centre, the UNHCR and the British Equality and Human Rights Commission were all admitted to intervene in Case C-411/10 *The Queen on the Application of N.S. v Secretary of State for the Home Department*, judgment of 21 December 2011, nyr, because they had been admitted as parties to the domestic proceedings before the Court of Appeal (England and Wales).

III RESPONSIVENESS THROUGH EFFICIENCY AND THROUGH ACCOUNTABILITY?

In a recent recommendation, the Committee of Ministers of the Council of Europe gave the following definition of the *efficiency* of a court: 'the delivery of quality decisions within a reasonable time following fair consideration of the issues'.[13] That definition can be applied to the Court of Justice as to any court, even though the parameters of 'reasonable time' and of 'quality decisions' are of course different for the Court of Justice, due to such factors as the multilingual nature of the proceedings and the occasionally constitutional character of the cases which it must decide. Among those elements of efficiency, the one for which the Court of Justice was most often criticised, in the course of its history, was the excessive length of its proceedings. This concern has been taken very seriously by the Court, especially in recent years. It has adopted a number of internal reforms and has requested adjustments of its Statutes and Rules of Procedure. It has now submitted to the political institutions further proposals for reform of the Statute and the Rules of Procedure,[14] where the main concern is, once more, to allow for a reduction in the duration of Court proceedings. As a result of these efforts, and also of the fortunate addition of 12 new judges since 2004, the Court of Justice (though not the General Court) has been rather successful recently in streamlining its procedures so as to provide timely justice to its users. It may be, though, that future increases in its workload will necessitate even more radical reforms which could, this time, affect the very architecture of the system of judicial protection in the EU.[15]

Efficiency, as was usefully recorded by the Council of Europe's recommendation quoted above, is about more than delivering speedy rulings. It also requires the 'delivery of quality justice' and 'a fair consideration of the issues'. Indeed, putting too much effort into reducing the duration of proceedings may negatively impact on those other elements of judicial efficiency. As Advocate General Sharpston recently remarked in an extra-judicial capacity, 'in a difficult case, speed may come at the expense of quality'.[16] This may seem a very commonsensical observation, but it was made in a manner and with an emphasis that suggest that, within the Court institution itself, some persons question the currently

[13] *Recommendation of the Committee of Ministers of the Council of Europe on Judges: Independence, Efficiency and Responsibilities*, CM/Rec (2010)12 of 17 November 2010, no 31.

[14] *Draft Amendments to the Statute of the Court of Justice of the European Union and to Annex 1 thereto*, of 28 March 2011, and *Draft Rules of Procedure of the Court of Justice*, of 25 May 2011. Both documents were posted on the Court's website: www.curia.europa.eu/jcms/jcms/Jo2_7031. See also the Editorial Comments, 'Delivering Justice: Small and Bigger Steps at the ECJ' (2011) 48 *CML Rev* 987.

[15] For discussion of some more radical reform proposals, see the Report of the House of Lords' European Union Committee, *The Workload of the Court of Justice of the European Union*, 14th Report of Session 2010–11, 6 April 2011.

[16] E Sharpston, 'Transparency and Clear Legal Language in the European Union: Ambiguous Legislative Texts, Laconic Pronouncements and the Credibility of the Judicial System' (2009–10) 12 *Cambridge Yearbook of European Legal Studies* 409, 418.

dominant concern for reduction of the duration of proceedings and take the view that the efficiency of a judicial institution cannot only be measured by its timely delivery of rulings. Indeed, it seems as if the ability of the Court to limit the time taken by its proceedings is accompanied by increasing criticism of the quality of its jurisprudence.[17] Of course, there have always been strong criticisms of aspects of the Court's case law, but it seems that the criticism is becoming more widespread. It takes the usual form of accusations of judicial activism (particularly in Germany[18]), but increasingly the criticism is focusing not so much on the outcomes reached by the Court but on the lack of sustained reasoning leading to those outcomes. Thus, it would seem that the Court of Justice tends to score less well on the 'quality' and 'fair consideration' criteria of efficiency. We will consider these allegations in more detail, in section V below, but for now we may observe that, if it wants to 'serve the citizens', the Court cannot be content with being efficient in the purely quantitative sense of keeping the processing time of cases within reasonable limits. There is also a qualitative side to efficiency, and therefore the need to find other ways in which the Court can seek to be responsive.

IV FORMS OF RESPONSIVENESS OF THE COURT

The responsiveness of a judicial institution can first of all be achieved, or at least demonstrated, by the way in which it is composed. The Court of Justice and the General Court have always comprised at least one judge from each Member State. This controversial principle is often criticised but it has the benefit, at least, of allowing those Courts to have direct and personal knowledge of the legal systems of the 27 Member States, and it also allows the Courts – in theory at least – to be aware of the impact and acceptability of the case law in each of those countries. Echoing national debates on whether the judiciary should reflect, in its very composition, the diversity of society, it has been argued that the composition of the European Court of Justice should also reflect societal diversity alongside the national diversity which it currently reflects.[19] Yet, this is nearly impossible under the current rules for the appointment of members of the Court of Justice and the General Court. Despite the formal rule that members of the European Courts are

[17] For a summary of the current critical debate about the quality of the Court's jurisprudence, see 'Editorial Comments – The Court of Justice in the Limelight Again' (2008) 45 *CML Rev* 1571.

[18] See several publications by Fritz Scharpf, among which his recent 'Legitimacy in the Multi-level European Polity' in P Dobner and M Loughlin (eds), *The Twilight of Constitutionalism?* (Oxford, Oxford University Press, 2010) 89, 109 ff. Also M Höpner, 'Usurpation statt Delegation – Wie der EuGH die Binnenmarktintegration radikalisiert und warum er politische Kontrolle bedarf', *MPIfG Discussion Paper* 08/12. See also the very radical statement by former German President (and chairman of the EU Charter Convention in 2000) Roman Herzog in *Frankfurter Allgemeine Zeitung*, 8 September 2008, and an English-language version of his argument in R Herzog and L Gerken, 'We Must Cure Brussels of its Centralising Fever', *Europe's World*, Summer 2007. And yet again, C Budras, 'Der lange Arm des EuGH', *Frankfurter Allgemeine Zeitung*, 2 September 2010.

[19] I Solanke, 'Diversity and Independence in the European Court of Justice' (2008–09) 14 *Columbia Journal of European Law* 89.

appointed by 'common accord' of the Member States, the reality is – and will remain – that each country puts forward their one and only preferred candidate, so that it depends on the individual choices of each of the 27 States whether, as a result, the overall composition of the Courts reflects to any extent the gender or ethnic composition of the European population. The introduction, by the Constitutional Treaty and then the Lisbon Treaty, of a panel of experts tasked with giving an opinion on the candidates' suitability to perform their judicial duty[20] will not remedy this situation, since the panel examines each individual appointee's credentials separately and cannot take an overall view of the desirable composition of the Courts. One may also note that, due to the continued insistence on the 'one country-one judge' principle, the Court of Justice and the General Court are currently composed of a large majority of members stemming from the smaller Member States, so that the equal representation of all national legal systems is now counterbalanced by a very unequal representation of the European population at large.

The panel of experts created under the Lisbon Treaty is clearly *not* an appointing commission like the one that now appoints judges of the UK Supreme Court. Its role is merely advisory and is presumably intended to weed out the more outrageous choices made by Member State governments. It has, in fact, already done so on a few occasions. The Panel does not meet and hear the candidates in public. Scrutiny of candidate judges by a committee of the European Parliament, as was suggested during the Convention on the Future of the Union (and also on earlier Treaty revision occasions) will not happen, and the European Union is certainly not moving in the direction of an American-style democratic selection process of judges.[21]

Whereas the European citizen has no knowledge of how and why the members of the Court of Justice are appointed, that citizen can observe to some extent how those persons hear the cases, at least if he or she is prepared to travel to Luxembourg. The Supreme Court of Canada has webcast all its hearings since 10 February 2009, and they remain freely accessible after the event. One can occasionally watch the arguments of the parties before the European Court of Human Rights. But there is no provision for the broadcasting or webcasting of some or all of the hearings in front of the European Court of Justice. *Europe by Satellite*, the EU's own information channel, announces on its website that it offers live coverage of 'significant rulings from the European Court of Justice', but in fact the only thing that can be seen live is the formal pronouncement of the operative part of the judgment, which is entirely incomprehensible to the informed, even legally trained, European citizen. Occasionally, Court rulings may form the object of

[20] Article 255 TFEU and Council Decision of 25 February 2010 relating to the operating rules of the panel provided for in Article 255 of the Treaty on the Functioning of the European Union [2010] OJ L50/18.

[21] For a critical discussion of current judicial selection mechanisms in the United States, see J Resnik, 'Judicial Selection and Democratic Theory: Demand, Supply, and Life Tenure' (2005) 26 *Cardozo Law Review* 579.

short presentations and discussions at the Commission's daily press conference, which is also transmitted live.[22] Furthermore, the Commission's Audiovisual Services unit produces a collection of videos about European affairs, which are accessible via the Internet, and which includes an extremely dull video of the swearing-in ceremony of new ECJ members, which took place on 10 May 2010. It is difficult to imagine one single European citizen (apart from those appearing in the video) who would want to sit out its full one hundred minutes.

Increasing the *visibility* of the Courts' activity may, admittedly, be rather difficult. A more interesting form of responsiveness may be found in the *accountability* mechanisms that apply to its activity; however, such mechanisms are largely absent. The 'accountability revolution'[23] that, for the last twenty years or so, has profoundly changed many national legal systems, has also affected the European Union legal order. But, whereas at the national level these reforms have often led to the emergence of new forms of *judicial* evaluation and other forms of judicial accountability,[24] at the European Union level accountability and deliberation debates and reforms have been confined to the *political* institutions and have not affected the EU's judiciary.[25]

First and most obviously, the Court of Justice's rulings are not subject to judicial control by any other court (not even, for the time being, by the European Court of Human Rights, as confirmed in the ECtHR's *Kokkelvisserij* decision[26]) – although of course the General Court's judgments are subject to the hierarchical scrutiny of the Court of Justice, a form of 'internal' judicial accountability which is of central importance in all national legal systems. The European Ombudsman can only open inquiries regarding the non-judicial activities of the Court (for example, on personnel issues). The European Court of Auditors audits the ECJ's administrative operations, but not its judicial 'value-for-money' performance. Documents produced in the course of judicial proceedings, such as submissions by intervening States, are excluded from the Treaty-based right of access to

[22] For example, on 8 September 2011, the ruling of the CJ in the *Monsanto* cases (Joined Cases C-58/10 to C-68/10) was shown live, but was also, more informatively, presented at the Commission's press conference.

See http://ec.europa.eu/avservices/ebs/schedule.cfm, for the date of 8 September 2011.

[23] A Le Sueur, 'Developing Mechanisms for Judicial Accountability in the UK' (2004) 24 *Legal Studies* 73, 73.

[24] R Mohr and F Contini, 'Judicial Evaluation in Context: Principles, Practices and Promise in Nine European Countries' (2007) 1 *European Journal of Legal Studies*, no 2 (online).

[25] On questions of accountability of the EU's political system, see among others: C Harlow, *Accountability in the European Union* (Oxford, OUP, 2002); W van Gerven, *The European Union – A Polity of States and Peoples* (Oxford, Hart, 2005) ch 2; D Curtin, *Executive Power of the European Union* (Oxford, Oxford University Press, 2009) ch 9; L Verhey, P Kiiver, S Loeffen (eds), *Political Accountability and European Integration* (Groningen, Europa Law Publishing, 2009). On deliberation with citizens in EU policy-making, see S Boucher, 'If Citizens Have a Voice, Who's Listening? Lessons from Recent Citizen Consultation Experiments for the European Union', *EPIN Working Paper* no 24, June 2009. And see now EU Reg 211/2011 of 16 February 2011 on the Citizens' Initiative [2011] OJ L65/1.

[26] EctHR, Appl No 13645/05, *Coöperatieve Producentenorganisatie van de Nederlandse Kokkelvisserij et al v Netherlands*, decision of 20 September 2009.

documents.[27] The European Parliament cannot call in the members of the European Court of Justice for a hearing about particular aspects of its case law, although there is nothing to stop it from commenting on that case law, which it very rarely does. What remains is a classical device of 'routine accountability',[28] namely the publication of the ECJ's annual report, which – among other things – contains data allowing for an evaluation of its 'productivity', but does not engage in a substantive discussion of the case law.

How, then, can the citizens' legitimate interest in the quality of European justice be articulated? Like Molière's Monsieur Jourdain, who discovered that he had spoken prose all his life without knowing it,[29] courts have practised forms of accountability long before the accountability language and ideology became fashionable. Those traditional accountability practices include:

> the fact that most courts sit in public; the common practice of giving reasoned, written judgments; the possibility that judgments are appealable to a higher judicial body; and the scrutiny meted out to judgments (and judges) by a more-or-less informed news media and scholarly work of academics.[30]

Those traditional forms are also practised by the Courts of the EU, although with certain limits: only the General Court's judgments are subject to appeal, whereas those of the Court of Justice are not; and the scrutiny by 'European legal opinion' is more attenuated than what happens at the national level, due to the fragmentation of the European Union legal field.[31] So, the main mechanism through which the ECJ accounts for its activity is the published reason-giving which accompanies its rulings, to which we turn in the next section.

V THE DUTY TO GIVE REASONED JUDGMENTS

Whereas the other EU institutions have a Treaty-based duty to give reasons for the acts which they adopt[32] (a duty which, contrary to what happens in most States, extends not only to administrative acts but also to legislative acts), the Court of Justice – the body that defines and develops the other institutions' duty to give reasons – is under a similar duty itself under its Statute. According to Article 36 of the Statute of the Court, 'judgments shall state the reasons on which they are based. They shall contain the names of the Judges who took part in the

[27] As confirmed in Joined Cases C-514/07 P, C-528/07 P and C-532/07 P *Kingdom of Sweden and others*, judgment of 21 September 2010, [2010] ECR I-8533, paras 79–82. Contrast this with the vigorous arguments by Advocate General Poiares Maduro for providing greater access to Court submissions (Opinion in the same case, paras 32 to 39).

[28] On this notion of 'routine accountability', see Le Sueur (n 23) 92.

[29] Molière, *Le bourgeois gentilhomme*.

[30] Le Sueur (n 23) 76.

[31] See B De Witte, 'European Union Law: A Unified Academic Discipline?' *EUI Working Paper* RSCAS 2008/34.

[32] Art 296 TFEU. On the content of this duty to give reasons, see P Craig, *EU Administrative Law* (Oxford, Oxford Univeristy Press, 2006) 382–84.

deliberations.' Unlike with the other EU institutions, however, the performance of the Court's duty to state reasons is controlled by itself, and 'the lack of an enforcement mechanism makes the implementation of the duty depend in large part on the Court's institutional self-understanding'.[33] This question has been extensively commented on in academic writing almost since the start. In the early years of the Community the Court of Justice used a very elliptic style, modelled on the French example, which was increasingly criticised by legal writers and national judges who were used to more discursive judgments in their own legal system. Gradually, the length of the Court judgments increased, and occasionally the Court now develops very elaborate and compelling arguments to support its rulings. The problem, though, is that it does not *always* provide good reasoning, and that the quality of the Court's reasoning has become, in the eyes of many observers, more uneven and unpredictable.

Thus, for example, the Court of Justice feels free not to answer some of the questions referred by a national court if it considers them superfluous in the case at hand, even though they may raise important general questions of EU law.[34] It also feels free to ignore arguments which an intervening State or the Commission have submitted to it; a recent example of this is the *Ruiz Zambrano* judgment in which the Court of Justice mentioned that all eight intervening States as well as the Commission proposed one interpretation, but then went on to adopt another interpretation, based on different premises, without bothering to discuss the arguments of the States and the Commission.[35] The lack of sufficient reasoning in what was a rather unexpected and innovative ruling has struck many of the early commentators of this judgment.[36] Similar criticisms, focusing more on the lack of sufficient reasoning than on the rulings themselves, were made of the *Mangold* and *Kücükdeveci* judgments on non-discrimination.[37]

[33] V Perju, 'Reason and Authority in the European Court of Justice' (2009) 49 *Virginia Journal of International Law* 307, 327.

[34] See, for example, Joined Cases C-171/07 and C-172/07, *Apothekerkammer des Saarlandes and others* [2009] ECR I-4171, in which the Court refused (para 62) to answer a question from the German court asking it to reconsider its *Costanzo* doctrine, according to which national administrative authorities have a duty to disapply national laws that conflict with directly effective norms of EU law. Although this is a very controversial doctrine (see the critical discussion by M Verhoeven, *The Costanzo Obligation – The Obligations of National Administrative Authorities in the Case of Incompatibility between National Law and European Law* (Antwerp, Intersentia, 2011)), the Court refused to deal with the question, because it had found the German legislation in the case at hand to be compatible with EU law, so that the duty to disapply national law was not triggered in that case.

[35] Case C-34/09, *Gerardo Ruiz Zambrano v Office national de l'emploi*, judgment of 8 March 2011, nyr, para 37 (reference to the views of the governments and the Commission), and paras 39–45 (the Court's own view).

[36] See for example the case comment by K Hailbronner and D Thym in (2011) 48 *CML Rev* 1253, 1259–64, and the editorial comment by N Nic Shuibhne, 'Seven Questions for Seven Paragraphs' (2011) 36 *ELR* 161.

[37] In relation to the implications of those two judgments for the horizontal direct effect of general principles of EU law, Eleanor Spaventa wrote: 'That such a dramatic constitutional development should happen through badly reasoned rulings is then all the more regrettable' (E Spaventa, 'The Horizontal Application of Fundamental Rights as General Principles of Union Law' in A Arnull, C Barnard, M Dougan and E Spaventa (eds), *Constitutional Order of States. Essays in EU Law in Honour of Alan Dashwood* (Oxford, Hart Publishing, 2011) 199, 215.

In many of the Court of Justice's judgments, there is a sense that the outcome is *inevitable* and the reasoning is, carefully or sometimes not so carefully, built so as to convey that sense of inevitability. This is in the best traditional style of some national legal systems, particularly the French. An alternative way of constructing a judgment would be for the Court to provide first a sympathetic account of the opposing views and interpretations, accepting that opposed interpretations of the law can be equally legitimate, before explaining, in a second stage, why it decides to back one interpretation rather than another. Such an approach would seem more responsive to the diversity of interests and values that characterises the European Union, and would leave more room for subsequent discussion by interested citizens. It has been argued, persuasively in my view, that it would also be beneficial for the Court's own authority if it were 'to include in the public reason giving process the substantive legal debate about doctrinal choices and jurisprudential visions that inform the Court's specific decisions and its overall case law'.[38] Vlad Perju, one of the advocates of a more discursive style in Court judgments, gives the example of the *Chacón Navas* judgment in which, according to him, the Court adopted a medical model of disability rather than a social model in interpreting the Employment Equality Directive 2000/78, without acknowledging the fact that there were those two competing models and that the latter model was supported by many scholars and some of the EU's political institutions.[39] Because of this, the ruling seemed unilateral and truncated and could not provide clear guidance for the future.

Another example is the Court's case law on free movement, in which it assumes often very quickly that a given Member State measure constitutes a restriction of free movement, and then moves on to consider whether there is a legitimate justification for that restriction, although the existence of a restriction is often quite doubtful. Indeed, as one attentive observer puts it, there is often 'a striking absence of analysis'[40] of this question. One could mention, by way of illustration, the *Idrima Tipou* judgment of 2010.[41] This case involved Greek legislation which makes shareholders of commercial television stations jointly liable for fines imposed on their broadcasting station for certain breaches of media law. This was an indistinctly applicable measure, affecting both Greek and foreign shareholders. The referring court had asked whether the rule was compatible with EU company law, since it formed an exception to the principle that shareholders are not liable for the obligations of the company. Instead, the Court chose to assess the facts under the heading of the freedom of establishment and the free movement of capital, without being asked so by the Greek court. The Court states, in paragraph

[38] Perju (n 33) 328.

[39] Ibid, 310–11. For a case comment on *Chacón Navas* that discusses those two contrasting models of disability, see L Waddington (2007) 44 *CML Rev* 487.

[40] C Barnard, 'Restricting Restrictions: Lessons for the EU from the US?' (2009) 68 *CLJ* 575, 597. The article argues, more generally, that the Court of Justice gives an unduly expansive meaning to the notion of restrictions of the fundamental freedoms.

[41] Case C-81/09 *Idrima Tipou AE v Ipourgos Tipou kai Meson Mazikis Enimerosis*, judgment of 21 October 2010, nyr.

58 of the judgment: 'although the measure is applicable without distinction to Greek investors and investors of other Member States, its deterrent effect is greater for investors from other Member States than for Greek investors'. But why is that? That conclusion seems unpersuasive in the absence of any further explanations concerning the state of the Greek media market.

Similarly, the Court of Justice never mentions political or academic disapproval of its earlier judgments and does not openly engage with it. For example, the recent *Bressol* case was widely seen as an opportunity for the Court to reconsider, or at least to explain better, the approach it had taken in *Commission v Austria* as regards cross-border access to higher education institutions. The latter judgment had been bitterly criticised in Austria for disrupting the policy choice, made by successive Austrian governments and parliaments, to keep access to higher education open and cost free for the students. When a similar Belgian case came before the Court shortly afterwards, one could have expected a responsive Court to acknowledge and discuss the criticisms, but the Court did not do so – nor did its Advocate General, who is in a better institutional position to canvass all the relevant legal and non-legal opinions concerning the case.[42] This refusal to acknowledge public debate about controversial cases may be inspired by the wish to remain aloof from popular or Member State pressure, or at least to preserve the image of aloofness and of a court guided by legal principle and nothing else. But it could also be due, in some cases at least, to an objective problem faced by the CJEU, namely the fact that it is not well equipped to follow public debate, or even informed scholarly debate, in all 27 States of the European Union. Despite the country briefings by its research and documentation directorate, the personal knowledge of the Court's members and their personal staff, and the (naturally biased) information conveyed by parties to the case or intervening Member States, the CJEU, in its 'fairy tale duchy of Luxembourg', remains far removed from the living legal and political reality of the single States. Hence, it is more concerned with the pursuit of its 'line' of cases than with the public debate that surrounds a case brought to Luxembourg.

A number of authors, including most recently Marcus Höreth[43] and Vlad Perju in his already-cited paper, advocate one major solution to achieve the aim of making the Court's rulings more discursive: the introduction of separate opinions in the Court, on the model of the European Court of Human Rights and many constitutional courts. The solution would probably be effective, in particular since it is widely known that some of the incoherence and blind spots in Court judgments result from the effort to reach a consensus on the collegiate judgment; the introduction of separate opinions would reduce the need to accommodate the

[42] Case C-73/08 *Nicolas Bressol and others v Gouvernement de la Communauté française* [2010] ECR I-2735. See also Advocate General Bot writing in his Opinion on Case C-555/07 *Seda Kücükdeveci* [2010] ECR I-365: 'we are all aware that *Mangold* has been the subject of criticism' (para 76), but without engaging in a discussion of that criticism.

[43] M Höreth, 'Richter contra Richter. Sondervoten beim EuGH als Alternative zum "Court Curbing"' (2011) *Der Staat* 191.

views of all judges within a single judgment and allow both the majority and potential dissenters to give better-reasoned opinions.[44] However, such a reform is unlikely in the foreseeable future; earlier proposals of this kind were fiercely resisted from within the Court, whose members generally take the view that the collegiate nature of its judgments has, historically, been a source of strength.[45] The collegiate and impersonal nature of the judgments hides from sight the possible internal divisions of the Court and shields its members from political pressure, so the traditional argument goes. One may note that, recently, researchers have started to look behind the opaque screen of the collegiate judgment in order to find traces of political preferences (often: national preferences) of individual members of the Court.[46]

Since the introduction of separate opinions is not going to happen in the foreseeable future, an evolution towards a more discursive reasoning in Court judgments will depend on extra efforts, from the side of the judges, to make sure that the search for consensus, which marks the deliberations of the Court, does not go to the detriment of the clarity and logic of its reasoning.

VI RESPONSIVENESS THROUGH POLITICAL OVERRULING?

Responsiveness to citizens may also mean, and perhaps above all, responsiveness to the arguments presented by the institutions representing the preferences of the citizens: national governments and parliaments, or the Council and the European Parliament, depending on the nature of the case. Procedurally speaking, the views of those institutions and States can be adequately conveyed to the Court thanks to the right of all those actors to intervene in all cases pending before the CJEU. Note, however, that the agents of the States and the EU institutions before the Court are trained lawyers who are 'repeat players' of the Luxembourg game and are often better trained in using the technical arguments of EU law than in articulating the legal policy views of their principals. Also, as was mentioned before, the Court does not always feel the need to respond to the arguments made by the intervening States.

[44] See, on this point, JHH Weiler, 'Epilogue: The Judicial Après Nice', in de Búrca and Weiler (eds) (n 5) 215, 225: 'One of the virtues of separate and dissenting opinions is that they force the majority opinion to be reasoned in an altogether more profound and communicative fashion. The dissent often produces the paradoxical effect of legitimating the majority because it becomes evident that alternative views were considered even if ultimately rejected.'

[45] But see the view of the current German judge at the Court of Justice, Thomas von Danwitz, who expresses mild support for the idea of separate opinions, whilst adding that this is not, in his view, a major question: T von Danwitz, 'Funktionsbedingungen der Rechtsprechung des Europäischen Gerichtshofes' (2008) *Europarecht* 769, at 779.

[46] See, eg, M Höpner, 'Warum betreibt der Europäische Gerichtshof Rechtsfortbildung? Die Politisierungshypothese' *MPIfG Working Paper* 10/2. The author mentions (at 8) the view, expressed by another author, that the *Laval* and *Viking* judgments were decided by a narrow majority comprising the judges of the new Member States who shared a 'national interest' in the outcome of the judgments. There is no concrete evidence for this view, but the fact that such speculations have become more frequent in recent years is indicative of a growing tendency to see the Court of Justice as a partisan political actor rather than an independent umpire.

In the national legal systems, the responsiveness of courts to political institutions is backed up by the possibility for those political institutions to overrule a judicial decision which they dislike. This creates a moderate form of 'political accountability' of courts, which forces them to adopt interpretations of existing law that are persuasive enough so as not to lead the legislator to set in motion the cumbersome and costly process of legislative overruling. The situation at the European level is not essentially different. When the Court offers a particular interpretation of EU legislation, it knows that the European legislator might be able to overturn its judgment by amending the legislation in a sense contrary to the Court's ruling. But, on a closer look, we can see that legislative overruling is much more difficult in the European Union than in most Member States. Indeed, there are no 'shortcuts' for adopting legislative amendments. Such amendments need to be processed through the normal legislative decision-making procedures, which in most cases require a qualified majority in the Council and the agreement of the Parliament through co-decision, and in some cases even unanimity within the Council. Those heavy requirements, which make sense as a restraint on *initial* EU legislation, make much less sense when applied to *amending* legislation and, anyway, they make the prospect of the political institutions 'correcting' the Court a rather remote one. Take, as an example, the fate of the EU's Working Time Directive. Many Member States' governments were upset by the Court's interpretation of that Directive to the effect that on-call duty of medical personnel should be counted as working time and not as resting time, thus increasing the cost of running hospitals.[47] When the Commission proposed to update the Directive on a number of points, a qualified majority of Member State delegations in the Council reached agreement on overturning the Court's interpretation by introducing a new clause stating that inactive on-call time by medical personnel should not be defined as working time. However, the amendment process of this Directive became charged with other politically controversial issues, and eventually the European Parliament blocked the reform at conciliation committee stage so that the revision of the Directive failed and the Court's interpretation of the original text of the Directive was preserved.

Political overruling of a Court judgment becomes even more difficult, immensely difficult indeed, when that judgment relates to the interpretation of *primary* EU law. Given the large amount of written and unwritten primary law, Court rulings often deal with primary law. Whereas at the Member State level, constitutional amendments responding to court cases usually require special majorities in parliament and are therefore difficult to achieve but not impossible, any amendment of the Treaties requires the unanimous agreement of all Member State governments, and universal ratification in each of the 27 States. It will rarely occur that a given Treaty interpretation by the Court is rejected by *all* governments, which makes the overruling of primary law interpretations almost impos-

[47] See the discussion of the case law by T Novak, 'The Working Time Directive and the European Court of Justice' (2008) 15 *Maastricht Journal of European and Comparative Law* 447.

sible.[48] One of the reasons why the *Laval* and *Viking* judgments became so controversial is the helplessness felt by the opponents after the judgment. Since the Court of Justice based those rulings, in large part at least, on a particular interpretation of the EC *Treaty* provisions on free movement rather than on secondary EU law, it became impossible, in practice, for the opponents of the rulings to try to overturn them – only the Court itself can decide to overrule or at least qualify its case law in this area.

The Court of Justice is, thus, rather uniquely immune from political pressure before it decides a case, and from political retaliation afterwards. It is very largely the master of its own fate and of its institutional practices, at least in the short run.[49] This does not mean that the Court of Justice is insensitive to the perceptions that the political actors (especially, the powerful Member States) may have of its case law, but at least it does not feel under an immediate threat of court-curbing because of particular rulings. Indeed, it is interesting to note that whereas *individual* Member State governments occasionally complain about judgments of the Court of Justice, especially when those judgments curtail that State's policy autonomy in a sensitive domain, the *collectivity* of the Member State governments have agreed, in each Treaty revision so far, to confirm and extend the far-reaching powers that the Court of Justice possesses for enforcing EU law. And yet, the Court's long-term authority and the effective application of EU law depend on the cooperative attitude of national courts, on the willingness of Member State governments not to engage in non-compliance tactics and even on an overall sympathetic reception of its case law by legal writing in the various countries of Europe. Most of the cases coming to Luxembourg are routine cases, which the Court can deal with according to its routine techniques. But every now and then, cases may arouse deep feelings among the parties and among sections of the citizenry of the countries concerned. The Court should perhaps take extra care, first in identifying such cases, secondly in drafting its judgments in such cases more carefully and discursively,[50] and, above all, in showing respect for careful political

[48] There seems not to have been a single instance of such a constitutional overruling, although the so-called 'Barber' Protocol to the Maastricht Treaty came close to it by entrenching a very restrictive interpretation of the Court's *Barber* judgment. See A Arnull, 'Me and My Shadow: The European Court of Justice and the Disintegration of European Law' (2007–08) 31 *Fordham International Law Journal* 1174, 1190. Overruling of a Court judgment is to be distinguished from the case in which the Member States refuse to *extend* the Court's powers to new areas of cooperation or seek to *constrain* its future activity by adopting specific language, such as the 'no direct effect' rule for Third Pillar instruments, which was inserted by the Treaty of Amsterdam. Such 'ouster clauses' can be imposed by a small number of Member States in the course of Treaty amendment negotiations.

[49] See, in this sense, the conclusions of the analysis by M Höreth, *Die Selbstautorisierung des Agenten – Der europäische Gerichtshof im Vergleich zum U.S. Supreme Court* (Baden Baden, Nomos, 2008). Other authors have made this point as well. See, eg, Arnull (n 48); KJ Alter, 'Who Are the "Masters of the Treaty"?: European Governments and the European Court of Justice' (1998) 52 *International Organization* 121; D Beach, *Between Law and Politics. The Relationship between the European Court of Justice and EU Member States* (Copenhagen, DJØF Publishing, 2001).

[50] As suggested by Sharpston,(n 16) 422: 'the Court needs to distinguish more readily, in terms of "required processing time", between a barely contested infringement action and a really awkward, delicate case..

deliberations that may have taken place either at the EU level or in a Member State, depending on the case. This is one practical way in which the Court can show itself to be responsive to the European citizens at large: if it could display such 'deliberation-respecting judicial review',[51] then much of the current criticism could subside.

There may be a small role to play here for legal academics and especially for the professional European Court watchers among them. Legal writers are no longer the predictably strong supporters of the Court of Justice of earlier times; one now tends to find comparable amounts of praise and blame in the comments written about Court judgments. By focusing not only on the outcomes of Court decisions, but also on the quality of the Court's reasoning and its ability to give fair consideration to all the interests at stake in a given case, academics could help to make the Court more responsive to the European citizen.

[51] See, in the United States context, WN Eskridge and J Ferejohn, 'Constitutional Horticulture: Deliberation-Respecting Judicial Review' (2008–09) 87 *Texas Law Review* 1273.

6

A Very Cosmopolitan Citizenship: But Who Pays the Price?

MICHELLE EVERSON

I AN AVANT-GARDE COURT

WRITTEN IN IMMEDIATE response to the Judgment of the Court of Justice of the European Union (CJEU) in *Ruiz Zambrano*,[1] one European legal journal notes in its editorial that:

> The Court is trying to do good things in individual cases; but it cannot continue to ignore the systematic legitimacy – and credibility – consequences of this choice. Thus, even if the outcome is right, has too high a price been paid?[2]

Bemoaning, in particular, the 'brief and opaque articulation' of the 'reasoning' which the Court deployed in order to justify its seeming reversal of age-old jurisprudence that limited the reach of citizenship of the European Union to contexts of cross-border movement,[3] the editorial nonetheless also appears to capture a far broader truth about the core nature of (legally constituted) citizenship: citizenship is a positive (constitutional) good, for which someone will nevertheless always pay a negative price.

In traditional terms, the 'costliness' of citizenship is to be found in its Janus-like face; its dual function as an instrument which confers not only rights but also status, and which thus ensures both the inclusion and the exclusion of the individual within a group. In the terminology of political theory, citizenship is 'intimately linked to the ideas of individual entitlement on the one hand and attachment to a particular community on the other'.[4] In other words, citizenship is a particularist vehicle and must be distinguished from a universal scheme of

[1] Case C-34/09 *Ruiz Zambrano v Office national de l'emploi*, judgment of 8 March 2011, nyr.
[2] N Nic Shuibhne, Editorial (2011) 36 *ELR* 161.
[3] Ibid, 162.
[4] W Kymlicka and W Norman, 'Return of the Citizen: A Survey of Recent Work on Citizenship Theory' in R Beiner (ed), *Theorizing Citizenship* (New York, State University of New York Press, 1995) 283, 283.

human rights: the entitlements of citizenship are granted by a bounded community with the express intention of giving the individual status within that community, and with the implicit consequence that such included status gains all the more in value because non-citizens or 'others' have been denied status, and are excluded from and dominated by community.[5]

In Hannah Arendt's analysis, where universal human rights are aporias, and what truly counts for the fate of the individual is a *political* or enabling relationship with a community founded within a geopolitical unit within which all citizens are protected, the consequences of a lack of citizenship – or 'the right to have rights'[6] – are catastrophic indeed.[7] As recent European history teaches us, the price to pay for the personal absence of citizenship, or statelessness, may and can be annihilation. In this exact regard, therefore, editorial critique of the CJEU, or the 'costliness' of its citizenship jurisprudence, must be immediately and very carefully distinguished.

In the modern law of the nation state, the duality of citizenship is concretised in the distinction that is drawn between nationality law and the laws apportioning the rights that attach to individual citizens. Nationality law governs the exclusionary facet of citizenship, delineating exactly who belongs and who does not belong to the community of citizens gathered together under the umbrella of one nation.[8] Thereafter, the inclusion of individual citizens within the enabled community – or sovereign State – is paradigmatically assured by means of a threefold scheme of civic, political and social rights, which fulfils Ralf Dahrendorf's dictum that citizens themselves can only become sovereign within the state – and, extrapolating, will only then owe and offer it allegiance[9] – where guaranteed entitlements insure against the vagaries of life such that the citizen always has a voice that might be asserted against fate.[10]

[5] For citizenship theorists, the enduring tragedy is one that this statement also holds true for liberally flavoured, contractual-based conceptions of citizenship: the 'unbounded' granting of rights nonetheless implies a contract of trust, of paction within and with the universal liberal ideal, which cannot but lead to domination as and between the liberal order and its non-liberal subjects. See, UK Preuß, 'Disconnecting Constitutions from Statehood: Is Global Constitutionalism a Viable Concept?' in P Dobner and M Loughlin (eds), *The Twilight of Constitutionalism* (Oxford, Oxford University Press, 2010) 23, for his analysis of the 'Achilles heel' within global constitutionalism; see, for illuminating commentary, C Volk, 'From Nomos to Lex: Hannah Ahrendt on Law, Politics and Order' (2010) 23 *Leiden Journal of International Law* 759.

[6] By virtue of the right to define the content of individual rights within the sovereign or *effective* political community; see, for discussion and details, Volk (n 5) 759–60; H Lindahl, 'Finding a Place for Freedom, Security and Justice: The European Union's Claim to Territorial Unity' (2004) 29 *ELR* 461.

[7] In terms both of the 'internal' withdrawal of citizenship and the 'external' refusal of nation states to recognise stateless individuals.

[8] Typically on one of two bases: a communitarian basis founded in race, language, culture or religion (*ius sanguinis*); or a contractual basis founded in concordance with the ideals of the *res publica* of citizens (*ius soli*).

[9] See, M Everson, 'The Legacy of the Market Citizen' in J Shaw and G More (eds), *New Legal Dynamics of European Union* (Oxford, Clarendon Press, 1995) 73; further, for justification of extrapolation, M Everson, '"Subjects" or "Citizens" of "Erewhon?" Law and Non-Law in the Development of a "British Citizenship"' (2003) 7 *Citizenship Studies* 57.

[10] R Dahrendorf, *Der moderne soziale Konflikt*, (Stuttgart, Deutsche Verlagsanstalt, 1992), building on the seminal work of, or 'story told' about, citizenship by Marshall, see TH Marshall (1953) *Citizenship and Social Class* (London, Pluto Press, 1992).

Citizenship is highly valuable, but it is also inexorably closed to the non-citizen, with all the issues of individual cost that that entails. Or is it? 'No', intones the CJEU: taking the unpromising material of the highly restricted and 'ancillary' citizenship of the European Union introduced by the Maastricht Treaty (now, Article 20 TFEU), the eternally activist Court of Justice has famously fashioned its own 'avant-garde' citizenship, thereby seemingly overcoming Hannah Arendt's assertion that the individual is inexorably located in 'time and space'.[11] In a series of ever more extraordinary cases, stretching from *Sala* to *Zambrano*, from *Chen* to *Grzelcyk* and to *Rottman*,[12] the Court has weaved its activist jurisprudential spell, interlacing borrowed human rights doctrines together with its own proportionality principle, in order both to decouple the enjoyment of EU citizenship from the award of nationality and to prise open once-closed national welfare settlements, so as to force them to provide social rights, or necessary succour, to the indigent stranger.

To the extent that the CJEU has overcome certain of the exclusionary facets of citizenship, has opened up the benefits of EU citizenship to non-Member State nationals and has extended social citizenship across national borders to forge a very particular form of trans-European solidarity,[13] the Court can be argued to be responding creatively to a 'progressive' zeitgeist within an increasingly globalised civil society. In this view, and where critique of the Court is also qualified in terms of approval of its final decision ('even if the outcome is correct') judicial avant-gardism is just as surely a mirror to, for example, post-modern rejections of constructed identity, or the cynically imposed social order that the introduction of a national norm of citizenship has so often implied: 'the historical "trick" to the rise of a nation state will be to find a horizontal solidarity for the existing [class] stratification and a rationale that using a state apparatus to protect the nation makes sense'.[14]

By contrast, in a post-national and individualised world, the CJEU is to be found in the vanguard of social movements that are chipping away at the false consciousness of constructed collectivism, and which are at last forging forms of citizenship that are responsive to individual realities and individual needs.

Yet, criticism is nonetheless telling. In common with all avant-garde movements, the Court's 'opaque' jurisprudence is an affront to structured legal form: the 'systematic legitimacy' of European law is undermined as the Court responds

[11] For Arendt, see Lindahl (n 6); for analysis of the avant-garde nature of EU citizenship, see G Rene De Groot and A Seling, *Case Comment* (Case C-135/08 *Janko Rottman*) (2011) 7 *European Constitutional Law Review* 150 (pro-CJEU); and HU Jessurun D'Oliveira, *Case Comment* (Case C-135/08 *Janko Rottman*) (2011) 7 *European Constitutional Law Review* 138 (anti-CJEU).

[12] Case C-85/96, *Maria Martinez Sala v Freistaat Bayern* [1998] ECR I-2691; Case C-200/02 *Zhu and Chen* [2004] ECR I-9925; C-184/99 *Grzelcyk v Centre Public d'aide sociale d'Ottignies-Louvain-la-Neuve* [2001] ECR I-6193; Case C-135/08 *Janko Rottman v Freistaat Bayern* [2010] ECR I-1449 (Grand Chamber).

[13] Again, viewed negatively, A Somek, 'Solidarity Decomposed: Being and Time in European Citizenship' (2007) 32 *ELR* 787.

[14] A cynicism identified, for example, by K Deutsch, paraphrased and cited in N Fligstein, *Euro-clash: The EU, European Identity and the Future of Europe* (Oxford, Oxford University Press, 2008) 130.

sympathetically, but arbitrarily, to adverse individual circumstance. The 'credibility' of European law is strained as the Court acts as a 'unilateral constitutional' actor, transforming EU citizenship from a status that is ancillary to national citizenship to one which has 'substance' of its own.[15] The CJEU is being revolutionary, but a price is also being paid for its citizenship jurisprudence, at least with regard to the coherence of EU law. Accordingly, the exact same question may be asked of recent CJEU jurisprudence that is asked of all avant-garde undertakings: is the challenge to legal form and structure which it entails sustainable and one which might be resolved within a new grammar and semantic of citizenship law? Alternatively, is the avant-garde moment just that; a *moment* of paradox, which will inevitably founder on its own contradictions?

In seeking to answer this question, however, this chapter comes to an uncompromisingly negative conclusion. The Court of Justice is undoubtedly seeking to ameliorate the exclusionary impacts of the vehicle of citizenship; nonetheless, and where its Article 20 case law is set in the far wider context of its multiple relationships with the European or 'potential' European – as consumer and as market citizen – the Court's jurisprudence begins to dissolve into a morass of unthinking sentimentality, aggressive Europeanism and an all-too-ready preparedness to equate the universalist aspirations of European law with the lowest common denominator of neoliberal socio-economic organisation. More particularly, taking on the mantle of Eugen Ehrlich's 'judge-king' in seeking to respond to social reality, but failing, at the same time, to find a coherent scheme of legitimation for its seemingly progressive law,[16] the Court has also placed the normative integrity of European law as a whole in doubt. Its sentimentality is particular, not general (section II). In common with traditional political regimes, it has instrumentalised citizenship for its own integrationist ends, or has – more radically – made a scientific unit of the European consumer (section III). It has also fatally conflated economic provision with legal entitlement (section IV). Certainly, the traditional concept of citizenship may appear incongruous in the current global social context. Nonetheless, the CJEU's effort to adjust its citizenship to the modern world around it has revealed only the limitations of law. Most importantly, the CJEU has thereby likewise overlooked one of Hannah Arendt's most fundamental insights: the vehicle of citizenship also encapsulates and reflects the establishment of a structured relationship between the legal and political system that guarantees the *voice* of the citizenry – and to the exact degree that the Court has forgotten 'our voice', we are all paying the price for EU citizenship (section V).

[15] Nic Shuibhne (n 2) 162.

[16] For the European battle to justify a law that responds appropriately to its social environment, see M Everson and J Eisner, with reference to Ehrlich and the free law tradition of the early 20th century, *The Making of a European Constitution: Judges and Law beyond Constitutive Power* (London, Routledge-Cavendish, 2007).

II THE COSMOPOLITAN CITIZEN BEYOND NATION AND HISTORY

Hans Lindahl has reminded us of just how powerful Arendt's concept of 'spatiality' is. The notion of space is:

> not merely a geographical term. It relates not so much, and not primarily, to a piece of land as to the space between individuals in a group whose members are bound to, and at the same time separated and protected from, each other by all kinds of relationships, based on a common language, religion, a common history, customs, and laws.[17]

Writing against the post-war backdrop of Europe's proven moral turpitude, its failure to secure the most basic of rights of the millions of murdered dead, who had seen their citizenship and concomitant protection negated, its continuing complicity in the mass displacement of the millions of individuals who had found themselves on the wrong side of redrawn borders, Arendt's sorrowful observation that 'Freedom, where it existed as tangible reality, has always been spatially limited',[18] her assertion that human security can only be found within time and place, was not an intentionalist statement of sovereign exclusion. Instead it was a highly ambivalent recognition that freedom is only ever secured within a substantive realm of collective nation and history – which contemporaneously and inexorably imperils freedom – and it is this ambivalence which has likewise led Hans Lindahl to conclude that, with its constitution of a legal space of European values, the EU has also reasserted, with all its negative connotations, a *place* of European nation and history, a European *place* of exclusion.[19]

In other words, a curiously differentiated legislative regime, whereby Union citizens are afforded specific, if limited, rights, third country nationals are afforded limited recognition,[20] and asylum seekers are subject to a common framework of control,[21] has not ended exclusion in Europe, but has rather reinforced it within a binary legal code, whereby the 'legally resident' take their stratified place within a European space, which protects individual Europeans, one from the other, and Europeans from *the* other, such that 'the illegal', both within Europe and without, are left bereft, knocking at the firmly closed doors of solidarity and recognition. The European other dies daily in the waters of the Mediterranean, or languishes in the no-man's-land of detention centres, just as the Lisbon Treaty promises its citizens 'an area of freedom, security and justice' without internal frontiers

[17] H Arendt, *Eichmann in Jerusalem: A Report on the Banality of Evil* (London, Penguin, 1994) 262. See, also, H Arendt, *The Human Condition* (Chicago, Chicago University Press, 1958) 52. Cited by Lindahl (n 6).

[18] *On Revolution* (London, Penguin Classics, 1990).

[19] Lindahl (n 6).

[20] As family members under Dir 2004/38 on the rights of Union Citizens and their family members [2004] OJ L158/77; and long-term residents under Dir 2003/109 concerning the status of third country nationals who are long-term residents [2004] OJ L16/44.

[21] See C Barnard, *The Substantive Law of the EU: The Four Freedoms* (Oxford, Oxford University Press, 2004) for comprehensive details on the disturbing differentiated categorisation of individuals in Europe.

(Article 67 TFEU). Spatiality and temporality have inexorably returned to haunt Europe and, with them, the pressing questions of which are the narratives of history and which are the narratives of nation, which are unfolding within our common realm of legal place.

For the CJEU, however, the immediate and judicially liberating answer to this question might be argued to be 'none': no history and no nation. From the inception of Union citizenship in the Maastricht Treaty, the Court's citizenship jurisprudence has surprised and acted as counterweight to the establishment of European spatiality: first, decoupling the right of free movement of European citizens (Article 20(2a) TFEU) from the more restrictive status of 'European as worker' under Article 45 TFEU (*Maria Martinez Sala*);[22] secondly, cutting the Gordian knot between citizenship and nationality, extending 'associative' rights of EU citizenship to TCNs or third country nationals (*Zhu and Chen*);[23] thirdly, questioning constructed solidarity and opening up closed national benefits systems to EU nationals and their associates (*Baumbast*);[24] and latterly, even seeming to suggest that rights of EU citizenship have 'substance' of their own and will accrue even where there is no question of movement across national borders (*Ruiz Zambrano*).[25] Vitally, and armed only with a hotchpotch of stated citizenship rights,[26] the CJEU has thereby defied the Council's imposition of European spatiality. Where the Council and its Member States have grudgingly granted legislative provision to allow for movement of EU citizens and legally resident TCNs throughout Europe – presumably in order 'to encourage labour migration as a way of increasing the European Union's competitiveness'[27] – the Court has deployed the human right to a 'family life' (Article 8 ECHR), together with the principle of proportionality, to unravel and to extend the limited protection afforded by EU citizenship and to begin to construct a cosmopolitan citizenship far beyond the reach of the imagined European Republic.

The key to this wonder, however, is also its weakness. Nation and history are discarded, not in a politically constitutive moment, but are instead swept aside in an emotionally founded *interpositio auctoritatis*, or situational assertion of legal meaning, in which European judges respond to individual circumstances and want. Facts and emotions matter. The decoupling of enjoyment of citizenship rights from nationality follows as the CJEU responds to a simple human happening, or to the birth of a child within the EU, allowing her mother and 'primary carer', a Chinese national, to travel freely with her across Member State frontiers so that she might in fact enjoy her newly won EU citizenship, granted by virtue of unlimited *ius soli* then operative in relation to the entire Irish island, and not only

[22] Case C-85/96 *Maria Martinez Sala v Freistaat Bayern* [1998] ECR I-2691.

[23] Case C-200/02 *Zhu and Chen* [2004] ECR I-9925.

[24] Case C-413/99 *R and Baumbast* [2002] ECR I-7901.

[25] Case C-34/09 *Ruiz Zambrano*, judgment of 8 March 2011, nyr.

[26] For example, in addition to the rights of free movement, guaranteeing such minor 'municipal rights as local voting rights and consular protection' (Art 20(2) TFEU).

[27] A Wiesbrock, 'Free Movement of Third-country Nationals in the European Union: The Illusion of Inclusion' (2010) 35 *ELR* 455, 455.

within the confines of the Republic of Ireland.[28] The nation founded either in pre-communitarian bounds of belonging or in concordance with the ideals of the founding republican moment, is hostile to both child and mother. The CJEU and its EU citizenship are not: the human right to a family life demands that Mrs Zhu must be allowed to travel with her daughter. National and historical indifference to the fate of the individual – or, the 'the blind-side' of exclusionary nationality law – must likewise cede to the compelling facts of personal need and to the legal contortions of an empathetic Court. An unemployed Somali mother of four children might claim a right to residence in the UK as the primary carer of her children, on the basis of a distant and very brief period of UK-based work enjoyed by her Danish spouse: the Council's recent efforts to restrict non-economic free movement to cases where the Union citizen is economically self-sufficient (Directive 2004/38)[29] cannot repeal or offer lesser protection than the earlier Regulation 1612/68, protecting the residency of EU workers – and, by association their associates – on the basis of their family's educational requirements.[30]

The cases are legion and, importantly, have also begun to extend their empathetic reach to the regime governing TCNs. Here, for example, any arbitrary distinctions drawn by Member States in order to delineate who might benefit from the right to family reunification under Directive 2003/86 will also be reviewed by the Court in the light of the proportionality principle, or rather, in the light of circumstances and sympathy. A Moroccan couple of over thirty years' standing may not be denied reunification simply because the Dutch government demands that TCNs possess a 'sufficient' income; a sufficiency that is – perversely – 120 per cent of the income deemed to be 'sufficient' for Dutch families.[31] The language of the Court's jurisprudence is a legal language; a formal language of human rights, equitable maintenance of protection and the principle of proportionality. But the grammar of the Court is a grammar of emotion, an emotion whose effects are electrifying: nation is shorn of hostile meaning and indifferent history is forgotten as the *ius Europeaum* furnishes 'the right outcome', or simply engages with the 'real' other far beyond imagined community.

With this, the CJEU – in counterpoint to the Council and the Member States – is responding to the post-national zeitgeist, or in a paraphrased Habermasian construction, appears to be including the other in a simple 'non-levelling and non-appropriating' act of recognition.[32] Nevertheless, the judge-kings of the CJEU are also only the sum total of their emotions and it is here that circumstance may challenge law as European Justices exhibit particular rather than universal

[28] Case C-200/02 *Zhu and Chen* [2004] ECR I-9925.

[29] It is important to note, however, that the Council has, for all of the reservations of the Member States, also responded to certain of the universalist aspirations of the Court – Dir 2004/38 may also be regarded as codifying the earlier case law of the CJEU (to the degree that the Directive deploys the term 'proportionality').

[30] Case C-310/08 *Harlow LBC v Ibrahim* [2010] ECR I-1065 (Grand Chamber).

[31] Case C-578/08 *Chakroun* [2010] ECR I-1839 (2nd Chamber).

[32] J Habermas, *The Inclusion of the Other: Studies in Political Theory* (Cambridge, Polity Press, 1998) 44.

sympathy and a budding cosmopolitan citizenship begins to fall victim to the arbitrary nature of the Court's empathic character. Failed Colombian asylum seekers in Belgium whose children become Belgian by virtue of their birth in that country – as well as their consequent loss of Colombian nationality – are afforded the protection of the *ius Europeaum*: they are primary carers and cannot be removed from Belgium, because this would negate the 'substance' of their children's EU citizenship (*Ruiz Zambrano*). Mrs McCarthy, a UK national, whose Jamaican husband is denied leave to remain in the UK, is less fortunate: Mrs McCarthy, it appears, was not exercising her right of free movement under Directive 2004/38, such that her husband could not benefit from her rights of EU citizenship.[33]

Efforts to distinguish the two cases in law seem doomed to failure. *McCarthy* is a purely 'internal' or national situation, with no element of cross-border movement, and would not trigger the rights of EU citizenship and their consequences for associates of EU citizens under established case law. But, so too, is *Ruiz Zambrano*, which has famously challenged this EU orthodoxy.[34] Equally, when her legal position is compared to that of a TCN claiming a 'human right' of family reunification (*Chakroun*),[35] Mrs McCarthy would seem doubly unfortunate: surely EU law should apply equally to TCNs and citizens, such that the UK's immigration regime might at the very least be subject to a test of proportionality, the non-application of the Family Reunification Directive within the UK notwithstanding?[36] The facts of the two cases are equally difficult to disentangle: certainly the Court might state that Mrs McCarthy, unlike the Zambranos, will not be forced by UK law to leave the EU; but surely she will be so by sentiment. Equally, it would prove difficult to regularise the residency of Belgium children in Colombia;[37] but, so too might it be difficult to regularise the status of Mrs McCarthy in Jamaica. The human right to a family life, unlike the Reunification Directive, is universal and should be enjoyed by all.

The sympathy failure and particularism of the Court is, above all, indicative of the difficulties that bedevil the acts of judge-kings and progressive law. Thus, for example, the adepts of the 'free law' methodologies of the early 19th century (*Freirechtslehre*) were undoubtedly correct in departing from formal legal method in order to adapt its precepts to the new reality of mass industrialisation.[38] The

[33] Case C-434/09 *McCarthy v Secretary of State for the Home Department*, judgment of 5 May 2011, nyr (Grand Chamber).

[34] Nic Shuibhne (n 2).

[35] Case C578/08 *Chakroun* [2010] ECR I-1839.

[36] Council Dir 2003/86/EC on the right to family reunification [2003] OJ L251/12. After all, the Court is quite remarkably prepared to subject national decisions to withdraw citizenship – the primary expression of the continuing sovereignty of the nation state – to the general application of the proportionality test within EU law, Case C-135/08 *Janko Rottman v Freistaat Bayern* [2010] ECR I-1449.

[37] This is all the more the case since it was not obvious that the parents could return safely to Colombia given the fact that they were asylum seekers and that their presence in Belgium was due to non-refoulement.

[38] Above all, the inappropriateness of notions of 'equality of bargaining power'; see for details, Everson and Eisner (n 16).

movement nonetheless remained forever vulnerable to Max Weber's critique that this 'materialisation' of law would, by virtue of its inevitable lack of coherence or structured method, undermine the authority of the legal system as a whole. Equally, however, the struggles of the Court are also a first indication of the deeper paradoxes that continue to bedevil all notions of cosmopolitan citizenship. As noted, citizenship is a valuable status precisely because it is a closed status – one which creates collective solidarity – and it is here that the sympathy failures of the CJEU, its inability to show empathy to the collective, become particularly telling.

Armed with its own brand of situational empathy, the CJEU has begun to establish a notion of 'European solidarity' through its notable efforts to expand the addressees of national solidarity collectives to include the figure of the impecunious, but needy, stranger. Importantly, it has done so in the face of Council opposition: predictably, Member State action to implement the right of free movement within the Union has seen the re-emergence of economic qualifications within the concept of European citizenship; this time, with regard to the assertion of the primacy of the national solidarity collective. Directive 2004/38 on free movement re-emphasises the closed nature of the national solidarity collective – or the exclusionary notion that the redistributive social benefits of citizenship are reserved for members of the nation alone – by granting EU citizens and their family members a right of residence throughout Europe only 'as long as they do not become an unreasonable burden on the social assistance system of the host Member State' (Article 6).

The operative word here, the measure of the willingness of the Member States to open up national solidarity to afford real succour to the indigent Union citizen, is to be found in the word 'unreasonable';[39] and is it is here, too, that the determination of the CJEU to pry open that door further is demonstrated. Prior to the implementation of Directive 2004/38, the Court had already firmly signalled its universalist welfare aspirations in cases such as *Grzelczyk*.[40] In *Baumbast*, where a German national had not satisfied UK requirements that he maintain sufficient sickness insurance for himself and his family, the Court accordingly declared that national legislation must be 'proportionate'.[41] As has been noted,[42] the imposition of the Union law principle of proportionality to all subsequent national legislation implementing Directive 2004/38 therefore also amounted to a 'constitutional review' of the efforts of the Council to set the legislative limits to national solidarity through the judicial frontline assessment of the impacts of a notion of 'unreasonable burden' in the light of everyday cases in individual Member States.

[39] M Dougan, 'The Constitutional Dimension to the Case Law on Union Citizenship' (2006) 36 *ELR* 613.

[40] Case C-184/99 *Grzelcyk v Centre Public d'aide sociale d'Ottignies-Louvain-la-Neuve* [2001] ECR I-6193, stating that the fact that Dir 93/96 regulating movement of students ([1993] OJ L317/59) did not provide for benefits for students, similarly did not preclude extension of national benefits to EU students where such students found themselves in the same needy circumstances as national students.

[41] Case C-413/99 *R and Baumbast* [2002] ECR I-7901.

[42] Dougan (n 39).

This constitutionally oriented aspiration to review the actions of the Council in setting limits to national solidarity collectives has also inexorably implicated the CJEU in a series of intricate and often contradictory judgments, concerning the intimate tax, benefits and financial dealings of a host of EU citizens from students to pensioners.[43] Nonetheless, such painstaking judicial labour has also brought with it immense benefits in terms of the pursuit of the Court's dedicated campaign to reorient Union citizenship in line with common understandings of the simple humanity that is due from man to man under circumstances of real human want. Contractual citizenship and solidarity is blind to Mr Baumbast's, or the geographical stranger's, need for immediate medical care for his family. This need not be so declares the CJEU: the measure of solidarity within Europe is not to be negated by spatially bounded history; still less is it to be found within a simple reciprocal display of solidarity between actuarial national calculations of cost and benefit in social provision.[44] Instead, a miracle of extra-European recognition is invoked into being as the Court's sympathetic act of observing and responding forensically to the needs of individual citizens transforms a once technical yardstick of procedural legal review, proportionality, into a far more indistinct realm of substantive adjudication, open to the emotionally founded *interposito auctoritas*, within which a 'miracle' of European solidarity is born – a miracle of unbounded love.[45]

Immediate critique of – or the notable degree of controversy and puzzlement about – the CJEU's inconsistency in social cases is thus readily explained:[46] a process whereby the identity of European citizens is negotiated in emotional reflex with a concrete other, is not easily explained in formal legal categories, still less easily recognised within a proceduralist legal paradigm – how can a collective national expression of shared love ever be proportionally balanced against the miracle of universal and unbounded solidarity? An emotionally non-systematic Court has once again fallen victim to Weber's critique of the materialist judge-king. At a deeper level of political theory, however, the Court's proven hostility to the Council, to the Member States and their closed solidarity collectives inevitably gives rise to its own contradictions and paradoxes: can collectively established love ever be tolerated, and, if not, how can love for the individual ever be *effectively* expressed?

[43] Here, it suffices to note only Case C-258/04 *Ioannidis* [2005] ECR I-8275, where the Court continued to struggle to identify 'an effective and genuine link' between applicant and host State.

[44] Both Dougan (n 39) and Somek (n 13) confirm – each in their own way – that the CJEU has moved beyond simple notions of reciprocity to justify its creation of European solidarity. In Somek, this idea is to be found in the notion that European solidarity is a 'miracle' drawn forth by virtue of empathetic empirical observation; within Dougan, the constitutional review of the actions of the Council, a European figure, provides us with a distinct European (ie not nationally reciprocal) form of solidarity.

[45] Somek (n 13) recalling Unger's description of social solidarity as an irrational act of collective love: *Law in Modern Society* (New York, Free Press, 1975).

[46] See, in particular, Somek's musings on the complex differences in the treatment of students, pensioners and what-have-you, in 'Solidarity Decomposed' (n 13).

As Alex Somek has convincingly argued,[47] one of the most telling cases in this regard is that of *Commission v Austria*.[48] At one level, *Commission v Austria* is a simple non-discrimination case with no connection to citizenship jurisprudence under Article 20 TFEU: the 'open-door' policy of university entry within Austria, guaranteeing university admission to all Austrians holding a high school diploma, regardless of grade, was held here to be indirectly discriminatory against non-Austrian EU nationals who were required to qualify themselves for admission in line with their own national practices. Nonetheless, the facts of the case do also encompass a measure of irrationality, or social love, a collective decision that 'everyone who has made it through school [should be] rewarded with a fresh start';[49] a measure of national empathy, with very real socially redistributive consequences, which closes the space of Austrian education to non-Austrians, just as it makes inclusive reparation for jointly experienced memories of adolescent self-discovery and academic underachievement. By the same token, then, the CJEU's brutally rational, but 'unsolicited . . . advice' to Austria 'to establish "entry examinations or the requirement of a minimal qualification to avoid the system's collapse"'[50] would seem also to entail a lack of emotional solidarity with the underachieving teenager of all of our pasts.

III THE EUROPEAN BURGHER AND A TECHNOLOGY OF CONSUMPTION

Encompassing not only a vision of individual security and individual empowerment, but also and vitally so, mechanisms – more particularly, the franchise – which foster the establishment of collective solidarity and a (redistributive) enabling notion of the 'common good', the vehicle of citizenship inevitably poses complex philosophical and practical challenges, ill suited to treatment within a judicial vocabulary of emotional response. Arendt's concerns, her reluctant identification of a paradigm of spatiality, remain valid, if highly uncomfortable: as Ralf Dahrendorf notes, the legal 'entitlements' of citizenship are distinct in their origins from the economic 'provisions' of the market economy; yet, following TH Marshall, the liberating and enabling core of a modern paradigm of citizenship remains its redistributive element, its reapportionment of economic provisions by means of the award of social rights, in order to give concrete effect to legal entitlements.[51]

At a practical political level, a socially democratic vehicle of citizenship accordingly entails a constant and difficult balancing act between the distinct but entwined entitlements of law and the provisions of the market: an entitlement

[47] Ibid.

[48] Case C-147/03 *Commission of the European Communities v Republic of Austria* [2005] ECR I-5969.

[49] Somek also notes the potentially regressive social impacts of the decision: are those failing to obtain a grammar school education (typically, from the less-advantaged Austrian classes) to be excluded from Austrian educational life?

[50] Somek (n 13).

[51] Dahrendorf (n 10).

that cannot be satisfied – perhaps because the market has been repressed by over-eager interventionism – is no entitlement at all. By the same philosophical token, however, the redistributive element within citizenship still defies all assaults upon its exclusionary characteristics that derive from universalist impulses: leaving aside all 'arbitrary' closure founded in pre-political ties of language, culture or blood, the act of redistribution nonetheless requires even the most republican or inclusive of citizenship communities to identify the finite polity, or political *space*, within which the politics of the common – redistributive – good can be fought out. The CJEU's strength – its ability to disregard nation and history – consequently becomes its weakness as its universalism blinds it both to the practical exercise of the balancing of provision against entitlement, and to the philosophical effort to establish the common good of the *res publica*.

But is this the whole picture? Recent eye-catching Article 20 TFEU jurisprudence, inspired by the universalism of human rights, represents only one short moment in the history of CJEU encounters with individual Europeans. Casting a far wider net and, in particular, focusing upon the notable relationship established between the CJEU and the European consumer, we are rewarded with contrasting insights into the Court's treatment of entitlements and provisions, and of its wider struggles to identify the European common good:

> The Member States must not crystallize given consumer habits so as to consolidate an advantage acquired by national industries concerned to comply with them (Case 178/84, *German Beer*).[52]

The story of the creation of the 'European consumer' by the CJEU is well documented[53] and once again striking in terms of the ability of the judge-kings of the Court to mirror a zeitgeist which has rebelled against the 'infantilising' of consumers within restrictive regimes of regulation and hierarchical consumer protection. Within this narrative, the Court's re-characterisation of the individual European as a 'rational', 'confident' and 'informed' consumer, as well as its championing of 'active' modes of European consumption, might be argued to reflect and reinforce an increasingly individualistic pattern of social organisation in which consumption is seen not simply as an expression of self-gratification, but rather as a diffusely liberating political act.[54]

Beyond such immediate social intervention, however, the Court's relationship with the European consumer similarly impacts upon an analysis of citizenship within the European Union: firstly, since its jurisprudence has reallocated economic

[52] Case 178/84 *Commission v Germany* [1987] ECR 1227.

[53] S Weatherhill, *EC Consumer Law and Policy* (London, Longman, 1997); M Everson, 'Legal Constructions of the Consumer' in F Trentmann (ed), *The Making of the Consumer Knowledge, Power and Identity in the Modern World* (Oxford, Berg, 2006); M Dani, 'Assembling the Fractured European Consumer' (2011) 36 *ELR* 362.

[54] 'Diffuse' in the sense that disconnected individual action nonetheless secures social change; most strikingly, within a vein of queer theory, which argues that the conspicuous act of 'sexual consumption' is a political act: see F Trentmann (ed), *The Making of the Consumer Knowledge, Power and Identity in the Modern World* (Oxford, Berg, 2006).

provisions within a distinctly European market, unravelling national conceptions of the 'citizen-consumer', and creating a European *space* of economic self-expression; and secondly, at a far deeper level of legal semantic, because the universalist impulses of the CJEU are now reborn within an 'economic technology', or a 'scientification' of the European consumer and of the European common good.[55]

Given the intensity of CJEU encounters with the European consumer, it comes as a surprise to find that the EU gained its first competence for consumer affairs with the advent of the Maastricht Treaty and, in particular, Article 129(a) guaranteeing a 'high level of protection' for European consumers. The Court had nonetheless been active long before this time, in particular, having been called upon to confront aggressively the 'nationally embedded' consumer during its great period of activism at the time of the creation of the European single market.[56] The core problem facing the economically integrationist judge-kings of the then European Court of Justice was the great swathe of materially interventionist economic regulation, which Member States had begun to introduce in the 1960s in the wake of the thalidomide crisis:

> The consumer is no longer seen merely as a purchaser and user of goods and services for personal, family or group purposes but also as a person concerned with the various facets of society which might affect him directly or indirectly as a consumer.[57]

The sentiments of the time, most cogently expressed by President Kennedy, were reproduced almost verbatim in an early EEC Council Resolution and coalesced around the figure of the 'citizen-consumer'. So, the argument ran, the mass industrialisation that followed World War II had alienated consumers from the means of production, such that the multiple characters of citizens as, say, producers, workers and purchasers of goods and services, had been detached the one from the other with all the usual socially regressive consequences of painful divorce. The figure of the citizen-consumer and a mass of interventionist regulation re-assembled the legion personalities of the citizenry, all the while redirecting the provisions of the market to a politically established programme of the common economic good. At the same time, however, and from the viewpoint of the European Court, the mass of national intervention – in areas as diverse as competition policy, labour law, product regulation and marketing control[58] – designed to ensure 'the freedom from harm'[59] of the citizenry had reinforced the distinctive nature of national economies, presenting immutable barriers to the completion of the European market.

At this one level, the response of the Court – its recourse to a principle of proportionality that subjects national intervention justified with reference to consumer

[55] See, for exhaustive consideration, M Everson and Ch Joerges, 'Consumer Citizenship in Postnational Constellations?' in K Soper and F Trentmann (eds), *Citizenship and Consumption* (New York, Palgrave Macmillan, 2007).

[56] Everson (n 53).

[57] EEC Council Resolution on a 'Preliminary Programme for a Consumer Protection and Information Policy ([1975] OJ C92/1).

[58] For the – inevitable – lack of coherence in the interventionist programme to secure the character of the citizen-consumer, see Everson (n 5).

[59] D Bollier and J Claybrook, *Freedom from Harm* (Washington, Public Citizen Project,1986) 31.

protection to a forensic examination which tests stated regulatory aims against their effects – can be welcomed as a long overdue rationalisation of stagnating and infantilising 'welfarist' regulation that merely protected entrenched industrial interests: additives in beer would not harm the health of German drinkers (*German Beer*);[60] much less would the addition of wholemeal to pasta undermine the welfare of Italian diners.[61] At yet another level, however, and as has been cogently noted,[62] the Court's rationalising *interpositio auctoritatis*, its efforts to de-culture the European consumer and prise him or her out of nationally constructed consumption culture, also entails a 'subjectification' of its own: that is, the remoulding of a European consumer as a confident and informed consumer,[63] as an active and frontier-busting consumer, [64] and, consequently, as a 'European burgher' who might forge the space of a specifically European market, and of Europe itself, through the atomistic act of consumption.

The modern conception of citizenship remains closely entwined with modern visions of the market economy and of the nation and, for all that the CJEU's encounters with the European consumer may also sound a faint echo of a pre-modern history – one which witnessed English judges unravel feudal relations through the creation of individual civic (contractual) rights[65] – they recall, far more, the nation-building law of the late 19th century. The CJEU's rational and active European consumer may accordingly be argued most strongly to resemble Bismark's burgher (*Wirtschaftsbürger*) or the 'sovereign consumer', upon whose 'commercial talent' and whose ability to overcome the limitations of parochial localised economies, the modern nation state would be built.[66] Within this nation-building model, 'freedom from harm' is instead pre-dated by contractual autonomy, or by an emphasis upon a neo-classical economic paradigm, within which the 'freedom to' of the talented Burgher furnishes the entrepreneurial impetus for the clearing of the space of the national economy and thus of the nation.[67]

To the degree that such a characterisation of the CJEU's encounters with the European consumer is convincing, it can similarly be argued that, in addition to

[60] Case 178/84 *Commission v Germany* [1987] ECR 1227.

[61] Case 90/86 *Zoni* [1988] ECR I-4285.

[62] Dani (n 53) 363, with reference to the work of Nikolas Rose.

[63] Under the principle of proportionality, 'labelling' of goods would act as a less competitively disruptive mode of consumer protection regulation, allowing for the movement of 'de-cultured' beer and wine across European frontiers.

[64] Case C-362/88 *GB-INNO-BM* [1990] ECR I-667: 'Free movement of goods concerns not only traders but also individuals. It requires, particularly in frontier areas that consumers resident in one Member State may travel freely to the territory of another Member State to shop under the same conditions as the local population.'

[65] TH Marshall (n 10).

[66] Everson (n 53): the sovereignty of the consumer was founded in contractual autonomy and legal refusals to intervene in private relations in order to protect consumers. Exemplary, late-19th century interpretation of the Swiss commercial code, 'The unitary conception of contract law "is justified by the far higher degree of equal access to education in Switzerland than in all other European nations and by the commercial talents of the Swiss people"' cited in E Kramer, 'Zur Konzeption des Konsumentenschutzes' (1986) 270 *Kritische Vierteljahresschrift* 270, 286.

[67] See Bollier and Claybrook, *Freedom from Harm* (1986) for the original, historical, transition from 'freedom to' to 'freedom from'.

emotion, the Court is also powered by a far more instrumentalist integrationist interest, wherein adjudication is less a matter of establishing legal entitlement and more a process of facilitation for unfettered market operation or for the establishment of economic provisions within a distinct European rather than national space. European citizens are subjectified and harnessed to the project of European market- and nation-building. Unravelling established national regulatory complexes which balance provision against entitlement – or, indeed, even negating conceptions of legal entitlement which emphasise the distinctness of (universal) legal right from (particular) economic provision – the judge-kings of an activist CJEU might thus be suggested to have reversed the post-war construction of national citizenship, reverting to an older instrumentalist conception in order to further the European integration project. But, far more challengingly, the Court may also be argued to have impacted upon a conception of a European common good, again seeking universalism beyond the politics of finite communities; in this context, however, within a legal methodology of scientification and economic technology.

Adjudicating in matters of consumer protection, for which the Union has long lacked a legal competence, and promoting a diffuse consumer interest, in which 'social-political expression' is atomised within a myriad of individual acts of self-gratification, the CJEU's judge-kings might nevertheless be argued to have been in structured pursuit of a conception of a European common good; one anchored within the putative universalism of market operation. Once again, the deployment of a principle of proportionality in order to assert the authority of the *interpositio auctoritatis* is central to the Court's efforts to readjust the strictures of formal law to social reality, or to integrationist demands; but, here, the moment of judicial decision is dominated not by emotion, but by rationality. In common with the early 20th-century adepts of free law methodologies, the Court looks beyond law to disciplines such as science and economics, which claim to reveal the objective truth of the world to law and which simultaneously preserve the coherence and thus legitimacy of legal method: 'The mechanism for the discovery of necessary legal change' was not one that might be 'discrete or casual'; instead, legal change, the adaptation of the abstract categories of law to social reality, should be 'organised and continuous in nature'.[68] In the world of European consumption, organisation is accordingly furnished by hard science, continuity by modern, predominantly neoliberal economics. Real rather than imagined dangers to the consumer can be identified by science, and an objective rather than constructed European common good can be found in economics: additives will not harm German or Italian consumers and all European – and, logically, non-European – citizens will benefit from 'limitless' consumer-driven growth.

The conundrum of an exclusionary citizenship is solved: objective universal truths displace the constructed political values of the finite community of citizens

[68] H Laski, *A Grammar of Politics*, 4th edn (London, Allen & Unwin, 1958) 545; paraphrased in Everson and Eisner n 16).

and open up the potential for wealth and welfare for all. Amen. Nonetheless, problems remain: the jurisprudence of the Court is founded within a particular personification of the European subject, that of the rationally confident and consuming individual. But what of the very real persona of the 'anxious consumer',[69] or the stubbornly 'ethical consumer';[70] and what happens 'when the science runs out'?[71] The answers to these questions are to be found in European cases tackling the thorny issues of advanced modern agricultural methods, or the presence of genetically modified organisms (GMOs) or growth hormones within processes of agricultural production.[72] In these cases, however, the disturbing factor is not one that the Court departs from its organised and continuous method and responds to the diffuse concerns of anxious and ethical European consumers in order to confirm European bans on GMOs and hormones by means of retreat into the transcendental nonsense of legal formalism;[73] but, rather that the Court has *no* language, *no* semantic within which it might directly engage with the concerns of the concrete, and often politically motivated European citizen. The *interpositio auctoritatis* has been filled with science and law reborn as an economic technology,[74] which exerts its decisional power to remould the character of now atomised Europeans, but which is similarly deaf to the political, social and ethical values which cannot be integrated within its own scientific and technological grammar.

IV *HOMO ECONOMICUS*

> It would be neither satisfactory nor true to the development of the case law to reduce freedom of movement to a mere standard of promotion of trade between Member States. It is important that the freedoms of movement fit into the broader framework of the objectives of the internal market and European citizenship. At present, freedoms of movement must be understood to be one of the essential elements of the 'fundamental status of nationals of the Member States'. They represent the cross-border dimension of the economic and social status conferred on European citizens.[75]

[69] Dani (n 53).

[70] Everson and Joerges (n 55).

[71] M Everson and E Vos, *Uncertain Risks Regulated* (New York, Routledge, 2008).

[72] See, for example, Case T-144/00 Biret International SA v Council of the European Union [2002] ECR II-17; Case T-13/99 Pfizer Animal Health SA v Council of the European Union [2002] ECR II-3305.

[73] For transcendental nonsense, see F Cohen, 'Transcendental Nonsense and the Functional Approach' (1935) *Columbia Law Review* 809; for similar conclusions in relation to GMOs and hormones, see Dani (n 53).

[74] The term is distilled from Foucault's concept of political technology; see, in particular, *Birth of Biopolitics: Lectures at the College de France, 1978–79* (London, Palgrave Macmillan, 2008).

[75] Opinion of AG Poiares Maduro in Joined Cases C-158 and 159/04 *Alfa Vita Vassilopoulos AE v Greece* [2006] ECR I-8135; cited in A Tryfonidou, 'Further Steps on the Road to Convergence among the Market Freedoms' (2010) 35 *ELR* 36, 36.

Recent developments in the field of the free movement of goods – in particular, the CJEU equalisation of the disparate elements of the EU's system of free movement[76] – are accompanied by a powerful rhetoric of citizenship liberation, which appears all the more remarkable when contrasted with our traditional narratives of citizenship formation. Above all, a shocking note of dissonance is sounded by the simple equation of economic rights (to provide goods, services etc) with the 'social status' of European citizens. TH Marshall's stirring story of the evolution of industrial citizenship within the United Kingdom, for example, subordinates economic rights (as a sub-category of civic rights) to social rights; or does so to the degree that social rights counterbalance economic rights thereby creating allegiance to the alienating state of modernity and the mass modern economy.

For Marshall, citizenship can be traced as a historical and a violent happening, which both creates and tames the market and the state: civic rights – including, most importantly, the right to contract – are medieval artefacts whose post-black death development shattered the feudal system and elevated the feudal subject to the status of a contractual party, who might then forge a new market-based economy; political rights are the child of the 17th century and the struggle by market burghers to assert their growing economic power by means of violent struggle for a share in the political powers of the sovereign; social rights are corrective, status-based mechanisms, politically hard-fought-for by the industrial classes of the 19 and 20 centuries in response to the necessary functional differentiations of the mass economy, as well as the abject indifference of a bourgeois state to inequalities of class. From subjecthood to contract to status: the historical antagonisms captured within the concept of citizenship are then, in turn, seemingly reconciled, as – following the formula given by Dahrendorf – civic, political and social rights are concentrically constitutionalised within the post-war national settlement, furnishing each reborn nation with a normative concept of citizenship, which both recognises its own historical class struggle, and holds it in permanent equilibrium; a concept of citizenship that guarantees not only the market, with its myriad inequalities, but also the means of its social correction within a politically inclusive State.

In such an analysis, rhetorical appeals to the liberating effects of economic rights, their simple equation with the social status of individual Europeans, might consequently be considered to amount to a declaration of war on the part of the judge-kings of the CJEU, a retrograde bourgeois effort to turn back the clock and – echoing Margaret Thatcher – to shatter institutions of class equilibrium for the purposes of economic revolution. The point is vital in practice, as well as elevated academic theory. The industrial class is wholly not dead within Europe, and as convincing sociological analysis has demonstrated,[77] has gained very little from a slow process of European economic integration that has deprived the European working class of ever more political influence; more particularly since it remains

[76] See, for full details, Tryfonidou (n 75).

[77] See Fligstein (n 14).

trapped in national paradigms of social organisation, whilst property-owning and entrepreneurial interests focus the core of their activities on decision-making centres in and around Brussels, rather than national capitals.

Given this conclusion, the analysis might also ask whether adjudicative European law – a confounding *Janus* that engages both in acts of emotional irrationality, just as it draws a rationalist veil of technology over its activities – has made its own particular contribution to the exclusion of the common European man from political sites of antagonistic European class conflict and whether it, too, and not just a diffuse process of economic differentiation, is actively engaged in the bourgeois colonisation of the normative framework of European law. In this context, striking judgments in *Viking*, *Laval* and *Rüffert* have become pivotal,[78] not simply since they have rejected the warnings given by Marx and, more recently, by Polanyi,[79] about the dire and violent consequences of forcing an industrial class into wage competition with itself. But rather, since they have also, with the aid of our old adjudicative friend of 'proportionality', once again excluded a European working class from any possible site of political contestation, within which its antagonistic interests might be presented and asserted. The adjudicative interplay between a Posted Workers Directive,[80] purportedly introduced by the Council in order to regulate potential social dumping within the European market, and primary European 'economic rights' (of establishment and service provision) have thus led in European law to:

(1) the creation of an absolute judicial prohibition against all international solidarity strikes against the hiring of cheap foreign labour (*Viking*);
(2) the imposition of a judicial value of 'proportionality' upon *all* national strikes called in defence of industrial bargaining agreements (*Viking* & *Laval*);
(3) the establishment of a prohibition on the enforcement of local bargaining agreements, as local and national authorities are precluded by the provisions of state aids law from tailoring their tenders in line with such agreements, and Article 3(1) of the Posted Workers Directive is deemed to give European protection only to *universal* provisions of national labour law, such as minimum wage requirements (*Laval* & *Rüffert*).

Not surprisingly, such judgments have drawn a host of outraged comment from scholars, not least since the European Court appears thus to have drawn a coach and horses through the social constitutional settlements of countries, such as Sweden, which, historically, have not maintained minimum wage legislation, but have, instead, reconciled antagonistic class struggle by means of governmental enforcement of union–employer negotiated bargaining agreements. At this one

[78] Case C-438/05 *International Transport Workers' Federation, Finnish Seamen's Union v Viking Line ABP, OÜ Viking Line Eesti* [2007] ECR I-1079; Case C-341/05 *Laval un Partneri Ltd v Svenska Byggnadsarbetareförbundet, Svenska Byggnadsarbetareförbundet, avd. 1, Svenska Elektrikerförbundet* [2007] ECR I-11767; Case C-346/06 *Rechtsanwalt Dr Dirk Rüffert v Land Niedersachsen* [2008] ECR I-1989.

[79] K Polanyi, *The Great Transformation* (1944) (New York, Beacon Press, 2001).

[80] Dir 96/71/EC [1996] OJ L18/1.

level, the CJEU would thus seem to have confirmed that the corporatist model of economic organisation within Europe is dead, and declared – the somewhat untimely – sovereignty of an Anglo-Saxon model of universal welfare provision.[81] Equally, however, the CJEU might thus appear to further have extended the bourgeois colonisation of the framework of European law.

The infamous and shocking historical analogy is the case of *Lochner v New York*, decided by the US Supreme Court in 1905,[82] in which the democratic right of the State of New York to set its own working conditions (including the rights of workers to strike) was overturned with reference to the US Constitution's absolute guarantee for property. Presented by the majority of the Court as a formalistic inevitability, driven simply by the hierarchical precedence of the Constitution over State legislation, the cracked veneer of formalist rationality within the Court was nonetheless readily exposed, as the dissenting judge, Justice Holmes, laconically observed that the democratic right of the States to legislate in this area was also guaranteed by the Constitution. The bourgeois sentiments of the US Supreme Court are readily identified; and so, too, are the bourgeois sentiments of European judge-kings who need not have decided as they did. Above all, bourgeois sentiment becomes most apparent as the useful precedents of a series of social insurance cases are rejected,[83] and the hands of national courts are tied, as our old friend 'proportionality' becomes the impossible yardstick against which social antagonism must be measured. Within earlier social insurance cases – primarily concerning professional 'trade agreements', rather than the industrial bargaining agreements more commonly concluded by the mass trades union movement – the core decision was one that such restrictive practices were per se legitimate mechanisms of social policy, and might only be reviewed under the European competition regime, with an eye to a procedural principle of proportionality, whereby such private arrangements would be reviewed by national courts in order to ensure that they were fair and not abusive in their composition and rates.[84] Such a procedural resolution was also conceivable in the case of collective bargaining agreements; however, here the formula is reversed. Collective bargaining agreements are per se restrictions on European rights; strikes will be contested in national courts in order to ascertain whether they are proportionate with those rights; but, will be so reviewed in their substance, and not in their conduct.

The effect of such a legal construction is a severe curtailment or even foreclosure of the legal strike: a strike, withdrawal of labour, is never substantively proportionate. Certainly, it may be illegally conducted and, here, proportionality may have a real legal meaning, allowing courts to review whether strike ballots

[81] See relevant references in C Joerges and F Rödl, 'Informal Politics, Formalised Law and the "Social Deficit" of European Integration: Reflections after the Judgments of the ECJ in Viking and Laval' (2009) 15 *European Law Journal* 1.

[82] *Lochner v New York* 198 US 45 (1905).

[83] Joined Cases C-180/98 to 184/98 *Poucet and Pistre* [2000] ECR I-6451; Case 67/96 *Albany* [1999] ECR I-5751; Joined Cases C-180/98 to C-184/98 *Pavel Pavlov* [2000] ECR I-6451.

[84] See M Everson, 'Social Pluralism and the European Court of Justice. A Court between a Rock and a Hard Place' (2003) 9 *Journal of Legislative Studies* 98.

were properly held. Beyond this, however, the strike is an irrational and disproportionate act, a concrete political expression of antagonistic class conflict, a modern continuation of the struggle that creates and undermines our market and our State, and a necessary site of reconciling conflict between antagonistic European classes. To this exact degree then, the CJEU may be argued to be undermining all of our historical citizenships, denying the political voice and political action of a distinct class of industrial workers.

But is it doing more? Eastern enlargement and the failure of Western Europe to afford a measure of democratically legitimated redistributive justice to its recently liberated Eastern cousins is the backdrop against which the cases were decided, and it is also the backdrop against which the formalistically flavoured *choice* of the Court to assert the hierarchical precedence of rights of establishment and service provision (Articles 49 and 56 TFEU), as well as competition law, above the constitutional traditions and democratic processes of the Member States was taken. Piercing the veil of the Court's somewhat questionable formalism – the assertion that extension of the doctrine of horizontal direct effect to the economic rights contained within the Treaty is a simple given[85] – the CJEU's *interposito auctoritas* is revealed, mostly clearly in the terms deployed by its Advocate General Maduro, as a curious but disturbing melange of sentimentality and economic technology. For all of his talk of the creation of a European social constitution, the measure of AG Maduro's notion of social justice in modern Europe is thus to be found in his promotion of social constitutionalism within a by-now dominant European economic model of 'allocative efficiency'; an ill-timed, emotional and technological *auctoritas interposito*, which reacts to the clearly disadvantaged position of Eastern European workers with a notion of 'social justice' that sees them work for less than Western workers, and Western workers denied access to their own jobs, all in pursuit of a more efficient economy.

Herein lies the far wider problem within the CJEU's increasingly inspirational and aspirational approach to the four freedoms (including the rights to work and to freely dispose of capital), as well as to the free movement of goods. Convergence between these economic freedoms and the notion of 'genuine'[86] EU citizenship – in essence a matter of elevating economic rights to the same 'immutable' status as citizenship rights and also enforcing them between private individuals – both fundamentally alters our perceptions of entitlements and of provisions, and recalls the processes of subjectification to which European consumers have been exposed.

[85] And certainly, this might appear logically systematic within European law, or might do so if the distinctive facts of earlier cases such as Case C-112/00 *Schmidberger* [2003] ECR I-5659 are ignored; nonetheless, at national constitutional level, horizontal direct effect of constitutional rights is restricted in general and rarely if ever extends to 'profit-driven' economic rights (beyond property rights): for details of the source of the constitutional theory of horizontal direct effect within the German tradition and the refusal of German justices to extend the doctrine to economic rights, see Joerges and Rödl (81); for examination of the then CJEU's disruption of the UK's limitation of the reach of economic rights by means of the imposition of the doctrine of State liability.

[86] Opinion of AG Poiares Maduro in Joined Cases C-158 and 159/04 *Alfa Vita Vassilopoulos AE v Greece* [2006] ECR I-8135.

The love of the CJEU for the individual European – the desire that all should be given opportunity – coincides happily with the frontier-busting universalism of neoliberal precepts and is transformed into a legal semantic of economic technology, which isolates and atomises the individual as a *homo economicus*. Rights are no longer legal entitlements but are rather to be viewed as legal mechanisms which facilitate – in line with economic theory – the 'never-ending' creation of economic provisions within the internal market. The European citizen is reborn as a unit of economic production and is divorced from the social collectives in which values of ethics and solidarity might be politically established and enforced. Certainly, the wealthy might still buy themselves a measure of private welfare protection, but all classes are impacted upon by a sentimentality and economic technology, which strives for universalism, but which – in its cool and calm logic – rejects all collective political efforts to humanise markets as retrograde manifestations of residual 'risk aversion' on the part of the populace.[87]

V THE COSMOPOLITAN REPUBLIC

> What is protected is the applicant's right to live freely and openly as a gay man. That involves a wide spectrum of conduct, going well beyond conduct designed to attract sexual partners and maintain relationships with them. To illustrate the point with trivial examples from British society: just as male heterosexuals are free to enjoy themselves playing rugby, drinking beer and talking about girls with their mates, so male homosexuals are to be free to enjoy themselves going to Kylie concerts, drinking exotically coloured cocktails and talking about boys with their straight female mates. *Mutatis mutandis* – and in many cases the adaptations would obviously be great – the same must apply to other societies. In other words, gay men are free to be as free as their straight equivalents in the society concerned to live their lives in the way that is natural to them as gay men, without the fear of persecution.[88]

As this quotation from the recent case law of the UK Supreme Court indicates, global society continues to change at an extraordinary rate; and with it law, at national, supranational and global level. In an ecstatically greeted move,[89] UK judges substantially widened the notion of discrimination laid down in the immediate post-war Vienna Convention on refugees, overturned a disturbing tendency in international law to define the homosexual solely in relation to the sexual act,[90] put to rest a history of anti-homosexual sentiment in the UK whose very concrete legal effects were still being felt less than a decade ago (age of consent), and similarly laid down a gauntlet to national and international courts to do the same. A

[87] Foucault (n 74).

[88] *HJ (Iran) and HT (Cameroon) v Secretary of State for the Home Department* [2010] UKSC 31 (United Kingdom Supreme Court).

[89] S Chevlan, 'Put Your Hands Up (If You Feel Love)' (2011) 23 *Journal of Immigration, Asylum and Nationality Law* 56.

[90] P Johnson, '"An Essentially Private Manifestation of Human Personality"': Constructions of Homosexuality in the European Court of Human Rights' (2010) 10 *Human Rights Law Review* 67.

return to a closed world of nation states, or, indeed, to inclusive notions of national citizenship founded in traditionally constructed class conflict and hostile to all 'others', be their exclusion a matter of nationality, ethnicity or lifestyle, is unthinkable. It is equally unimaginable that a return might be made to a Europe where Kylie records and exotic cocktails are unavailable because of trade barriers.

Yet, the quotation also tells us far more. Firstly, with regard to the political-legal culture which it reflects. Judicial tolerance for homosexual lifestyles cannot be ascribed to any particular liberality on the part of the UK legal profession. Gay liberation is an unfolding social movement – founded in violence (Stonewall riots), art (*Brokeback Mountain*), consumption (the pink lifestyle) and politics (in the UK, Clause 22) – which is received *explicitly*, though always slowly and, importantly, 'imperfectly' within the law; it is after all to be doubted that all gay men feel that the apex of gay culture is formed by Kylie Minogue. Secondly, with regard to legal method: here, where a substantial change is being made to UK law, the language of legal change is not one of law but of the language of the political culture that is demanding it.

Equally, however, where the gauntlet is thrown down to other national laws and to international law to follow suit, no hierarchy is imposed, no normative superiority is claimed. In its efforts to mould a 'genuine' Union citizenship, the CJEU is responding to a zeitgeist, and its sincerity, at least in relation to Article 8 ECHR, cannot be doubted. Yet, its efforts fatally disregard the often overlooked triad in Arendt between the law, politics and culture of her republic: Roman law, so Arendt, was born to dominate and conquer.[91] Founded only in the sovereign power of 'objectively-universal' legal method, the *lex Romana* remained a monolith, unable to adapt to the cultural changes and challenges spawned by ever increasing (universal) empire, and thus doomed to collapse under the weight of its own contradictions. Ever at odds with the liberal rights theorists of her era, Arendt declaimed that the only stable and inclusive republic would be one in which sovereign power is discarded and, more importantly, hierarchies between law, politics and culture are broken down. Today, given the Habermasian dedication to the declaration of the co-originality of law and politics, Arendt's prescriptions might appear more liberal than they once did, but her core and immutably republican insights about the essential vibrancy of politics and culture surely bear repeating.

The efforts of the CJEU to implement a universally flavoured Union citizenship as against the politics of the Council or the political culture of the Member States are mired in their own contradictions. The Court has forgotten the particularist limitations of its own prejudices; worse still the Court's judge-kings have mislaid the most telling insight of the free law movement. Free law was all about breaking down the hierarchies between law, society and politics. To the extent that political economy acted as law's window on the world, it did so *only* to the degree that it

[91] See Volk (n 5) for full details.

gave law a 'moral insight' into the limitations of its own formal methodology.[92] Where law has descended into economic technology, has subjectified the European as a *homo economicus*, the worst of all legal hierarchies has been established, a hierarchy that denies and destroys the politics and the culture of the *res publica*. As the UK Supreme Court demonstrates, it is possible for law to make – always imperfect – cosmopolitan changes to our world and our concept of citizenship; but, it can only do so in a 'non-levelling and non-appropriating' relationship with a vibrant political culture. The judges of the CJEU are not engaging with and asserting themselves against medieval feudalism; instead, they should never forget that they are forging their own cosmopolitan citizenship against the backdrop of the very real and valuable attainments of post-war European nation states – vibrant and politically inclusive republics within which culture, art and communication give law insights into the concrete particulars of our changing lives that can and must be asserted against abstractly exclusionary universalisms.

[92] Laski, *A Grammar* (1958); explanatory details in Everson and Eisner (n 16).

Part III

The Citizen's Policy Agenda?

7

Europe in Times of Economic Crisis: Bringing Europe's Citizens Closer to One Another?

FABIAN AMTENBRINK*

I INTRODUCTORY REMARKS

DESPITE ITS HUGE consequences for European integration, European Economic and Monetary Union (EMU) has not, until recently, gained the attention of as many legal academics as other supposedly more mainstream areas of European Union law. Even after the establishment of the European System of Central Banks (ESCB) and the introduction of a single currency, the implications of EMU are primarily discussed in terms of the effectiveness and efficiency of the legal framework and its economic implications. While the shortcomings of the present regulatory system, which have contributed to the Eurozone debt crisis since 2010, certainly justify such analyses, they deflect from the question whether and to what extent EMU actually contributes to European integration, as defined by the Treaty on European Union in terms of a 'process of creating an ever closer union among the peoples of Europe. A Union in which decisions are taken as openly as possible and as closely as possible to the citizen'[1] and that promotes economic, social and territorial cohesion, and solidarity among its Member States and its citizens.[2] It is at least not self-evident that EMU actually contributes to the identification of the citizens of the Member States with the European project. In fact, one may wonder whether the Eurozone debt crisis actually provides evidence to the contrary.

* The author would like to thank the participants at the 'Empowerment and Disempowerment of the European Citizen. The Citizen's Policy Agenda?' workshop, held at the University of Edinburgh on 10 December 2010, for their comments on an earlier draft of this chapter. All errors and omissions remain those of the author. This contribution reflects mainly on the development prior to the establishment of the 'Six Pack' and the Fiscal Compact.

[1] Art 1(2) TEU.

[2] See Preamble and Art 3(3) TEU.

The present contribution explores whether and to what extent in times of (economic) crisis the policies exercised at the supranational level have the potential to contribute to or indeed undermine the appreciation of the European Union (EU) by its citizens and, in the long term, the emergence of a transnational citizenship beyond the creation and upholding of rights. In addressing these questions, two fairly distinct topics in European integration studies are connected, namely the conduct of macroeconomic and monetary policy in the EU and the discourse on the existing or perceived lack of identification with and ownership by the citizens in relation to European policies and supranational integration as such. In this chapter, therefore, the debate on the existence or emergence of a European demos is first recalled, thereby reflecting on the notion of the 'European citizen' and exploring the role that common goods and solidarity may have in this context. Thereafter, it is explored whether and to what extent EMU pursues 'common goods' that bring citizens closer to Europe and each other, thereby creating solidarity among Europeans. Finally, the chapter seeks an answer to the question whether the current Eurozone debt crisis is uniting Member States and their citizens in solidarity in pursuing these common goods in defence of the aims of European integration. The legal analysis will be enriched with relevant references to political science and political economy scholarship, adding a multidisciplinary dimension to the chapter.

II IN SEARCH OF THE 'EUROPEAN CITIZEN'

In the spring 2011 Eurobarometer, 62 per cent of the respondents agreed with the statement that 'You feel you are a citizen of the EU'.[3] Yet, what remains unclear in this survey is exactly what connotation those that responded link *positively* with being a citizen of the Union. Is this primarily an acknowledgment of the fact that they hold the nationality of a State that, for better or for worse, is part of the EU, or the acceptance of an identity and belonging apart from that linked to their own country and that unites them with their compatriot citizens of the other Member States of the Union?

The complexity of finding an answer to this question equals that of defining the notion of 'European citizen'. Indeed, with regard to the latter, two quite distinct associations can be made which are by no means congruent. First, there is the legal concept of 'European citizenship' that is directly linked to primary Union law and namely Article 20 TFEU, which establishes citizenship of the Union. While Union citizenship is conditional on holding the nationality of a Member State and thus conditional on national citizenship, it is a well-documented fact that the Court of Justice of the European Union (ECJ) has added substantial weight to the concept of European citizenship by assigning rights to this status which, arguably, are not in all instances directly linked to the free movement pro-

[3] European Commission, 'Eurobarometer 75: Public Opinion in the European Union', August 2011, 51

visions in primary and secondary Union law.[4] Next to this normative definition, 'European citizen' can also be given a somewhat more philosophical connotation related to the rationale for the introduction of the legal concept of citizenship by the Maastricht Treaty, that is, to bring Europe closer to its citizens.[5] The expression 'European citizen' may thus describe a state of affairs pertaining to the level of integration of the citizens of the Member States in the European constitutional order, which is characterised by the emergence of a transnational citizenship beyond the creation and upholding of rights and obligations. As such, the existence or emergence of European citizens can be placed in the context of the debate on the European demos and the integrative function of the European constitutional order.[6]

The existence of such a transnational citizenship or European demos is highly doubtful. Indeed, Europe's vision of 'an ever closer Union' has, for a long time, been pursued by means of the establishment of a supranational legal order and corresponding institutions, rather than by facilitating the creation of a demos in the sense of belonging and common (political) identity.[7] The European populace is that of the participating Member States rather than that of the European Union.[8] Citizens rarely claim ownership of European policies and decision-making. What is missing is an identification with, commitment to and appreciation of policies and decisions that are supposedly formulated and implemented in the citizen's best interest.[9] The top-down approach to the establishment of a (political) community beyond the State that could be witnessed from the very beginnings of the European project has come under pressure in the last two decades, as the laissez-faire attitude of the citizens of the Member States has given way to a more conscious and critical approach to the supranational legal order. It is no coincidence that, for the best part of the last 20 years, European politics and law have been increasingly geared towards the a posteriori construction of a

[4] See generally CWA Timmermans, 'General Aspects of the European Union and the European Communities' in AM McDonnell, PJG Kapteyn, K Mortelmans, CWA Timmermans (eds), *The Law of the European Union and the European Communities*, 4th edn (Alphen aan de Rijn, Kluwer Law International, 2008) 53, 98 ff. For a critical view of this state of affairs, see D Kochenov, 'Ius Tractum of Many Faces: European Citizenship and the Difficult Relationship between Status and Rights' (2009) *Columbia Journal of European Law* 15, 169.

[5] The introduction by the same Treaty of the European Ombudsman is another such initiative that can be placed in this context.

[6] Throughout this chapter, the author takes the view, in line with the jurisprudence of the ECJ, that the Treaties, and thus primary Union law, can be referred to as the constitutional foundation of the EU. Generally on European constitutional principles, see, eg, A von Bogdandy and J Bast (eds), *Principles of European Constitutional Law* (Oxford, Oxford University Press, 2006).

[7] See, however, U Beck, 'Reinventing Europe – A Cosmopolitan Vision' in C Rumford (ed), *Cosmopolitanism and Europe* (Liverpool, Liverpool University Press, 2007) 39, 41, who wonders whether and to what extent 'the nation-states themselves still have a homogeneous populace or citizenry'.

[8] See in this context W Wallace, 'The Sharing of Sovereignty: the European Paradox' (1999) XL VII *Political Studies* 503, 521, who refers to the absence of 'a coherent European narrative'.

[9] F Amtenbrink, *Continuation or Reorientation. What Future for European Integration*, Erasmus Law Lectures No 9 (The Hague, Boom Juridische Uitgevers, 2007).

European demos, not least through the introduction of the concept of European citizenship.[10]

The path towards the (at least partial) abandoning of the exclusive status of the national constitutional order as the source of identity and belonging in favour of the 'anchoring of citizens' sense of attachment and allegiance along the lines of constitutional patriotism'[11] at the European level is anything but straightforward. In the absence of commonalities such as history, language, culture and ethnicity:

> in the EU the focus has come to rest on the formulation of common values, the establishment of concrete rights and the creation of a legal framework on the basis of which citizens can, in the words of Closa, 'articulate their discourses and, from these, they can develop feelings of attachment and allegiance'.[12]

Considering that, despite its autonomous role, the European concept of citizenship is still closely linked to the economic and social rights of the internal market, as developed in the case law of the ECJ, it is hardly surprising that it has not substantially contributed to the creation of a (political) community or identity beyond the participating Member States. Indeed, if the upholding of fundamental rights standards and internal market freedoms were sufficient, the participation of all Member States in the European Convention on Human Rights and its recognition by primary Union law,[13] as well as the upholding of fundamental (economic) rights and values by the ECJ should have created such a European identity or indeed patriotism a long time ago.

National constitutional orders of the Member States thus continue to fulfil an important integrative function in the EU. Whether written or unwritten, they allow the citizens of a country to identify with a particular political and social order, thereby making 'a major contribution to a sense of order and coherence' and a feeling of being integrated in and belonging to a particular society.[14] This ability 'to bring together identity and order, legitimacy and community, national economy and national welfare within a single framework'[15] is arguably still at large in the European legal order. European citizens are indeed united in diversity,[16] rather than in sharing a common identity. The vision expressed in the Schuman Declaration of the 'coming together of the nations of Europe' has made

[10] F Amtenbrink, 'The Multidimensional Constitutional Legal Order of the European Union – A Successful Case of Cosmopolitan Constitution-Building?' (2008) XXXIX *Netherlands Yearbook of International Law* 3.

[11] C Closa, 'Deliberative Constitutional Politics and the Turn Towards a Norms-Based Legitimacy of the EU Constitution' (2005) 11 *European Law Journal* 411, 431, with reference to the works of Jürgen Habermas.

[12] Amtenbrink (n 10) 62, with reference to Closa, ibid, 419.

[13] See Art 6 TEU.

[14] F Amtenbrink and PAJ van den Berg, 'Lost in Translation? On the Role of National Constitutions in the European Constitutional Order' in F Amtenbrink and PAJ van den Berg (eds), *The Constitutional Integrity of the European Union* (The Hague, TMC Asser Press/Berlin, Springer, 2010) 1, 2.

[15] W Wallace, 'The Sharing of Sovereignty: The European Paradox' in R Jackson (ed), *Sovereignty at the Millennium*, (Malden, MA, Blackwell, 1999) 81, 98.

[16] This was the motto of the EU as foreseen in the failed Treaty establishing a Constitution for Europe [2004] OJ C310/1.

place for a more lifelike reference to an ever closer union of the 'peoples' of Europe.[17] Ironically, the attempts in the failed Treaty establishing a Constitution for Europe to address the issue by means of constitutional symbolism have created unity, in an unwanted direction, as citizens in the Member States seemed to have at least partially joined ranks in their rejection of what they (mis-)interpreted as being an attempt at State-building in disguise.[18]

Creating compassion among the citizens of the Member States for the ideals underpinning European integration and, moreover, for one another in these conditions, is a complex process. Attempts in the Treaty on European Union (TEU) and the Treaty on the Functioning of the European Union (TFEU) to create such benevolence through the notion of solidarity have arguably had little effect. The preamble to the TEU refers to the desire of the Member States 'to deepen the solidarity between their peoples while respecting their history, their culture and their traditions'. Article 3(3) TEU refers to the aims of the Union as being to 'promote economic, social and territorial cohesion, and solidarity among Member States' and, in the area of the Common Foreign and Security Policy, reference is made in the TEU to the 'mutual political solidarity among Member States'.[19] According to Article 80 TFEU, the Union's policies on border checks, asylum and immigration must be based on 'the principle of solidarity and fair sharing of responsibility, including its financial implications, between the Member States'.[20] Article 222 TFEU on the duty of the Union and Member States to assist a Member State that is the subject of a terrorist attack or the victim of a natural or man-made disaster is even referred to as a 'Solidarity Clause'. In concrete terms, economic, social and territorial cohesion in the Union is supported inter alia through action taken through Structural Funds and the European Investment Bank. Yet, apart from the fact that a clear definition of the concept of solidarity is missing,[21] the current state of affairs suggests that these – in parts, long-standing – arrangements have not succeeded in bringing the citizens of the beneficiary countries closer to those of the benefactor countries. Quite the contrary: politicians in the latter category of countries often emphasise the (undesirable) status of their States as major net payers in the EU, at times triggering a defiant response from beneficiary countries. As will be highlighted hereafter, a similar pattern can also be observed for EMU in the context of the Eurozone debt crisis.[22]

Rights and privileges created by the European legal order are often at best perceived as individual rights and privileges, rather than convictions and achievements that all citizens of the EU share among themselves, that tie their fates

[17] Art 1(2) TEU.

[18] In particular, in the Netherlands, on the grounds of the loss of national identity and the creation of a European super state. See Wetenschappelijke Raad voor het Regeringsbeleid (Scientific Council for Government Policy), *Europa in Nederland* (Amsterdam, Amsterdam University Press, 2007).

[19] eg Art 24(2) TEU.

[20] A similar provision can be found in Art 194 TFEU for Union policy on energy.

[21] This is observed by, eg, I Hartwig and P Nicolaides, 'Elusive Solidarity in an Enlarged European Union' (2003) 3 *Eipascope* 19, 19.

[22] See section IV below.

together and that set them apart from others. Yet, this is not to say necessarily that the supranational legal order does not in any way reflect any commonalities among the citizens of Europe. Rather than through the construction of an (artificial) European constitutional gospel, and even the establishment of rights and political participation, citizens may be unified in their recognition and pursuit of common goods. It can be argued that it is from such common convictions that belonging and solidarity beyond the scope of any legal concept in EU law may eventually arise.[23] If the pursuit of common goods by the Union may actually hold the promise of paving the way towards a closer union of the people of Europe,[24] then the defence of such common goods in times of crisis should only intensify this effect.

III EUROPEAN ECONOMIC AND MONETARY UNION – IN PURSUIT OF A COMMON GOOD?

The introduction of a single currency in parts of the European Union and the current Eurozone debt crisis may provide clues as to whether the premise of the previous section is indeed accurate or rather results from an overtly idealistic view of the dynamics of European integration. Put differently, the question addressed here must be: Is the operation of EMU geared towards a common good?

A The Objectives of EMU as a Common Good

Article 2(3) TEU calls upon the Union to work for the sustainable development of Europe based on balanced economic growth and price stability, as a highly competitive social market economy, aiming at full employment and social progress. The Union is moreover supposed to promote economic, social and territorial cohesion, and solidarity among Member States. While the citizens of the Member States may not easily agree on the exact mix or prioritisation of these aims, it seems safe to assume that there is a fairly large degree of agreement on the importance of these issues. In fact, in the spring 2011 Eurobarometer, respondents named 'unemployment' and 'the economic situation' as the two most important general issues facing their country, followed in third place by 'rising prices and inflation'.[25] When it comes to the most important issues facing the Union, the pattern is broadly the same: the economic situation was mentioned most often, followed by unemployment, the state of the public finances in Member States, and inflation and rising prices.[26]

[23] See in this regard eg C Barnard, 'EU Citizenship and the Principle of Solidarity' in E Spaventa and M Dougan (eds), *Social Welfare and EU Law* (Oxford, OUP, 2005) 157.

[24] See eg JPJ White, 'Rethinking Transnational Solidarity in the EU' (2003) 11 *Perspectives* 1, 40.

[25] Eurobarometer (n 3) 21.

[26] Ibid, 23.

Article 2(4) TEU states that the Union establishes an economic and monetary union whose currency is the euro. To the extent that EMU pursues the aims set out in primary Union law, thereby addressing the concerns of the citizens, this policy area may actually defend a good shared by many citizens and, thus, a common good. Arguably, in the citizen's perception, the euro is a synonym for EMU. This is verified by the outcomes of the spring 2011 Eurobarometer. When asked what the EU means to them personally, 47 per cent of the citizens of the Member States of the Eurozone referred to the euro. This was the highest score.[27] Even for citizens outside the Eurozone, the euro came in an impressive third place. Linking these results to those on the personal concerns of citizens, it can be argued that the single currency and especially its stability actually are a common concern of European citizens. Indeed, looking back, the prospect of introducing such a stable currency has certainly been the prime attraction of EMU for countries such as Greece, Italy, Portugal and Spain, with a history of high inflation and – in some instances – repeated devaluations of the domestic currencies. The single currency can also be linked to a second common good identified by many European citizens, that is, free movement within the internal market. The single currency has removed barriers to trade in the shape of high transaction costs and exchange rate risks. In fact, a stable euro even has advantages for the intra-Union trade of those Member States that remain outside the Eurozone. The extent to which a currency can be societally embedded could arguably nowhere be better witnessed than in Germany with regard to the Deutsche Mark. Throughout its lifetime, that currency became the synonym for the German post-war economic success story and, moreover, constituted a major motivation among East German citizens for a fast unification with West Germany. The example of Germany also highlights that trust in and identification with (macro-)economic policy and the institutions in charge thereof (in this example, the German Bundesbank) are not built instantly, but rather over time and through accomplishments. At the heart of the common good lies an economic rationale the pursuit and defence of which unites people.

Yet price stability is not the only common good in the economic and monetary sphere. In fact, the spring 2011 Eurobarometer suggests a rather more complex picture, as a one-sided focus on price stability would not necessarily match other personal concerns voiced by citizens, namely with regard to the economic situation and unemployment. Sound government finances, an objective that is most prominently expressed in Article 126(1) TFEU regarding the prohibition on Member States from running excessive government deficits, is also a major concern of citizens in the EU. An astonishing two-thirds of those participating in the survey (EU 27 average) totally agreed with the statement that measures to reduce the public deficit and debt in their own country cannot be delayed.[28] However a more diverse picture emerges when taking into account the response to the statement that it is necessary, given the economic crisis, to increase public deficits to

[27] Ibid, 31–32, followed by the response 'Freedom to travel, study and work anywhere in the EU'.

[28] European Commission, 'Eurobarometer 75: Europeans, the European Union and the Crisis', August 2011, 23.

create jobs. In the Eurozone, 40 per cent of the respondents agreed with this statement.[29] However, in the non-Eurozone countries, a majority of respondents were in favour of a more lenient monetary policy.[30]

B Effectively Defending Common Goods?

To the extent that price stability, sound government financing and employment may be classified as common goods that bring the citizens of the EU together, the question is whether, and to what extent, they are indeed effectively pursued by the Union.

Article 127 TFEU defines price stability as the primary objective of the ESCB and of the European Central Bank (ECB). Support for the general economic policies of the Union, with a view to contributing to the achievement of the objectives of the Union, is a secondary objective that is subordinated to price stability. Yet, whether the price stability objective necessarily coincides with economic growth and employment is questionable. Proponents of the current focus of monetary policy argue that monetary policy contributes to the development of the economy by providing for low inflation and stable prices.[31] Proof for the fact that this view is not necessarily shared by all comes in the shape of the United States Federal Reserve System, which has as its objective the promotion of maximum employment, stable prices, and moderate long-term interest rates.[32] Given the importance of the secondary objective of the ECB, it is not entirely unexpected that the question has been raised as to exactly how the ECB contributes to the general economic policies of the Union other than by maintaining price stability. In particular, in the regular so-called monetary dialogue between the president of the ECB and members of the European Parliament committee on economic and monetary affairs, democratically elected parliamentarians regularly demanded more consideration of the secondary objective, including an adjustment of the ECB's stands on interest rates.[33]

The clear preference that has been given to a certain type of fiscal discipline can also be seen for the economic policies of the Union and the Member States as defined in primary and secondary Union law. The economic 'Union', as defined in the previous paragraph, has to comply with a number of guiding principles. As well as price stability, this also includes sound public finances and monetary con-

[29] Ibid, 24; 45% EU 27 average.

[30] 53%.

[31] See, eg, DT Brash, 'Central Banks: What They Can and Cannot Do', speech delivered to the Trans-Tasman Business Circle, Sydney, 30 March 2001, available at www.rbnz.govt.nz/speeches/0102706.html.

[32] See Federal Reserve Act, 12 USC 225a. As added by Act of November 16, 1977 (91 Stat 1387) and amended by Acts of October 27, 1978 (92 Stat 1897); August 23, 1988 (102 Stat 1375); and December 27, 2000 (114 Stat 3028).

[33] F Amtenbrink and CPS van Duin, 'The European Central Bank before the European Parliament: Theory and Practice after Ten Years of Monetary Dialogue' (2009) 34 *ELR* 561, 575 ff.

ditions, and a sustainable balance of payments. More specifically, Article 126(1) TFEU demands that Member States avoid excessive government deficits, as defined in the Protocol on the excessive deficit procedure annexed to the TEU and TFEU. Leaving aside the question whether the actual reference values are necessary from an economic point of view,[34] the one-sided numeric fixation on government budgetary positions raises the question whether this comes at the expense of other aims of the EU, such as growth and employment.

While citizens across the Union generally seem to be united in the issues that they identify as important, and while the Union, in principle, recognises these issues in formulating its objectives, it may be argued that citizens in the Member States are split as to the perceived benefits of EU membership even if a tiny majority of the respondents in the spring 2011 Eurobarometer take a favourable view on this.[35] This divide also becomes apparent when observing the level of trust that citizens have in the EU.[36] Asked about which (international) institution is best able to take effective actions against the effects of the financial and economic crisis, no uniform picture emerges. Overall the EU receives the highest score, compared to national governments, the International Monetary Fund and the G20, something very much emphasised by the European Commission in its report on the spring 2011 Eurobarometer.[37] Yet, the margin between the EU and the national governments is very small indeed.[38] It can thus hardly be argued that the Union takes a convincing lead in this regard. While the legal framework on EMU may thus at least partially be geared towards pursuing common goods that are to a certain extent shared by the citizens across Member States, the very same citizens are not united in their belief that participation in the EU is a good thing and that its policies have a positive impact on their lives. Applying this more specifically to the Eurozone and the single currency, beyond elitist arguments about the lack of knowledge and appreciation of EU policies by citizens, this may have much to do with the serious deficiencies of the present system that have resulted in negative sentiments and even distrust between Member States and, ultimately, in the current Eurozone debt crisis.

An analysis of the current legal framework in primary and secondary Union law raises questions as to the legal commitment actually to defend these common goods. Despite what the name of Title VIII of the TFEU may suggest, Union law does not foresee an economic union characterised by a single economic and fiscal policy that is geared towards the aims laid down in Article 2 TEU. Instead, the economic policy of the Union effectively relies on the adoption by the Member States of 'an economic policy which is based on the close coordination of Member States' economic policies, on the internal market and on the definition of

[34] See, eg, W Buiter, 'De budgettaire voodoo van Maastricht' (1992) *Economisch Statistische Berichten* 268.

[35] 52%.

[36] Eurobarometer (n 3) 35 and 43–44.

[37] European Commission (n 28) 11.

[38] Ibid, 9; EU: 22%, national governments: 20%.

common objectives, and conducted in accordance with the principle of an open market economy with free competition.'[39] Moreover, employment policy is even listed separately from EMU and only amounts in effect to the coordination of national strategies and the application of soft-law instruments.[40]

Yet, apart from falling short of integrating important policy fields that are given a high priority by citizens, such as inter alia fiscal, labour market and social policy, the current legal framework on EMU also lacks sufficiently stringent procedures to enforce the existing fiscal rules. This sentiment was even shared by some Member States, and by Germany in particular, which drove a hard bargain in the wake of the negotiations for the Treaty of Amsterdam to reinforce the Treaty rules on economic coordination.[41] The resulting Stability and Growth Pact, and more specifically its two regulations on the strengthening of the surveillance and coordination of budgetary positions and on speeding up and clarifying the implementation of the excessive deficit procedure, have since become the core of the system of economic coordination in EMU.[42] The fundamental disagreement between countries, namely Germany and France, about the general direction of economic policy and especially the need to focus on fiscal soundness, found its expression in the inclusion of an explicit reference to economic growth in the Stability and Growth Pact.[43] Doubts about the effectiveness of the system nevertheless remained and were soon to be confirmed by actual events.[44]

The multilateral surveillance procedure included in Article 121 TFEU (ex Article 99 EC), which used to empower the Council[45] to issue an early warning to a Member State with an economic policy that is inconsistent with the broad economic guidelines also issued by the Council, has proven to be ineffective. The multilateral surveillance procedure does not establish any instrument actually to enforce fiscal discipline, as a result of which it cannot prevent the emergence of excessive deficits. Added to this, until now there has not always been the necessary political consensus in the Council even to apply the existing weak rules. Under the pre-Lisbon legal arrangements, European Commission recommendations for the application of the early warning procedure were not put to the vote in the Council

[39] Art 119(1) TFEU.

[40] Albeit in their current form, the Broad Economic Policy Guidelines issued by the Council in accordance with Art 121(2) TFEU include employment policy.

[41] Report by the ECOFIN Council to the European Council, 'The Preparation for Stage Three of EMU', Annex I, Presidency Conclusions, Dublin European Council, 13 and 14 December 1996.

[42] [1997] OJ L209/1, last amended by Council Regulation 1055/2005, [2005] OJ L174/1, amending Regulation (EC) 1466/97 on the strengthening of the surveillance of budgetary positions and the surveillance and coordination of economic policies; and [1997] OJ L209/6, last amended by Council Regulation 1056/2005 [2005] OJ L174/5), amending Regulation (EC) No 1467/97 on speeding up and clarifying the implementation of the excessive deficit procedure. Resolution of the European Council on the Stability and Growth Pact Amsterdam of 17 June 1997, [1997] OJ C236/1.

[43] F Amtenbrink, 'Economic, Monetary and Social Policy' in McDonnell, Kapteyn, Mortelmans and Timmermans (eds) (n 4) 881, 912.

[44] See P Maillet, 'Le pacte de stabilité de croissance: portéet limites du compromis de Dublin?' 404 (1997) *Revue du Marché Commun et de L'Union Européenne* 5. H Hahn, 'The Stability Pact for European Monetary Union: Compliance with Deficit Limit as a Constant Legal Duty' (1998) 35 *CML Rev* 77.

[45] Before the Treaty of Lisbon, this task was assigned to the Council; see ex Article 99 TEC.

on several occasions, despite a clear danger of the emergence of excessive deficits in the countries concerned.[46] By amending the early warning procedure in the Treaty of Lisbon, nowadays vesting the task of issuing an early warning in the European Commission where a national economic policy is not consistent with the Union's broad economic guidelines or if they risk jeopardising the proper functioning of economic and monetary union, the politicising of the system has actually been conceded.[47] While the excessive deficit procedure described in Article 126 TFEU, in contrast to the multilateral surveillance procedure, does in principle foresee a strict procedure that can ultimately even result in the financial sanctioning of a Member State that does not effectively address its excessive deficit, the absence of automatic sanctions has placed the effectiveness of the procedure in the hands of the Member States united in the Council.

Even when considering the special circumstances caused by the global financial and economic crisis, it is still a sign of the failure of the system that, by October 2011, 23 countries were subject to an excessive deficit procedure. Recent attempts to repair these deficiencies through the introduction of stricter rules – for reasons that cannot be further elaborated here – are unlikely to change this assessment of the state of affairs of economic coordination in the EU fundamentally.[48] Thus, to the extent that EMU can be considered to reflect a common good, the existing legal framework falls short of effectively defending them. Rather than accommodating a common (European) good by adjusting their economic policies accordingly, Member States can be seen using their influence to escape the application of the multilateral surveillance and excessive deficit procedure in pursuit of their individual domestic (political) interests.[49] This has resulted in rifts between Member States. In particular, some smaller Member States found it unacceptable that, in the light of their own (successful) efforts to reach a balanced or even surplus budget, large Member States could effectively escape the EU budgetary regime. What is more, the system has not been able to keep a number of Member States, most notably Greece, from ending up on the edge of de facto insolvency, as the lax application of the rules went hand in hand with a flawed system for the verification of economic data submitted by the Member States.[50] The effects of this large-scale failure of economic coordination and, linked thereto, the public skirmishes of (national) politicians (on the workings of EMU and the Union in

[46] In February 2002, this concerned Germany and Portugal and, in July 2004, Italy. See 2407th Council meeting (ECOFIN), Brussels, 12 February 2002 (6108/02 (Presse 28)) and 2594th Council meeting (ECOFIN), Brussels, 5 July 2004 (10888/04 (Presse 213)).

[47] To be sure, in the context of the early warning procedure, the Council still remains in charge of issuing recommendations to the Member State concerned.

[48] Reference is made to five new regulations and one directive aimed at strengthening the Stability and Growth Pact and addressing economic imbalances in the Eurozone, the so-called 'Six pack'.

[49] I Begg, D Hodson and I Maher, 'Economic Policy Coordination in the European Union' 183 (2003) *National Institute Economic Review* 66. See also in this context, Case C-27/04 *Commission v Council* [2004] ECR I-6649. See, eg, I Maher, 'Economic Policy Coordination and the European Court: Excessive Deficits and ECOFIN Discretion' (2005) 29 *ELR* 831.

[50] In the past, Eurostat could be seen correcting national data on several occasions.

general) on the public perception of Europe should not be underestimated, especially in the Eurozone Member States. In fact, the high priority that citizens gave to the euro when asked what the EU means to them personally, as outlined earlier, may not only be explained by a broad acceptance of the European single currency and its benefits. Even the European Commission concludes in its report on the spring 2010 Eurobarometer that the citizen's concern about the euro 'provides further evidence of the extent to which the debt crisis may have impacted on public *sentiment*'.[51] Interestingly, the Commission avoids linking these concerns to the workings of economic coordination in EMU.

What the European Commission chooses to describe as 'sentiments' are actually well-founded doubts about the future of the single currency that result from the interconnectedness of economic and monetary policy. From the outset, it has been observed that the weakness of the system of economic coordination, together with diverging economic situations in the Member States, may result in spill-over effects not just on the economies of other Member States, but also on the single monetary policy in the Eurozone and the single currency itself. Indeed the ECB 'may feel forced to tighten or loosen its monetary policy standards, thereby also affecting those Member States whose economic situation may require a different monetary policy stance'.[52] In the worst case scenario, the ECB ends up intervening in the bond market in order to 'bail out' a Member State in financial distress through the purchasing of debt of these countries.[53] By now, this can actually be witnessed in practice, as the ECB has, since 2010, engaged in a rather controversial course of purchasing the sovereign debt of some Member States on the secondary market.[54] Uncertainty in the financial markets about the ability of the EU to address the precarious fiscal position of Eurozone Member States effectively has not only put the external value of the euro under pressure, but has also generated, or at least increased, the ambivalent feeling of citizens towards this still relatively young currency. This is not without risks, as Issing rightly observed long before the present crisis that 'the life of a currency depends on the trust of the population in the stability of the money!'[55]

IV UNITED IN TIMES OF CRISIS?

It has been said that 'the measure of a country's greatness is its ability to retain compassion in times of crisis'.[56] While the EU naturally cannot be equated with a

[51] Emphasis added. European Commission, 'Eurobarometer 73: Public Opinion in the European Union', August 2010, 17.

[52] Amtenbrink (n 43) 928.

[53] F Amtenbrink and J de Haan, 'Economic Governance in the European Union – Fiscal Policy Discipline Versus Flexibility' (2003) 40 *CML Rev* 1075, 1093.

[54] See Decision of the European Central Bank of 14 May 2010 establishing a securities markets programme (ECB/2010/5), [2010] OJ L124/8.

[55] Ottmar Issing during the 1998 European Parliament hearing for his installation as a member of the Executive Board of the ECB.

[56] Judge J Marshall in his concurring opinion in *Furman v Georgia* (408 US 238).

country, the question nevertheless arises, is the current Eurozone debt crisis uniting the Member States and, more importantly, their citizens in solidarity? Observing the events surrounding the sovereign debt crisis in the Eurozone, especially in Greece, suggests that the opposite is the case. Indeed, frequent public demands have been made to oust Greece from the Eurozone or even from the Union as a whole. Greece has been criticised not only for fraudulently obtaining access to the Eurozone by deliberately submitting false economic data, but also for totally failing to implement necessary structural economic reforms to prevent the financial meltdown.[57] It has even been reported that politicians in (economically better-off) Member States such as France and Germany have, behind the scenes, threatened that their countries could unilaterally withdraw from the Eurozone and reintroduce their former national currency if a rescue were not to take place on their terms.[58]

Others have criticised the lack of solidarity of such countries with the Member States in distress. Germany, in particular, has been condemned for its long indecisiveness in 2010 with respect to establishing a rescue package for the ailing Greece, thereby – in the view of some – contributing to a further deterioration of the Greek fiscal position. Yet the initial behaviour of Slovakia may best highlight how, in the face of crisis, solidarity seems to crumble away, in particular in the Eurozone. Despite considerable pressure, namely from the European Commission, the democratically elected parliamentarians in Slovakia initially blocked the financial participation of their country in the European Financial Stability Facility (EFSF), which together with the European Financial Stability Mechanism (EFSM) has until now formed the main financial instrument to support Member States in distress.[59] Fears of a so-called 'transfer union' have been aired in several Eurozone Member States. The phrase, which has been adapted from the German constitutional principle according to which there must be a 'reasonable equalization of the disparate financial capacities' between the federal states (*Bundesländer*), has a somewhat negative and politically loaded connotation.[60] In Germany, this system is heavily criticised for its one-sided burdening of the economically better-off

[57] On the (lack of) reliability of Greek government deficit and debt statistics, see European Commission, 'Report on the Greek Government Deficit and Debt Statistics', January 2010 (COM (2010) 1 final). Available at http://epp.eurostat.ec.europa.eu/cache/ITY_PUBLIC/COM_2010_REPORT_GREEK/EN/COM_2010_REPORT_GREEK-EN.PDF.

[58] As reported, for example, for Germany by *The Guardian* on 3 December 2010. Available at www.guardian.co.uk/world/2010/dec/03/angela-merkel-germany-abandon-euro. The report was immediately contradicted by the German government. For France, see the report at www.europeanvoice.com/article/2010/05/sarkozy-threatened-to-leave-eurozone/67979.aspx.

[59] EFSF Framework Agreement of 7 June 2010. Available at www.efsf.europa.eu/attachments/20111019_efsf_framework_agreement_en.pdf (as amended). EFSF has been set up as a *société anonyme* incorporated in Luxembourg. See also Reg 407/2009 establishing a European financial stabilisation mechanism [2010] OJ L118/1.

[60] The system is laid down in Art 107 of the Basic Law of the Federal Republic of Germany (*Grundgesetz*). For a brief, neutral account of this system, see, eg, Bundesministerium der Finanzen, *The Federal Financial Equalisation System in Germany*, available at www.bundesfinanzministerium.de/nn_4480/DE/BMF__Startseite/Service/Downloads/Abt__V/The_20Federal_20Financial_20Equalisation_20System_20in_20Germany,templateId=raw,property=publicationFile.pdf.

states in favour of the economically weaker regions. In the EU context, economically strong Member States are concerned about a permanent EU system obliging them financially to support the structurally weak economies of the Eurozone.

Despite the Treaty provisions on solidarity outlined earlier, primary Union law on EMU at least partially supports this rather dismissive attitude towards financial solidarity between Member States. Article 123 TFEU categorically rules out overdraft facilities or any other type of credit facility with the ECB or with the central banks of the Member States in favour of central governments, regional, local or other public authorities, other bodies governed by public law, or public undertakings of Member States. Article 124 TFEU adds to this a prohibition of privileged access by central governments, regional, local or other public authorities, other bodies governed by public law, or public undertakings of Member States to financial institutions. As a rule, government deficit financing must thus strictly take place at market conditions. The rationale for this approach is that the potential withdrawal of confidence of the financial markets in the creditworthiness of a Member State, inter alia expressed in the sovereign debt ratings of major credit rating agencies, should be an incentive for any Member State to strive for sound economic policies. Failure to do so results in sanctions by financial markets, as witnessed in 2010 and 2011 and not only in Greece. A number of Member States with excessively high government deficits have to service considerably higher interest rates on their sovereign debts than, for example, Germany. It is hardly surprising in such circumstances that these Member States are the main advocates of the introduction of European bonds on behalf of all 17 Eurozone Member States, as they would potentially benefit from lower interest rates on their debts. At the same time, Article 125 TFEU makes clear that neither the Union itself nor another Member State is 'liable for or [may] assume the commitments of central governments, regional, local or other public authorities, other bodies governed by public law, or public undertakings of any Member State, without prejudice to mutual financial guarantees for the joint execution of a specific project'. This prohibition has arguably been introduced into primary law to rule out perverse incentives on the part of Member States with a lax fiscal policy. Any hopes for a bailout by other Member States or the EU would in principle be excluded. As such, this provision thus actually propagates quite the opposite from a transfer union and seems to rule out solidarity with Member States in financial distress.

The only easing of this strict approach to liability for national government deficits and debts can be found in Article 122 TFEU, according to which, first, the Council on a proposal from the Commission may decide, in a spirit of solidarity between Member States, upon the measures appropriate to the economic situation; in particular if severe difficulties arise in the supply of certain products, notably in the area of energy. Moreover the Council, on a proposal from the Commission, may grant, under certain conditions, Union financial assistance to a Member State that is in difficulties or is seriously threatened with severe difficulties caused by natural disasters or exceptional occurrences beyond its control. It goes beyond the scope of this chapter to address the rather controversial question as to whether Article 122(2) TFEU is actually a valid legal basis for the EFSM agreed upon by the Council in May 2010[61] and, moreover, whether the activities of the ECB in the government bond market are in breach of primary Union law.[62]

However that may be, the extent to which the Eurozone Member States have been willing to explore the outer limits, to say the least, of Union law in order to come to the rescue of failing Member States seems to counter any critique about a missing solidarity among Member States. After all, despite the at times dismissive rhetoric, Eurozone Member States have actually been willing to put taxpayers' money on the line by initially providing bilateral loans to Greece and, subsequently, by providing irrevocable and unconditional guarantee commitments as part of the EFSF, which actually provides the financial support to several euro-area Member States in conjunction with the IMF. Yet, rather than pursue sublime aims of solidarity among Member States and compassion for fellow citizens in the EU, the real motives for this course of action may be much more egotistic. Leaving aside the fact that such loans are not, in fact, interest free, rescuing Member States in financial distress arguably serves first and foremost all other Eurozone Member States, namely those with an equally precarious financial situation, as financial markets are (supposedly) reassured and the euro is stabilised. What is more, the rescue also turns out to be an indirect 'bailout' of the financial sector in countries such as France, Germany and Belgium, where banks have a known large exposure to borrowers in the countries in crisis. A *de facto* insolvency of such a Eurozone country could trigger the next banking crisis.

The Eurozone debt crisis has revealed that the irrevocable fixing of the exchange rates of the currencies of 17 Member States and the introduction of a single currency, paired with the internal market and financial market liberalisation, have resulted in a somewhat involuntary, yet inescapable, solidarity between Member States and ultimately the (taxpaying) citizens of the Union. Yet, it would be wrong to conclude that this factual economic and financial connectedness brings the citizens of the Union closer to one another. In fact, it may be argued that the Eurozone debt crisis splits the Member States and the citizens of the Union into

[61] Council Reg (EU) No 407/2010 of 11 May 2010 establishing a European financial stabilisation mechanism [2010] OJ L118/1. The main question is whether this solution is in breach of Art 125(1) TFEU, the so-called non-bailout clause. See eg H Kube and E Reimer, 'Grenzen des Europäischen Stabilisierungsmechanismus' (2010) *Neue Juristische Wochenschrift* 1911; W Frenz and C Ehlenz, 'Schuldenkrise und Grenzen der europäischen Wirtschaftspolitik' (2010) *Europäisches Wirtschafts- und Steuerrecht* 211; T Jeck, 'Euro-Rettungsschirm bricht EU-recht und deutsches Verfassungsrecht', cepStudie, 5 July 2010, available at: www.cep.eu/fileadmin/user_upload/Kurzanalysen/Euro-Rettungsschirm/CEP-Studie_Euro-Rettungsschirm.pdf; C Herrmann, 'Griechische Tragödie – der währungsverfassungsrechtliche Rahmen für die Rettung, den Austritt oder den Ausschluss von überschuldeten Staaten aus der Eurozone' (2010) *Europäische Zeitschrift für Wirtschaftsrecht* 413.

[62] See eg M Seidel, 'Der Ankauf nicht markt- und börsengängiger Staatsanleihen, namentlich Griechenlands, durch die Europäische Zentralbank und durch nationale Zentralbanken – rechtlich nur fragwürdig oder Rechtsverstoß?' (2010) *Europäische Zeitschrift für Wirtschaftsrecht* 521. See also the reply by C Herrmann, 'EZB-Programm für die Kapitalmärkte verstößt nicht gegen die Verträge – Erwiderung auf Martin Seidel' (2010) *Europäische Zeitschrift für Wirtschaftsrech* 645.

two halves: those that demand solidarity and those that are expected to practise solidarity. These groups cannot be easily reconciled, as they both lack compassion for each other's points of view. Those that require financial assistance criticise, in the name of solidarity, those that have to come to the rescue for their lack of commitment or alleged delaying tactics in taking the necessary steps. This view is rebutted by reference to the lack of adherence to the fiscal rules agreed upon in primary Union law. It is argued that the Member States in distress have, in the past, shown little or no solidarity with their fellow Eurozone Member States in not taking the necessary measures to ensure a sound budgetary position. In small and struggling economies, such as Slovakia, the sentiment is that these countries are expected to pick up the tab for unsound economic policies of other, comparatively bigger economies.

The over-simplified image that is created by politicians and communicated to citizens at this time is that of a divided EU in which the citizens of the Member States in financial distress effectively live off the backs of the citizens of those Member States that have managed to better observe the agreed-upon EU fiscal rules and undertake any necessary structural economic reforms. Citizens are left with the impression – often based on public statements by national politicians – that they have to foot the bill for the extravagant lifestyle of other Europeans. What is seldom explained is that this is the natural outcome of a system of economic governance that has been put in place by elected politicians. With the introduction of a single currency, the participating Member States and hence also their citizens have become companions in faith, whereby a seriously deteriorated budgetary position of one Member State is contagious in the Eurozone and thus sooner or later affects all other Member States and their citizens as well.

What is more, this division in the Eurozone manifests itself not only in the issue of coming to the financial rescue of other Member States, but also in the question of how to reform the system of economic governance in the EU to prevent future euro crises. Few seem to disagree that fundamental reforms are needed. Yet rather than choosing a cohesive approach, new, partly complementary and partially contradictory proposals are publicised almost daily by national and European political leaders (including inter alia the President of the European Council, the President of the European Commission, the President of the euro group, the President of the ECB and heads of state and government) for the best way forward, including inter alia the suspension of voting rights of Member States with excessive deficits, automatic (financial) sanctions, the issuing of Eurobonds and a liability for investors in government bonds (letting the financial markets foot any future bailout of Member States). The contents of these proposals highlight the differences in understandings of solidarity within the Eurozone. While those likely to be burdened with the financial consequences of future bailouts favour a policy of deterrence and severe sanctions, potential future recipients of such aid may argue in favour of a quasi Europeanisation of financial risks in the Eurozone. Overall, this cacophony in times of crisis signifies the extent to which (national) differences prevail despite the existence of common goods.

V CONCLUDING REMARKS

This chapter set out to explore whether and to what extent in times of (economic) crisis the policies exercised at the supranational level have the potential to contribute to or indeed undermine an appreciation of the European Union by its citizens and, in the long term, the emergence of a transnational citizenship beyond the creation and upholding of rights. The formulation of this research question already implies the (partial) absence of a 'European citizen' that shares with his compatriot citizens of all Member States a sense of belonging and common (political) identity. It has been argued that the latter not only requires the creation of rights and obligations on the part of the citizens of the Member States but also the pursuing of common goods with which citizens actually identify.

While the substantive provisions of EMU, and especially those relating to sound government financial positions and price stability, are arguably geared towards common goods with which citizens in the Member States can identify, the current legal system governing EMU is insufficient to defend these common goods effectively. What is more, despite extensive macroeconomic integration in the area of monetary policy, the legal framework does not in any major way propagate solidarity in the area of EMU. Instead, in the face of the debt crisis in several Eurozone Member States, national and European politicians reluctantly had to accept and contribute to rescue measures first and foremost to keep the crisis from spreading to their own doorstep.

It would be over-optimistic to conclude that the crisis has stimulated solidarity among Member States and compassion among citizens of the Union. In fact, the crisis may very well have had the opposite effect. Debates have been characterised by an 'us against them' or 'everybody for themselves' mentality and national interests prevail. EMU has thus certainly not reached its full potential in promoting economic, social and territorial cohesion, and solidarity among Member States and its citizens. Rather, the extent to which the Eurozone debt crisis at times has brought out the worst in sentiments and chauvinism is a painful reminder of the limitations of the ambitious European project.

8

Can the EU Deliver on Citizen Expectations in the Fight against Climate Change?

JOANNE SCOTT

. . . we need to strengthen efforts to work with our international partners, to push and encourage them so that we can achieve the level of ambition needed to put global efforts on track to secure the real limitation of climate change to which we are all committed.[1]

I INTRODUCTION

THE LANGUAGE OF citizen expectations is present in the Laeken Declaration on the future of the European Union.[2] This reports that 'citizens want a common approach on environmental pollution, climate change and food security . . . transnational issues which they instinctively sense can only be solved by working together'. For climate change, this claim is borne out by the results of Eurobarometer surveys, which are intended to serve as a means of keeping the EU in touch with citizen expectations.[3] Three special surveys on climate change have been produced, each of which attests to the intensity of citizen concerns and to the widely shared view that the European Union ought to be doing more in the fight against it.[4] The headline figures in the most recent report are telling in this respect. This records that Europeans consider that

[1] European Commission, 'Analysis of Options to Move Beyond 20% of Greenhouse Gas Emission Reductions and Assessing the Risk of Carbon Leakage' COM (2010) 265, 13.

[2] 15th December 2001, available at www.ena.lu/laeken_declaration_future_european_union_15_december_2001-020003970.html.

[3] See the European Parliament page entitled 'The EP and the expectations of European citizens' at www.europarl.europa.eu/parliament/public/staticDisplay.do?language=EN&id=40.

[4] These surveys can be accessed at http://ec.europa.eu/public_opinion/archives/eb_special_en.htm. They are numbered 300 (September 2008); 313 (July 2009) and 322 (November 2009). The surveys cover 'the population of the respective nationalities of the European Union Member States, resident in each of the Member States and aged 15 years and over'. Since the submission of this chapter, a later special Eurobarometer report on climate change has been published. See Report No 372 published in October 2011.

climate change is the second most serious problem in the world today, and that a clear majority (55 per cent) believe that the EU is not doing enough to address it.[5]

This chapter begins with a brief evaluation of EU policies in tackling climate change. It then goes on to examine a recent shift in EU climate change policy in favour of climate unilateralism. The chapter offers several examples of this and highlights the common features that these disparate examples share. This overview of EU climate unilateralism makes readily apparent the important but controversial place that is occupied by the EU in shaping the global climate change 'regime complex'.[6]

II ARE CITIZENS RIGHT TO BE CONCERNED?

At first glance, this expression of citizen dissatisfaction with the EU's performance seems hard to understand. It follows close on the heels of the adoption by the EU of its climate and energy package, which commits the EU to achieving a unilateral 20 per cent reduction in greenhouse gases (GHG) by 2020 relative to a 1990 baseline.[7] Although this falls short of the kind of commitment that would be required by developed countries to have a chance of limiting the increase in global temperature to 2 degrees Celsius,[8] the EU's commitment is nonetheless more stringent than those put forward by most other developed states.[9] With the adoption

[5] Survey no 322 (n 4) 21 and 86–87. Citizens consider poverty, lack of food and drinking water to be the most serious problems. 30% consider that the EU is doing about the right amount to address climate change.

[6] On this concept, see RO Keohane and DG Victor, 'The Regime Complex for Climate Change', Kennedy School Discussion Paper 10/33 (January 2010).

[7] This was agreed in December 2008 and formally agreed on 23 April 2009. The fieldwork for the third climate change survey was conducted between August and September 2009. A Citizens' Summary of this is available at http://ec.europa.eu/clima/summary/docs/climate_package_en.pdf. This is accompanied by a commitment to increase this reduction to 30% within the framework of an ambitious and comprehensive global agreement on condition that other developed countries undertake to achieve comparable emission reductions and that the economically more advanced developing countries make a contribution commensurate with their respective responsibilities and capabilities. See European Commission (n 1).

[8] This is the goal agreed at Copenhagen as well as by the Major Economies Forum and the G8. The EU has accepted this. See also the World Resources Institute's recent analysis, which cites the Intergovernmental Panel on Climate Change (IPCC)'s finding that a reduction of between 25% and 40% would be required of developed countries in order to stabilise carbon dioxide concentrations at 450ppm, the level associated with a 26%–78% risk of overshooting the 2°C goal. World Resources Institute, 'Comparability of Annex I Emission Reduction Pledges' ((February 2010), 2, available at http://pdf.wri.org/working_papers/comparability_of_annex1_emission_reduction_pledges_2010-02-01.pdf.

[9] The EU is willing to reduce its emissions by 30% as opposed to 20% compared to a 1990 baseline if other developed countries commit to a comparable figure and developing countries contribute adequately according to their respective responsibilities and capabilities. Because this benchmark has not yet been achieved, the European Parliament voted against raising the EU's commitment to 30% on a unilateral basis on 5 July 2011. See Art 28 of Dir 2003/87 OJ [2003] L275/32 (as amended). For details of the pledges made by other developed countries, see World Resources Institute (n 8) 2. Japan has made a commitment of between 10% and 25% and Norway of between 30% and 40%. However, the comparable figure for the US is 5%; for Canada, 19%; and for Russia between 22% and 25% (all relative to a 1990 baseline).

of the energy and climate package, the EU is said to be on track to achieve this 20 per cent emission reduction goal.[10]

On closer inspection, however, the EU's performance seems less than impressive and thus seems to substantiate citizen concerns. The EU's 20 per cent emission reduction target is less ambitious than it might first appear, in significant part because the choice of a 1990 baseline serves the EU very well. Had a 2005 or 2000 baseline been chosen instead, the headline reduction figure for the EU would have been halved (from 20 per cent to 10 per cent), while the comparable figure for the United States would have increased from 5 per cent to between 17 and 21 per cent.[11] It is likewise the case that the method of accounting used in calculating emission reductions is production rather than consumption based, and consequently that emissions associated with the production of imported goods are not included in the EU account. It has been suggested that nearly one-quarter of all carbon dioxide emissions produced from burning fossil fuel are emitted during the production of goods that are consumed elsewhere.[12] China is by far the biggest exporter of emissions that are 'embodied' in traded goods, while the largest net importers of embodied emissions are the United States, Japan, the United Kingdom, Germany, France and Italy.[13] In the largest economies of Western Europe, net imported emissions amount to 20–50 per cent of the emissions associated with the consumption of goods.[14]

It is also widely known that the EU's flagship emissions trading scheme (ETS) has contributed little by way of emission reductions to date.[15] During the second trading phase (2008–12), the ETS is anticipated to generate 'negligible net [emissions] abatement',[16] and to generate a price signal that is too weak to incentivise significant investment in low carbon technology.[17] A combination of an excessively high

[10] See the most recent European Environment Agency report on 'Tracking Progress Towards Kyoto and 2020 Targets in Europe' (Report 7/2010 at www.eea.europa.eu/publications/progress-towards-kyoto), which observes that 'the EU is well on track to achieve its 2020 reduction target of 20% with domestic emission reductions only, provided that Member States fully implement the EU climate and energy package adopted in 2009', 5. In 2009, EU27 emissions stood 17.3% below 1990 levels.

[11] World Resources Institute (n 8) 13–14. It is widely accepted that emission reductions that took place in Central and Eastern Europe in the early 1990s account for a significant part of the reduction in the EU and that substantial reductions also took place in France and the United Kingdom during this time.

[12] SJ Davis and K Caldeira, 'Consumption-based accounting of CO2 emissions' (2010) 107/12 Proceedings of the National Academy of Science 5687, 5688, available at www.pnas.org/content/early/2010/02/23/0906974107.abstract.

[13] Ibid, 5689.

[14] Ibid, 5690. This falls to 17.8% in the case of the US and 10.8% in the case of Japan.

[15] For an excellent, in-depth account, see Sandbag, 'Cap or Trade? How the EU's ETS risks locking in carbon emissions' (September 2010) available at www.sandbag.org.uk/site_media/pdfs/reports/caportrap.pdf.

[16] Ibid, 44. See also A Ellerman, F Convery and C de Perthuis, *Pricing Carbon: The European Union Emissions Trading Scheme* (Cambridge, Cambridge University Press, 2010), who conclude that Phase 1 of the EU ETS drove between 120Mt and 300Mt of abatement in Phase 1, with a best guess of 210Mt.

[17] The price of carbon is currently hovering around the €12 mark, whereas the National Audit Office has estimated that demonstration carbon capture and storage projects would cost in the region of €60–90 per tonne of carbon dioxide abated between 2012 and 2015. See National Audit Office, 'European Emissions Trading Scheme' (National Audit Office, 2009) 44.

emissions cap, a recession leading to a substantial and unexpected reduction in production, and the ready availability of large quantities of cheap 'offsets' derived from emission reduction projects abroad, has created the possibility of continued growth in the domestic emissions of ETS-covered sectors.[18] Add to this concerns about the authenticity (additionality) of many of the putative emission reductions associated with project offsets,[19] and the EU's record seems to somewhat undermine its claim that it will lead global action against climate change to 2020 and beyond.[20]

Disappointing through the EU's contribution to addressing the threat of climate change has been, there is a limit to what emission reductions achieved within the territory of its Member States can achieve. European Union GHG emissions represent 11–12 per cent of global GHG emissions,[21] and, in 2008, emissions from developing countries surpassed emissions from developed countries for the very first time.[22] Emissions from China and the United States alone amount to 41 per cent.[23] While European emissions are falling, emissions from Asia, the Middle East and Latin America are subject to continued and significant growth.[24] It has been estimated that a *global* 50 per cent decrease in emissions will be required by 2050 if there is to be a chance of limiting climate change to an increase of 'only' 2°C.[25]

III EU GLOBAL CLIMATE LEADERSHIP FROM COPENHAGEN AND BEYOND

In view of the global nature of the climate change challenge, and the inability of the EU to achieve results while acting alone, the capacity of the EU to shape the direction of climate change mitigation policies beyond its own borders will be key. Traditionally, in the area of climate change, the EU has sought to lead by example, engaging in 'directional leadership' in the hope that unilateral action will create demonstration effects and spur regulatory action elsewhere.[26] The EU's

[18] See Sandbag (n 15), concluding that the EU's domestic emissions in ETS covered sectors could grow by 34% between 2010 and 2016.

[19] Ibid. See also, M Wara, 'Is the Global Carbon Market Working' (2007) 445 *Nature* 595.

[20] European Commission, 'EU Action against Climate Change: Leading Global Action to 2020 and Beyond' (2009), available at http://ec.europa.eu/clima/publications/docs/post_2012_en.pdf. For a recent appraisal framed in the language of leadership, see CF Parker and C Karlsson, 'Climate Change and the European Union's Leadership Moment' (2010) 48 *Journal of Common Market Studies* 923.

[21] European Environment Agency, 'Greenhouse Gas Emission Trends and Projections in Europe 2009' (EEA Report 9/2009), 8, available at www.eea.europa.eu/publications/eea_report_2009_9/ghg-trends-and-projections-2009-summary.pdf.

[22] International Energy Agency, *CO2 Emissions from Fuel Combustion* (2010 Edition) 7.

[23] Ibid, 9.

[24] Between 2007 and 2008, EU emissions fell by 2%, while developing country emissions increased by 6%. Ibid, 7.

[25] This is relative to a 1990 baseline and requires also that emissions peak in the next decade. This is based on research undertaken by the Climate Active Research team from the Sustainability Institute, the MIT Sloan School of Management and Ventana Systems. See http://climateinteractive.org.

[26] For a discussion see Parker and Karlsoon (n 20). The language of directional leadership is taken from O Young, 'Political Leadership and Regime Formation: On the Development of Institutions in International Society' (1991) 45 *International Organization* 281. Of course, in the light of the discussion above, one can question how good an example the EU has turned out to be.

unilateral commitment to reduce emissions by 20 per cent by 2020 is consistent with this approach, as indeed is its promise to raise the level of its commitment to 30 per cent in the event of an appropriate mitigation effort elsewhere.[27] Similarly, the EU's pioneering efforts to build a domestic carbon market, and to offer the prospect of international linkage for other comparable schemes,[28] can be viewed as an effort to lead by example in a bid to demonstrate the 'feasibility, value and superiority' of carbon trading as a cost-effective policy response.[29]

At Copenhagen, however, the EU's bid for directional leadership came unstuck. The EU's preference for a top-down, target-driven approach had to give way to a process sometimes characterised as 'pledge and review'.[30] Also, no agreement was reached on emissions from international aviation and maritime transport and no meaningful framework for monitoring, review and verification of emissions was put in place.[31] Even before Copenhagen, there were signs that the EU's leadership style was beginning to change. Increasingly, the EU seems to be willing to use the size of its internal market to create incentives for global regulatory engagement. In so doing, it is exhibiting 'structural leadership',[32] seeking to use its material power to alter the cost-benefit consequences of climate change mitigation action or inaction elsewhere. Four examples of this are outlined briefly below.[33]

The first example concerns the inclusion of aviation activities in the European ETS. From 2012 and subject only to limited exceptions, flights arriving at or departing from an EU airport will be obliged to surrender emission allowances within the framework of this scheme.[34] They will be required to do so in relation to the entire journey and not only in respect of that part of the journey which takes place in European airspace. However, a possible escape route is provided in the legislation. Where a third country adopts measures for reducing the climate change impact of flights departing from that country which land in the EU, the Commission may adopt amendments to exclude such flights from the ETS.[35] Similarly, where agreement is reached on global measures to reduce

[27] Recall the language in n 9 above.

[28] Art 25 Dir 2003, n 9 above.

[29] Parker and Karlsson (n 20) 926.

[30] This involves Parties associating themselves with the Copenhagen Accord and registering their emission pledges. These pledges are non-binding and are at any rate accompanied by many qualifications and conditions. For an overview of the pledges registered, see the World Resources Institute, 'Comparability of Annex I Emission Reduction Pledges' at www.wri.org/publication/comparability-of-annexi-emission-reduction-pledges.

[31] For an overview, see the Pew Center summary, available at www.pewclimate.org/docUploads/copenhagen-cop15-summary.pdf.

[32] See Young (n 26), and Parker and Karlsson (n 20), 926. The latter suggest that structural leadership 'rests on the ability to take actions or deploy power resources that create incentives, costs and benefits in a particular issue area'.

[33] These are not the only examples. In relation to maritime emissions, for example, the EU is committed to pursuing an international agreement, but 'will take steps to move forward if no such agreement has been agreed by 31 December 2011'. See European Commission (n 1) 8.

[34] See Annex 1 Dir 2003/87 and Art 2(3) defining the concept of attributed aviation emissions (n 9 above).

[35] Ibid, Art 25a(1).

GHG emissions from aviation, the Commission shall consider amending the Directive.[36]

The second example is more tentative but potentially more sweeping in its overall effect. Under the recently amended Emissions Trading Directive, the Commission is required to prepare an analytical report assessing the situation of those energy-intensive sectors or subsectors that have been found to be exposed to a significant risk of carbon leakage.[37] It is anticipated that this report may be accompanied by a proposal to include importers of energy-intensive products of this kind in the ETS.[38] In this event, it is conceivable that emission allowances would have to be surrendered in respect of emissions 'embodied' in the production of products which are manufactured in third countries but sold in the EU. Again, however, a possible escape route is put in place: 'Any binding sectoral agreements which lead to global greenhouse gas emissions reductions of the magnitude required to effectively address climate change, and which are monitorable, verifiable, and subject to mandatory enforcement arrangements shall . . . be taken into account when considering what measures are appropriate'.[39] The implication here is that a particular sector may be exempted from these requirements if an adequate regulatory framework has been negotiated and put in place elsewhere.

The third example is more complicated to describe and concerns trade in 'project offsets' rather than trade in tangible goods. The European emissions trading scheme is linked to the global carbon market as a result of a 'linking Directive'.[40] This makes it possible for Certified Emission Reductions (CERs), often known as project offsets, to be used towards achieving compliance with emission reduction obligations under the emissions trading regime. During the years 2008–20, as much as half of the EU-wide emission reduction burden may be met by using project offsets of this kind.[41] Despite serious concerns about the adequacy of the regulatory framework governing project offsets under the Kyoto Protocol, EU law has in the main been parasitic upon this international regime.[42] This, however, is about to change. An EU

[36] Ibid, Art 25a(2).

[37] Ibid, Art 10b. Carbon leakage occurs when domestic action leads to a shift in market share towards less efficient installations elsewhere, thereby amounting to increased emissions globally. See European Commission (n 1) 10. See Art 10a(15) Dir 2003/87 (n 9) for the criteria to be applied in determining whether a sector is at significant risk of carbon leakage.

[38] Art 10b(1)(b) Dir 2003/87, n 9 above. See also the discussion of this in European Commission (n 1) 11–12. Here the Commission recognises a number of potential difficulties, including the increasing cost of imported inputs for EU manufacturers, developing country objections, and the danger that measures of this kind be circumvented by delivering cleaner products to the EU market, while 'keeping "dirtier" production for their own domestic use' (11).

[39] Art 10(3) Dir 2003/87, n 9 above.

[40] Dir 2008/101 OJ [2008] L8/3 amending the basic instrument, Dir 2003/87, n 9 above.

[41] Art 11a(8) Dir 2003/87, n 9 above.

[42] For an overview of these concerns, see L Schneider, 'Is the CDM fulfilling its environmental and sustainable development objectives? An evaluation of the CDM and options for improvement' (Öko Institut, 2007). The main concern is that a substantial proportion of these offsets may not be 'additional' in that the emission reductions they represent would anyway have occurred according to a business-as-usual scenario. Since the start of the ETS, the EU has not allowed for nuclear or land use/ land-use change credits to be used. It has also imposed additional requirements in relation to large hydro projects, requiring that these be in compliance with relevant international standards, including

ban on project offsets derived from industrial gas projects will be imposed in the post-2012 European emissions trading scheme.[43] In addition, and in contrast to earlier legislation, the recently amended Emissions Trading Directive confers power on the Commission to adopt delegated legislation restricting the use of credits from specific project types with effect from the start of 2013.[44] And most importantly, according to the recently amended Directive, no new projects will be capable of yielding offsets for use in the European scheme except those which are situated either in least-developed countries (LDCs) or in countries which have concluded agreements with the EU 'specifying levels of use'.[45] For non-LDCs, the bottom line is that in the absence of a global agreement on climate change, no new projects will be capable of yielding project offsets for compliance in the EU unless a bilateral agreement with the country in question has been reached.[46]

The fourth and final example concerns the introduction by the EU of sustainability criteria for biofuels.[47] The Renewable Energy Directive establishes a 10 per cent target for renewable energy in transport to be achieved by Member States by 2020. Deep-seated concerns about whether biofuels lead to genuine GHG emissions savings and about their broader social and environmental effects induced the EU to elaborate sustainability criteria of this kind.[48] While these criteria do not apply as a condition of market access, they must be met in order for biofuels to count towards attainment of the renewable energy targets laid down. Among the sustainability criteria is a requirement that GHG savings of at least 35 per cent be secured,[49] and a requirement that biofuels should not be derived from land of high biodiversity value or high carbon stock.

In general, it will be for economic operators to demonstrate to the importing Member State that the sustainability criteria have been met.[50] Again, however, a type of escape route is put in place. It is open to the Commission to conclude a bilateral or multilateral agreement with a third country and to decide that an agreement of this kind serves to demonstrate that biofuels originating in the country concerned automatically comply.[51] It is similarly open to the Commission

those agreed by the World Commission on Dams. On the latter, and the process of voluntary harmonisation to which it gave rise, see J Scott, 'In Legal Limbo: Post-Legislative Guidance as a Challenge for European Administrative Law' (2011) 48 *CML Rev* 329.

43 See Commission Reg 550/2011, [2011] OJ L149/1.

44 Art 11a(9) Dir 2003/87, n 9 above.

45 Ibid, Art 11a(6). The Directive stipulates that any such agreement may also provide for the use of credits where the baseline used is below the level of free allocation under the measures referred to in Article 10a or below the levels required by Community legislation'. The meaning and significance of this will be explained later.

46 See also the discussion in European Commission (n 1). Here, there is more information about what the content of a bilateral agreement might be.

47 See Art 17 Dir 2009/28, [2009] OJ L140/16.

48 For a discussion of these concerns, see H Lee, WC Clark and C Devereaux, 'Biofuels and Sustainable Development' HKS Working Paper No RWP08-049 (October 2008) available at SSRN: http://ssrn.com/abstract=1282111.

49 This rises to 50% from 2017.

50 Art 18(1) Dir 2009/28, n 47 above.

51 Ibid, Art 18(4).

to decide that a voluntary national or international scheme setting standards for biofuels contain accurate data to demonstrate compliance with some or all of the sustainability criteria laid down.[52]

IV STRUCTURAL LEADERSHIP: THE EU AS A NORM ENTREPRENEUR

While there is wide variation in the examples outlined above, each uses (or contemplates using) trade-related environmental measures to secure compliance with EU law on the part of commercial operators who are situated abroad: be it American airlines in the ETS or biofuel producers in Brazil. To this extent, they represent actual or threatened instances of robust unilateralism on the part of the EU. However, there is more going on than that. The EU measures do not represent instances of pure, unadulterated unilateralism in that they provide for an escape route that would obviate the need to demonstrate compliance with the EU norm. In the event that adequate domestic regulation is adopted, or where a bilateral or global deal is struck, the EU backstop measures may cease to apply. Consequently, the EU's ultimate goal is not to enforce compliance with EU rules on the part of operators situated abroad, but it is on the contrary to galvanise or incentivise regulatory engagement elsewhere. One way of thinking about this is in the language of 'regulatory penalty defaults':[53]

> A regulatory penalty default is a harsh or quasi-punitive regulatory requirement that applies as the default rule if parties fail to reach a satisfactory alternative arrangement. Like their counter-parts in contract theory, regulatory penalty defaults have an information-forcing character: by creating incentives for regulated entities to contract around the default rule, they also create corollary incentives for the parties to produce and disclose such information as may be necessary to win approval for alternative proposals. Regulatory penalty defaults can also introduce accountability into such agreements if they are structured to establish threshold standards of environmental performance.[54]

In relation to each of the four examples above, the nature of the EU's regulatory penalty default is plain to see. For aviation and potentially for energy-intensive sectors exposed to a significant risk of carbon leakage, foreign operators are or may be required to surrender permits under the ETS. For biofuels, operators are required to demonstrate compliance on a shipment-by-shipment basis with the sustainability criteria that the EU has laid down. The punitive nature of the backstop rule is most apparent in relation to European-level regulation of the Clean Development Mechanism (CDM). From the start of the third trading phase, the

[52] Ibid.

[53] For a good discussion, see B Karkkainen, 'Information-forcing Regulation and Environmental Governance' in G de Búrca and J Scott (eds), *Law and New Governance in the EU and the US* (Oxford, Hart Publishing, 2006) 293.

[54] B Karkkainen, 'Adaptive Eco-System Management and Regulatory Penalty Defaults: Towards Bounded Pragmatism' in J Chen (ed), *The Jurisdynamics of Environmental Protection:* (Environmental Law Institute, 2003) 51.

only offsets derived from new projects that will be able to enter the emissions trading scheme will be those from projects that are situated in LDCs. The substance of each of these measures is captured in Table 1 below.

Table 1: The EU's regulatory penalty defaults

Aviation	Surrender credits under ETS for whole journey
Energy-intensive sectors	Surrender credits under ETS for emissions embodied in production
CDM	No offsets from new projects from start of third trading phase other than those situated in LDCs
Biofuels	Demonstrate compliance with EU sustainability criteria on a shipment-by-shipment basis

Less easy to grasp, and certainly less than clear, is the content of the performance benchmarks which are put in place to permit escape from the regulatory penalty default. These are often defined in the only the vaguest of terms.[55] To give just one example, offsets from new CDM projects may be included in the emissions trading scheme in the event that an international agreement on climate change is concluded or where a bilateral agreement has been concluded with a third country which specifies their level of use.

There is no indication of what the EU means when it speaks of emission reductions of a magnitude required to 'effectively address climate change', or what it has in mind when it talks of bilateral agreements regulating 'the level of [offset] use'. It is only in relation to biofuels that the substance of the required behaviour is clearly defined. A bilateral or multilateral agreement, or a voluntary certification programme, may be recognized as demonstrating compliance with the sustainability criteria where they contain measures that correspond to them. Even here, however, the Commission is also empowered to take a variety of extraneous factors into account.[56]

[55] It is also the case that the EU decision-maker often enjoys considerable discretion in deciding when these performance benchmarks have been met and in determining what the result of this should be in relation to the relaxation of the regulatory penalty default. For example, in relation to energy-intensive sectors, binding sectoral agreements *shall be taken into account* in considering what measures are appropriate, while in relation to aviation, the Commission *may* adopt amendments to the Emissions Trading Directive following the adoption of third country measures reducing the climate change impact of flights.

[56] For example, in assessing a bilateral or multilateral agreement from this perspective, Art 18(4) of the Renewable Energy Directive (Directive 2008/28, note 47 above) provides that '. . . due consideration shall be given to measures taken for the conservation of areas that provide, in critical situations, basic ecosystem services (such as watershed protection and erosion control), for soil, water and air protection, indirect land-use changes, the restoration of degraded land, the avoidance of excessive water consumption in areas where water is scarce and to the issues referred to in the second subparagraph of Article 17(7)'.

Table 2: An Overview of the EU's performance benchmarks constituting escape routes from the regulatory penalty default

	Aviation	Energy-intensive sectors	CDM	Biofuels
Global agreement	Global agreement to reduce GHG emissions from aviation.	The nature of the Commission's analysis and proposals regarding the inclusion of energy-intensive sectors in the ETS will be determined 'in the light' of the outcome of international negotiations and the extent to which these lead to global GHG emission reductions	International agreement on climate change	Multilateral agreement containing sustainability criteria corresponding to those in the Renewable Energy Directive and demonstrating compliance with the sustainability criteria
Bilateral agreement	None	None	Agreement with third country specifying level of use	Bilateral agreement as above
Third country measures	Third country measures to reduce the climate change impact of flights departing from that country which land in the EU	None	None	Voluntary national scheme setting standards for the production of biomass products demonstrating compliance with the sustainability criteria
Private governance	None	Binding sectoral agreements which lead to global greenhouse gas emissions reductions of the magnitude required to effectively address climate change, and which are monitorable, verifiable and subject to mandatory enforcement arrangements	None	Voluntary international scheme as above

In thinking about what it is that the EU is hoping to achieve by way of global emission reductions, it is necessary to look outside the formal legislative framework and to the international policy domain. The EU's standpoint in ongoing global negotiations does provide some clues. The EU's general stance is characterised by a willingness to increase its emission reduction commitment from 20 per cent to 30 per cent provided that other developed countries commit themselves to comparable emission reductions and that developing countries contribute adequately according to their responsibilities and respective capabilities'.[57] Still this remains quite vague.

The EU has offered some additional guidance as to what this might require on the part of both developed and developing countries. In its view, keeping below a temperature rise of 2 degrees requires that global emissions peak by 2020 at the latest, and that they be reduced by at least 50 per cent below 1990 levels by 2050 and that they continue to decline thereafter. As such, and in keeping with the findings of the UN Intergovernmental Panel on Climate Change (IPPC), developed countries should reduce their emissions by 25%–40% by 2020 (and by between 80%–95% by 2050[58]), and developing countries should achieve a substantial deviation below the currently predicted emissions growth rate, in the order of 15%–20% by 2020.[59]

There is then room in the EU's contingent unilateralism for a differentiated response. With the exception of biofuels, where the environmental performance benchmarks are relatively clearly defined, the point at which the regulatory penalty default can be lifted could and should be different for China and for the United States. There is ambiguity on this point in relation to aviation in the emissions trading scheme. While the body of the Emissions Trading Directive is vague, requiring States to adopt measures to address the climate change impact of flights, the preamble to the Directive seems to suggest that measures that are equivalent to those of the EU in terms of environmental effectiveness would be required. This differentiation dimension will be absolutely key if the EU is to act in conformity with the by now well-established, though contested, principle of common but differentiated responsibilities and respective capabilities.[60]

One thing that does seem clear about the EU's structural leadership approach is that as the prospect for a comprehensive global agreement on climate change

[57] Appendix I at http://unfccc.int/home/items/5264.php. This commitment was first made by the Council of the European Union in 2009 before the Copenhagen climate change meeting. See the Information Note from the General Secretariat of 11 November 2009, available at www.consilium.europa.eu/uedocs/cmsUpload/ST15838_09.pdf, 2.

[58] Inforrmation Note, ibid, 5.

[59] Joint Council and Commission letter of 28 January 2010 at: http://ec.europa.eu/unitedkingdom/press/press_releases/2010/pr1005_en.htm.

[60] The fairness dimension to EU contingent unilateralism is a theme that I am addressing in my current work. For a good introduction to the debate on common but differentiated responsibilities, see L Rajamani, 'The Reach and Limits of The Principle of Common but Differentiated Responsibilities and Respective Capabilities In the Climate Change Regime' in N Dubash (ed), *Handbook on Climate Change and India* (London, Routledge, 2012).

fades, EU policy is increasingly predicated upon a sectoral approach.[61] In each of the four examples above, progress at a sectoral level may suffice to permit escape from the regulatory penalty default. While this is explicit in three out of the four examples (aviation, energy-intensive sectors and biofuels), it is also implied in relation to the fourth (European-level regulation of the CDM). The oblique language of agreements which establish 'levels of use' in relation to project offsets may be viewed as code for the construction of a sectoral offsetting mechanism. This would create opportunities for countries that over-perform in relation to sectoral emissions targets to sell the resulting emissions as offsets in the EU:[62] 'Credits could be awarded for beating reinforced ambition levels, while no penalties would be imposed for missing these ambition levels' (no-lose targets).[63] The focus for the EU would be on 'key sectors' where emissions are rising rapidly or which form part of competitive world markets.[64]

One of the interesting questions arising in relation to the EU's regulation-based approach is the scope or reach of the regulation that third countries must adopt to escape from the regulatory penalty default. The EU's approach is characterised by variation in this respect. In the aviation and biofuels examples, third country regulation which is confined to flights or biofuels destined for the EU market can suffice to relax the regulatory penalty default. Likewise, in relation to European-level regulation of the CDM, it seems likely that the focus of the bilateral agreements in question would be on the operation of plants which seek to generate offsets for European use. Consequently, these EU measures do not require third country-wide, across-the-board, regulatory reform.[65] This approach carries with it the danger that 'EU imports [may be] delivered by the "cleanest" third country producers, while keeping "dirtier" production for their own domestic use'.[66]

By contrast, were the ETS to be extended to include imports from energy-intensive sectors, more could be required: namely, global emission reductions of the magnitude necessary to address climate change effectively. Where reductions on this scale cannot be achieved by focusing on emissions embodied in goods produced for export to the EU, further third country emission reductions may be deemed necessary as a precondition for lifting the regulatory penalty default. Here, the environmental performance benchmark is not defined exclusively by reference to the regulation of EU-destined goods, and the level of the EU's ambition in terms of its capacity to leverage regulatory change is increased.

[61] For an overview of sectoral approaches, see C Egenhofer and N Fujiwara, 'Sectoral Approaches to Address Climate Change: More than Wishful Thinking?' (2009) 8 *European Review of Energy Markets* 1.

[62] SEC (2009) 101 final, Annex 17, 117.

[63] Ibid.

[64] Ibid.

[65] Nonetheless, the EU regulatory penalty default may well galvanise the emergence of normative resources which can subsequently be applied also in relation to the production of goods which are not intended for export to the EU. In this sense, the EU's approach may facilitate regulatory endeavours which go beyond the scope of what is formally required to escape the EU's regulatory penalty default.

[66] European Commission (n 1) 12.

V CONCLUSION

The shift in favour of structural leadership on the part of the EU, and the associated implication that the EU is prepared to use the size of its internal market in a bid to galvanise global regulatory change, will be controversial; including as a matter of international law. We see this most clearly in relation to the aviation example. Already the Air Transport Association of America and a number of major US airlines are challenging the aviation extension to the ETS on the basis of international and European law. The case reached the Court of Justice following a reference for a preliminary ruling on validity from the High Court of England and Wales.[67] It is equally clear that the biofuels example raises issues of legality under WTO law.[68]

But there may nonetheless be reasons to favour this kind of 'contingent unilateralism', based on a combination of a fixed regulatory penalty default and the possibility for escape from it when other states adopt adequate climate regulations of their own. Acting alone, the EU cannot achieve its climate change goals. At the same time, the prospects of achieving a comprehensive global climate change deal seem increasingly remote. Perhaps then the best we can hope for today is a 'climate change regime complex' of the kind that Keohane and Victor advocate and describe, comprising 'loosely coupled systems of institutions' operating at different levels of governance and in relation to narrowly drawn, discrete but often overlapping, issue areas.[69]

Keohane and Victor posit their regime complex approach as not only politically feasible but also in some ways as representing a preferable policy response. They argue that it brings with it the advantage of flexibility/adaptability and that it may serve to overcome the counter-productive rigidities often associated with a comprehensive global response. In charting the policy implications of this approach, Keohane and Victor venture out on a limb, arguing in favour of the introduction by States of carbon border tax adjustments, specifically conceiving these as creating incentives for participation in a global carbon-trading scheme.[70] Keohane and Victor situate their regime complex somewhere in the middle of a continuum between an integrated, comprehensive global regime and an entirely fragmented response.[71] In so doing, they set out a number of criteria for evaluating a regime

[67] See Case C-366/10 *The Air Transport Association of America, American Airlines, Inc, Continental Airlines, Inc, United Airlines, Inc v The Secretary of State for Energy and Climate Change* OJ [2010] C260/9. Judgment was delivered on 21 December 2011, after the submission of this chapter.

[68] For a good discussion, see International Food and Agricultural Trade Policy Council Discussion Paper, 'WTO Disciplines and Biofuels: Opportunities and Constraints in the Creation of a Global Marketplace' (October 2006), available at www.agritrade.org/Publications/DiscussionPapers/WTO_Disciplines_Biofuels.pdf.

[69] See again Keohane and Victor (n 6) 3 and 26 for a graphic representation.

[70] Ibid, 18.

[71] Ibid, 3.

complex,[72] arguing that it is on this basis that its normative justifiability can be evaluated and assessed.

Keohane and Victor's position represents a kind of in-between stance that has much to offer in thinking about the position of the EU. They would neither denounce the EU's contingent unilateralism out of hand, nor exempt it from evaluation on the basis of the criteria they lay down. Theirs is a constructive position that acknowledges the reality of regime fragmentation and that sets out to appraise and improve rather than simply to condemn. If nothing else, a normative appraisal of this kind would require of the EU a more developed narrative about what it is doing and why, and about the normative basis underpinning its increasingly numerous trade-supported policy demands.

The EU is willing to concede that its climate unilateralism is driven in part by the need to level the competitive playing field for EU businesses that compete with businesses abroad, but a citizenship perspective on climate change reminds us that the EU faces demands for effective climate action not just from the commercial sector but from ordinary citizens as well. Opposition to EU climate unilateralism is beginning to heat up,[73] and it remains to be seen how the EU will balance the demands of industry and of powerful trading partners in the face of these intense citizen concerns.

[72] The six criteria they list are coherence, accountability, determinacy, sustainability, epistemic quality and fairness (ibid, 16).

[73] A quick search for 'EU ETS' on the Aviation Law Prof Blog (http://lawprofessors.typepad.com/aviation/) brings up numerous stories about different countries and other actors speaking out against the aviation extension in the ETS. It seems that the hearing in the aviation case before the Court of Justice on 5 July 2011 (n 67 above) served to focus attention on this measure, which had already been in place for more than two years.

9

Is the Citizen Driving the EU's Criminal Law Agenda?

ESTER HERLIN-KARNELL*

I INTRODUCTION

THE LISBON TREATY has elevated criminal law to a central constitutional place. Institutionally this has been a reformation. Indeed, the abolition of the complex pillar system and the extended jurisdiction of the Court of Justice to cover this area have been of great importance for the credibility of the area of freedom, security and justice (AFSJ) project. The present chapter's starting point is, however, slightly different. It will try to investigate to what extent these constitutional changes as brought about by the Lisbon Treaty – and as witnessed in the case law of the Court of Justice – have been driven by genuine concerns for the individual. In other words, this chapter explores the extent to which the individual could be said to drive the agenda in contemporary EU criminal law and policy. Of particular relevance for such an examination is the recent Stockholm Programme,[1] which stipulates the goals to be achieved within the AFSJ, and as such is the follow-up to the previous Hague Programme.[2] The Stockholm Programme claims to be serving and protecting the citizen as well as placing citizens at the heart of EU activities. However, if one looks more closely at this Programme, the importance of increasing the effectiveness of existing European crime policies seems to overshadow other objectives such as the protection of human rights at the EU level. The Stockholm Programme states, for example, that

* Thanks go to Professor Niamh Nic Shuibhne for her invaluable comments on this chapter as well as to all the participants at the workshop 'Empowerment and Disempowerment of the European Citizen', 10 December 2010, Edinburgh Europa Institute, for useful suggestions. Some of the ideas outlined in the present chapter were also presented at the Uppsala University European Law Colloquium on Freedom, Security and Justice on 13–14 January 2011 under the title 'EU Criminal Law Relocated: Recent Developments'; thanks also to those participants for comments. The usual disclaimer applies.

[1] European Council, 'The Stockholm Programme: An Open and Secure Europe Serving and Protecting the Citizen' [2009] OJ C115/1.

[2] European Council, 'The Hague Programme: Ten Priorities for the Next Five Years' [2005] OJ C236.

'faced with cross-border crime, the administration of justice must not be impeded by differences between the Member States' judicial systems'. Yet the focus on speedy prosecutions may undermine the values it seeks to protect: namely the guarantee of due process and procedural safeguards for the individual. In other words, the EU embraces a number of principles in theory that in practice may be rendered nugatory.

This chapter is structured as follows. It begins by identifying the general framework for the protection of the individual in EU criminal law. This obviously means that it is not only defence rights that are looked at but also the protection of EU citizens from criminal activity. After all, the very concept of creating an AFSJ suggests that the EU really wants to guarantee its citizens a crime-free European sphere. Secondly, the chapter then tries to outline the concept of citizenship rights within the AFSJ and explores the extent to which greater emphasis on those rights might enhance the credibility of European criminal law. Recent case law will be discussed in order to illuminate the many questions that are currently confronting the EU in this context. Finally, the chapter looks at some recent legislative instruments in this area and questions the degree to which they are driven by the concerns of citizens. The research questions explored in the chapter are, first, what are the underlying rationales for the EU and, secondly, what do those rationales tell us about the relationship between the individual and the EU with regard to the AFSJ? As frequently pointed out by others, the safeguarding of someone's security might constitute a restriction of someone else's freedom.[3] The primary rationale is then, perhaps, the concept of justice. This chapter seeks to examine just what that means in a transnational setting by investigating the role and function played by the individual.

II THE INDIVIDUAL AND THE AFSJ

The EU places the individual at the centre of the stage. After all, Article 2 TEU reminds us that:

> The Union is founded on the values of respect for human dignity, freedom, democracy, equality, the rule of law and respect for human rights, including the rights of persons belonging to minorities. These values are common to the Member States in a society in which pluralism, non-discrimination, tolerance, justice, solidarity and equality between women and men prevail.'

And Article 3 TEU makes it clear that not only shall the Union aim to promote the well-being of its peoples, but it shall also offer its citizens an AFSJ without internal frontiers, in which the free movement of persons is ensured in conjunction with appropriate measures with respect to, among other things, the prevention and combating of crime. Moreover, Article 6 TEU stipulates that the Union recognises

[3] On security and the AFSJ, see S Peers, *EU Justice and Home Affairs* 3rd edn (Oxford, Oxford University Press, 2011) ch 1.

the rights, freedoms and principles set out in the Charter of Fundamental Rights. It is also provides that, notwithstanding the statement that fundamental rights constitute general principles of EU law, the Union shall accede to the ECHR. In addition, the strong focus on citizens' rights within the AFSJ is manifested in the Stockholm Programme, 'An Open and Secure Europe and Protecting the Citizen'. In this Programme, it is pointed out that a growing number of citizens are involved in criminal proceedings in a Member State other than their country of origin. For this reason, the Commission has recently published a proposal for a Directive on the rights, support and protection of victims' rights.[4] This Directive cross-refers to the Commission's reports on EU citizenship from 2010,[5] and seeks to contribute to the broader ambition of the dismantling of obstacles to citizens' rights. Therefore the Commission stipulates that the strengthening of procedural rights of suspects or accused persons in criminal law proceedings reflects this approach. There is thus a strong focus on the protection of 'rights' as a key element of the development of EU criminal law.

Before the entry into force of the Lisbon Treaty, there had been a clear implementation imbalance with regard to the former third pillar, which was not only characterised by the infamous limited jurisdiction of the Court of Justice as stipulated by ex Article 35 TEU, but the question of enforcement within this sphere was left to a general loyalty obligation (in the wake of the *Pupino*[6] case, which insisted on a Communitarised reading of the former third pillar) to refrain from ineffective action from a Union perspective.

Consequently the Lisbon Treaty represents an important change here, with the constitutionalisation of EU criminal law, even though the AFSJ will remain work-in-progress for some time. In particular, the Lisbon Treaty provides for a whole new framework as regards the approximation of legal safeguards and the jurisdiction of the Court of Justice, to which we will now turn.

A EU Criminal Law and the Lisbon Treaty: Key Reforms

It is fitting to begin by briefly setting out the basic legal framework of EU criminal law after Lisbon.[7] The crucial provisions are Articles 82 (procedural criminal law) and 83 (substantive criminal law) TFEU. These provisions need, however, to be read in the light of Chapter 1 of Title V TFEU, which sets out the general goals to be achieved in this area. More specifically, Article 67 TFEU stipulates that the Union shall constitute an area of freedom, security and justice with respect for fundamental rights and the different legal systems and traditions of the Member States. Moreover, it provides that the Union shall endeavour to ensure a high level

[4] European Commission, 'Proposal for a Directive establishing minimum standards on the rights, support and protection of victims of crime' COM (2011) 275 final.

[5] European Commission, 'Dismantling the Obstacles to EU Citizens' Rights' COM (2010) 603 final.

[6] Case C-105/03 *Pupino* [2005] ECR I-5285.

[7] For a recent comprehensive analysis, see Peers (n 3).

of security through measures to prevent and combat crime, racism, and xenophobia, and through measures for coordination and cooperation between police and judicial authorities and other competent authorities, as well as through the mutual recognition of judgments in criminal matters and, if necessary, through the approximation of criminal laws. So the importance of ensuring a high level of security plays an important role here.

i Procedural Criminal Law: Basics I

Article 82 TFEU stipulates that judicial cooperation in criminal matters shall be based on the principle of mutual recognition and should include the approximation of the laws and regulations of the Member States in the areas referred to in paragraph 2 of the same provision. That paragraph, in turn, states that the European Parliament and the Council may establish minimum rules to the extent necessary to facilitate mutual recognition of judgments and judicial decisions as well as police and judicial cooperation in criminal matters having a cross-border dimension. Such rules shall take into account the differences between the legal traditions and systems of the Member States. Article 82(2) TFEU then sets out a list of areas within which the EU has legislative competence, including the mutual admissibility of evidence between the Member States, the rights of individuals in criminal proceedings, and provisions regarding the rights of victims. Furthermore, the provision contains a so-called 'general clause' stating that any other specific aspect of criminal procedure, which the Council has identified by (unanimous) decision in advance, would qualify for future approximation. Finally, Article 82(2) states that the adoption of the minimum rules should not prevent Member States from maintaining or introducing a higher level of protection for individuals.

It remains to be seen whether this constitutes a far-reaching and sufficiently consistent solution as regards the protection of the individual. In particular, it remains arguably unclear to what extent a Member State could insist on higher levels of protection of the individual under the so-called non-mandatory exceptions granted by the European Arrest Warrant (EAW)[8] and therefore refuse to surrender. After all, there is no general human rights exception under the EAW. Instead the notion of mutual recognition (and trust) is the main rule here but – as will be seen – the Court has started to loosen the scope of its requirements within EU criminal law by stressing the (from a traditional EU law perspective, quite clear) assumption that mutual recognition is not absolute.

ii Substantive Criminal Law: Basics II

Article 83(1) TFEU concerns the regulation of substantive criminal law and stipulates that the European Parliament and the Council may, by means of directives,

[8] Council Framework Decision 2002/584/JHA of 13 June 2002 on the European arrest warrant and the surrender procedures between Member States [2002] OJ L 190/1.

establish minimum rules concerning the definition of criminal law offences and sanctions in the area of particularly serious crime with a cross-border dimension resulting from the nature or impact of such offences or from a special need to combat them on a common basis. Thereafter, this provision sets out a list of crimes in respect of which the EU shall have legislative competence such as terrorism, organised crime, and money laundering. It also states that the Council may identify other possible areas of crime that meet the cross-border and seriousness criteria. Furthermore, and interestingly, Article 83(2) establishes that the possibility exists for approximation if a measure proves essential towards ensuring the effective implementation of a Union policy in an area that has already been subject to harmonisation measures.

iii The Court's Jurisdiction: Basics III

One of the most significant changes introduced by the Lisbon Treaty is the extension of the Court's jurisdiction also to cover the former third pillar area. This is obviously one of the most important constitutional restructurings under the Lisbon Treaty and one of the most crucial changes for the individual. It should perhaps be recalled that prior to the entry into force of the Lisbon Treaty, Member States based jurisdiction on a voluntary declaration as to whether to accept the Court's jurisdiction in accordance with Article 35 TEU.[9] The Lisbon Treaty changes this, significantly extending the Court's jurisdiction within the AFSJ field. The Lisbon Treaty Protocol on Transitional Provisions provides for a five-year transition – or alteration – period before existing third pillar instruments will be treated in the same way as other Union instruments.[10] Therefore, despite the entry into force of the Lisbon Treaty and, thereby, the merging of the pillars, there will remain 'echoes' of the third pillar through the Protocol and its five-year transition period. Obviously, this means that the Commission will not have the power to bring infringement proceedings against Member States as regards alleged breaches of pre-existing measures during this period.[11] It also means that the complex inter-pillar structure that has characterised European criminal law will remain

[9] eg, E Denza, *The Intergovernmental Pillars of the European Union* (Oxford, Oxford University Press, 2002) ch 9 and A Hinarejos, *Judicial Control in the European Union* (Oxford, Oxford University Press, 2009).

[10] Art 10 of this Protocol stipulates that: '1. As a transitional measure, and with respect to acts of the Union in the field of police cooperation and judicial cooperation in criminal matters which have been adopted before the entry into force of the Treaty of Lisbon, the powers of the institutions shall be the following the date of entry into force of that Treaty: the powers of the Commission under Article 258 of the Treaty on the Functioning of the European Union shall not be applicable and the powers of the Court of Justice of the European Union under Title VI of the Treaty on European Union, in the version in force before the entry into force of the Treaty of Lisbon, shall remain the same, including where they have been accepted under Article 35(2) of the said Treaty on European Union. 2. The amendment of an act referred to in paragraph 1 shall entail the applicability of the powers of the institutions referred to in that paragraph as set out in the Treaties with respect to the amended act for those Member States to which that amended act shall apply. 3. In any case, the transitional measure mentioned in paragraph 1 shall cease to have effect five years after the date of entry into force of the Treaty of Lisbon.'

[11] Peers (n 3) 62.

influential for some time. Moreover, as a result of the transitional rules, there will be mixed jurisdiction over different measures concerning the same subject matter, and the most feasible regime (and favourable from the perspective of the individual) should then be preferred. The crucial question seems to concern the definition of when an act is 'amended'. It seems likely that in the absence of any *de minimis* rule or any indication that acts are in any way severable as regards the Court's jurisdiction, any amendment – no matter how minor– – would suffice.[12] In the light of the Court's history in promoting European integration, the Court would conceivably favour the most inclusive reading of when an act is 'amended'.

Most importantly, the Lisbon Treaty introduces the possibility of expedited procedures for persons in custody.[13] Article 267 TFEU provides that if a question is raised in a case pending before a court or tribunal of a Member State with regard to a person in custody, the Court shall act with a minimum of delay. This is obviously an extremely important change and reflects the debate on speedier justice in Europe. However, despite the reformation of the Court of Justice's jurisdiction effected by the Lisbon Treaty, the Court will still not have the power to review the validity or proportionality of operations carried out by the police or other law enforcement agencies of a Member State, or the exercise of responsibilities incumbent upon Member States with regard to the maintenance of law and order and the safeguarding of internal security.

B Accession to the ECHR and the Legally Binding Status of the Charter of Fundamental Rights: Good for the Individual

The Lisbon Treaty stipulates that the EU shall accede to the European Convention on Human Rights (ECHR).[14] Such an accession requires unanimity in the Council and ratification by the Member States. Article 6(2) TEU adds that accession shall not affect the Union's competences as defined in the Treaties. It is clear that this accession has great symbolic value, particularly in the area of criminal law. An important question is, of course, to what extent the ECHR as such is a sufficient guardian of the individual in criminal law. After all, the *Bosphorous*[15] case law told us that 'equivalent protection' might not mean that much in practice because both the Luxembourg and Strasbourg courts are – expressed in simplified terms – 'cautious' about criticising each other. The practice of cross-referencing between the ECtHR and the Court of Justice has been the main theme here. Interestingly, it was recently argued that ECHR cases are not designed to create common

[12] Ibid, 64.

[13] For detailed discussion, see E Herlin-Karnell, 'The Lisbon Treaty and the Criminal Law: Anything New under the Sun?' (2008) 10 *European Journal of Law Reform* 321.

[14] On the EU's accession to the ECHR, see, eg, T Lock, 'Walking on a Tight Rope: The Draft ECHR Accession Agreement and the Autonomy of the EU Legal Order' (2011) 48 *CML Rev* 1025.

[15] *Bosphorus Hava Yollari Turizm ve Ticaret Anonim Sirketi v Ireland* (45036/98) 2006 42 EHRR 1 (ECHR). See, eg, S Douglas-Scott, 'A Tale of Two Courts: Luxembourg, Strasbourg and the Growing European Human Rights Acquis' (2006) 46 *CML Rev* 629.

principles for reference so that their scope should be confined with specific reference to the individual case decided by the ECtHR and they are, therefore, not intended to construe general binding principles.[16] This would distinguish ECtHR case law very sharply from Court of Justice jurisprudence. In any case, a significant difference between both Courts is that the ECtHR takes up cases only after all domestic remedies have been exhausted and it gives judgments on overall fairness. It obviously remains to be seen how this relationship will be shaped by the EU's accession to the ECHR when the EU becomes a signatory. The Court of Justice will continue to be the guardian of the autonomous EU legal order; but, strictly speaking, it will be subordinated to the ECtHR as a matter of Treaty law when it comes to EU law compliance with the ECHR. Plausibly, and if the two Courts manage to avoid the political sensitivity of these issues, 'equivalent' protection will become 'maximum' protection.[17]

In addition, through the ratification of the Lisbon Treaty, the Charter of Fundamental Rights has finally become legally binding. It is stated in Article 6 TEU, however, that the provisions of the Charter shall not extend the EU's competences. Also, Article 51 of the Charter makes it clear that it is directed at the Union's institutions and at the Member States when they are 'implementing' Union law. Given this formulation, it could perhaps be questioned what the point of the Charter is. This is particularly the case since the Charter also, in Article 52, distinguishes between principles and rights, where rights have been given a 'higher' status. The problem is how to identify fully justiciable rights as opposed to partially justiciable principles. Interestingly, for example, the principle of legality is referred to as a 'principle' in the Charter while Article 7 ECHR refers to the ban on retroactive criminal law[18] as an absolute right.[19]

Moreover, even if the application of the Charter is confined to the implementing of Union law, it still has an important function as a source of interpretation. With respect to criminal law, Articles 47–50 of the Charter could have a huge influence as they guide the Union's action in this area and provide an overarching theoretical framework. Most importantly, Article 49 provides for the guarantee of legality and proportionality in a more extensive way than the ECHR. Also, Article 47 of the Charter guarantees the right to a fair trial, while Article 48 stipulates the presumption of innocence and the right of defence. The latter provision also makes it clear that the severity of penalties must not be disproportionate to the criminal offence. This is actually a more extensive guarantee than the ECHR framework (and its promise via Article 6 ECHR – of a fair trial – as the only

[16] S Allegrezza, 'Critical Remarks on the Green Paper on Obtaining Evidence in Criminal Matters' (2010) 6 *Zeitschrift für Internationale Strafrechtsdogmatik* 569, 575.

[17] For a critical analysis of the ECHR, which emphasises that not all problems are solved automatically with EU accession, see A Williams, 'Burying, Not Praising the European Convention on Human Rights: A Provocation', in N Walker, J Shaw and S Tierney (eds), *Europe's Constitutional Mosaic* (Oxford, Hart Publishing, 2011) ch 4.

[18] The only exception being war crimes, as drafted in the aftermath of World War II.

[19] See E Herlin-Karnell, 'The Lisbon Treaty. A Critical Analysis of its Impact on EU Criminal Law' (2010) *European Criminal Law Association Forum* 58.

guarantee of proportionality). Indeed, the Commission is firm in this regard, as it ensures in its Communication on the Stockholm Programme (discussed below) that it will apply a 'Zero Tolerance policy' as regards any violations of the Charter.[20] In particular, the Commission recognises that mutual trust will be essential to making real progress. This requires the establishment of minimum standards of procedural protection.

It is therefore likely that the binding status of the Charter will have both a significant symbolic status and a real substantive impact on the criminal law. Although one may well speculate as to whether the Court will use its traditional case law on general principles and view the Charter as part of this, such an interpretation would run counter to the express will of the Member States. As pointed out by Dougan,[21] it is possible that the Court will continue to apply and develop its case law based on general principles and then have a separate agenda for the EU's institutions and the Member States when implementing EU law. It could therefore be argued that the Charter, consequently, not only underlines and clarifies the legal status and freedoms of the Union's citizens when facing the institutions of the Union, but also gives the Union and, in particular, the policies regarding the AFSJ a new, explicit normative foundation.[22]

III EU CRIMINAL LAW AND EU CITIZENS

The question of citizen rights in the context of EU criminal law could, in a straightforward manner, be described as concerned with procedural rights in criminal law proceedings. The most obvious example is the fundamental requirement of access to justice as forming part of Article 6 ECHR and Article 47 of the Charter regarding the right to fair hearing, the provision of resources for interpretation and so on, as discussed above. As explained in section II, the entry into force of the Lisbon Treaty means that the pillars of the Union have been abolished (though note the interim effects of the transitional Protocol). Naturally, this means that the notion of citizenship as stipulated in Article 20 TFEU will now explicitly apply to the former third pillar area, the most obvious example being the criminal law cooperation instruments such as the EAW and the principle of mutual recognition in this area. The application of mutual recognition raises familiar questions about the implications of free movement within the area of EU criminal law cooperation as well as the constitutional dimension of citizenship in EU criminal law. It could perhaps be argued that the most essential aspect has been of a symbolic nature, ie simply recognising the relevance of citizenship. After

[20] European Commission, 'Communication from the Commission to the European Parliament, the Council, the European Economic and Social Committee and the Committee of the Regions – Delivering an Area of Freedom, Security and Justice for Europe's Citizens: Action Plan Implementing the Stockholm Programme' COM (2010) 171, 3.

[21] M Dougan, 'The Treaty of Lisbon 2007: Winning Minds, Not Hearts' (2008) 45 *CML Rev* 613.

[22] I Pernice, 'The Treaty of Lisbon and Fundamental Rights' in S Griller and Z Ziller (eds), *The Lisbon Treaty: EU Constitutionalism without a Constitutional Treaty?* (New York, Springer, 2008) 235.

all, it could be argued that there was a need to recognise that a system based on enforcement and mutual recognition also needed the other side of the coin, namely substantial principles of non-discrimination and the recognition of citizenship rights.

Nevertheless, there had been a general assumption that, before the entry into force of the Lisbon Treaty, the question of Union citizenship was not significant outside the first pillar setting. I have previously argued this is not the whole truth.[23] Citizenship and non-discrimination were relevant to third pillar criminal law cooperation – and continue to be during the transitional period – not only because of the depillarisation trend starting with *Pupino*,[24] as mentioned above, but mainly because fundamental rights applied across the pillars as proclaimed in ex Article 6 TEU. Accordingly, the Member States and the EU institutions are under a duty to apply the same standards as regards human rights when acting in the AFSJ. It is also quite obvious that the notion of non-discrimination is of the utmost importance in criminal law cooperation as forming part of the concept of a fair trial in a broad sense. Furthermore, there has always been a clear first pillar aspect here: citizens cross borders and therefore there is a free movement dimension regardless of whether a matter also concerns, for example, an EAW order.

In what follows, this chapter will try to look more closely at recent judgments concerning the individual and the wider implications of EU legal evolution for EU criminal law proceedings in the context of citizenship and non-discrimination. These cases highlight the bigger debate concerning the application of mutual recognition to European criminal law and the AFSJ dimension to classic citizenship case law. The main issue concerning the mutual recognition cases has been the task of creating mutual trust in this area. For this reason, the chapter will try to map recent developments in the area of EU criminal law cooperation, which illustrate the Court's attempts to construct a European web of criminal law by, inter alia, embracing the principles of non-discrimination and citizenship in this dynamic area.

A Free Movement Rights, the Individual and Criminal Law: the Case of the EAW

As indicated above, EU criminal law cooperation touches upon free movement rights. It concerns not only the difficulties of applying mutual recognition in criminal law as such but also the consequences of free movement rights more broadly, ie that some of these rights have been exercised in the wrong way. In other words, there is a need to enforce criminal law cooperation at the EU level precisely because EU free movement rights have facilitated criminal activity.

Indeed, as also indicated above, one of the most controversial instruments in this area has been the EAW Framework Decision, which has been debated for

[23] E Herlin-Karnell, 'The EAW and the Principles of Non-discrimination and EU Citizenship' (2010) 73 *MLR* 460.

[24] Case C-105/03 *Pupino* [2005] ECR I-5285.

quite some time.[25] In the early days, academics pointed out that this mutual recognition flagship of EU criminal law had been adopted too early, without adequate protection of the individual and without sufficient mutual trust in this area.[26] Several constitutional courts in Europe, most prominently in Germany, either declared the national law implementing the EAW unconstitutional[27] or, on the contrary, upheld it as part of the speedy process of criminal law cooperation in Europe (for example, the Czech Republic).[28] In other words, those challenges to the constitutionality of the EAW concerned the national measure implementing it or its application in a particular case. In *Advocaten voor de Wereld*,[29] the Court had to deal with the (probably) most difficult issue of them all: the validity of the EU instrument itself. The Court concluded that the EAW did not breach the principle of legality. Further, the Court stipulated that even if the Member States were to reproduce word-for-word the list of the categories of offences set out in the Framework Decision for the purposes of its implementation, the actual definition of those offences and the penalties applicable are those which follow from the law of 'the issuing Member State'. Nonetheless, the lack of a coherent approach to the fair trial guarantee in these cases raised several issues of concern with regard to the EAW and the very phenomenon of mutual recognition.[30]

In seeking to understand the tension between free movement rights and the application of mutual recognition in this (former third pillar) area, it is useful to turn to the *Wolzenburg* judgment.[31] That ruling concerned the EAW and the scope of possibility for the Member States to refuse to surrender a request issued under Article 4(6) EAW. In *Wolzenburg*, the Netherlands had made a so-called voluntary opt-out under Article 4(6) EAW. This means that if an arrest warrant has been issued for the purposes of executing a custodial sentence or detention order, where the requested person is staying in or is a national or a resident of the executing Member State, that State undertakes to execute the sentence or detention order in accordance with its domestic law. Therefore, the question arose as to whether it constituted discrimination to distinguish between a State's own nationals and non-nationals in this regard and whether an additional administrative burden – such as a residence permit – was in line with the axiom of non-discrimination in EU law. In

[25] See eg V Mitsilegas, 'The Constitutional Implications of Mutual Recognition in EU Criminal Law' (2006) 43 *CML Rev* 1277 and Peers (n 3).

[26] eg, S Peers, 'Mutual Recognition and Criminal Law in the European Union: Has the Council Got It Wrong?' (2004) 41 *CML Rev* 5; S Aleagere and M Leaf, 'Mutual Recognition in European Judicial Cooperation: A Step Too Far Too Soon?' (2004) 11 *ELJ* 200.

[27] eg, Mitsilegas (n 25).

[28] eg, E Guild (ed), *Constitutional Challenges to the EAW* (The Hague, Asser Press, 2006).

[29] Case C-303/05 *Advocaten voor de Wereld*, ECR [2007] I-3633. For commentary, see, eg, E Herlin-Karnell, 'In the Wake of Pupino: Advocaten voor der Wereld and Dell'Orto' (2007) 8 *German Law Journal* 1147.

[30] See eg E Spaventa, 'Opening Pandora's Box: Some Reflections on the Constitutional Effects of the Decision in Pupino' (2007) 3 *European Constitutional Law Review* 5, and M Fichera, *The Implementation of the European Arrest Warrant in the European Union: Law, Policy and Practice* (Antwerp, Intersentia, 2011) as well as A Suominen, *The Principle of Mutual Recognition in Cooperation in Criminal Matters* (Antwerp, Intersentia, 2011).

[31] Case C-123/08 *Wolzenburg* [2009] ECR I-09621.

this case, the Court of Justice stipulated that non-discrimination was applicable in the (now former) third pillar area, as there was a clear free movement dimension to the EAW. This has important implications from the perspective of rehabilitation issues and the possibilities of integrating into society.[32] The Court in *Wolzenburg* seems to have applied a reasoning that is directly reflected in the Citizenship Directive, Directive 2004/38.[33] One may therefore say that the Court used Directive 2004/38 as a template in the context of the EAW and its intersection with former third pillar law. In relying on the Directive, the Court in *Wolzenburg* appears to have adopted a restrictive approach towards residence requirements in line with the case law on student benefits.[34] Clearly, this raises the familiar question of the extent to which secondary legislation should prevail over Treaty-based rights as provided in the Treaty, ie the relationship between primary and secondary EU law.[35] Whatever the status of citizenship might be at present, it seems clear that cases such as *Teixeira* and *Ibrahim*[36] albeit in the context of the free movement of workers and education of children in the host State, confirm the special status of minor children as also reaffirmed by the recent judgment in *Ruiz Zambrano*.[37] Interestingly, Mr Wolzenburg was about to become a father, but in his case, the question was whether or not he should be entitled to access to a Dutch prison instead of serving the remainder of his sentence in the issuing State, namely his native Germany.

Nevertheless, in spite of the restrictive reading of the residence requirement as interpreted by the Court, it is submitted that the *Wolzenburg* case is not about limiting rights but expanding them. After all, at the time this judgment was delivered, it was not even clear that citizenship and non-discrimination applied to the former third pillar even though there had always been a clear free movement dimension to the EAW. More crucially, it highlighted the extent to which mutual recognition was absolute in the former third pillar domain and to what extent other concerns, such as attention to the principle of proportionality, could be taken into consideration. It seemed as if the concept of managed recognition, which for a long time had been applicable in the classic EU law domain, was largely forgotten in the former third pillar.[38]

[32] Ibid, Opinion of AG Bot, para 65.

[33] Dir 2004/38/EC on the right of citizens of the Union and their family members to move and reside freely within the territory of the Member States *[2004] OJ L158/77*.

[34] Case C-158/07 *Förster* [2008] ECR I-8507.

[35] S O'Leary, 'Equal Treatment and EU Citizens: A New Chapter on Cross Border Educational Mobility and Access to Student Financial Assistance' (2009) 34 *EL Rev* 612 and E Spaventa, 'Seeing the Wood Despite the Trees? On the Scope of Union Citizenship and its Constitutional Effects' (2008) 45 *CML Rev* 13. For a strict application of the residency requirements as stipulated in Dir 2004/38, see, eg, Case C-158/07 *Forster* [2008] ECR I-8507.

[36] Case C-480/08 *Teixeira* [2010] ECR I-1107 and Case C-310/08 *Ibrahim* ECR [2010] ECR I-1065; for commentary, see C O'Brien, Annotation (2011) 48 *CML Rev* 203 as well as N Nic Shuibhne, 'The Third Age of EU Citizenship: Directive 2004/38 in the Case Law of the Court of Justice' in P Syrpis (ed), *The Judiciary, the Legislature and the EU Internal Market* (Cambridge, Cambridge University Press, 2012) ch 13.

[37] Case C-34/09 *Ruiz Zambrano*, judgment delivered on 8 March 2011, nyr, regarding the purely internal situation and citizenship.

[38] On managed mutual recognition, see K Nicolaidis, 'Trusting the Poles? Constructing Europe through Mutual Recognition' (2007) 14 *Journal of European Public Policy* 682.

Yet, crucially, in the judgment in *IB*,[39] concerning the operation of the EAW and trial in absentia, the Court confirmed that mutual recognition is not absolute. In paragraph 50 of this judgment, the Court pointed out that while it is true that the EAW is based on the principle of mutual recognition, that recognition does not, as is clear from Articles 3 to 5 of the Framework Decision, mean that there is an absolute obligation to execute the arrest warrant that has been issued. The Court stressed the importance of allowing for some national discretion in this area and especially the importance of enabling particular weight to be given to the possibility of increasing the requested persons' chances of reintegrating into society. The Court held that, against the background of these interests, the arrest warrant should also include a sentence imposed in absentia, as there was nothing indicating that the EU legislator wished to exclude trials in absentia from the scope of the possibilities of including extra procedural safeguards. This represents an important step. After all, the previous assumption seems to have been that the notion of mutual recognition in this area was absolute and that any hesitation by the Member States to surrender on the grounds of human rights concerns would conflict with the *Pupino*-created[40] obligation of loyalty. Moreover, in the *Mantello*[41] case, concerning the scope of the mandatory options for non-execution of arrest warrants under Article 3(2) of the EAW, the Court stated that the *ne bis in idem* principle should be given an autonomous interpretation in EU law. Furthermore, the Court made it clear that whether a person has been 'finally' judged is determined by the law of the Member State in which the judgment was delivered. In the light of the fact that Article 50 of the Charter prescribes the right not to be punished twice, such reaffirmation appears perhaps less controversial.

In any case, it could be argued that criminal law in the free movement context seems odd, in the sense that the Court appears not to be too enthusiastic about the idea of extending free movement rights unreservedly. Interestingly, it should perhaps be mentioned that in *Tsakouridis*[42] the Court stipulated that an expulsion decision can be taken on imperative grounds of public policy against a citizen who has resided on the territory of the host State for the previous ten years if criminality is at stake. So when drug dealing is in question, the Court is willing to agree that there are no unlimited citizenship rights.[43] It could be cautiously asked if this represents a new trend where citizenship rights presuppose law-obeying nationals. Although a case such as *Tsakouridis* concerned the Member States' possibilities of derogation from free movement rights on the grounds of public policy (in an illegal drugs-related context), it shows the character of criminal law in this area as being very different from other areas of law and constantly interacting

[39] Case C-306/09 *IB*, [2010] I-0000.

[40] Case C-105/03 Criminal proceedings against Maria Pupino [2005] ECR I-5285.

[41] Case C-261/09 *Mantello*, judgment of 7 September 2010, nyr.

[42] Case C-145/09 *Tsakouridis* judgment of 23 November 2010, nyr. For a more recent confirmation of this 'new' trend see, Case C 348/09, *PI* judgment of 22 May 2012, nyr, where it was stated that crimes listed in Article 83 TFEU are considered 'serious' criminality and may justify expulsion measures on the ground of public security.

[43] See however Case C-348/96 *Donatella Calfa* [1999] ECR I-11.

with the free movement law. This case law shows the challenges for the Court of Justice in the future. On the on hand, it is just 'classic' free movement rights at stake and an orthodox approach adopted by the Court in its application of these rights. In its purest meaning, 'citizenship' in this area is taken as guaranteeing the right to non-discrimination and fair trial rights but does not seem to extend as far as also ensuring preferences for where to serve a prison sentence when it is not directly connected to the possibility of reintegrating into society. On the other hand, cases such as *IB* and *Mantello* demonstrate that the Court is taking the lead (also) by guiding EU criminal law towards a non-absolute concept of mutual recognition and by cautiously touching upon the phenomenon of the beginning of an autonomous interpretation in this area.

But perhaps more importantly, the case law discussed above also touches upon the question of what values the EU seeks to protect. As noted in section II, Article 2 TEU reminds us that the values the EU seeks to protect are, inter alia, respect for human rights, non-discrimination and justice. Article 3 TEU sets out the AFSJ mission in further detail by linking it to the need to fight crime. Thus, there is a need to find a means of balancing these sometimes conflicting values. The Commission's recent evaluation of the implementation of the EAW is interesting in this regard.[44] In its assessment, the Commission points out that the effective application of the EAW has been undermined by the systematic issuing of EAWs for the surrender of persons sought in respect of often very minor offences. Therefore, the Commission states that there is now a need to apply a proportionality test to make sure that offences that are not serious enough to justify the measures and cooperation that the execution of an EAW requires are excluded. As was demonstrated above, though, it could be argued that the principle of proportionality already forms part of the very notion of a 'managed' mutual recognition concept as such. In addition, it could perhaps be argued that the concept of justice is interlinked with a general proportionality requirement in this area. Indeed, it demonstrates the complex state of play created when former intergovernmental acts such as the EAW had very little focus on the individual and, for some reason, also neglected the overarching umbrella principle of proportionality. Instead, the main focus has been to create a judicial web based on trust so as to facilitate mutual recognition mechanisms. Indeed, the very notion of an autonomous interpretation of EU criminal law is closely connected with the wider aspiration of creating trust. In the *Gözütok and Brügge*[45] cases, in the context of the interpretation of *ne bis in idem*, the Court stated that there is a necessary implication that the Member States have mutual trust in their criminal justice systems. Yet in spite of the reassurance in *IB* that mutual recognition is not absolute, it seems still too

[44] European Commission, 'Report from the Commission to the European Parliament and the Council: On the Implementation Since 2007 of the Council Framework Decision of 13 June 2002 on the European Arrest Warrant and the Surrender Procedures between Member States' COM (2011) 175 final.

[45] Joined Cases C-187/01 and C-385/01 *Gözütok and Brugge* ECR [2003] I-1354; see also Case C-436/04 *Criminal Proceedings against Leopold Henri Van Esbroeck* [2006] ECR I-2333.

early to speak of an autonomous European criminal law that fully respects fundamental rights. The entry into force of the Lisbon Treaty provides steps in the right direction, as it offers a framework as a starting point from which EU criminal law can develop. But, as will be shown below, part of this trust mission now involves placing the individual at the centre of the debate. It is for this very reason that highly fragmented cases, from a citizenship perspective, are still of significance since they constitutionalise criminal law towards being in conformity with the existing EU *acquis*. But even if it is true that the creation of trust remains work in progress, as well as the creation of a European criminal law space more broadly, the very existence of Union citizenship and its application in the former third pillar area is an important change in the right direction. The next section will try to illuminate the Stockholm Programme from this perspective.

IV THE STOCKHOLM PROGRAMME: SERVING THE CITIZEN?

The Stockholm Programme is the latest development in the EU's Justice and Home Affairs agenda.[46] It continues the process of furthering not only European criminal law cooperation but also asylum and civil law cooperation in family matters. As noted above, while the Lisbon Treaty opens up a new chapter for the development of EU criminal law, the recent Stockholm Programme, which has to be read in the light of the entry into force of the Lisbon Treaty, is remarkable for several reasons. First, it is remarkable because it claims to be serving the citizen in a way not previously seen in earlier Justice and Home Affairs (JHA) agendas. Secondly, this Programme stresses the importance of more effective and better enforcement in EU criminal law. Thirdly, it highlights the importance of better regulation in this area in specifically tying this debate to concerns of the individual.

An initial question, against the background of an increased focus on security issues within the Union, is obviously: does the Stockholm Programme serve the citizen?[47] Whatever the answer, the Commission's Communication on the Stockholm Programme points to the current success with respect to EU involvement in the criminal law area. But it is also pointed out that the desired progress has been comparatively slow because of the limited jurisdiction of the Court – and thus because the Commission has been unable to bring infringement proceedings – which has led to considerable delay in the transposition of EU legislation at national level. However, the Communication states that the main focus for the future is building a citizen's Europe. Another question is that of 'emotional' regulation, in that the EU wants to create a common sense of justice.[48] A compre-

[46] European Council, 'The Stockholm Programme: An Open and Secure Europe Serving and Protecting the Citizen [2009] OJ C115/1.

[47] Discussed more fully in E Herlin-Karnell, 'The Integrity of European Criminal Law Cooperation: The Nation State, the Individual and the AFSJ' in F Amtenbrink and P van den Bergh (eds), *The Constitutional Integrity of the European Union* (The Hague, TMC Asser Press/Springer, 2010) ch 10.

[48] T Elholm, 'Does EU Criminal Law Cooperation Necessarily Mean Increased Repression? (2009) 17 *European Journal of Crime, Criminal law and Criminal Justice* 191, 223–25 discussing European

hensive discussion on this issue is beyond the scope of this chapter, but it can be noted that the Stockholm Programme has at least some elements that could tentatively be described as 'emotional' elements of regulation. I draw this parallel with what commentators have previously pointed out in the context of the Commission's approach to sanctions, where it has been suggested that it would help to give the general public a shared sense of justice in order to impose sanctions at EU level.[49]

According to the Stockholm Programme agenda, the main focus of the Union's action in the coming years will be 'Advancing a People's Europe', ensuring that citizens can exercise their rights and fully benefit from European integration. Here, the Commission's action plan for implementing the Stockholm Programme is illuminating.[50] The Commission emphasises that a criminal justice strategy, fully respecting subsidiarity and coherence, should guide the EU's policy for the approximation of substantive and procedural criminal law. It should be pursued in close cooperation with the European Parliament, national parliaments and the Council, and acknowledge that focus will remain primarily on mutual recognition while the harmonisation of offences and sanctions will be pursued for selected cases. More specifically, this Programme includes the following objectives:

- promoting citizens' rights – a Europe of rights;
- making life easier – a Europe of Justice;
- protecting citizens – a Europe that protects;
- promoting a more integrated society for the citizen – a Europe of solidarity.

These ambitions are very promising, albeit extremely wide ranging, and the Commission deserves a lot of credit for having taken on board the main criticisms advocated by academics.[51] According to the Commission, the internal security strategy must be construed around three complementary and now inseparable fields of activity: stronger police cooperation, a suitably adapted criminal justice system, and more effective management of access to the EU territory. Thus, the Commission stresses the need for a criminal justice system that serves to protect the public. Hence, it concludes that 'faced with cross-border crime, the administration of justice must not be impeded by differences between the Member States' judicial systems'.[52] So there is an apparent need to establish a successful crime-fighting agenda at the EU level. The question remains as to what extent the citizen is genuinely driving this agenda and to what degree such an agenda is driven by other aspirations such as the establishment of an autonomous EU system of criminal law.

Commission, 'On the Approximation, Mutual Recognition and Enforcement of Criminal Sanctions in the European Union' COM (2004) 334. For similar points, see also K Nuotio, 'On the Significance of Criminal Justice for a Europe "United" in Diversity' in K Nuotio (ed), *Europe: In Search of Meaning and Purpose* (University of Helsinki, 2004) 171.

[49] Elholm, ibid, 223.
[50] European Commission (n 20).
[51] Among the many critics, see eg Steve Peers's many contributions posted at www.statewatch.org.
[52] European Commission (n 20) 5

Regardless of the answer, the Commission identifies the need to strengthen mutual trust by enhancing procedural safeguards for the individual. The problem is that, although the Commission is trying its best, the Stockholm Programme contains so many general wishes and statements that, for the individual, it remains unclear to what extent this programme is genuinely driving citizens' rights in this area. For this reason, the Commission's recent Communication ('Towards an EU Criminal Policy: Ensuring the Effective Implementation of EU Policies through Criminal Law') is particularly interesting.[53] This Communication explicitly mentions not only the need to develop a coherent system of EU criminal law policy, but also highlights the concerns of EU citizens. Part of the justification for this Communication is, therefore, the added value of EU criminal law, in line with the wishes of EU citizens. Indeed, the latest Eurobarometer[54] places the fight against crime high in the EU chart-list of what the citizens want to the EU to tackle effectively. As such, it was ranked fourth after concerns about fixing the debt crisis, immigration policy and health policy.

For this reason, it is interesting briefly to reflect on the strong focus on the citizen in the light of the new mechanism of the Citizens' Initiative outlined in Article 11 TEU, and on the degree to which such citizen participation is viable in EU criminal law. Article 11 gives citizens and representative associations the opportunity to participate in Union decision-making through the direct right to bring a citizens' initiative, signed by not less than one million citizens who are nationals of a significant number of Member States.[55] It is a symbolic provision in the sense that it tries to bridge the alleged lack of democracy in the Union, by strengthening the claim in Article 10 TEU that the Union is founded on the principle of representative democracy.[56] Cautiously, however, it should be noted that 'initiatives' could have strange consequences as well as good consequences. There is no one-sided truth and in criminal law, and in particular in political debate on criminal law, penal populism is not uncommon.[57] So imagine that citizens would submit an initiative calling for extremely harsh penalties, perhaps because they have been misled by empirical data (which was not collected in a sound way, either at the EU or national level). Such an approach might not necessarily lead to a more effective criminal law system. On the contrary, it could be a dangerous direction for the EU criminal law policy debate. That said, however, it is obvious that the very existence of citizens' initiatives may prove to be of crucial importance as regards, for example, the protection of the victim and an adequate level of safeguards for the individual in criminal law proceedings.

[53] European Commission, 'Towards an EU Criminal Policy: Ensuring the Effective Implementation of EU Policies through Criminal Law' COM (2011) 573 final.

[54] Eurobarometer 75, spring 2011; available at http://ec.europa.eu/public_opinion/archives/eb/eb75/eb75_en.htm.

[55] Reg 211/2011/EU of the European Parliament and of the Council on the citizens' initiative [2011] OJ L65/1.

[56] JC Piris, *The Lisbon Treaty: A Legal and Political Analysis* (Cambridge, Cambridge University Press, 2010) 133.

[57] See, eg, M Nolan, 'Law Reform, Beyond Mere Opinion Polling and Penal Populism' in A Norrie et al (eds), *Regulating Device* (Oxford, Hart Publishing, 2009) 165.

A The Options for Creating a Citizens' Agenda in EU Criminal Law

The question of empowering European citizens in the criminal law context seems to be connected to the overall ambition of strengthening mutual trust in EU criminal law cooperation in general.[58] Interestingly, in the recent proposals for a directive on the right of access to a lawyer in criminal proceedings and protection of the victim respectively (developed as part of the Council's roadmap initiative, outlined below),[59] the Commission specifically links the subsidiarity principle to the importance of mutual trust. According to the Commission, only action taken by the European Union will establish consistent common minimum standards that apply throughout the whole of the EU and thereby enhance trust. One reason for current mistrust in this area has been the lack of sufficient underlying criminal law protection of the individual. For this reason, the Stockholm Programme and the action plan[60] implementing it set out to remedy this problem by stating the need for a so-called roadmap of safeguards for the individual within criminal law procedure. The Council roadmap[61] for strengthening the procedural rights of suspected or accused persons in criminal proceedings is one of the latest developments in this area. This roadmap forms part of the Stockholm Programme mission. The roadmap focuses on certain areas of particular importance:

- Translation and interpretation;
- Information on rights and information about the charges;
- Legal aid and legal advice;
- Communication with relatives, employers, and consular authorities;
- Special safeguards for suspected or accused persons who are vulnerable.

Clearly the EU deserves a lot of credit for being active here, but it is regrettable that, in relation to the objectives, there is no clarification regarding the precise procedural stage at which they should be guaranteed.[62]

It could be also asked how much of this really differs from existing ECHR case law in this area. Most of this case law means that the right to a fair hearing applies also to pre-trial scenarios.[63] Of course, as is so often pointed out,[64] the Member

[58] See, eg, The Stockholm Programme (n 46).

[59] European Commission, Proposal for a Directive on the right of access to a lawyer in criminal proceedings and on the right to communicate upon arrest COM (2011) 326/3; 'Proposal for a Directive establishing minimum standards on the rights, support and protection of victims of crime' COM (2011) 275 final.

[60] European Commission n 20).

[61] Presidency of the Council of the EU, 'Roadmap with a view to Fostering Protection of Suspected and Accused Persons in Criminal Proceedings', Brussels, 1 July 2009, document No 11457/09, DROIPEN 53, COPEN 120. For commentary, see M Jimeno-Bulnes, 'The EU Roadmap for Strengthening Procedural Rights of Suspected or Accused Persons in Criminal Proceedings' (2009) *European Criminal Law Association Forum* 59.

[62] See, eg, Jimeno-Bulnes (n 61).

[63] A Ashworth and M Redmayne, *The Criminal Process*, 3rd edn (Oxford, Oxford University Press, 2005) 28.

[64] eg, Douglas-Scott (n 15) 642.

States of the EU are no 'saints'; most of them continue to have cases pending in front of the ECtHR and it is, therefore, good to have as much protection stipulated as possible. At a more sophisticated level, it could however be argued that the most important objective is to create a European common sense of fairness, which genuinely cares for the individual. Part of this mission involves pinning down just what shared values the EU has.[65] As explained above, we already know that Article 2 TEU states that the EU respects values founded on human rights, but it is somewhat unclear what this means in the context of procedural safeguards in criminal law. It goes without saying that this is obviously what the very ambition of the creation of mutual trust is about. Also, it seems clear that in order to create such trust, there is a need for some kind of a general legislative framework for the adoption of legal safeguards, which is why the Lisbon Treaty is welcome since it provides for legislative competence in this regard. The problem is that things have happened very quickly (for example, the adoption of the EAW in the aftermath of 9/11) and the EU is still trying to catch up with the establishment of a coherent regime that respects criminal law procedural safeguards. Consequently, in the next section, I investigate two areas where legislative action appears particularly fast-moving and where there is an acute need to ensure that adequate protection of the individual is safeguarded at the EU level.

V EXAMPLES OF LONG-LASTING CLASHES

The Stockholm Programme stresses the importance of increasing security within the Union. It is stated that Europe is facing growing cross-border criminality and that it is the Commission's obligation to do its utmost to ensure that EU citizens can live in a secure environment.[66] This section will look at some concrete examples of where the EU's approach does *not* seem to be driven by citizen concerns. Instead, the main focus of the EU in this area seems to be on security and effectiveness endeavours.

A Brief Comment on Data Protection and the Individual

The question of data protection in the criminal law context plays a central role in the Stockholm Programme, where it is repeatedly stressed[67] that the notion of data protection needs to be strengthened. More specifically, it is stated that the Union must ensure that the fundamental right to data protection is consistently applied and that the Union must therefore respond to the challenge posed by the increasing exchange of citizens' personal data and the need to ensure the protec-

[65] An examination of some of these values is found in A Williams, *The Ethos of Europe* (Cambridge, Cambridge University Press, 2010), in particular ch 1.

[66] Stockholm Programme (n 46) 4–5.

[67] Ibid, 10.

tion of privacy. Since 2008, the general framework for the protection of personal data in police and judicial cooperation has been covered by Framework Decision 2008/977.[68] The scope of this measure is limited to the processing of personal data transmitted or made available between Member States.[69] The most important change in this regard is the inclusion of Article 16 TFEU. That provision not only contains an individual right of the data subject to the protection of his or her personal data, but it also obliges the European Parliament and Council to provide for data protection in all areas of European Union law.[70] Article 16 TFEU stipulates that everyone has the right to the protection of personal data concerning him or her. This applies to all areas, ie also to the AFSJ (unlike the Data Protection Directive,[71] which excluded criminal law from its scope. Article 16 TFEU mirrors Article 8 of the Charter, which also proclaims the right to data protection. In addition, Declaration 21 attached to the Lisbon Treaty states that specific rules on the protection of personal data and the free movement of such data in the fields of judicial cooperation in criminal matters and police cooperation based on Article 16 TFEU may prove necessary because of the specific nature of these fields. Interestingly, it has been suggested that Article 16 TFEU is drafted in a way that echoes citizenship.[72] It is true that Framework Decision 2008/977 still applies in this area but it is not as far reaching as Article 16 TFEU. As pointed out by Hijmans and Scirocco, it could be argued that Framework Decision 2008/977 does not fulfil the criteria of Article 16 TFEU since it does not apply to all processing of data (domestic processing is excluded from it). This is therefore an area with an interesting future, where the right to data protection, and by extension citizenship rights, needs to be balanced against the need to fight crime effectively.

B Joint Investigation Orders

The initiative for a Directive on a European Investigation Order[73] offers – in procedural rather than substantive criminal law – an interesting narrative with respect to clashes between the efficiency of criminal law cooperation and the protection of the individual. Moreover, the recent Communication from the

[68] Framework Decision 2008/977/JHA on the protection of personal data processed in the framework of police and judicial cooperation in criminal matters [2008] OJ L350/60.

[69] Yet according to Protocol 21, the United Kingdom and Ireland shall not be bound by the rules laid down on the basis of Article 16 TFEU, which relate to the processing of personal data by the Member States when carrying out activities which fall within the scope of Chapters 4 or 5 of Title V, ie criminal law and police cooperation.

[70] H Hijmans and A Scirocco, 'Shortcomings in EU Data Protection in the Third and Second Pillars: Can the Lisbon Treaty Help Close the Gap?' (2009) 46 *CML Rev* 1485.

[71] Dir 95/46/EC on the protection of individuals with regard to the processing of personal data and on the free movement of such data [1995] OJ L281/31.

[72] Hijmans and Scirocco (n 70).

[73] Initiative for a Directive of the European Parliament and of the Council regarding the European Investigation Order in criminal matters, 2010/0817 (COD) Brussels 29 April 2010. Also discussed in E Herlin-Karnell, 'The Development of EU Precautionary Criminalization' (2011) 1 *European Criminal law Review* 149, 165.

Commission on 'EU Counter-Terrorism Policy: Main Achievements and Future Challenges' is relevant in the present context.[74]

The recent initiative for a European Investigation Order would repeal (the politically sensitive and long-debated[75]) European Evidence Warrant (EEW)[76] Framework Decision by proposing an initiative for a new directive on the basis of Article 82(2) TFEU. Accordingly, this means that, first, the proposed directive is subject to mutual recognition. Secondly, it means that the so-called emergency brake, under which the Member States could pull a brake if the legislation at issue were to affect fundamental principles of their criminal justice systems (see Articles 82(3) and 83(3) TFEU respectively) and where a Member State can request a draft directive be referred to the European Council, would not apply. The reason for this is that general issues concerning the operation of the mutual recognition rule under the proposed directive as stipulated in Article 82(1) TFEU do not entail the emergency brake possibility. The reason for this is that the emergency brake applies to Article 82(2) TFEU only, but not to the very application of mutual recognition as such. Given the controversy with mutual recognition and the long-standing question of trust-building in this area, such a divergence seems highly regrettable.[77] Furthermore, somewhat interestingly, the sacred notion of *ne bis in idem* is abolished, as is the role of territoriality, where Member States have had the option to investigate and punish crimes committed on their territory. Although the proposed directive ensures in Article 1 that it complies with fundamental rights and that it would not require the Member States to breach fundamental rights, there is a risk that the general efficiency focus will have a negative impact in this regard and undermine rights without necessarily serving effectiveness and security. As pointed out by Peers, the reassurances given are too vague to be taken adequately seriously.[78]

The other recent example worth mentioning is the recent Communication on EU Counter-Terrorism Policy.[79] This Communication is to be read in conjunction with a Commission staff working paper, 'Taking stock of EU Counter-Terrorism Measures'[80] and with the Stockholm Programme. The Commission staff working paper includes a table with concrete achievements and future challenges to be achieved by focusing on four prestigious words, 'prevent, protect, pursue and respond'. The Communication points to success with current instruments, such as the EAW and the Third Money Laundering Directive,[81] as well as a whole range of

[74] Communication from the Commission to the European Parliament and the Council, 'The EU Counter-Terrorism Policy: Main Achievements and Future Challenges' COM (2010) 386 final.

[75] For a detailed account, see V Mitsilegas, 'The Third Wave of Third Pillar Law. Which Direction for EU Criminal Justice?' (2009) 34 *EL Rev* 523.

[76] Framework Decision 2008/978/JHA on the European evidence warrant [2008] OJ L350/72.

[77] See also S Peers, 'EU Criminal Law and the Treaty of Lisbon' (2008) 33 *EL Rev* 507.

[78] Analysis by S Peers, 'The Proposed European Investigation Order: Assault on Human Rights and National Sovereignty' available at www.statewatch.org/analyses/no-96-european-investigation-order.pdf.

[79] COM (2010) 386 final. Also discussed in Herlin-Karnell (n 74) 166.

[80] SEC (2010) 911 final.

[81] Dir 2005/60/EC [2005] OJ L309.

legislative measures for the prevention of the use of the Internet for terrorist purposes;[82] all of which have, however, been criticised from a human rights perspective.[83] For this reason, the Commission points out that the relationship between the many interacting instruments and the mechanism for information exchange needs to be evaluated. The argument is centred on effectiveness concerns coupled with the need to prevent, pursue and protect. Admittedly, there are also good aspects of this Communication, such as the explicit recognition of the need to respect fundamental rights; it is highlighted that it is a priority to ensure that any measure complies with the Charter. Yet in the light of EU history on the fight against terrorism since 9/11, it is easy to have the impression that such reassurance appears fluffy and vague.[84] At least it remains to be seen in practice. The problem, as discussed above, is that the preventive emphasis easily leads to measures that do not adequately respect fair trial rights.

Thus, it is cautiously submitted that these measure are not driven by safeguarding the individual but by security and efficiency concerns to enable speedy justice in Europe. These legislative developments might sound paradoxical when considering the increased focus on the citizen's participation and the empowerment of the EU in this area, as discussed above.

VI CONCLUSION

This chapter presented three key points. First, the general framework of EU criminal law and how it has changed after the Lisbon Treaty was outlined, reflecting on the extent to which citizens are placed at the centre of these developments. The conclusion here was that although the situation is improving considerably, much of the focus at present remains driven by other concerns such as effectiveness and security. Accession to the ECHR and the legally binding status of the Charter constitute extremely important developments, but do not solve the deficit automatically. It is their proper implementation and application that will matter. The same goes for the far-reaching albeit vague proclamation of the Union's values in the Preamble to the Lisbon Treaty and in Articles 2 and 3 TFEU.

Thereafter, the chapter investigated the implications of citizenship in the area of EU criminal law by looking at recent case law. I concluded that the development of citizenship rights (although already applicable to the former – and still existing in terms of the transitional Protocol), even though the case law is still very fragmented, constitutes an extremely important symbolic change in this area. The chapter then discussed the recent Stockholm Programme and pointed out that although the Commission is trying its best to create a genuine EU agenda in criminal law, this

[82] Such as Council Framework Decision 2008/919/JHA on combating terrorism [2008] OJ L330/21.
[83] Peers (n 78).
[84] On the fight against terrorism at the EU level in general, see, eg, the introduction in C Eckes, *EU Counter-Terrorist Policies and Fundamental Rights: The Case of Individual Sanctions* (Oxford, Oxford University Press, 2009) chapter 1.

Programme is far too open ended and general to be taken adequately seriously. Particularly, the strong focus on security and effectiveness seems somewhat in disharmony with the objective of creating a true area of freedom and justice.

Finally, data protection and joint investigation orders were outlined as examples of policy initiatives where the current development of EU criminal law has *not* been driven by citizen concerns but by efficiency needs and a security focus. Perhaps the greatest difficulty (the UK/Ireland opt-out in this area aside) will be to decide the exact content of the emerging regime of EU criminal law. There are many and various documents produced by the EU and they all aim to embed citizenship rights in the criminal law policy agenda, but it remains to be asked to what extent the individual – including the defendant – fully benefits from the complex web of EU criminal law as it currently stands. Perhaps one (short-term) solution, as frequently suggested by others, but deserves repeating, would be the creation of a European defence lawyer,[85] as a counterpart to the possible creation of a European public prosecutor (Article 86 TFEU).

This is all work in progress. But one thing seems clear: the future of EU criminal law is an exciting one and the points raised in the present chapter should therefore be seen as an attempt to raise awareness of the sensitive nature of criminal law rather than as one-sided criticism of the current state of play.

[85] See B Schünemann, 'Alternative-Project for a European Criminal Law and Procedure' (2007) 18 *Criminal Law Forum* 227.

10

For Better, For Worse: The Relationship between EU Citizenship and the Development of Cross-border Family Law

HELEN STALFORD*

I INTRODUCTION

THE EU HAS, for over a decade now, been legislating on cross-national family justice issues. This is to accommodate the increasing incidence of international relationship breakdown and to determine procedures for ensuring that divorces and other parental responsibility agreements reached in one Member State can be enforced easily in any other Member State to which any of the parties move. In that sense, the development of EU family justice has always been associated with EU citizenship insofar as both respond to, and are largely triggered by, the exercise of free movement between the Member States. It is the free movement imperative that justified EU intervention in the family justice arena to begin with: the increasing prevalence of private relationship formation between individuals of different nationalities, itself a product of the progressive 'normalisation' of cross-national migration among young adults in particular, reinforces the need for an effective supranational legal and administrative response when such relationships break down.

EU-wide marriage and divorce statistics bear testimony to the successes and pitfalls of the EU's citizenship/free movement project: there are an estimated 16 million international married couples in the EU (ie where the parties are of a different nationality to one another). The most recent data, from 2007, recorded 2.4 million new marriages in the EU that year of which approximately 310,000 (13 per cent) were international. In the same year, there were 1,047,427 divorces across the EU, of which 137,000 (again, 13 per cent) had an international element, continuing an upward trend in the number of new international divorces since

* I am indebted to Ruth Lamont, Michael Dougan, Roderic O'Gorman and Paul Beaumont for their very helpful comments on previous drafts of this chapter. The usual disclaimer applies.

2000. Added to this, there are an estimated 3.5 million married couples who have moved to other Member States, 28,000 of which divorce every year, often prompting return migration to their country of origin for at least one of the parties.[1]

The EU's traditional preoccupation with securing economic and political integration limited the EU's legal competence or, indeed, inclination to legislate on family matters per se. Thus, until the late 1990s at least, family-related provision had a merely facilitative function: to enable the migrant worker to live and work in other Member States.[2] The 'Communitarisation' of EU family justice measures by the Treaty of Amsterdam added fresh momentum to this agenda, prompting swift implementation of a range of binding measures. This coincided with a growing judicial readiness to hew more family-friendly contours into the free movement provisions, primarily through increasingly liberal and social interpretations of EU citizenship, which would benefit third country national family members in particular.[3] In that sense, the articulation of family entitlement under the EU free movement provisions could be viewed as the precursor to the development of more discrete, focused EU family justice legislation. Certainly, protecting and sustaining free movement remains an important imperative underpinning the latter. The primary aim of EU family provision is thus twofold: to protect individuals from the potentially injurious consequences of free movement, notably by ensuring that individuals do not exploit the EU's fluid policy on free movement to frustrate the legitimate enforcement of family decisions across countries; and to sustain free movement opportunities in the face of and, indeed, because of, personal family crises by ensuring that decisions relating to divorce, legal separation and parental responsibility are automatically recognised and enforced in any Member State to which either of the parties subsequently moves. In short, the free movement of persons and families remains inoperable in many cases unless accompanied by the free movement of decisions regulating the organisation of their personal relationships.

Despite the irrefutable free movement imperative shared by EU citizenship and EU family law, academic and judicial scrutiny of these areas has been pursued on largely discrete tracks. There has been virtually no attempt to explore the parallels

[1] European Commission, 'Impact Assessment: Accompanying Document to the Communication from the Commission to the European Parliament, the Council, the European Economic And Social Committee and the Committee Of The Regions Bringing Legal Clarity to Property Rights for International Couples' SEC (2011) 327, 12 and 59.

[2] Art 10 Reg 1612/68 [1968] OJ L257/2. Rights pertaining to the migrant worker's children are now enshrined in Art 10 of the revised version of this instrument, Reg 492/2011 on freedom of movement for workers within the Union [2011] OJ L141/1. The entitlement of other accompanying family members is captured by Arts 1 and 2(2) Dir 2004/38 on the right of citizens of the Union and their family members to move and reside freely within the territory of the Member States [2004] OJ L158/77.

[3] See notably, Case C-60/00 *Carpenter v Secretary of State for the Home Department* [2002] ECR I-6279; Case C-413/99 *Baumbast and R* [2002] ECR I-7091; Case 291/05 *Eind* [2003] ECR I-10719; Case C-200/02 *Zhu and Chen* [2004] ECR I-9925; Case C-127/08 *Metock* [2008] ECR I-6241; Case C-310/08 *LB Harrow v Nimco Hassan Ibrahim* [2010] ECR I-1065; Case C-480/08 *Teixiera* [2010] ECR I-1107. For a critical examination of these judgments, see C O'Brien, 'Case C-310/08 *Ibrahim*, Case C-480/08 *Teixiera*' (2011) 48 *CML Rev* 203; and S Currie, 'Accelerated Justice or a Step Too Far? Residence Rights of Non-EU Family Members and the Court's Ruling in Metock' (2009) 34 *EL Rev* 310.

between the two regimes or, indeed, to challenge the rationale for applying distinct conceptual and operative tests to each. The aim of this chapter is, therefore, to draw these two areas of scholarship together in order to explore both the benefits and the disadvantages of further convergence between the two regimes. Following a very brief overview of the EU family justice framework in section II, section III pinpoints the extent to which it overlaps, conceptually and operationally, with the EU citizenship framework. In doing so, the discussion critically assesses the currency that both regimes attach to the relationship of individuals not only with the host State, but with their family members also. Section IV examines how some of the more recent developments in EU family law, notably in the context of applicable law, point towards a more empowering articulation of individuals' rights. Section V moves on to explore the interaction between EU family law and EU citizenship in practice before concluding, in section VI, with a consideration of the potential for, and value of, a more uniform or at least complementary approach to the two areas in the future.

II A BRIEF OVERVIEW OF THE EU FAMILY JUSTICE REGIME

Historically, cross-national family disputes within the EU were regulated through a network of bilateral agreements, intergovernmental conventions and private international laws.[4] Since the late 1990s, however, EU family law has evolved into a much more coherent discipline in its own right, prompted largely by the Treaty of Amsterdam which conferred law-making competence on the EU institutions in relation to cross-national family issues by transferring matters relating to inter alia administrative cooperation in civil and commercial matters into the former EC Pillar.[5] What followed was a flurry of legislative activity aimed at transposing the previous measures into uniformly applicable law, accompanied by judicial clambering to clarify the precise scope and practical application of such measures.

Currently, (intra-EU) cross-border issues relating to divorce, legal separation, annulment, parental responsibility and maintenance are regulated by four main instruments, themselves the product of extensive, often strained negotiations and revisions.[6] The first instrument, Regulation 2201/2003, commonly referred to as 'the Brussels II*bis* Regulation', governs cross-national jurisdiction, recognition and enforcement of judgments both in matrimonial matters (divorce, separation,

[4] Previously applicable instruments include the 1970 Hague Convention on Divorces and Legal Separations, and the 1980 European Custody Convention. The 1996 Hague Protection Convention on Jurisdiction, Applicable Law, Recognition, Enforcement and Co-operation in respect of Parental Responsibility and Measures for the Protection of Children of 19 October 1996 continues to apply to private international law disputes between the EU Member States and third countries.

[5] Ex Art 65 EC, now Art 81 TFEU.

[6] For a critical review of this process, see P McEleavey 'The Brussels II Regulation: How the European Community has Moved into Family Law' (2002) 51 *ICLQ* 883; H Stalford 'Regulating Family Life in Post-Amsterdam Europe' (2003) 28 *EL Rev* 39; and N Lowe, 'Negotiating the Revised Brussels II Regulation' (2004) *International Family Law*, November, 205.

annulment) and matters of parental responsibility (including custody, access and parental child abduction), regardless of the marital status of the parents.[7] Importantly, this, like virtually all EU family law, is formally limited to *procedural* harmonisation as opposed to harmonisation of *substantive* family law measures; once the jurisdiction competent to rule on a particular cross-national dispute has been determined by reference to the instrument, it is up to the courts of that jurisdiction to apply its national rules accordingly. Any decisions made thereafter have to be uniformly recognised and enforced across all of the Member States to which either of the parties subsequently moves. In that sense, the factors originally driving the development of EU family law are analogous to prohibitions on duplicate regulatory processes imposed on the Member States in the context of the free movement of individuals, products or services. In a free movement of goods context, for instance, it was argued that a product, when crossing borders, should generally only have to undergo one regulatory procedure in its State of origin. To require otherwise would imply subjecting imported goods to the 'double-burden' of two separate domestic regulatory processes – one in the State of origin, and one in the destination State – thereby hindering free movement and fuelling mistrust between the regulatory authorities.[8] The same is true of family justice measures: if orders for divorce, child custody, access and maintenance are legitimately enacted and judicially endorsed in one Member State, and are underpinned by a set of values that are common to all EU family systems – values such as fairness, equality and accommodating individual 'needs' – there is no reason why such decisions should not be upheld and respected within other jurisdictions to which the parties move.

EU family law legislation enacted subsequently followed the same logic. The second instrument, Regulation No 4/2009, governs jurisdiction, enforcement, recognition and, for the first time, applicable law, relating to maintenance obligations.[9] Again, this finds its origins in earlier, much broader conflicts of laws

[7] Reg 2201/2003 concerning jurisdiction and the recognition and enforcement of judgments in matrimonial matters and in matters of parental responsibility [2003] OJ L338/1. This is a revised version of the previous 'Brussels II Regulation' on jurisdiction and the recognition and enforcement of judgments in matrimonial matters and in matters of parental responsibility for the children of both spouses [2000] OJ L160/0019. This, in turn, is a revised version of the intergovernmental Convention on jurisdiction and the recognition and enforcement of judgments in matrimonial matters [1998] OJ C221. The Brussels II*bis* Regulation also supersedes the private international law measures that previously regulated these matters between Member States of the European Union, aside from the 1980 Hague Abduction Convention, which still operates in the context of child abduction proceedings between EU Member States.

[8] E Spaventa, 'From *Gebhard* to *Carpenter*: Towards a (non-)economic European Constitution' (2004) 41 *CMLRev* 743, citing as an illustration of the point Case 120/78 *Rewe-Zentrale AG-Bundesmonopolverwaltung für Branntwein* (*Cassis de Dijon* Case) [1979] ECR 649. The same rationale has been applied successfully to the free movement of workers, the self-employed or services to allow, for example, the exportability and recognition of foreign professional and academic qualifications: Case C-55/94 *Reinhard Gebhard v Consiglio dell'Ordine degli Avvocati e Procuratori di Milano* [1995] ECR 1-4165; Dir 2005/36/EC of 7 September 2005 on the Recognition of Professional Qualifications [2005] OJ L255/22.

[9] EU Reg No 4/2009 on jurisdiction, applicable law, recognition and decisions and cooperation in matters relating to maintenance obligations [2008] OJ L7/1.

legislation,[10] but has been substantially revised with a view to streamlining, simplifying and clarifying procedures for enforcing spousal and parental maintenance decisions cross-nationally.[11] Accompanying this instrument are harmonised measures on applicable law concerning divorce and legal separation concluded within the scope of Brussels II*bis*[12] as well as a directive relating to the provision and enforcement of mediated decisions (including family mediation).[13]

These developments have already attracted extensive judicial, political and academic attention[14] and, still, the corpus of EU family law measures continues to expand: in 2010, the Commission, in highlighting how uncertainty surrounding the property rights of international couples constricts the exercise of free movement rights, proposed a series of remedial measures.[15] These include proposals for regulations concerning the division of matrimonial property (Rome IV),[16] the property consequences of registered partnerships,[17] and the rules governing jurisdiction, applicable law, recognition and enforcement of decisions relating to succession.[18]

[10] Initially, maintenance was included within the intergovernmental Brussels Convention (EC) on Jurisdiction and the Enforcement of Judgments in Civil and Commercial Matters [1968] OJ L299/32, which was subsequently transposed into Reg (EC) No 44/2001 on jurisdiction and the recognition and enforcement of judgments in civil and commercial matters [2001] OJ L12/1.

[11] See further P Beaumont, 'International Family Law in Europe – The Maintenance Project, the Hague Conference and the EC: A Triumph of Reverse Subsidiarity' (2009) 73 *RabelsZeitung Band* 509, 545; and M Harding 'The Harmonisation of Private International Law in Europe: Taking the Character out of Family Law?' (2011) 7 *Journal of Private International Law* 203, 211.

[12] Reg 1259/2010 [2010] OJ L343/10 (commonly referred to as 'Rome III'). See also Council Decision of 12 July 2010 authorising enhanced co-operation in the area of the law applicable to divorce and legal separation [2010] OJ L189/12.

[13] Dir 2008/52/EC of the European Parliament and of the Council of 21 May 2008 on certain aspects of mediation in civil and commercial matters in [2008] OJ L136/3. For further analysis of the practical application of this instrument in the context of family justice, see H Stalford, 'Crossing Boundaries: Reconciling Law, Culture and Values in International Family Mediation' (2010) 32 *Journal of Social Welfare and Family Law* 155.

[14] Examples of this now extensive body of work include A Borras, 'From Brussels II to Brussels II*bis* and further' in K Boele-Woelki and C González Beilfuss (eds), *Brussels IIbis: Its Impact and Application in the Member States* (Antwerp, Intersentia, 2007); D Bradley, 'A Family Law for Europe? Sovereignty, Political Economy and Legitimation' (2004) 1(3) *Global Jurist Frontiers*; and A Fiorini, 'Rome III – A Step Too Far for the Europeanisation of Private International Law?' (2008) 22 *International Journal of Law, Policy and the Family* 178. A state-by-state insight into the impact of EU regulation of family law is also provided by the many cross-national comparative studies undertaken by the expert network, the Commission on European Family Law, available at www.ceflonline.net/.

[15] European Commission, 'EU Citizenship Report 2010: Dismantling the Obstacles to EU Citizens' Rights', COM (2010) 603 final; See also European Commission, 'Bringing Legal Clarity to Property Rights for International Couples' COM (2011) 125.

[16] Proposal for a Council Regulation on jurisdiction, applicable law and the recognition and enforcement of decisions in matters of matrimonial property regimes, COM (2011) 126.

[17] Proposal for a Council Regulation on jurisdiction, applicable law and the recognition and enforcement of decisions regarding the property consequences of registered partnerships, COM (2011) 127. This is a particularly welcome development given the divergence in the Member States' approach to registered partnerships, only 14 of which legally recognise registered partnership.

[18] Proposal for a Regulation of the European Parliament and of the Council on jurisdiction, applicable law, recognition and enforcement of decisions and authentic instruments in matters of succession and the creation of a European Certificate of Succession, COM (2009) 154.

This very brief overview highlights how EU family law has evolved incrementally, from a combination of private international law and EU intergovernmental instruments, towards a tighter, more coherent body of law, albeit still confined to the procedural aspects of cross-border family disputes between the Member States and still operating in parallel with private international law vis-à-vis non-EU Member States.[19] And yet, despite the historical and legal complexity of EU family law, the fundamental internal market rationale it shares with EU citizenship has led to a notable level of operational and conceptual convergence between the two regimes. The nature of this convergence, as well as the benefits and potential problems generated by it, are the subject of the next section.

III THE OPERATIONAL AND CONCEPTUAL LINKS BETWEEN EU FAMILY JUSTICE AND EU CITIZENSHIP

The basic premise for this discussion is that the EU citizenship and EU family regimes share a fundamental common objective: to provide a regulatory framework for determining the status and entitlements of EU nationals and their family members following a move to another country. In that sense, both regimes operate together as a complete 'migration-enabling' package, with the former facilitating equal access to employment and social benefits on a par with nationals, and the latter providing a transparent administrative and judicial process to enable legal decisions relating to the negotiation of family relationships to be transported and applied across jurisdictional boundaries. While the judicial and legal rhetoric might vary between the two regimes, the underlying principles and objectives are virtually the same and can be summarised as follows: first, the operation of both regimes relies extensively on establishing a connection between the individual/s concerned and the host State; and secondly, respect for human rights, and particularly the right to family life, seems now firmly embedded in both. Taken together, it could be argued that, as has occurred in the context of citizenship, the needs and fundamental rights of the individual are increasingly at the centre of developments in EU family justice, over and above the broader interests and objectives of the internal market. To illustrate this, each of these principles will now be considered in turn.

A The Importance of Establishing a Connection with the Host State

The rights enshrined in EU family justice law, like those associated with EU citizenship, are abstract and nebulous until applied within a particular national

[19] There is insufficient scope within this chapter to discuss this point in any detail, suffice to say that Denmark is not party to any EU family legislation; the UK is not bound by the applicable law rules relating to the Maintenance Regulation; while the latest rules on applicable law relating to Brussels II*bis* proceedings also concern only 14 of the 27 Member States, as discussed further below.

framework, their quality and substance entirely determined by the national laws and policies with which they interact. The ability of an individual to demonstrate some connection with a Member State to which access is sought has become a keystone of both regimes, aimed, somewhat cynically, at curbing strategic and unprincipled welfare or forum shopping. This, in turn, reinforces Member States' authority to determine the conditions by which individuals can access their legal or welfare entitlement; only those with a genuine relationship with the Member State concerned, be that through economic, social or personal investment, should be entitled to benefit from their family justice or support system.[20]

In the context of EU citizenship, this requirement is manifested in the 'real link' test. This test has been developed by the Court to the extent that it is now no longer confined to demonstrating the exercise of some economic activity in the territory of the host State but extends to other social, cultural and even civic associations with the State in question.[21] This case law has dispensed with nationality or even long-term residence as a basic precondition for establishing such a link.[22] A similar approach has developed in the context of family justice, although the connecting factor is determined largely in accordance with the 'habitual residence' test instead.[23] For example, where competing divorce, legal separation or annulment proceedings are issued by the parties in different Member States, the question of which Member State has jurisdiction to decide on such matters is ascertained primarily by reference to the State in which the party/parties are habitually resident.[24] Habitual residence carries even more weight in the context of competing parental responsibility proceedings. In such cases, jurisdiction is determined primarily in accordance with the State in which the child/ren is/are habitually resident.[25] The same is true of the child abduction provisions, which, save in the most exceptional circumstances,[26] support a blanket policy of returning the child (and the case) to

[20] A Somek, 'Solidarity Decomposed: Being and Time in European Citizenship' (2007) 32 *EL Rev* 787; and C O'Brien, '*Real links, Abstract Rights and False Alarms: The Relationship between the Court of Justice's "Real Link" Case Law and National Solidarity*' (2008) 33 *EL Rev* 643. O'Brien argues that the regulatory framework put in place by the EU is merely concerned with establishing a transparent and uniform *procedure* by which nation states can conduct these assessments.

[21] Case C-184/99 *Grzelczyk* [2001] ECR I-6193; Case C-148/02 *Garcìa Avello* [2003] ECR I-11613; Case C-353/06 *Grunkin and Paul* [2008] ECR I-07639; Case C-499/06 *Halina Nerkowska* [2008] ECR I-3993.

[22] Case C-224/98 *D'Hoop* [2002] ECR I-6191; Case C-138/02 *Collins* [2004] ECR I-2703; Case C-209/03 *Bidar* [2005] ECR I-2119; Case C-212/06 *Government of the French Community and Walloon Government v Flemish Government* [2008] ECR I-1683.

[23] For a recent, thorough analysis of habitual residence in the context of private international law, see P Beaumont and P McEleavy, *Anton's Private International Law*, 3rd edn (Edinburgh, W. Green, 2011) 175–209.

[24] Art 3 Reg 2001/2003.

[25] Arts 8(1) and 9(1) Reg 2201/2003. An alternative jurisdiction can be used in certain limited circumstances (set out in Arts 9(2), 12(1), 12(3) and 15)) but even then, it has to be demonstrated that the child has a 'substantial connection' with the alternative jurisdiction and that it is in the best interests of the child to hear the case there.

[26] These exceptions are set out in Arts 10 and 11 Reg 2201/2003 and relate to the length of time during which a child has been absent from the state of habitual residence, to the acquiescence of the other parent to the child's removal in the first place, to the withdrawal of the application for return, to the expressed wishes of the competent child to remain with the abducting parent, and to concerns that the child's welfare will not be safeguarded in the country of habitual residence.

the State in which the child was habitually resident prior to the wrongful removal so that parental responsibility matters can be thrashed out there.[27]

The significance of habitual residence to the application of the Brussels II*bis* jurisdictional rules has prompted calls for a clearer articulation of what factors might be taken into account in family cases and, more specifically, whether it should merely conform to the established definition of habitual residence applied to other areas of EU law, notably in relation to the coordination of social security provision. In *Swaddling*, for example, the Court of Justice stated that the notion of 'habitual residence' denotes the individual's principal or habitual centre of interests and 'has a Community-wide meaning'.[28] Here, the Court acknowledged that the length and continuity of residence is an important factor in determining where an individual's 'centre of interests lies', but that it is not the only factor. Thus, the fact that a person had not resided in a Member State for 'an appreciable period' should not, in itself, be used as a basis for denying him or her access to a particular benefit. More recently, in *Kozlowski*, concerning the application of the European Arrest Warrant, the Court advised that habitual residence should be determined in the light of 'various objective factors characterising the situation of that person, including, in particular, the length, nature and conditions of his presence and the family and economic connections which that person has with the executing Member State'.[29]

EU family law cases have presented other opportunities to further refine and 'sensitise' the habitual residence test in a way that responds more closely to the dynamics of individuals' cross-border family relationships. The case of *A*,[30] for example, concerned care proceedings issued under Article 20(1) of the revised Brussels II Regulation in respect of three children whose family had lived a nomadic life, mainly on caravan sites, between Finland and Sweden. The children had previously been in care in Finland but were taken into care for a second time following evidence that they had been left alone while their parents visited Sweden, that they were not attending school, and that their living conditions posed a serious threat to their physical and psychological welfare. The mother, A, appealed against the care order arguing that the children were, in fact, habitually resident in Sweden and that, therefore, the determination of any child protection issues were a matter for the Swedish authorities.

One of the questions directed to the Court of Justice concerned the interpretation of 'habitual residence' as the primary connecting factor for determining jurisdiction in cross-national parental responsibility disputes (and, in this case, child protection measures) under Brussels II*bis*. Echoing the approach of the Advocate General, the Court offered a lucid and illuminating definition of habit-

[27] See, eg, Case C-195/08 PPU *Rinau* [2008] ECR I-05271.

[28] Case C-90/97 *Swaddling* [1999] ECR I-1075.

[29] Case C-66/08 *Kozlowski* [2008] ECR I-6041; see also, Case C-123/08 *Wolzenburg* [2009] ECR I-9621.

[30] Case C-523/07 *A* [2009] ECR I-2805.

ual residence in this context, asserting that it requires more than mere presence in the territory, but rather a stable connection between the individual and the State. This, it concluded, is to be determined by the national court 'by reference to all the relevant circumstances', including the 'duration, regularity, conditions and reasons for the stay on the territory of a Member State and the family's move to that State, the child's nationality, the place and conditions of attendance at school, linguistic knowledge and the family and social relationships of the child'.[31] In reaching this conclusion, the Court in *A* explicitly stated that it would be inappropriate to transpose existing, largely residence-based interpretations of habitual residence onto emotionally sensitive and socially complex cross-national family cases, particularly those involving young children.[32] In making this distinction, the Court paved the way for a more nuanced conceptualisation of habitual residence – one that takes into account a range of personal and social factors to demonstrate an individual's connection with a particular State.[33]

It would seem reasonable to assume, following this decision, that the same interpretation of habitual residence extends to other areas of EU law to which the test is relevant, notably EU migrants' access to social welfare provision or the application of the European Arrest Warrant. Indeed, to do otherwise would surely lead to the undesirable and confusing situation whereby different interpretations of habitual residence would be applied depending on the area of law at issue; it would certainly militate against the uniform, 'Community-wide' definition of habitual residence envisaged by the Court of Justice in *Swaddling*. This more individualised approach to habitual residence impacts, in turn, upon assessments as to the accessibility and scope of EU citizenship entitlement. Specifically, since 'habitual residence' has been commonly deployed as a means of supporting or, indeed, rebutting an individual's claim to have a 'real link' with a Member State under the citizenship case law, it follows that the 'real link' test might be more easily satisfied by those who can similarly demonstrate personal and emotional connecting factors other than residence.[34] In that sense, the family justice jurisprudence marks the gradual convergence of the real link and habitual residence tests through a more consistent alignment of the factors to be taken into account in both contexts.

[31] Ibid, para 39, cited in R Lamont, 'Case C-523/07, A, Judgment of the Court of Justice (Third Chamber) of 2 April 2009, not yet reported' (2010) 47 *CML Rev* 235, 238.

[32] R Lamont, 'Habitual Residence and Brussels II*bis*: Developing Concepts for European Private International Family Law' (2007) 3 *Journal of Private International Family Law* 261.

[33] This approach was confirmed and expanded upon in Case C-497/10 PPU *Mercredi*, judgment of 22 December 2010, nyr. It has also been discussed in the context of proposals to develop cross-border succession rules; see n 18 and Beaumont and McEleavey (n 23) 1064–65.

[34] Case C-138/02 *Collins* [2004] ECR I-2703; Case C-209/03 *Bidar* [2005] ECR I-2119. In such cases, the Court has reaffirmed that habitual residence requirements are a legitimate means by which Member States can ascertain whether there is a 'real link' between the individual claimant and their employment market before granting particular benefits, provided that such a test can be objectively justified.

B The Influence of Human Rights

The second feature of EU family law that resonates with EU citizenship discourse, and which points to the progressively individualised approach to citizens' entitlements, relates to the increasing weight attached to international human rights standards. Wider human rights developments at EU level imply that every regulatory area is now routinely subject to a degree of human rights auditing. This is manifested most recently in the elevated status afforded to fundamental rights by the Lisbon Treaty,[35] which has catalysed the process of EU accession to the ECHR[36] and prompted the development of a more robust human rights auditing strategy within the framework of the Charter of Fundamental Rights of the European Union.[37] All of these developments have important implications for both citizenship and EU family law insofar as any new legal and policy developments are now routinely subject to the scrutiny of the institutions to ensure their compatibility with the Charter.

This process of fundamental rights 'mainstreaming' has occurred fairly organically in both an EU family justice context and an EU citizenship context, notwithstanding the fact that the initial motivation for introducing harmonised procedures in relation to jurisdiction, recognition and enforcement of decisions was as much political (encouraging mutual recognition and cooperation between Member States' authorities) as it was personal (enabling individuals to conduct their family relationships cross-nationally). By the same token, EU citizenship and free movement were as much driven by a desire to remove administrative and legal barriers for people, products and services wishing to move between the Member States as to enable EU nationals and their family members to experience the benefits (and associated responsibilities) of living in other Member States. The Court of Justice then added a more explicit human rights component, notably the right to private and family life enshrined in Article 8 ECHR (and Article 7 of the Charter), to the mix of critical factors to be taken into account when determining the validity of internal restrictions on free movement.[38] The result is that free movement laws must be applied by the Member States in a manner that is consistent with individuals' fundamental rights, even if the link with facilitating the free movement of EU citizens is relatively tenuous, and even if this undermines otherwise lawful national immigration restrictions. This is illustrated by the case of *Ruiz Zambrano*,[39] which concerned a Columbian national who entered Belgium with his wife and child under a visitors' visa before making a series of

[35] Specifically, Art 6 TEU.

[36] Art 6(2) TEU.

[37] European Commission, 'Strategy for the Effective Implementation of the Charter of Fundamental Rights by the European Union' COM (2010) 573/4.

[38] *Carpenter* and *Metock*, n 3. For more detailed critique of the Court's reasoning in *Carpenter*, see Spaventa (n 8) 766–771. On *Metock*, see Currie (n 3), and C Costello, '*Metock*, Free movement and "Normal Family Life" in the Union' (2009) 46 *CML Rev* 587.

[39] Case C-34/09 *Gerardo Ruiz Zambrano v Office national de l'emploi*, judgment of 8 March 2011, nyr.

unsuccessful claims for asylum. Despite having been issued with an order to leave, Mr Ruiz Zambrano secured irregular employment in Belgium. Mrs Ruiz Zambrano subsequently gave birth to two more children, both of whom automatically acquired Belgian nationality (and, by implication, EU citizenship) by virtue of Belgian law, a status which the father sought to rely on to regularise his right of residency in Belgium. In a decidedly pragmatic and humane interpretation of EU citizenship, the Court upheld the father's residence claim in order to give effect to the children's rights of residence as citizens of the Union. Furthermore, it concluded that the granting of a work permit to Mr Ruiz Zambrano was necessary if he was to have any prospect of accumulating the necessary resources to enable the family to continue to qualify for residence in Belgium.[40] While this reasoning chimes with previous case law,[41] it is seen as further evidence of the growing prominence of fundamental rights over and above market integration insofar as the family had never actually moved between the Member States to trigger their free movement entitlement in the first place.

The progression from the administrative and legal pragmatism, not to mention the economic rationale, of free movement towards a more distinctly rights-based approach is equally reflected in the evolution of EU family law. This process has been less contentious, however, not least because EU family law is, by its very nature, implicitly responsive to a number of the human rights principles endorsed by the Charter, notably the right to respect for private and family life (Article 7), the right to marry and to found a family according to national laws (Article 9), the right to property (Article 17), the right to protection against discrimination (Article 21), the welfare and rights of children (Article 24), as well as a right to an effective legal remedy and to a fair trial (Article 47).[42] Indeed, the appraisal of more recent EU family law proposals, in accordance with the Strategy for the Effective Implementation of the Charter of Fundamental Rights,[43] has been a relatively painless formality.[44] The weightiness of EU family law's allegiance to fundamental rights is also attributable to the fact that it is largely derived from private international law instruments and case law within which such principles and values are firmly embedded.[45] As a result, family law has presented new opportunities for the EU to engage with a range of human rights principles that

[40] Ibid, para 44.

[41] Notably *Chen*, n 3.

[42] The latter standard is reflected, in particular, in the proposals regarding applicable law, considered below.

[43] Note 37 above.

[44] European Commission, 'Explanatory Memorandum accompanying Proposal for a Council Regulation on jurisdiction, applicable law and the recognition and enforcement of decisions in matters of matrimonial property regimes' COM (2011) 126/2, 4–5.

[45] For more detailed analysis of EU family law from a human rights perspective, see H Stalford, 'EU Family Law: A Human Rights Perspective' in J Meeusen, M Pertegás, G Straetmans and F Swennen (eds), *International Family Law and the Internal Market* (Antwerp, Intersentia, 2006); and L Walker, 'The Impact of the Hague Abduction Convention on the Rights of the Family in the Case Law of the European Court of Human Rights and the UN Human Rights Committee: The Danger of *Neulinger*' (2010) 6 *Journal of Private International Law* 629.

have previously remained firmly outside its purview. Children's rights provide a notable example: EU family law, and specifically the Brussels II*bis* Regulation, is peppered with references to the obligation to act in the best interests of the child and to hear the views of children in cross-national family proceedings (in accordance with their age and/or capacity). Insofar as these obligations are central canons of the UN Convention on the Rights of the Child 1989 (Articles 3 and 12 respectively), they are now entrenched in most Member States' domestic family law systems and are the main source of inspiration for Article 24 of the EU Charter. Moreover, they are embedded in the Hague Conference instruments by which the Brussels II*bis* instrument is so heavily inspired. The integration of these principles within EU family law not only achieves consistency with Member States' parallel obligations under international law, but also potentially pulls the Court into the hitherto largely uncharted territory of considering children's rights in its interpretation and application of EU law.

There are, however, clear limits on how far the *Court of Justice* is willing to go in this regard. This is illustrated by *Detiček*.[46] The main question considered in this case was whether a child protection order issued in Italy could be enforced cross-nationally following the mother's unlawful removal of the child to Slovenia, notwithstanding the fact that the mother had subsequently been granted provisional custody of the child by a Slovenian court. These new, provisional measures had been put in place on the grounds that it would be both in the best interests of the child to remain with her mother as opposed to being returned to a children's home in Italy, and that the child (who was deemed to be sufficiently capacitous) had expressed a strong desire to remain with her mother. The specific question addressed to the Court was whether the Slovenian court was authorised to issue new interim measures in respect of the child, effectively usurping the protective measures that had already been put in place and declared enforceable by the Italian courts. What is most significant about this judgment is the way in which the Court deliberated on the matter: while acknowledging that the welfare of the child was an important consideration in determining whether new measures should be put in place to enable her to stay with her mother, it robustly upheld the Italian court's jurisdiction to determine the custody of the child. In doing so, the Court remained loyal to the procedural and political objectives of the Regulation: to achieve mutual recognition between the Member States, and to preclude an abducting parent from gaining any legal advantage from their wrongdoing.[47] In doing so, it resolutely declined to indulge in any qualitative assessment of the child's welfare or rights, deferring to the domestic courts' absolute competence in this regard.

This approach was confirmed in the subsequent case of *J McB*,[48] which concerned a custody dispute between an unmarried Irish father and British mother in respect of their three children. The father had immediately instituted custody

[46] Case C-403/09 PPU *Detiček v Sgueglia* [2009] ECR I-12193.

[47] Ibid, paras 44–49.

[48] Case C-400/10 PPU *J McB v L E*, judgment of the Court of 5 October 2010, nyr.

proceedings before an Irish court following the couple's separation (the mother moved out with the children, alleging domestic violence), but before the application could be served on the mother and the jurisdiction of the Irish court officially seised, she took all of the children to England without the consent of the father. As a precondition for issuing an order for the return of the children to Ireland under the abduction provisions of Brussels II*bis*, the father was required to obtain a declaration from the Irish court that the mother's removal had been wrongful. The Irish court declined to provide such a declaration on the grounds that, at the time of the children's removal, the father had not officially been awarded custody of the children and that, as the couple were not married, the father was not automatically presumed to have custody of them. The question referred to the Court of Justice was whether the father could be precluded from relying on the child abduction provisions of the Brussels II*bis* Regulation (which would have achieved the automatic return of the children to Ireland) solely on the basis that he had not acquired custody of the children primarily because of his marital status.[49] The Court of Justice reaffirmed the authority of the national family justice process, concluding:

> [The Brussels II*bis* Regulation] does not determine which person must have such rights of custody as may render a child's removal wrongful . . . but refers to the law of the Member State where the child was habitually resident immediately before its removal or retention the question of who has such rights of custody. Accordingly . . . Regulation 2201/2003 must be interpreted as meaning that whether a child's removal is wrongful for the purposes of applying that regulation is entirely dependent on the existence of rights of custody, conferred by the relevant national law, in breach of which that removal has taken place.[50]

In reaching this conclusion, it was acknowledged that the rights of unmarried fathers and children who have a *de facto* family life are protected by Article 8 ECHR and, by implication, Article 7 of the Charter, regardless of marital status. However, it reminds us that the Charter should be taken into consideration solely for the purposes of interpreting *EU* law, within the limits of the powers conferred on the EU institutions, rather than for defining the reach or human rights compatibility of national law.[51] Accordingly, while concerns around the status of unmarried fathers under Irish law, as well as around the children's welfare, are central to the proceedings at issue in *J McB*, the Court seizes the opportunity to demarcate the boundaries between EU and national competence to determine such substantive issues in family justice proceedings. In doing so, it simultaneously acknowledges the importance of interpreting EU law in the light of fundamental rights, whilst also conceding authority to the national courts to give effect to those rights. Ultimately, EU law will be interpreted in the light of what those

[49] Under Irish law, a biological unmarried father does not automatically have rights of custody in respect of his child unless those rights are conferred on him by agreement with the mother or by a court order. Conversely, mothers automatically acquire custody of their children.

[50] Note 48, paras 43–44.

[51] Ibid, para 52.

national decisions dictate on the presumption that human rights have been upheld or are accessible, but it will not usurp their function as a human rights arbiter, at least not under the pretext of applying EU family instruments.

The Court's concern to respond to the political exigencies of mutual trust over and above the human rights considerations is demonstrated even more starkly in the subsequent case of *Zarraga.*[52] The case involved a custody dispute between a Spanish mother and German father in respect of their daughter. The father had initially been awarded custody of the child in Spain whilst the mother, who had since moved back to Germany with her new partner, had access during the holidays. The mother failed to return the child to the father at the end of the first access visit, resulting in complex and protracted return proceedings under the Brussels II*bis* child abduction provisions. Notwithstanding strong evidence that the child had both settled in Germany and voiced strong objections to returning to live with her father, the Court upheld the return order on the basis that such objections should be put before the competent jurisdiction of the child's former habitual residence (Spain). In other words, the Court refused to deviate from the principle of mutual recognition underpinning EU family law, even though the child's objections can serve as a legitimate exception to return under Brussels II*bis.*[53]

The Court of Justice's concern to contain the influence of human rights in the context of EU family law is also re-emerging in the context of EU citizenship. The decisions in *McCarthy*[54] and *Dereci*[55] provide two notable illustrations of this counter-trend. *McCarthy*, which was decided soon after *Ruiz Zambrano,*[56] concerned an Irish national who had always been resident in the UK. She was refused the possibility of using her EU citizenship status to enforce her right to family life, in this case to allow her Jamaican husband to stay in the UK with her. The decision was distinguished from *Ruiz Zambrano* on the basis that the children in the latter case would have been effectively deprived of exercising their EU citizenship rights had the family been deported to Colombia, at least until they reached an age at which they could move independently. Mrs McCarthy, on the other hand, had an unconditional right to remain in the UK and, indeed, to move to another Member State if she so desired. As such, unlike in *Ruiz Zambrano*, the national measures at issue did not directly preclude her from exercising her citizenship rights.

[52] Case C-491/10 PPU *Joseba Andoni Aguirre Zarraga v Simone Pelz*, judgment of 22 December 2010, nyr.

[53] Indeed, the European Court of Human Rights had already asserted in another child abduction case (determined under the 1980 Hague Abduction Convention) that upholding the rights of the child was paramount, even if it serves to trump the principle of mutual recognition; see *Neulinger and Shuruk v Switzerland* (Application No 41615/07) ECHR [2010]. For further analysis of the emerging dissonance between the Court of Justice and the European Court of Human Rights in their interpretation of child abduction law, see L Walker and P Beaumont, 'Shifting The Balance Achieved by the Abduction Convention: The Contrasting Approaches of the European Court of Human Rights and the European Court of Justice' (2011) 7 *Journal of Private International Law* 231.

[54] Case C-434/09 *McCarthy*, judgment of the Court of 5 May 2011, nyr.

[55] Case C-256/11 *Murat Dereci and Others v Bundesministerium für Inneres*, judgment of the Court of 15 November *2011, nyr.*

[56] Note 39 above.

In a similar vein, *Dereci* concerned the joined appeals of five third country nationals against the Austrian authorities' refusal to grant them residence permits despite the fact that they were the family members of EU citizens residing in Austria. Admittedly, most of them had entered and remained in Austria illegally either before or after marrying Austrian nationals and, in some cases, having children with them. The claimants sought to rely on the ruling in *Ruiz Zambrano*, in which the Court confirmed that EU citizenship as enshrined in Article 20 TFEU 'precludes national measures which have the effect of depriving Union citizens of the genuine enjoyment of the substance of the rights conferred by virtue of that status'.[57] The Court qualified its ruling in *Ruiz Zambrano* by reasserting the meaning of 'genuine enjoyment' for the purposes of this test. For the test to be satisfied, the Union citizen must be in a situation where he has in fact to leave not only the territory of the Member State of which he is a national but also the territory of the Union as a whole.[58] In doing so, the Court makes a clear distinction between situations where the family's reunification within the Member State is *essential* for the enjoyment of EU citizenship rights (in other words, the family would otherwise be forced to leave the EU territory), from those in which it is merely 'desirable' (in which case they might possibly pursue family life in another Member State).[59] Moreover, in a remark that resonates with the subsidiarity-sensitive family law jurisprudence, the Court of Justice confirmed that the question of whether or not national immigration law unduly interferes with the enjoyment of EU citizenship rights is to be determined by the national courts.

C The Expansive Nature of the Free Movement Imperative

The starting point for examining the relationship between EU family justice and EU citizenship is that both regimes were initially concerned with stimulating and sustaining free movement, an essential cog driving the internal market. The discussion up to now has highlighted how they have evolved into rather more than that in recent years. With regard to EU citizenship, this is evidenced in the case law from the late 1990s onwards, which saw the progressive detachment of citizenship rights initially from the economic imperative and latterly, it seems, from the migration imperative too.[60] The enhanced role of fundamental rights as discussed above, the integration of social welfare and security measures within the legislative scope of EU citizenship,[61] not to mention the extensions to the political

[57] Ibid, para 64.

[58] Note 55, para 66.

[59] Ibid, para 68. See further, A Lansbergen and N Miller, 'European Citizenship Rights in Internal Situations: An Ambiguous Revolution? Decision of 8 March 2011, Case C-34/09 *Gerardo Ruis Zambrano v ONEM*' (2011) 7 *European Constitutional Law Review* 287.

[60] See E Spaventa, 'Seeing the Wood Despite the Trees? On the Scope of Union Citizenship and its Constitutional Effects' (2008) 45 *CML Rev* 13 and the contribution to this volume by S O'Leary; but for an opposing perspective, see N Nic Shuibhne, 'The Resilience of EU Market Citizenship' (2010) 47 *CML Rev* 1597.

[61] Art 21(3) TFEU.

dimension of EU citizenship following the Treaty of Lisbon,[62] all bear testimony to the progressively far-reaching effects of this status.

EU family justice seems to be following a similar trajectory, albeit in a much more subtle way. This is apparent, first, in the amendments to the legal basis for the adoption of EU family justice measures, brought about by the Treaty of Lisbon. Article 81(2) TFEU now allows the EU to enact measures '*particularly* when necessary for the proper functioning of the internal market'. This replaces the previous, more restrictive wording of ex Article 65 EC whereby such measures could only be enacted '*in so far as* is necessary for the proper functioning of the internal market'. This implies that it is no longer necessary to establish a firm link between the achievement of the EU's internal market objectives (namely the free movement of persons) and the development of harmonised family justice measures.

This development could be viewed as a constitutional endorsement of what we have already witnessed in the context of EU citizenship jurisprudence; the 'exportation' case law to have emerged over the past decade – which allows individuals effectively to retain or 'export' benefits acquired in one Member State even when a move to another Member State is not imminent – raises questions as to whether migration remains the key condition to trigger EU citizenship entitlement. Moreover, it has paved the way for the legitimate curtailment of domestic policies which have merely a *prospective* rather than an actual impact on the exercise of rights by EU citizens.[63] By the same token, the amendments brought about in Article 81(2) TFEU could conceivably lead to EU restrictions on *substantive* domestic family laws that inhibit individuals' enjoyment of their free movement rights or, indeed, unfairly disadvantage individuals or families who have a reasonable prospect of moving in the future. An example of this might be applications by custodial parents to relocate with their children from one Member State (where the non-custodial parent is living) to another EU Member State. Currently different Member States' courts adopt diverse approaches to this issue. In England and Wales, for instance, considerable weight is attached to the reasonable wishes of the custodial parent (usually the mother), such that requests for relocation are commonly granted. Domestic courts might legitimately refuse such applications in the light of child welfare concerns.[64] The elevation of EU citizenship to a

[62] Notably the introduction of the Citizens' Initiative in Art 24(1) TFEU.

[63] Case C-224/98 *D'Hoop* [2002] ECR I-6191; Case C-192/05 *Tas Hagen* [2006] ECR I-10451; Cases C-11–12/06 *Morgan and Bucher* [2007] ECR I-9161; Case C-499/06 *Halina Nerkowska* [2008] ECR I-3993. See further, M Dougan, 'Expanding the Frontiers of Union Citizenship by Dismantling Territorial Boundaries of National Welfare States' in C Barnard and O Odudu (eds), *The Outer Limits of EU Law* (Oxford, Hart Publishing, 2009) 119.

[64] Guidelines for assessing the merits of relocation requests before the English courts were established in *Payne v Payne* [2001] 1 FLR 1052. For a summary of the UK-based case law, see C Renton, 'International Relocation of Children – Part 1', *Family Law Week* available at www.familylawweek.co.uk/site.aspx?i=ed61748. See also R George, 'The Shifting Law: Relocation Disputes in New Zealand and England' (2009) 12 *The Otago Law Review* 107; and R George, 'Practitioners' Views on Children's Welfare in Relocation Disputes: Comparing Approaches in England and New Zealand' (2011) 23 *Child and Family Law Quarterly* 178.

'fundamental status',[65] however, and the increasing alignment between free movement decisions and human rights principles, may mean that refusals to grant a request for relocation to another Member State could be more easily challenged on the basis that they unduly interfere with the operation of free movement by EU citizens. Only the most persuasive of fundamental rights arguments (the right to maintain contact with the non-custodial parent; the right of the child to retain links with their cultural and linguistic heritage; or the need to maintain continuity in their educational and social activities) may be proffered as objectively justifiable derogations from the internal market imperative.

There are some further interesting signs of EU law encroaching on the application and development of *domestic* family law provision on the pretext of achieving uniform application of EU measures. For example, the Brussels II*bis* Regulation requires that national courts hear the views of all parties concerned in relation to any decision or appeal falling within its scope as a precondition of recognising and enforcing that decision in other Member States.[66] Particular importance is attached to hearing children's views on matters relating to custody, access and return. Recital 19 of the preamble sets the tone as follows: 'The hearing of the child plays an important role in the application of this Regulation, although this instrument is not intended to modify national procedures applicable.' Although this commitment to child participation is worded cautiously (mindful of the EU's legal incapacity to supplant existing national consultation procedures with harmonised measures), it is reinforced by other substantive provisions. For instance, Articles 23(b) and 41(2)(c)[67] caution that failure to consult with a competent child in the course of family proceedings can be used as a basis for non-recognition and enforcement of parental responsibility decisions. The principle is further echoed in the provisions relating to parental child abduction,[68] which make the enforcement of any order to return the child to the country from which they have been abducted conditional upon giving the child an opportunity to be heard.[69] This is a significant provision insofar as it *actively obliges* Member States to consult with children as a *sine qua non* of issuing a return order, subject to the child's age or degree of maturity.[70]

While the case of *Zarraga*[71] demonstrates the Court of Justice's reluctance to exploit this provision to its full potential, the domestic courts have been rather

[65] Case C-184/99 *Grzelczyk* [2001] ECR I-6193.

[66] Arts 22, 23(c), 35, 41(2), 42(2) Reg 2201/2003.

[67] Concerning automatic recognition and enforcement of rights of access.

[68] Arts 10–11, 40 and 42. Note that Arts 12 and 13 of the Hague Convention on the Civil Aspects of International Child Abduction of 25th October 1980 are applied to actions brought within the scope of Art 11 of Regulation 2201/2003, subject to the amendments set out in paragraphs 2–8 of Art 11.

[69] Arts 11(2) and 42(2)(a).

[70] This represents a subtle amendment to Art 13(2) of the Hague Convention, which does not impose an explicit obligation on national courts to consult with a child but, rather, allows the judicial or administrative authorities to refuse to order the return of the child if it finds that the child objects to being returned and has attained an age and degree of maturity at which it is appropriate to take account of its views. The effect of this provision is to place the onus firmly on the child to submit their objections to return, rather than on the national courts to actively seek the child's views.

[71] Note 52 above.

more open to deploying it to advance the status of children in family justice, and particularly child abduction, proceedings.[72] Such obligations have, therefore, served to enhance the 'auditing' function of the Regulation, prompting Member States to adopt a more rigorous and consistent approach to their child consultation procedures, not only to facilitate the smooth application of the instrument, but more widely in relation to consultation practices in purely internal family cases. Significantly, such developments are consistent with the growing prominence of children's rights in the judicial deliberations of EU citizenship referred to above, whereby the substantive rights and welfare of children (notably in relation to their education or EU citizenship identity) exert a profound influence on residence assessments under the free movement provisions, effectively 'anchoring' their parents' residence in the host State.[73]

IV DEVELOPMENTS IN THE FIELD OF APPLICABLE LAW: EMPOWERING THE CITIZEN?

A further manifestation of the progressive 'Europeanisation' of domestic family law – or, alternatively, the 'domestification' of EU family law – is the provisions aimed at harmonising Member State laws on applicable law, adopted in relation to divorce and legal separation proceedings under Brussels II*bis* and in relation to cross-border maintenance claims. These provisions seek to address the confusion and, in some cases, unfairness arising out of the complex interplay not only between different Member States' family law regimes, but also between states' parallel conflict-of-laws (or 'applicable-law') regimes. To put it another way, establishing jurisdiction in a particular State does not necessarily mean that the dispute in question will be governed by that State's domestic family law; it merely enables the courts of that State to determine which national law will be applicable to a given cross-national case by reference to its own conflict-of-laws rules. Some Member States automatically apply their own national laws to a given case once they acquire jurisdiction on the matter (as is largely the case in territories of the UK); other Member States may apply another State's family laws to settle an issue in the light of factors such as the couple's habitual residence during their marriage, or their nationality.

The legal maze created by the divergent applicable-law rules in operation across the Member States makes it difficult for most families to make an informed and confident choice about which country's system might best respond to their interests, inevitably adding to delays and the legal costs associated with such proceed-

[72] *Re F (Abduction: Child's Wishes)* [2007] EWCA Civ 468; *Re D (Abduction: Rights of Custody)* [2006] UKHL 51 [2007] 1 FLR 961 and the Court of Appeal decision in *Klentzeris v Klentzeris* [2007] EWCA Civ 533. For a detailed review of the 'child objections' cases, see P McEleavey, 'Evaluating the Views of Abducted Children: Trends in Appellate Case Law' (2008) 20 *Child and Family Law Quarterly* 230.

[73] See notably, *Chen* and *Baumbast*, referred to in n 3, and *Ruiz Zambrano* n 39. This same principle is codified in Art 12(3) Dir 2004/38. See further, H Stalford, 'The Relevance of EU Citizenship to Children' in A Invernizzi and J Williams (eds), *Children and Citizenship* (London, Sage, 2008).

ings. The Commission sought to address this problem with a proposal for a new Regulation, initially aimed at amending the existing Brussels II*bis* rules on jurisdiction and including harmonised rules on applicable law.[74] The intended effect was that the law governing the end of marriage would be designated by common rules regardless of which jurisdiction was invoked by the parties. The proposed Regulation received a mixed reaction, with many arguing that it represented a breach of subsidiarity and threatened the sanctity of domestic family law regimes.[75] Unsurprisingly, therefore, it failed to attain the unanimity required for its adoption, although enhanced cooperation measures were authorised for the 14 Member States who did express a desire to standardise their applicable rules in this regard.[76] Significantly, these new measures place much of the decision-making regarding applicable law in the hands of the parties themselves, essentially enabling them to specify that the laws of a State with which they share a 'close connection' should apply.[77] While this instrument reinforces the need to prove a sufficiently close connection between the party and the State through established mechanisms such as habitual residence or nationality, it achieves this with a rather more positive objective in mind: to reinforce the autonomy and integrity of the parties and to offer them as much choice as possible.[78] In that sense, it represents a refreshing shift in tone and rhetoric, away from top-down legal, judicial and administrative prescription towards a more bottom-up approach that affords greater independence and legal certainty to the parties. [79] The preamble is telling in this respect:

> Increasing the mobility of citizens calls for more flexibility and greater legal certainty. In order to achieve that objective, this Regulation should enhance the parties' autonomy in the areas of divorce and legal separation by giving them a limited possibility to choose the law applicable to their divorce or legal separation.[80]

[74] European Commission, 'Proposal for a Council Regulation amending Regulation No 2001/2003 as regards jurisdiction and introducing rules concerning applicable law in matrimonial matters' COM (2006) 399 final.

[75] Harding (n 11) 212; see also Beaumont (n 11) 511.

[76] Spain, Italy, Luxembourg, Hungary, Austria, Romania, Slovenia, Bulgaria, France, Germany, Belgium, Latvia, Malta and Portugal. The remaining 13 states will continue to apply their own conflicts-of-laws rules to determine which national laws will govern such matters. Reg 1259/2010 [2010] OJ L343/10 (commonly referred to as 'Rome III'). See also Council Decision of 12 July 2010, authorising enhanced co-operation in the area of the law applicable to divorce and legal separation [2010] OJ L189/12.

[77] Reg 1259/2010, Art 5.

[78] This is supported by measures that seek to ensure that up-to-date legal information is available on the national family laws of the various Member States: Reg 1259/2010, recital 17 of the Preamble and Art 17. The Regulation safeguards the ethics of legal certainty and fairness even where the parties decline to choose the applicable law. In such cases, the Regulation determines which conflicts-of-laws rules will apply to the divorce by reference to a scale of successive connecting factors based on the existence of a close connection between the spouses and the law concerned (Reg 1259/2010, recital 21 of the Preamble and Art 8).

[79] See further, European Commission, 'Explanatory Memorandum accompanying Proposal for a Council Regulation on jurisdiction, applicable law and the recognition and enforcement of decisions in matters of matrimonial property regimes' COM (2011) 126/2, 5.

[80] Reg 1259/2010, recital 15 of the Preamble.

> The informed choice of both spouses is a basic principle of this Regulation. Each spouse should know exactly what the legal and social implications of the choice of applicable law are. The possibility of choosing the applicable law by common agreement should be without prejudice to the rights of, and equal opportunities for, the two spouses. Hence judges in the participating Member States should be aware of the importance of an informed choice on the part of the two spouses concerning the legal implications of the choice-of-law agreement concluded.[81]

These developments point to a distinctly individualised and empowering approach to EU family law: one which endows citizens with decision-making authority and gives them the resources to utilise those powers – an approach that is likely to be rolled out through the other proposed applicable-law rules referred to above.[82] In that sense, developments in EU family law could be viewed as ascribing an additional set of attributes to EU citizenship to those already associated with the status, notably attributes of legal certainty and autonomy. But while such developments may be laudable in the abstract, whether or not they will be used for the mutual benefit of the parties is another issue. Family litigation, by its very nature, is usually the product of months or even years of emotional and financial wrangling between the parties, such that many of those who engage in litigation are well beyond the kind of consensual approach to determining jurisdiction that the applicable rules described above imply. Without close judicial scrutiny of how the parties exercise their enhanced autonomy under the new rules, it remains likely that the party with the resources to secure the best legal advice as to which system best meets their interests will continue to dictate the outcome of proceedings, rendering the weaker party decidedly disempowered.[83]

V TOWARDS A MORE UNIFORM SYSTEM OF EU FAMILY JUSTICE AND EU CITIZENSHIP?

The observations made so far point to the conceptual and ideological overlaps between EU citizenship and EU family law. There are some rather more significant operational links between the two regimes, however, that warrant further consideration and that arguably support a more coherent approach to their application and development.

[81] Reg 1259/2010, recital 18 of the Preamble.

[82] See nn 16, 17 and 18. It is worth noting, however, that the applicable laws recently introduced only apply to those who have agreed to the enhanced cooperation measures, the other 13 Member States opting instead to apply their own applicable-law rules. The result is effectively a two-tier system of applicable law, arguably maintaining confusion and inconsistency rather than enhancing autonomy and clarity.

[83] Although Beaumont has confidently noted that similar applicable law rules in the field of maintenance (referred to in n 9) should operate to restrict the choice of jurisdictions available to debtors to modify maintenance decisions. See n 11, 513.

In economic terms, the ease with which EU citizenship functions will have a direct impact upon the extent to which parties will have to rely on family justice measures. In other words, the accessibility and nature of State support available in one country may well determine the extent to which one party may have to apply for and enforce the matrimonial/parental responsibility obligations of the other party living in another State. Conversely, the ease with which a custodial parent can enforce the non-custodial parent's maintenance or caring obligations will have a bearing on whether recourse to State support will be necessary to cover the financial shortfall. A series of cases concerning the cross-border application of social security provision provides a good illustration of the interaction between the cross-national enforceability of maintenance orders and reliance on exportable social entitlement.[84] However, failure to enforce financial orders from non-custodial parents also inevitably impacts on a family member's need to access welfare support in the *host* State under the citizenship provisions.[85]

Changes in family relationships also carry some significant consequences in terms of individual family members' ongoing *legal* status under the free movement provisions. EU citizenship provision offers some protection for family members (including those of third country nationality) who would otherwise be vulnerable to deportation following divorce from, or the departure of, an EU migrant worker from whom they derived their entitlement in the first place.[86] However, this protection remains largely conditional upon having sufficient independent resources to support the family in the host State.[87] It therefore follows that the extent to which the financial obligations of the non-custodial parent (typically the father) can be enforced, either internally or cross-nationally, will largely determine whether the family can continue to be self-sufficient and, therefore, remain under the protective cloak of EU citizenship law.[88] Equally, the citizenship status of EU migrant workers may also be called into question as a result of family breakdown; their economic and employment situation may well be jeopardised in the process of meeting cross-national maintenance and contact responsibilities, such that they no longer meet the basic resources requirement imposed by the free movement provisions.

[84] See notably, Case C-255/99 *Humer* [2002] ECR I-1205; Joined Cases C-245/94 and C-312/94 *Hoever and Zachow* [1998] ECR I-2691; Case C-85/99 *Offermanns* [2001] ECR I-2261.

[85] *Martinez Sala* may well have been one such case; Case C-85/96 *Maria Martinez Sala* [1998] ECR I-6193.

[86] Case C-413/99 *Baumbast and R* [2002] ECR I-7091, now codified in Art 13 Dir 2004/38.

[87] Art 13 of Dir 2004/38 provides ongoing residence rights to such family members subject to the conditions set out in Art 7(1)(b), ie provided that their children are enrolled in an educational establishment in the host State, and that they have sufficient resources and sickness insurance cover to avoid becoming burden on the host State's social assistance system. Art 13(b) further provides that family members will retain a right of residence if it is necessary to facilitate contact between the non-custodial parent and their children, or if the relationship breakdown was triggered by 'particularly difficult circumstances' such as domestic violence.

[88] Although note that the Court of Justice has confirmed that the right of a non-EU parent to reside in a host State is not conditional on the parent having sufficient means to avoid becoming a burden on the social welfare system of that host state; see the judgment in *Ibrahim*, n 3. See further O'Brien (n 3).

Conversely, relationship breakdown followed by the migration of one party to another Member State, in conjunction with the enforcement of cross-border financial obligations, may bring the other party within the scope of EU citizenship entitlement in the home State. This is demonstrated by the *Schempp* case, which involved a claim by a German national resident in Germany that he was subject to unfavourable tax regulations as a result of his former wife having moved to another Member State.[89] Mr Schempp successfully argued that the German tax authority's refusal to regard the maintenance paid to his former spouse as tax-deductible expenditure, on the basis that she was no longer resident in Germany, was incompatible with ex Articles 12 and 18 EC.

These examples demonstrate the intimate, rather more pragmatic relationship between the application of EU family justice provision and the enjoyment of EU citizenship entitlement. This begs the question whether two distinct regulatory regimes relating to each sphere are really necessary or whether access to EU family justice provision could be subsumed within the EU citizenship framework more formally.

VI REGULATING CROSS-BORDER FAMILY JUSTICE UNDER THE EU CITIZENSHIP FRAMEWORK?

We are reminded that EU family law, rather like citizenship, is composed of two main components: the ability to export and enforce entitlement from one Member State to another; and the ability to access the family justice system in a Member State in which the parties are habitually resident. In relation to the first component, the emergence of the exportation case law in the context of EU citizenship demonstrates the ease with which benefits acquired from one Member State can be transported to another Member State if there is a sufficiently persuasive link with EU law.[90] It does not require a huge leap of imagination to argue that the ability to export legal decisions surrounding marital status and parental responsibility implies the same process. Indeed, EU measures to harmonise applicable law in the context of cross-border maintenance claims already allow those who had a right to free legal aid in the country in which an order for maintenance was initially ordered to export this same entitlement to the Member State in which they wish to enforce the order.[91] EU family law goes a step beyond EU citizenship in reinforcing the solidaristic obligations of States' authorities towards migrants insofar as the right is initially *acquired* from the State of origin but is then *enforceable* against the new State of residence and enforcement.[92]

[89] Case C-403/03 [2005] ECR I-06421 23.

[90] For a detailed analysis, see Dougan (n 63); and AP van der Mei, *Free Movement of Persons within the European Community: Cross-border Access to Public Benefits* (Oxford, Hart Publishing, 2003).

[91] Art 47(2) Reg 4/2009.

[92] See generally, C Barnard, 'EU Citizenship and the Principle of Solidarity' in M Dougan and E Spaventa (eds), *Social Welfare and EU Law* (Oxford, Hart Publishing, 2005) 157.

In relation to the second component, concerning *access* to family justice in the host State, it is now accepted that citizenship has progressed beyond the right to equal access to employment and welfare entitlement on the same basis as nationals to incorporate a range of other social, civil and legal advantages.[93] Accessing the family justice system in the host Member State could be seen as simply an extension of this – no different, in fact, to accessing criminal justice, social welfare provision or legal aid.[94] Again, a good illustration of how this duality of approaches has already been achieved is in the context of EU social security coordination for individuals moving between the Member States. Regulation 1408/71,[95] now Regulation 883/2004,[96] established detailed rules on the material and personal scope of cross-border social security entitlement, enabling citizens to retain their claim to a range of (primarily work-related) benefits, such as invalidity benefits, work-related accident pensions, early retirement payments and paternity benefits, even following a move to another Member State. The complex, restrictive nature of the EU's cross-border social security regime, however, prompted a number of claims for cross border access to such benefits on the alternative, relatively expansive basis of EU citizenship; citizenship was being effectively used to trump the normal, in some cases more restrictive, application of the social security legislation.[97] As a consequence, benefits deemed inexportable, or exportable in only limited circumstances under the Social Security Regulation (such as war benefits, student grants and unemployment benefits), suddenly appealed to the liberalised interpretation of EU citizenship and were mobilised. In the process, as Dougan observes, EU citizenship has served to reconfigure the boundaries of national solidarity by generating a wide-reaching, supranational entitlement to welfare support that is no longer contingent on either nationality of or residence within the paying State.[98]

In the same way, it could be argued that orders made in one Member State in relation to divorce, child contact or maintenance should be transportable with the individual citizen, not by virtue of a distinct and rather complex system of EU private international law, but as part and parcel of that individual's package of citizenship entitlement. It would produce exactly the same effects – enabling obligations undertaken in one Member State to be enforced notwithstanding their move to another Member State, and enabling citizens to become more active protagonists, not just in the cross-border welfare system,[99] but in the cross-border justice system too. The 'brakes' already established to curtail the use of EU citizenship (notably

[93] Case C-148/02 *Garcìa Avello* [2003] ECR I-11613; Case C-524/06 *Huber [2008]* ECR *I-09705;* Case C-357/98 *Yiadom* [2000] ECR I-9265; Cases C-482 and 493/01 *Orfanopoulos* [2004] ECR I-5257.

[94] Case C-27/96 *Bickel and Franz* [1998] ECR 1-7637; Case C-348/96 *Calfa* [1999] ECR 1-11; Case 186/87 *Cowan* [1989] ECR 195.

[95] [1997] OJ L28/1.

[96] [2004] OJ L200/1.

[97] Case C-85/96 *Maria Martínez Sala* [1998] ECR I-2691; Case C-138/02 *Collins* [2004] ECR I-2703.

[98] Dougan (n 63) 129. Admittedly, more recent cases have demonstrated a growing reluctance on the part of the Court of Justice to endorse such legal cherry picking and to reassert the authority of the Social Security Regulation, but it is still very much possible to pursue social security claims independently under the EU citizenship regime if it is likely to result in a more positive outcome for the claimant.

[99] Ibid.

objective justification, proportionality, public policy and fundamental rights) could continue to regulate cross-national family disputes in much the same way as they do currently where the interests of individual parties demand derogations from the free movement of such decisions.

Such arguments might seem fairly persuasive, but one must not overlook the range of factors that guard against too much convergence of the two regimes. First, EU family justice provisions do not necessarily interact with substantive national provisions to quite the same extent as EU citizenship. Rather, they are still overwhelmingly limited to procedural matters, namely to ascertaining which jurisdiction is competent to determine how matters pertaining to divorce and parental responsibility should be resolved and to ensuring that such decisions are recognised and enforced in any other Member State to which the parties move. EU family justice has no direct authority to dictate how substantive domestic family law is developed or administered, nor does it necessarily entitle individuals to access the family justice system of the host State on the same basis as resident nationals; the factors taken into account to establish jurisdiction, such as the first-seised rule, the habitual residence rules and the need to prove 'close connection', often mean that the case has to be pursued through the courts of another Member State. This is in contrast with EU citizenship which entitles individuals to access core national benefits in the host State and, indeed, from the home State[100] on the basis of equality with resident nationals.[101]

Secondly, EU family justice is concerned with enhancing cooperation and mutual respect between the Member States' authorities (notably the judicial and central authorities rather than the welfare authorities). In that sense, you could argue that it operates in a rather horizontal fashion, not only through fluid judicial and administrative communication, but also by enabling 'agreements' between private individuals (albeit often with the helping hand of a judge) to be honoured. EU citizenship, on the other hand, operates in a more vertical fashion insofar as it is more intimately concerned with promoting nation states' responsibility towards individuals, effectively negotiating the relationship between EU nationals and the host State in which they reside through the provision of a range of social and political rights.[102] These different levels of correspondence have taken time to develop and are now well established, such that it would probably be counterproductive and unduly complicated, not to mention administratively burdensome and potentially disempowering for the individuals concerned, to incorporate family justice into the EU citizenship regulatory framework.

Thirdly, EU family justice sits at the intersection between an existing international regulatory framework (notably the Hague Conference and the Council of Europe) and domestic family law regimes, selectively usurping the former whilst retaining a healthy distance from the latter. That said, judicial interpreta-

[100] Ibid.

[101] Art 18 TFEU.

[102] H Verschueren, 'European (Internal) Migration Law as an Instrument for Defining the Boundaries of National Solidarity Systems' (2007) 9 *European Journal of Migration and the Law* 307.

tions at EU and domestic level are still heavily inspired by developments at Hague Conference and Council of Europe level, and EU family justice legislation continues to interact closely with corresponding Hague Conference measures.[103] Citizenship, on the other hand, offers a unique supranational status in its own right and a controlled alternative to a parallel system of social security coordination, whilst also relying on national systems to dictate the means by which individuals qualify for such a status.[104] It has not superseded national citizenship, nor does it imply a transfer of status from the national to the supranational level,[105] but it does impose a new level of democratic legitimacy and identity. In that sense, you could say that citizenship is more evolutionary in nature, developing in line with the EU's vision of its own political, economic and social functions. By contrast, family justice is rather more pragmatic than ideological, offering practical solutions to the jurisdictional, recognition and enforcement problems faced by those engaged in cross-national family justice processes within the EU.

A final factor supporting the retention of two separate regimes is that, despite the preponderance of claims brought by EU nationals on the basis of their status as EU citizens, EU citizenship technically operates in a more discriminate way than EU family justice insofar as it is bestowed exclusively on those who are nationals of a Member State[106] and their qualifying family members.[107] EU family justice measures technically apply to everyone who moves lawfully between the Member States regardless of whether they are an EU national or not. Incorporating family justice into the EU citizenship framework would, therefore, require a separate intra-EU regulatory framework for those seeking to access cross-national family justice but who fall outside the scope of EU citizenship because of their third country nationality, and would only exacerbate and obstruct access to an already complex and multi-layered system of law.[108]

VII CONCLUSION

This chapter has sought to identify the common features underpinning EU citizenship and EU family justice. Of course, individuals may well engage with

[103] On a substantive level, Arts 12 and 13 of the Hague Convention 1980 are still applied to intra-EU child abduction cases under Reg 2201/2003. On a procedural level, negotiations regarding the content and scope of the EU Maintenance Regulation (4/2009) were heavily informed by preceding agreement with the Member States concerning the content and scope of the parallel Hague Convention on the International Recovery of Child Support and Other Forms of Family Maintenance, 23 November 2007. See Beaumont (n 11), who points out that this had an impact on substantive, rather than merely procedural issues, particularly vis-à-vis access to legal aid.

[104] *Chen*, n 3; Case C-369/90 *Michelletti* [1992] ECR I-04239.

[105] Art 20(1) TFEU.

[106] Art 20(1) TFEU.

[107] Arts 1 and 2(2) Dir 2004/38.

[108] Although, admittedly, this has not prevented differential legislation being applied in the context of social security coordination depending on whether the claim concerns a third country national (Reg 1408/71) or an EU national (Reg 883/2004).

EU citizenship on the one hand, and EU family justice on the other, in rather different ways: while EU citizenship rights are, to some degree, pursued by EU nationals, *because of* their migration decisions, EU family justice rights are imbued with the rather more negative function of enforcing fulfilment of individuals' responsibilities *in spite* of free movement. However, the fact that both regimes are reconciled through the EU's internal market vision, and are concerned with managing access to legal solutions and support at Member State level, creates an inevitable synergy between them. The evolution and application of both regimes are, therefore, necessarily underpinned by common core objectives and values. And yet these shared characteristics have been somehow overlooked, or even obscured to date. The rhetoric of 'real link' associated with citizenship, on the one hand, and 'habitual residence' associated with family justice, on the other, provides a good example of how the Court expresses the same thing but in different ways. Scratching beneath the surface of these differences reveals much greater potential to cross-reference between the two regimes, to learn lessons and perhaps achieve greater consistency in judicial interpretation and development of these two areas. Certainly, it is clear that both areas appear to be evolving along a similar trajectory, in both conceptual and operational terms, not least through their gradual departure from an exclusively free movement-driven agenda towards a more earnest focus on the fundamental rights and interests of the individual.

Additionally, while the mutual recognition imperative of EU family law seems to reinforce and extend the authority of the State and judiciary over the individual even beyond territorial boundaries, more recent developments, particularly in the field of applicable law, offset this by enabling the parties themselves to determine which States should exercise that authority. In doing so, EU family law might be lauded for adding some new attributes to the current citizenship menu of fundamental rights, equality and solidarity: attributes of autonomy, legal certainty and predictability. Whether these will serve to empower all EU citizens engaged in family litigation or merely to reinforce existing inequalities inherent in many personal relationships remains to be seen. In any case, EU family law appears to be gradually redefining and extending the geographical boundaries of citizens' relationship with the judicial and administrative authorities in much the same way that EU citizenship has extended citizens' welfare relationship beyond the territorial boundaries of a single State. Ultimately, then, the two regimes operate in tandem with a view to achieving a common ideal: not only to serve the interests of the internal market but, more significantly, to enhance citizens' autonomy to determine the national regulatory framework that responds best to their material, emotional and social interests.

Part IV

New Modes of Citizenship Participation

11

How Could the New Article 11 TEU Contribute to Reduce the EU's Democratic Malaise?

LUIS BOUZA GARCÍA

I INTRODUCTION

THE PARTICIPATORY INNOVATIONS for the European Union agreed at the European Convention 2003 have recently entered into force. Whereas the reasons that justified their creation have not changed since 2003, the perceived distance between the EU and its citizens has grown so much that any possible democratic tool seems too weak and too belated to redress it. The chapter will not reproduce the debate about the nature of the EU's democratic problems.[1] However, it starts by pointing out that the EU has officially recognised the need to bridge the gap with the citizens,[2] and will address the issue from a broader legitimacy perspective, encompassing among other things the absence of a European public space, rather than assuming that these democratic problems can be solved merely via institutional reform.

This chapter evaluates the democratic innovations recently introduced by the Lisbon Treaty in the European Union by combining a theoretical and empirical approach which does not focus on the innovations' institutional or legal effect but on how the EU political system actors may put them into practice. The chapter considers that despite the negative evaluations that could be extrapolated from existing EU civil dialogue or citizens' initiatives at the national level, the attitudes of the Commission and civil society actors may give Article 11 TEU innovations a relevant effect, in particular possibly increasing the participatory system inclusiveness and

[1] For the arguments for and against the existence of a European democratic deficit, see A Follesdal and S Hix, 'Why There is a Democratic Deficit in the EU: A Response to Majone and Moravcsik' (2006) 44 *Journal of Common Market Studies* 533; A Moravcsik, 'What Can We Learn from the Collapse of the European Constitutional Project?' (2006) 47 *Politische Vierteljahresschrift* 219.

[2] European Commission, White Paper on European Governance (27 July 2001); European Commission, 'The Commission's Contribution to the Period of Reflection and Beyond: Plan D for Democracy, Dialogue and Debate' (13 October 2005).

enlarging the European public sphere. The chapter exploits data from a PhD on a decade of debate on participatory democracy in the EU[3], going from the first discussions on the role of NGOs in 1997 to the consultation on how the European Citizens' Initiative (ECI) is to be implemented in 2011. It thus relies on the analysis of about 100 position papers and 40 in-depth interviews.

The first part of the chapter examines the decade-long debates on how to make the EU more participatory and points to the influence of civil society in the definition of two distinct participatory mechanisms: civil society consultation and the ECI. Following some criteria proposed by analysts of democratic innovations,[4] it is suggested that the ability to make participation more inclusive, more significant in terms of policy outputs and to reach beyond Brussels may be significant criteria when it comes to evaluating the impact of this Article on European civil society. The chapter's argument is that the new Article 11 TEU, and particularly paragraph 4, has a strong potential to make the relation between civil society organisations and the European Commission more inclusive, empowering and to step beyond specialised publics to contribute to the emergence of a general public sphere. However some potential threats which could make these instruments inefficacious or even counterproductive in each of the three mentioned dimensions are pointed out, the most unexpected of which is a measure of disinterest for the ECI from well-established civil society organisations and the inadequacy of the existing consultative structures to accommodate outsider organisations.

II IS INSTITUTIONALISATION ENOUGH TO CREATE A PARTICIPATORY MODEL?

The Lisbon Treaty has introduced in the EU's primary legislation an article that had been drafted by the European Convention under the heading of participatory democracy. Article 11 TEU reads as follows:

1. The institutions shall, by appropriate means, give citizens and representative associations the opportunity to make known and publicly exchange their views in all areas of Union action.
2. The institutions shall maintain an open, transparent and regular dialogue with representative associations and civil society.
3. The European Commission shall carry out broad consultations with parties concerned in order to ensure that the Union's actions are coherent and transparent.
4. Not less than one million citizens who are nationals of a significant number of Member States may take the initiative of inviting the European Commission, within the framework of its powers, to submit any appropriate proposal on matters where citizens consider that a legal act of the Union is required for the purpose of implementing the Treaties.

[3] L Bouza Garcia, *The role of specialised groups in the debate about the European constitution* (Doctoral Thesis, Robert Gordon University, 2012).

[4] G Smith, *Democratic Innovations* (Cambridge, Cambridge University Press, 2009).

The procedures and conditions required for such a citizens' initiative shall be determined in accordance with the first paragraph of Article 24 of the Treaty on the Functioning of the European Union.

By commanding institutions to maintain an open dialogue with civil society and the Commission to consult stakeholders this Article seems to fulfil civil society organisations' old demand to institutionalise civil dialogue.[5] The history of the institutionalisation of civil dialogue can be summarised as the evolution from ad hoc relationships between the EU institutions and interest groups towards relations structured by norms.[6] Whereas in the early years civil dialogue was conceived as an exchange of policy support against access to policy-making between stakeholders and the Commission, across time and in particular after the White Paper on Governance,[7] both sides have mutually elaborated this dialogue as an element of a new participatory governance model.[8]

The White Paper on Governance was followed by the adoption of a series of rules ensuring the dialogue's transparency and to some extent a balanced representation of interests[9] that can be considered minimalistic from a democratic perspective as it is limited to consultation.[10] A few years later, additional expectations were raised by the Commission's 'Plan D',[11] which conceived civil dialogue as a way of getting citizens interested in the EU. Although Plan D rules did not substantially change civil dialogue, it has been shaped by more recent projects such as the European Transparency Initiative.[12] This initiative created a voluntary register of interest representatives that (despite not being mandatory) tries to provide incentives for organisations to sign up by suggesting that contributions from unregistered organisations are considered equal to contributions by individual citizens and more recently by suggesting provision of a permanent access to the European Parliament's premises.

The ECI, which entitles at least one million citizens from at least seven Member States to ask the Commission to start legislation, has a shorter and distinct history. Although it seeks to mobilise large numbers of citizens, its inclusion in the Treaties was not the result of active mobilisation by millions of citizens but of

[5] L Bouza García, 'From Civil Dialogue to Participatory Democracy: The Role of Civil Society Organisations in Shaping the Agenda in the Debates on the European Constitution' (2010) 6 *Journal of Contemporary European Research* 85.

[6] S Smismans, 'European Civil Society: Shaped by Discourses and Institutional Interests' (2003) 9 *European Law Journal* 482.

[7] European Commission (n 2).

[8] B Kohler-Koch, 'Is there an EU Model for Participatory Governance and Does it Hold its Promises?' (paper presented at the conference *What Can Canada and the European Union Learn from Each Other?* held at the University of Victoria in 2010).

[9] E Fazi and J Smith, *Civil Dialogue: Making it Work Better.* (Civil Society Contact Group, 2006) available at http://act4europe.horus.be/module/FileLib/Civil%20dialogue,%20making%20it%20work%20better.pdf; V Cuesta López, 'The Lisbon Treaty's Provisions on Democratic Principles: A Legal Framework for Participatory Democracy' (2010) 16 *European Public Law* 123; Kohler-Koch (n 8).

[10] M Parés and C Castellà, 'Una propuesta de criterios de calidad democrática para evaluar los procesos participativos' in M Parés (ed), *Participación y calidad democrática* (Barcelona, Ariel, 2009) 241.

[11] European Commission (n 2).

[12] European Commission, Green Paper on the European Transparency Initiative (2006).

efficient lobbying by citizens' organisations in the Convention.[13] It is particularly important that the Initiative and Referendum Institute (IRI) and Mehr Demokratie, the organisations that were most active in demanding the inclusion of the ECI in the Treaty did not participate in consultations between 1996 and 2003,[14] although an interview with a representative of IRI suggested that they are far from being complete outsiders.

It has been argued that Article 11 TEU is an answer by the EU to democratic deficit criticisms.[15] However, it can be challenged whether Article 11 TEU was specifically designed to increase citizens' participation according to Graham Smith's definition of democratic innovation,[16] as it is now well documented that it was essentially the result of an incremental process of exchange between civil society organisations lobbying for participatory democracy for over a decade,[17] as well as the entrepreneurship of actors in the EU institutions.[18] This chapter argues that the recognition of two different participation instruments, as well as the existence of other consultation mechanisms such as social dialogue, online consultations or expert consultation is not a contradiction and that these instruments may be mutually reinforcing. However, it is necessary to consider whether the EU has a clear objective in the recognition of two participatory democracy mechanisms providing substantially different contributions to the EU's legitimacy.

EU institutions have expected participatory mechanisms to contribute both to input and output legitimacy[19] as well as to the emergence of a European public sphere. The White Paper on Governance[20] and its subsequent rules for consultation[21] aimed at improving the EU's input legitimacy by giving stakeholders and concerned organisations a bigger role in the policy-making process and structuring the relations with civil society by norms about fairness and transparency in the consultation.[22] The aim was to improve the opportunities of all relevant actors to

[13] J de Clerck-Sachsse, 'The Emergence of the European Citizens' Initiative in the European Convention' (paper presented at the conference *The European Citizens Initiative – A First Assessment* held at the College of Europe in 2011).

[14] Bouza Garcia (n 5).

[15] S del Río Villar, *La sociedad civil y su progresiva participación en la construcción europea: de la Conferencia Intergubernamental de 1996 a la Convención constitucional. Un proceso constituyente para la Unión, un referéndum para el demos europeo* (Doctoral Thesis, Universidad del País Vasco, 2004).

[16] Smith (n 4) 1.

[17] C Will, *The Challenges of Translation: The Convention and Debates on the Future of Europe from the Perspective of European Third Sectors* (London, Third Sector European Policy Working Papers, 2005); C Will and J Kendall, 'A New Settlement for Europe: Towards "open, transparent and dialogue with representative associations and civil society"?' in J Kendall (ed), *Handbook on Third Sector Policy in Europe: Multi-Level Processes and Organized Civil Society* (Cheltenham, Edward Elgar, 2009); Bouza Garcia (n 5).

[18] S Saurugger, 'The Social Construction of the Participatory Turn: The Emergence of a Norm in the European Union' (2010) 49 *European Journal of Political Research* 471.

[19] FW Scharpf, *Governing in Europe: Effective and Democratic?* (Oxford, Oxford University Press, 1999).

[20] European Commission (n 2).

[21] European Commission, 'Towards a Reinforced Culture of Consultation and Dialogue – General Principles and Minimum Standards for Consultation of Interested Parties by the Commission (11 December 2002).

[22] Smismans (n 6).

have their say in order to achieve a balanced and broad policy debate: 'In this context, civil society organisations play an important role as facilitators of a broad policy dialogue.'[23] However this process goes hand in hand with the philosophy of the 'better regulation package',[24] which considers that the stakeholders' contribution to the policy-making process is their input in terms of expertise, which contributes to improving the quality of the policies rather than their ability of mobilisation. Finally, EU institutions have also considered dialogue with civil society as a way to enlarge the European public sphere and to engage in an interactive dialogue on EU policies with citizens.[25]

This chronological analysis shows that Article 11 TEU is the result of the evolution of the EU's expectations about civil society consultation mechanisms. Originally conceived as managerial tools allowing the Commission to improve external expertise and thus contributing to better policy-making, these tools are now formulated as a way of contributing to the EU's input legitimacy via increased participation of citizens and organisations. It is necessary to analyse whether these tools are fit for their new purpose. The next section addresses the question of how to assess the potential contribution of Article 11 TEU to the EU's legitimacy.

III EVALUATING ARTICLE 11 TEU

The consequence of participatory innovations being considered a complement for representative democracy is often that the analysis of their effects is limited to the political system level, ignoring or minimising the consequences for society at large. In Benjamin Barber's argument for participatory democracy,[26] talk (recalling the Athenian isegoria) is a key aspect for establishing a dialogical relationship between the citizen and his community, whereas Pateman recalls that participation is at the core of democracy theories because it has an education and socialisation effect making democracy self-sustainable.[27] Furthermore, participatory mechanisms are thought to contribute to strengthening civic attitudes and civil society, as well as to include excluded groups and bring representatives closer to the people.[28] This chapter examines the potential effects of Article 11 TEU on three key dimensions on which current participation arrangements have tended to score quite low:[29] its ability to foster wider participation or inclusion; to empower actors such as civil society and citizens at large; and to increase the reach

[23] European Commission (n 21) 5.

[24] European Commission, 'Action Plan on Simplifying and Improving the Regulatory Environment' (2002); European Commission, 'Communication from the Commission on impact assessment' (2002).

[25] European Commission (n 2); European Parliament, 'Report on the Perspectives for Developing Civil Dialogue under the Treaty of Lisbon'(2008).

[26] B Barber, *Strong Democracy. Participatory Politics for a New Age* (Berkeley, University of California Press, 2003).

[27] C Pateman, *Participation and Democratic Theory* (Cambridge, Cambridge University Press, 1970).

[28] M Parés and P Resende, 'Tipos y prácticas de participación promovidas por la administración pública: sus límites y radicalidades' in Parés (n 10).

[29] Kohler-Koch (n 8).

of political discussion on the EU. Following the rationale of the research suggested in the introduction, the chapter deals with the more straightforwardly legitimacy-related of the criteria that have been suggested to analyse participatory innovations, rather than assessing their political efficacy or transferability (for instance).[30] A further difference with recent analyses of democratic innovations is that these criteria do not refer to individual citizens,[31] but to the role of civil society organisations. This is in a way a minimalist approach which assumes that the real addressees of these instruments are civil society organisations since they are already mobilised at EU level and citizens are still unlikely to be significantly involved in an individual capacity. The expectation is rather that these instruments can transform the role and attitudes of civil society organisations, which could have democratic positive effects on their members.

In terms of inclusion, existing participation arrangements have been criticised as unable to reach beyond Brussels-based organisations. This is linked to the lack of resources[32] and to the structure of political opportunities at the EU level.[33] Kohler-Koch considers that, far from mobilising the citizens, civil society organisations are entrenched within EU institutions: 'Organised civil society, however, contributes little to the formation of a grass roots based European civil society; it is instrumental to "better legislation" and in order to be efficient and effective it is becoming part of the EU elite system.'[34] Although the strong entrenchment of civil society organisations in the EU's political system contributes to increasing their ability to contribute to policy output, it does little to make ordinary citizens participate in the EU political system, be it directly or indirectly via internal control in their organisations. The landmarks of an eventual increase in inclusiveness and openness of the EU's participatory model and social groups would be increased representativeness and diversity of participants and whether there are de facto biases.[35]

The second question is the ambiguous evaluation of current participatory arrangements in terms of real empowerment since it is very unclear how institutions respond to civil society demands. Although institutions are not obliged to satisfy demands by civil society, feedback is extremely important for the Commission's accountability and for organisations to know how their contribution was used. Otherwise civil dialogue becomes something of a 'window dressing exercise'.[36] Although the ECI has been praised as 'a singular opportunity to bring

[30] Parés and Resende (n 28) 92–100; Smith (n 4) 20–27.

[31] Smith (n 4) 2.

[32] I Sudbery, 'Bridging the Legitimacy Gap in the EU: Can Civil Society Help to Bring the Union Closer to its Citizens?' (2003) 26 *Collegium* 75.

[33] C Mahoney, 'Networking vs Allying: The Decision of Interest Groups to Join Coalitions in the US and the EU' (2007) 14 *Journal of European Public Policy* 363; M Hooghe, 'The Political Opportunity Structure for Civil Society Organisations in a Multilevel Context: Social Movement Organisations and the European Union' in W Maloney and J Van Deth (eds), *Civil Society and Governance in Europe. From National to International Linkages* (Cheltenham, Edward Elgar, 2008).

[34] Kohler-Koch (n 8) 13.

[35] Subirats, Parés, and Blanco, (n 10).

[36] Fazi and Smith (n 9) 48–49.

the Union closer to the citizens and to foster greater cross-border debate about EU policy issues',[37] interviews carried out with EU civil servants and civil society officials reveal that influential policy actors do not expect it to have any meaningful impact on EU affairs. A 'de minimis' expectation is that Article 11 TEU will contribute to making the policy-making process more transparent and accountable by providing direct access to decision-making to citizens, civil society and stakeholders. In this sense recent moves to enhance the EU transparency agenda have been linked to the participatory democracy agenda.[38] The chapter follows a more demanding assessment criterion by addressing the new mechanisms' ability to foster participation beyond information and communication into policy influence by participants.[39]

Finally, civil society consultation has strongly motivated the emergence of pan-European civil society networks. The Commission has not only fostered a consultation policy but also the emergence of European civil society partners by encouraging and funding European umbrella organisations[40] in order to facilitate consultation. However, the emergence of these networks has not contributed to fostering social capital or to mobilising citizens, since these organisations are not able or do not need to mobilise citizens at the grassroots levels to obtain influence in Brussels.[41] On the other hand, a series of pan-European networks not active in Brussels and closer to grassroots citizens may be emerging in the form of alter-globalisation and alter-EU movements around European social forums[42] and of nationally based organisations feeling excluded by the Commission.[43] Thus the chapter addresses the relationship between the exercise of participatory mechanisms and the emergence of the traits of a European society. On the one hand, the weakness of the European identity, of transnational political movements and causes, and of the European public space is the biggest of obstacles to the exercise of participatory democracy in the EU. On the other hand, the usage of participatory mechanisms by civil society organisations contributes to the emergence of some of the traits of a pan-European society. Whereas this may extend in the long

[37] European Commission, 'Proposal for a regulation of the European Parliament and of the Council on the citizens' initiative' (31 March 2010) 3.

[38] J Greenwood, 'The Lobby Regulation Element of the European Transparency Initiative: Between Liberal and Deliberative Models of Democracy' (2011) 9 *Comparative European Politics* 317; I de Castro Asarta, 'Transparency Register: The Negotiation between Three Different Views of Lobbyists' Legitimacy' (paper presented at *New Frontiers in European Studies: UACES Student Forum 12th Annual Conference* held at the University of Surrey, 30 June–1 July 2011).

[39] Parés and Castellà (n 10).

[40] J Greenwood, *Interest Representation in the European Union*, 2nd edn (Houndmills, Palgrave Macmillan, 2007); R Sánchez-Salgado, *Comment l'Europe construit la société civile* (Paris, Dalloz, 2007).

[41] Sudbery (n 32).

[42] E Feron, 'The Anti-globalisation Movement and the European Agenda' in L Giorgi, I Von Homeyer and W Parsons (eds), *Democracy in the European Union: Towards the Emergence of a Public Sphere* (London, Routledge, 2006); E Agrikoliansky, 'Une autre Europe est-elle possible ? Les altermondialistes français et la Constitution: les conditions d'une mobilisation ambigüe' in A Cohen and A Vauchez (eds), *La Constitution Européenne. Elites, mobilisations et votes* (Brussels, Editions de l'Université de Bruxelles, 2007); D Della Porta (ed), *Another Europe: Conceptions and Practices of Democracy in the European Social Forums* (Abingdon, Routledge, 2009).

[43] Interview with a member of Red de Ciudadanas de Europa (Madrid, November 2011).

run to the emergence of pan-European civil society networks, the diffusion of social capital across European borders and eventually to making the EU less distant from citizens and contributing to a growing sentiment of ownership of the EU policy process, the chapter assesses only the new mechanisms' most immediate contribution to the emergence of a general public sphere.

The immediate question is how the recognition of civil dialogue by the Treaties and the introduction of a relatively modest tool such as the ECI may contribute to reversing the above-mentioned critical remarks on the EU's existing participatory mechanisms. It can be argued that these mechanisms may have a relevant effect on the actors' strategies because of a convergence of expectations and norms and competition between different actors and forms of collective action. To start with the expectations and the norms, the enforcement of the Lisbon Treaty is a further step in the decade-long process that has seen the evolution of ad hoc mechanisms for the relations with interest groups into legitimisation mechanisms.[44] This confirms that participation is increasingly becoming a norm that EU institutions and civil society have to comply with. In this sense the mutual pressure from each actor increases, the Commission being asked to pay more attention to participatory mechanisms and civil society organisations being watched more closely in terms of their participation track record. An additional mechanism at play may be the diversification of the European actors and increasing competition among different types of actors and collective action strategies. The new mechanisms, and in particular the ECI, may make other actors' collective action strategies more appreciated at EU level and thus attract them to participate in EU politics. These actors may additionally be more able to engage citizens directly at national level. This second point is not just a theoretical expectation but is grounded on the example of the recent consultation of civil society precisely on the Green Paper on the ECI.[45] This consultation process attracted a majority of organisations not registered in the European Transparency register (70 against 62), which suggests that these organisations are not frequent contributors to European policy-making. Furthermore, contributions from unregistered organisations reflect a bigger diversity, they are written in a wider range of languages with a weaker predominance of English (37 per cent of contributions against 57 per cent for registered organisations) and higher politicisation, including a number of national and regional political parties and social movements, than those of registered organisations.

[44] Smismans (n 6); P Magnette, 'Democracy in the European Union: Why and How to Combine Representation and Participation' in S Smismans (ed), *Civil Society And Legitimate European Governance* (Cheltenham, Edward Elgar, 2006); H Michel, 'Les groupes d'intérêt et la consultation sur le livre blanc: objectivation et institutionnalisation de la 'société civile' in D Georgakakis and M de Lasalle (eds), *La nouvelle gouvernance européenne. Genèses et usages d'un livre blanc* (Strasbourg, Presses Universitaires de Strasbourg, 2007); J Greenwood, 'Review Article: Organized Civil Society and Democratic Legitimacy in the European Union' (2007) 37 *British Journal of Political Science* 333.

[45] European Commission, 'Green Paper on a European Citizens' Initiative' (11 November 2009).

IV INCLUSION

As has just been discussed, the first way in which Article 11 TEU could contribute to making the EU more legitimate is by contributing to diversify the range of contributors to its participatory arrangements.

A Including Citizens in Civil Dialogue: How Could Citizens Acquire a Bigger Role in Civil Society Dialogue?

In terms of inclusion the major drawback of civil dialogue so far is that it has somehow reduced the participation scope to a narrow Brussels constituency of civil society offices relatively distant from the general public and their grassroots members. Presenting civil dialogue as a form of citizens' participation in the EU policy-making process implies that, civil society organisations being a manifestation of the free will of their members to advocate a cause or interest, the participation of organisations in policy consultations provides an opportunity for citizens' participation. However, as legitimate as civil society organisations consultation may be, the involvement of civil society organisations in policy-making is not a form of citizens' direct participation unless members of the organisations are effectively consulted and involved in the process. Consequently, when organisations participate in policy-making they are not providing a direct participation opportunity to their members but *representing* them. The perception that EU-level civil dialogue is not inclusive is particularly clear in interviews with civil society organisations based at the national level or simply not usually involved in EU politics.[46]

Civil dialogue is certainly a valuable tool from a democratic point of view, in particular comparing it with traditional lobby strategies.[47] However the question to be addressed is why some organisations should obtain the right to be consulted and thus possibly influence policy-making on certain topics. The response that the Commission has traditionally given is that this should be the result of a combination of expertise and representativeness. The reason for expertise is fairly evident, and to put it in the European Citizenship Action Service's (ECAS) terms: 'There is little point in public authorities dancing with a representative partner who has nothing to say.'[48] Representativeness is relevant from a participatory point of view not only from the numerical perspective (number of organisations, members and Member States where the organisation is active) but also from a

[46] Interviews with members of RCE and ADICAE in Spain (November 2009 and May 2010). Analysis of the papers reveals a division between some European citizens' organisations weakly demanding greater inclusion of nationally based organisations; business organisations consider that this should remain strictly bound to European organisations.

[47] Smismans (n 6); Fazi and Smith (n 9).

[48] European Citizenship Action Service, 'ECAS Contribution to the Commission's Consultation Document 'Towards a Reinforced Culture of Consultation and Dialogue' (2002) 3.

substantive point of view, since it is assumed that larger organisations are able to 'download' Brussels' debates to their members.

The latter dimension could be of great importance because, despite the technicality of most affairs discussed in Brussels, these appeal to some citizens' primary interests and concerns. In this sense, debates on EU topics within civil society may contribute to the vertical Europeanisation of some sectors of the public space (for instance, citizens concerned by agriculture, health or environment concerns) rather than to a horizontal and politically mediated Europeanisation of the public space. This contributes to the participation of grassroots members of citizens' organisations in debates on the EU and may thus contribute not only to deliberation, but as well to fostering social capital and ownership of the EU.

However, as has already been said, the main problem is that numerical representativeness does not ensure a fluid relation with grassroots members. Organisational complexity, consultation procedures and deadlines, encroachment in the EU's institutional system and members' disinterest make it extremely difficult for organisations to consult their members before taking a decision. In this sense, it is probably necessary to reconsider how EU-level civil society organisations represent their members.

This issue seems to have been addressed by Article 11 TEU as it commends dialogue with 'representative associations and civil society', giving place to several interpretations as to whether this might imply dialogue with unorganised civil society or even whether the EU has a definition of civil society at all.[49] Although it has been argued that this wording is due more to clumsiness than to intentionality,[50] interviews with different organisations interested in this Article during the Convention reveal that this was a real issue for them.[51]

However, the analysis of civil society position papers shows that this is problematic because these organisations have for a long time rejected the idea of being representatives of their members as they consider that the representation function belongs to elected politicians. Most of the citizens' organisations which lobbied the Convention for inclusion of the principle in Union primary law do not consider themselves to represent their members but rather to represent causes or broad sectors of society and thus tend to reject the notion of representativeness, whereas the social partners do stress their ability to represent their members and thus consider that representativeness should be a key criterion in consultation processes.

Several organisations consider that representativeness criteria impose the force of numbers and formal authorisation logics, which are very difficult to adapt to the kind of interests that they advocate, as excluded citizens' or general interest causes can hardly be consulted or authorisation demanded from them. From a

[49] The 'European Commission and Civil Society' website refuses to endorse any definition and refers to 'interested parties': see http://ec.europa.eu/civil_society/apgen_en.htm#5.

[50] Greenwood (n 44) 336.

[51] In particular, a representative of Business Europe (formerly UNICE) claims credit to this organisation's insistence on the recognition of the need of representativeness (interview held on 8 July 2009).

pluralist point of view, participation in consultations does not need any other criterion of justification where anyone interested can participate. However in a democratic approach where civil society is invited as a representative of citizens' concerns and may potentially influence policy decisions, the problem is that in most situations civil society organisations cannot act as delegates of a group, and they usually act with a high degree of independence. From a democratic perspective this distance between the principals (the citizens) and the agents (the organisations) is a problem.[52] In Pitkin's classical typology,[53] these organisations' representativeness must be considered to the extent that they substantially *stand for* a cause or a group of people.

Although the difficulty of representing causes and excluded groups is to be given due attention, this cannot, however, imply abandoning criteria on representativeness, at least inasmuch as civil dialogue is considered as a democratic process where influence over public policies is justified in terms of popular support and not only in terms of expertise, as may be the case in simple consultation. These should rather be adapted to the diversity in the relationships between the principal and the agents in each case.[54] In this sense, the substantive ability to stand for a cause or group is often advocated by civil society organisations. It has been suggested that representativeness criteria do not make sense when the main contribution expected from civil society is a contribution to public discourse.[55] However, from a democratic perspective, the organisations' ability either to consult their members or to mobilise general publics should be assessed too. The chapter argues that this can be included in an innovative representativeness criterion, which is proposed in the final section. Additionally, systematic feedback should be a relevant issue in the consultation process in order to allow civil society and citizens to hold the Commission to account regarding its responsiveness to citizens' organisations' demands.

B Who May Use the ECI to Participate in the EU?

Given the importance of the constituency of EU-level organisations, one might expect that the main users of the ECI will be EU-level civil society organisations, just as organised interests are successful promoters of equivalent provisions existing in other polities.[56] However this section highlights an unexpected obstacle to the generalisation of the ECI: the well-established European civil society organisations are unlikely to use the ECI because they have a preference for alternative

[52] B Kohler-Koch, 'Civil society and EU Democracy: "Astroturf" Representation?' (2010) 17 *Journal of European Public Policy* 100.

[53] HF Pitkin, *The Concept of Representation* (Berkeley, University of California Press, 1972) 232–33.

[54] D Castiglione and ME Warren, 'Rethinking Representation: Seven Theoretical Issues' (paper presented at the *Midwest Political Science Association Annual Conference* held in Chicago in 2005) 10–12.

[55] Kohler-Koch (n 53).

[56] Smith (n 4) 121.

participatory mechanisms, namely civil dialogue. By contrast, organisations rather less active at EU level may be better able to fill this void.

When the forms of action and advocacy of civil society organisations active at EU level are considered, it appears that signature collection and initiatives are infrequent in contrast with a high degree of involvement in stable participatory systems. To start with, if one considers the 22 organisations that were most active in the above-mentioned consultations on participatory democracy in the EU, only three of them asked the Convention to include principles of direct democracy in the draft Constitutional Treaty. The aim of the majority of these organisations was to promote a system of institutionalised access of civil society organisations to the Union institutions. Regarding the ECI, the position of these organisations could be summarised in the following extract from an interview with a member of the Social Platform, one of the leading organisations in the above-mentioned group: 'We did not ask for the citizens' initiative, it was a very open process, and that came from other people . . . It was not our idea, but we were very happy that it was included.'[57] This quote is a good summary of the position of these organisations towards the ECI: it is considered a positive evolution, but not as the main mechanism of the model of participatory democracy that they were promoting.

Turning now to the reactions of these civil society organisations to the consultation on the Green Paper on the ECI,[58] it is noticeable that only eight organisations out of the above-mentioned 22 did actually contribute to this consultation. This confirms that the ECI is far from being a priority for the organisations that were involved in the definition of the civil dialogue frame.

Qualitative analysis of these contributions shows a generally positive but distant attitude. Four of these contributions are very supportive of the principle. However, another group of four organisations write to ask the Commission to carry out action as well on other participatory tools. The following example from the Social Platform position paper stands out as a confirmation:

> Social Platform welcomes the Green Paper on the citizens' initiative. As a response, Social Platform calls on the European Commission to launch a public consultation on how to implement the first part of the Lisbon Treaty article 11 on civil dialogue. . . . This would ensure that both parts of the article are properly implemented. Social Platform would like to stress that the right to petition [*sic*] is not the only new instrument related to participatory democracy that the Treaty of Lisbon introduces into EU decision making processes.[59]

It thus appears that there is little appropriation of the ECI by the organisations that had advocated better access to the Union institutions for organised European civil society. It can be argued that this attitude is connected to the modest place

[57] Interview with a member of the Social Platform, carried out in Brussels on 3 February 2009.

[58] European Commission (n 45).

[59] Platform of European Social NGOs, 'Re: Green Paper on Citizens' Initiative – Complement it with a Consultation on How to Organise the Dialogue with Civil Society Organisations, as Provided by Article 11 of the Lisbon Treaty' in contribution of the Platform of European Social NGOs to the consultation on the Green Paper on a European Citizens Initiative (2010) 1.

that mobilisation of activists, supporters and grassroots members in general plays in the collective action register of these organisations in contrast with their embedding into the EU institutional system because of mechanisms such as civil dialogue. This results in EU-level civil society having little interest in organising campaigns akin to citizens' initiatives.

By contrast, the ECI may attract organisations that so far have not been interested in the EU by choice or by a lack of valuable resources but which, unlike most EU-level actors, are able to mobilise public opinion and thus turn the ECI into a significant tool, since a campaign's ability to influence decision-making processes depends on the capacity of its promoters to build up a coalition able to put political pressure on decision-making institutions.[60] In this sense the ECI may contribute to increasing the diversity of civil society organisations active at the EU level, thus increasing the EU's policy-making arena inclusiveness. Somehow, paradoxically, this may be the result of a competition between different kinds of organisation, since the new participatory mechanisms may significantly transform the relative value of the different collective action registers in the EU. If, as suggested above, civil dialogue value decreases in favour of an increased political weight for the ECI, the initiative may become a frequently used mechanism despite its weak legal rank. In fact, as mentioned above, the ECI's ability to attract outsider organisations has been confirmed by the consultation on the ECI. The fact that the promoters of the initiative (Initiative and Referendum Institute and Mehr Demokratie) signed up to the Commission's register of interest representatives, which they had not done before, suggests that the ECI may have a restructuring effect in the European civil society field.

V EMPOWERMENT

It is common to criticise democratic innovations in that they may give a voice to citizens who do not usually participate, but it remains up to political elites to choose whether to listen to this voice or not.[61] Article 11 TEU similarly creates a series of soft mechanisms whereby citizens and their organisations are just consulted or allowed to invite the Union institutions to act. This section discusses whether and how these new tools may acquire a higher de facto than de jure saliency.

A Civil Dialogue: Increased Legal Rank but Same Democratic Problems

The Lisbon Treaty provides civil dialogue with a legal rank that civil society organisations have sought for more than a decade. Interviews with some members of the EU civil society organisations that influenced the inclusion of Article

[60] KW Hula, *Lobbying Together. Interest Group Coalitions in Legislative Politics* (Washington DC, Georgetown University Press, 1999) 49.

[61] Smith (n 4) 22–24.

11 TEU consider this as an important achievement. One of the main reasons is that this change makes consultation a mandate of the Treaties and not dependent on the Commission's goodwill, with failure to consult possibly unleashing the possibility of judicial review: 'The European Court of Justice should in the future determine to what extent the inobservance of these procedural practices could be challenged by civil society organisations as an infringement of the principles of participatory democracy.'[62]

The expectation of these organisations is that, with this change, the participatory governance agenda will become more systematic and that practices will be somehow unified among the different Commission services, in particular, opening up possibilities in Directorates-General (DGs) that have been so far rather difficult to access for civil society organisations, as well as the establishment of structured dialogue with more reluctant institutions such as the European Parliament and the Council. Furthermore the core meaning of these organisations' discourse on civil dialogue has been the creation of a horizontal political dialogue with the Commission, beyond the policy-oriented consultations, similar to the existing social dialogue with trade unions and business organisations. To some extent this horizontal dialogue seems to be supported by Article 11(2) TEU, which calls upon the Union institutions to 'maintain an open, transparent and regular dialogue with representative associations and civil society'.

That said, the organisations that contributed to shaping civil dialogue are dissatisfied with the Commission's engagement with it. In this sense the Social Platform's contribution to the Green Paper on the ECI urges the Commission to take action on civil dialogue. In any event, an interview with a Commission official dealing with civil society consultation suggests that the Commission may adopt a low-profile reading of the Treaty articles on civil society dialogue:

> *Luis Bouza García*: Contributions asked the Commission that civil dialogue be included in the Treaty.
>
> *Interviewee*: Yes, but it wasn't . . . What the [Social] Platform would like is a social dialogue on the civil society field . . . This is not in the Treaty; this civil dialogue is not there . . . What is there is a different thing; it is an article saying that there are consultation mechanisms, dialogue mechanisms, but not a civil dialogue in the sense of the social dialogue.[63]

Finally it seems that the recognition of civil dialogue does not solve the problem of this tool's distance from ordinary citizens. In this sense it must be pointed out that the Lisbon Treaty has not turned participation in civil dialogue into a substantive citizens' right.[64] This may be particularly negative for this instrument since 'participation of civil society organisations in the policy-making can never replace widespread political participation through representation'.[65] Thus it could

[62] Cuesta López (n 9) 135.
[63] Interview with a Commission official (Brussels, May 2009).
[64] Cuesta López (n 9).
[65] Ibid, 138.

be argued that, although the above-mentioned attitude by the Commission towards civil dialogue may have different reasons, from a democratic-legitimacy perspective it contrasts strongly with the quick action undertaken to regulate the ECI. A plausible hypothesis may be that the Commission's expectations to obtain legitimacy from civil dialogue have decreased and that it now places bigger expectations on the ECI, which allows a much larger citizens' participation. In this sense, it seems that civil society organisations' increased role in the EU through strengthened citizen participation needs an increased democratic justification beyond its traditional contribution to stakeholder consultation and output legitimacy. The next section addresses exactly the question whether civil dialogue could contribute to larger participation, precisely through the concept of representation.

B Citizens' Initiative: Weak in Terms of Structures and Responsiveness and Difficult to Use

The most significant aspects of Regulation 211/2011 on the ECI[66] are addressed as a structure of costs and opportunities influencing the relation between the Commission and the promoters of initiatives. The degree of responsiveness of EU institutions in relation to the organisers is addressed subsequently.

At first sight the ECI is rather generous: the threshold of participants is only one million, ie just 0.2 per cent of the total population of the EU, which makes it far easier to collect the necessary number of signatures than it is at national level in many countries with similar schemes.[67] However, this does not mean that gathering signatures will be easy. The weakness of general European publics being the main challenge, the regulatory framework of the initiative is decisive for a successful instrument. Although observers of the early stages of the institutional debate on Regulation 211/2011[68] have pointed out that the Commission's proposal established major hurdles for the initiative, the final legislation makes the ECI easier to implement following the intervention of the European Parliament. In this sense the most relevant issue was the definition of what constituted a 'significant number of Member States' from where the signatures must be gathered. Whereas signatures from a high number of Member States would ensure that causes are genuinely European, and thus contribute to the emergence of a public space, it is the very weakness of the European public space which makes it difficult to organise initiatives. It would have been paradoxical to establish a demanding threshold (one-third of Member States, such as in the Commission's initial

[66] [2011] OJ L65/1.

[67] V Cuesta López, *Participación directa e iniciativa legislativa del ciudadano en democracia constitucional* (Pamplona, Aranzadi, 2008).

[68] B Kaufmann, *The European Citizens' Initiative Handbook* (Luxembourg, Green European Foundation, 2010) 6–10 and 67; L Bouza García, *Democracia participativa, sociedad civil y espacio público en la Unión Europea* (Madrid, Fundación Alternativas, 23 December 2010) 26–31.

proposal) for the sake of the emergence of pan-European debates – thereby turning the device into a highly impractical one.

A second major cost that has been partially waived consists in the 'admissibility check', that is, whether proposed initiatives pursue one of the objectives of the Treaties and fall within the powers of the Commission. The Commission's initial proposal established an important cost for the organisation, in that 300,000 signatures had to be gathered before the Commission proceeded to check whether the proposed initiative fell within the powers of the Commission. This requirement was extremely costly since it obliged organisers to launch the campaign and obtain one-third of the signatures for a potentially unacceptable initiative. Regulation 211/2011 establishes that, although the Commission will discard initiatives *manifestly* beyond the scope of its powers in the registration phase, it will only proceed to a detailed analysis on the admissibility after signature collection has been completed. However, dismissing an initiative with one million signatures on purely formal grounds is still a possibility that introduces uncertainty as to the effect of successful campaigns and increases the costs of using the ECI.

Additionally, Regulation 211/2011 includes some dispositions that could be considered as 'cost waivers', in that they facilitate the process of launching an ECI. The most obvious one, which was present in the first version of the Commission's proposal, is the possibility to collect statements of support online. This is most likely to change the very conception of signature collection campaigns: it can be expected that online campaigns relying on social media and viral diffusion will significantly reduce the time and effort needed to collect the signatures. The second one is the requirement to set up an organisation committee, which is a formal recognition of the promoters of the initiative. Although this recognition is a soft one when compared to several national frameworks, because there are no provisions about cost reimbursement nor the right to withdraw the initiative if the promoters do not agree with the way it is handled by the institutions as it happens under Swiss law,[69] the possibility for a group of citizens to be involved at some point of the decision-making process by formally presenting the initiative to the institutions is a significant novelty for the EU political system.

It thus appears that Regulation 211/2011 is relatively user-friendly in that it sets a series of hurdles but includes as well some significant innovations to waive the costs. However such reflections must be linked to the expected responsiveness of the Commission. Since the outcome of the ECI is a mere invitation to the Commission to act, the requisites imposed on the organisers cannot be disproportionate in comparison to such an outcome. In this sense it appears that, despite the low threshold in terms of the number of signatures, the ECI may prove to be beyond the capacities of most organisations in Europe.

Gathering signatures and submitting them to the Commission for consideration is something that citizens could already do before the entry into force of the Lisbon Treaty. In fact the inclusion of the ECI in the draft Constitutional Treaty

[69] Cuesta López (n 68) 225–33.

of 2003 seems to have attracted a number of organisations which launched up to 25 informal initiatives before the ECI had even entered into force.[70] The number of informal initiatives launched suggests that the importance of the ECI may lie beyond its capacity to obligate the Commission as well as the difficulty of meeting the demands of Regulation 211/2011.

The biggest difficulty of the ECI seems to be reaching one million signatures. Out of the 25 informal initiatives launched since 2003, only four could gather one million signatures.[71] The most significant failure was the inability of the European Trade Union Confederation (ETUC), which represents 60 million workers across Europe, to reach this number in support of its call to defend public services. Furthermore one million signatures is a number difficult to reach but easy to dismiss as not really representative of the European population. An example is provided by the dissatisfaction of one of the promoters of 'One million for disability', one of the first successful campaigns, with the European Parliament's dismissive attitude toward its proposal.[72]

The second and probably more delicate obstacle for the achievement of successful ECIs is that these have to be presented on matters and issues on which the Commission can act. In this sense ECIs can only address matters which can be included in the legislative agenda and thus which fall within the Union's competences according to the Treaties. Consequently it is highly likely that a number of initiatives will be unacceptable because they address European matters highly important for some publics but beyond the scope of Union law. In this sense a consideration of the subject matter of the informal initiatives presented so far[73] shows that at least seven of the 25 initiatives required a Treaty change and one was beyond the Commission's legislative powers. Of course this has to be interpreted carefully, since promoters wanting to use the ECI to achieve an EU policy objective have not yet had the opportunity to use the official system provided for under Regulation 211/2011.

It thus appears that the ECI is a weak device in terms of its capacity to oblige the Commission to act and yet a relatively cumbersome instrument, even for big professionalised organisations such as ETUC. The ECI does not have a great potential for bringing citizens' concerns to the agenda because of its institutional limitations and the organisational burdens it imposes on its promoters, in particular compared to its potential to deliver concrete achievements. This should lead us to a negative evaluation of the ECI from the democratic point of view. However, as suggested above, it may have unexpected effects on political inclusion and on the public sphere and thus have a greater de facto political weight.

70 Kaufmann (n 69).

71 Ibid. Also: C Fischer and T Lichtbau, 'Chapter 8: European Citizens' Initiative – Interim Results' in JW Pichler (ed), *We Change Europe! The European Initiative – Art 8b(4) Treaty of Lisbon* (Vienna, Neuer Wissenschaftlicher Verlag, 2008).

72 Interview with a member of the European Disability Forum (30 November 2009).

73 Fischer and Lichtbau (n 72; Kaufmann (n 69).

VI ARTICLE 11 TEU AND THE EUROPEAN PUBLIC SPHERE: DANGERS, OPPORTUNITIES, TRADE-OFFS AND COMPLEMENTARITIES

From the point of view of the European public space, each of the mechanisms of Article 11 TEU could worsen the EU's democratic legitimacy crisis by outlining the distance between the EU discourse on participation and the eventuality that Article 11 TEU could be too costly and would not significantly empower citizens. This section points out, however, that there are both analytical reasons to expect a relevant impact of the ECI in enlarging the general European public sphere and normative reasons to recommend the Union institutions to link these tools closely and develop an open attitude towards the ECI.

A The ECI and the Public Sphere

The effect on the public sphere of the ECI becoming a frequently used tool would be far from negligible. By arguing that the ECI is 'a singular opportunity to bring the Union closer to the citizens and to foster greater cross-border debate about EU policy issues',[74] the Commission's expectation seems to be that, by joining in petitions, citizens will be better informed on what the EU does and will become more knowledgeable of the EU. However citizen initiatives are political participation and interest aggregation mechanisms rather than deliberation ones,[75] and it can be challenged that signing in support for a campaign will make citizens better informed or engage in debates on the EU. Firstly, signing a petition can be quite an individual action whereby citizens endorse their previously held positions with little or no public deliberation. In terms of cost and benefits, promoters are more likely to look for already convinced citizens than to try to convince new ones. Furthermore the extent to which signatories will follow the issue after they endorse a specific initiative is likely dependent on the promoters' activism to keep them informed. Thus this tool will not create a sort of vertical relationship between citizens and EU institutions, as the Commission seems to expect, but a mediated one, where citizens will be informed, mobilised and asked to participate by organisations, including political parties, seeking to have an influence on the EU. It may contribute to the fragmented Europeanisation of the public sphere, where citizens concerned by issues addressed by civil society may become involved in EU affairs, whereas large sections of the public remain aside, in particular since the media may have no particular incentive to focus on the ECI.

Furthermore, competition with outsider organisations using the ECI may give EU civil society organisations a strong motivation to inform, involve and mobilise their members and public opinion at large, which would in turn contribute to a generalisation of public sphere-oriented participation tools. The consequence

[74] European Commission, 'Proposal for a regulation of the European Parliament and of the Council on the citizens' initiative' (31 March 2010) 3.

[75] Smith (n 4) 131–32.

may be that Commission–civil society relations would turn from a low-saliency, expertise-oriented and consensus-seeking regime towards a more public-opinion and mobilisation and contested regime. Thus the expectation is not that the ECI will in itself make citizens better informed, but that it will unleash a degree of mobilisation and competition among different civil society organisations for the citizens' interest and support of their causes, which may in turn make the public more interested in EU matters.

Granting a way of access to outsider organisations and causes may introduce a controversial approach in a consensus-prone polity. The question about the EU's politicisation is controversial because it deals directly with the transformation of the public's attitudes towards the EU:[76] it is incompatible with the permissive consensus approach, but it may on the contrary confirm that the EU is a mature polity allowing a space for contestation to emerge.[77] In particular, granting a space for contestation and opposition may contribute to fostering citizen ownership through 'normalisation' of the EU, ie the possibility to contest its policies without contesting the polity.

The ECI could clearly contribute to worsening the impression that 'the EU does not listen to its citizens'. The first and most obvious risk regards initiatives dealing with specific European or even EU topics on which the Commission cannot act. The best example is the initiative seeking to move the European Parliament from Strasbourg to Brussels. The Parliament's seat being established by the Treaties, such a proposal would seem unacceptable as a formal ECI. This risk was particularly acute in the first version of the Regulation implementing the ECI, where the Commission suggested checking admissibility after around one-third of the necessary signatures had been gathered, for the sake of fostering European debates. It may be argued that failed initiatives, whether they fail because they do not meet the one-million-signature threshold or because the Commission does not eventually endorse them, would nevertheless contribute to fostering debates on the EU. Whereas this is certainly true, it would unleash a second risk, as the national experience in many countries proves that sustained rejection of successful initiatives, as has been the case in Spain and Italy (for instance),[78] turns citizens' initiatives into irrelevant and finally unused instruments.[79] This situation could be worsened at the EU level since the irrelevance of the instrument would reinforce the view that the Union institutions are not accessible to its citizens.

[76] L Hooghe and G Marks, 'A Postfunctionalist Theory of European Integration: From Permissive Consensus to Constraining Dissensus' (2009) 39 *British Journal of Political Science* 1.

[77] D Della Porta, 'The Europeanization of Protest: A Typology and Empirical Evidence' in B Kohler-Koch and B Rittberger (eds), *Debating the Democratic Legitimacy of the European Union* (Lanham, Rowman & Littlefield, 2007).

[78] Cuesta López (n 68).

[79] C Mallaina García, *Nuevos desafíos democráticos: hacia una iniciativa legislativa popular efectiva,* (Fundación Alternativas, 11 November 2009).

B Overcoming the Opposition between Civil Dialogue and the ECI

The structure of the chapter may have suggested that civil dialogue and the ECI are radically opposite mechanisms with different origins and totally different purposes. However, both are democratic innovations that can provide citizens and organisations with a way of access to the EU. This section considers what may be their common contribution to the EU and how they could be implemented in a mutually reinforcing way.

Regarding the broader social dimension, the civil dialogue scheme does not seem capable of fostering debate beyond the organisations already well established and interested in European policy-making. There is a risk of a sort of 'participatory autopoeisis', where the recognition and inclusion into the Treaties of an already existing practice would turn a governance-inspired tool into a participatory mechanism, bringing the EU closer to the citizens by the mere virtue of being included in the Treaties.

A sign of such a trend is the increasing usage of digital forums as a complement to stakeholder consultations.[80] That said, it seems that these instruments suffer from the same problems as 'conventional' civil dialogue. Kohler-Koch reports that here too practices are very variable from one DG to another, in particular, regarding inclusion of the general public:

> The market-related DGs have been hesitant to use the instrument of online-consultations and when they use it the consultation is mostly addressed to 'stakeholders' and not to the 'general public'. General Directorates with a broader reach such as employment and social affairs or are in charge of a newly established EU policy field such as culture or public health are eager to engage the wider public in their consultations and, accordingly, use online-consultations and open hearings and conferences extensively.[81]

Additionally, this policy seems to be conceived as an information and communication one rather than a participatory one.[82]

Civil dialogue is a relevant instrument for building relations (hence trust) between EU officials and civil society organisations, conveying expertise and providing transparent access to the Union institutions at a relevant moment of the policy-making process. However it lacks support and control from grassroots citizens. On the contrary, the ECI has a potential for building bottom-up campaigns that contribute to raising awareness and build ownership among sections of the general public, even though it may be relatively ineffective as a policy-making device. From this perspective the mechanisms are not mutually exclusive but perfectly complementary.

[80] A Michailidou, 'Vertical Europeanisation of Online Public Dialogue: EU Public Communication Policy and Online Implementation' in C Bee and E Bozzini (eds), *Mapping the European Public Sphere. Institutions, Media and Civil Society* (Aldershot, Ashgate, 2010).

[81] Kohler-Koch (n 8) 9.

[82] Michailidou (n 81).

Civil dialogue is a participatory mechanism rather undeveloped at the national or regional level but is particularly relevant at the EU level and linked to the Commission's role and the nature of its policy communities and debates. For this reason discarding it as an instrument would be quite counterproductive at this stage, in particular knowing that the alternative may well be traditional lobbying. Since the Commission seems to be expecting a lot from the ECI, whereas it seems that European civil society is not strongly interested in this new device, it could be recommended that the Commission should link any future reflection on the democratic evolution of civil dialogue to the ECI. In this sense, participation in ECI campaigns and other forms of citizen mobilisation, in particular internal consultation of members, could be taken into account as a way to measure the representativeness of civil society organisations participating in civil dialogue.[83] This measure would thus reward organisations able to deliver goods that the Commission is expecting from civil society, namely the ability to engage in debates on the EU with citizens. This would certainly transform the nature of civil dialogue, whose focus would move from technical policy discussion to a rather more politically oriented debate. In this sense policy consultations could still be organised mainly for expertise-gathering purposes, while a more general debate could be organised with representative organisations defined in this sense. This would significantly contribute to fostering competition between organisations for citizens' attention on EU matters.

Regarding the ECI, its main weakness is the lack of certainty about the outcome of the promoters' efforts. Organisations will only invest resources in using the ECI if the initiative acquires a bigger weight in terms of Commission responsiveness. This depends on the Commission's attitude towards incoming initiatives: if it wishes to see a significant usage of the ECI in order to foster debates on the EU, the Commission could be advised to take the political step to clarify the political signification of the ECI by giving all acceptable initiatives, that is, those complying with the Treaties and Regulation 211/2011, a de facto mandatory force in terms of brining forward proposals for Union action, even when they are manifestly against its own political agenda.[84] This practice would give the ECI a real participatory content beyond the mere freedom of expression and which, if done systematically, would not challenge the Commission's original role in the decision-making process.

The joint adoption of these two recommendations would turn the ability to mobilise and inform citizens into a rewarded capacity, since organisations using the ECI would be empowered in civil dialogue and the ECI would become a real opportunity to shape the EU's agenda. This in turn may contribute to decreasing the radicalism of the initiatives, since promoters knowing that their proposal will make it to the decision-making institutions, the European Parliament and the Council, will tend to present politically acceptable proposals. Furthermore, it

[83] Bouza Garcia (n 69).

[84] Ibid.

would contribute to holding the democratically elected institutions to account, since it will be clear that the Commission is not taking the final decision on the matters submitted by the citizens.

VI CONCLUSION

This chapter has addressed three paradoxes related to Article 11 TEU. The first one is the paradoxical nature of the provision's mechanisms as democratic innovations, in that none of them can be said to have been purposely designed to redress democratic legitimacy problems. In fact they are rather the result of the convergence of the demands of well-established civil society actors with the discourse of the Commission on Union governance. The second paradox is that, since the context in which the instruments were included in the Treaties has changed significantly, these instruments are now a real democratisation opportunity. Although democratic legitimacy problems were apparent in 2003, the situation in 2011 (after three failed referendums on EU reform treaties in France, the Netherlands and Ireland) makes it urgent to redress this question. In this sense the main challenge is whether mechanisms designed to improve the EU's governance can be oriented towards democratic participation. Although this is certainly difficult given the tendency of governance approaches to minimise conflict, it is possible to consider criteria according to which governance tools contribute to democratic participation.[85] The third paradox is that, although the instruments have serious drawbacks in terms of policy influence and their capacity to foster institutional responsiveness, they may provide an important opportunity for the inclusion of new actors and for fostering larger social effects, in particular, the emergence of a European public sphere.

Considering these paradoxes, the chapter has approached civil dialogue and the ECI from three complementary perspectives. It seems that civil dialogue's main weakness, its inability to foster citizens' direct participation and its tendency to exclude some groups, could be complemented by the ECI, and vice versa. However, these tools not only have intrinsic difficulties, but could by themselves contribute to worsening the EU's gap with its own citizens. In this sense, the chapter has considered that participants in civil dialogue should be able to demonstrate their ability to represent causes or constituencies; and recommended that the ability to foster democratic debates could be an alternative measure of representativeness, which could be operationalised by considering (among other things) the organisations' usage of the ECI to promote its causes. The chapter has also recommended that the Commission adopt a policy of presenting proposals based on all successful initiatives, in order to reward organisations that have succeeded in mobilising citizens, to foster pan-European debates and to provide a real democratic content to the new ECI. This should not substantially penalise

[85] Subirats, Parés and Blanco (n 35).

organisations representing a cause rather than a constituency, because the ECI does precisely make them able to mobilise supporters who are not necessarily members of the organisations.

Although these recommendations can be dismissed as unrealistic on a first reading, they do not undermine the Commission's role, but suggest adapting it to a situation of increased politicisation. Furthermore, they are considered plausible since they are compatible with the Commission's recent discourse on civil dialogue, and could furthermore contribute to limiting some of the dangers of these innovations, albeit increasing their potential beyond the institutional framework.

12

The European Citizens' Initiative: A New Institution for Empowering Europe's Citizens?

GRAHAM SMITH

I INTRODUCTION

AS OF APRIL 2012, the citizens of the European Union are empowered to launch European Citizens' Initiatives (ECIs). Should any proposal attract one million signatures from their fellow European citizens from across a range of Member States, the European Commission will be required to formally respond to the organisers, explaining how it intends to act (or otherwise). In the official press release welcoming the speed of agreement between the European Parliament and Council on the realisation of this new democratic innovation, Maroš Šefčovič, Vice-President for Inter-institutional Relations and Administration states:

> The ECI will introduce a whole new form of participatory democracy to the EU. It is a major step forward in the democratic life of the Union. It's a concrete example of bringing Europe closer to its citizens. And it will foster a cross border debate about what we are doing in Brussels and thus contribute, we hope, to the development of a real European public space.[1]

This is bold rhetoric: the ECI is viewed as a significant institutional response to the EU's perceived democratic deficit – the difference and distance between the subjectivity, motives and intentions of citizens and European policy-makers who make decisions in their name.[2] The Commission itself has recognised the problem of the disconnection between citizens and decision-makers in Brussels, perhaps most vividly in the 2006 European Communications Policy White Paper:

[1] European Union Press Release, 'Commission welcomes agreement on European Citizens' Initiative' available at www.europa.eu/rapid/pressReleasesAction.do?reference=IP/10/1720&format=HTML&aged=0&language=EN&guiLanguage=en.

[2] P Culpepper and A Fung, 'Do All Bridges Collapse? Possibilities for Democracy in the European Union' (2007) 48(4) *Politische Vierteljahresschrift* 730.

> People feel remote from these decisions, the decision-making process and EU institutions. There is a sense of alienation from 'Brussels', which partly mirrors the disenchantment with politics in general. One reason for this is the inadequate development of a 'European public sphere' where the European debate can unfold. Despite exercising the right to elect members of the European Parliament, citizens often feel that they themselves have little opportunity to make their voices heard on European issues, and there is no obvious forum within which they can discuss these issues together.[3]

This chapter investigates whether this new institutional design is likely to play the role that Šefčovič suggests in empowering Europe's citizens. It begins with a short account of the emergence of the ECI, recognising that although the Commission and other European institutions have been concerned with the question of engaging citizens, the ECI was *not* part of an explicit plan of democratisation. Rather, the innovation emerged late in the day – and somewhat to the surprise of those lobbying on its behalf – in the Convention on the Future of Europe. Its presence in the aborted draft Constitution ensured that it was included without debate in the later Lisbon Treaty of 2009.

The chapter then lays out the main elements of Regulation 2011/211, which implements the ECI,[4] before turning its attention to whether such a democratic device is likely to empower European citizens. In the first place, the wording of the Regulation suggests that this new transnational institution will bring with it some unintended consequences in terms of the equality of access and impact for citizens across different Member States. Secondly, since the ECI bears more than a passing family resemblance to direct legislation practised across a number of liberal democratic States, it is possible to draw on the extensive body of scholarship on the theory and practice of direct democracy to offer speculative thoughts on the extent to which the ECI is likely to empower citizens. The final substantive section of the chapter asks whether the European Union is missing an opportunity to enhance its participatory institutions by linking the ECI to recent experiments in deliberative engagement that took place following the failed Constitution process.

II EMERGENCE OF THE ECI

The introduction of the ECI was not preceded by a widespread public debate or significant analysis on the part of European and national decision-makers in the various policy forums of the EU. Rather it emerged very much at the last minute from the Convention on the Future of Europe, which was charged with drafting a Constitution for the European Union in 2002–03, following effective lobbying by a small group of NGOs and members of the Convention.[5] During the Convention

[3] European Commission, 'White Paper on a European Communication Policy' COM (2006) 35.

[4] [2011] OJ L65/1.

[5] This account of the Convention process draws on a presentation by and subsequent discussion with Jens Nymand Christensen, a Secretariat-General of the European Commission, at a conference on the ECI, Liverpool University, 6 April 2011 and the account of the process offered by Democracy International available at www.democracy-international.org/eci.html.

process, a group of NGOs led by the Initiative and Referendum Institute Europe (IRI Europe)[6] proposed significant direct democratic reforms, in particular a Europe-wide referendum on the Constitution and new direct legislation devices such as a citizens' initiative (including binding ballot) and obligatory referendums for constitutional amendments. These ideas were picked up and promoted strongly by two members of the Convention, Jürgen Meyer (Social Democrat representative of the German Bundestag) and Alain Lamassoure (a French Conservative Member of the European Parliament). But these extensive reform proposals were rejected by the presidium led by Giscard d'Estaing. The response from the NGOs and Convention members was to offer a compromise draft on the ECI – an institution that would allow citizens to propose policy and legislative changes, but without a popular ballot process. But again this was rejected by the presidium. It appeared that no significant participatory institutional reform was going to emerge from the Convention process.

However, on the final day of the Convention (12 June 2003), d'Estaing announced a series of last-minute amendments to the proposed Constitution. To the surprise of participants, the intensive lobbying had been successful and the amendment on the compromise version of the ECI was included within Article I-46, 'the principle of participatory democracy':

> No less than one million citizens coming from a significant number of Member States may invite the Commission to submit any appropriate proposal on matters where citizens consider that a legal act of the Union is required for the purpose of implementing the Constitution. A European law shall determine the provisions for the specific procedures and conditions required for such a citizens' initiative.[7]

Having made a late entry into the final version of the Treaty Establishing a Constitution for Europe, the popular votes against the proposed Constitution in France and the Netherlands appeared to put an end to the institutionalisation of the ECI. However, it was back on the agenda at the Intergovernmental Conference (IGC) charged with agreeing the 'Reform Treaty' (the future Lisbon Treaty), which aimed to salvage elements of the aborted Constitution. To avoid unravelling the complex trade-offs that had been necessary to reach agreement in 2003, the Angela Merkel presidency decided that much of the proposed Constitution would not be reopened for debate unless there was *unanimity* amongst Member States to do so. This high threshold meant that there was little modification to many of the elements of the Constitution and therefore, with little or no public debate, the ECI passed into Article 11 of the revised Treaty on European Union.

From that point on, the institutionalisation of the ECI has been fairly rapid. Anticipating the entry into force of the Lisbon Treaty, the Commission adopted a Green Paper in 2009 and launched a public consultation. The final structure of Regulation 211/2011 was then agreed, again relatively quickly, between Council

[6] See www.iri-europe.org/.

[7] [2003] OJ C169.

and Parliament, coming into force in February 2011. The first initiatives were launched officially from April 2012.

III DESIGN OF THE ECI

There have been fairly significant changes made to the design of the ECI from the initial proposal to its final incarnation. We will not rehearse all the differences and disagreements between parties here; rather this section lays out the main elements of how the ECI will operate based on Regulation 211/2011.[8]

The ECI is explicitly transnational in its ambition, requiring significant support – one million signatures – from citizens from across a number of Member States. It is this feature that particularly distinguishes the ECI from the existing European Parliament Petition (EPP) which can be proposed by a single signatory.

The first stage in the ECI process is the establishment of a citizens' committee, which must include residents from at least seven Member States. It is this committee that officially provides the wording of the proposed initiative to the Commission. The Commission then has two months to either register or reject the proposal. Rejection can be for a number of reasons, including the composition of the committee or on the grounds that the proposal falls outside the powers of the Commission, 'is manifestly abusive, frivolous or vexatious' or 'manifestly contrary to the values of the Union'.[9] In its original formulation of the ECI, the Commission had suggested that registration should take place after a significant number of signatures have been collected to indicate that there is support for the proposal, but it was recognised that the rejection of an initiative at that point could cause considerable public disquiet.

If a proposal is registered and made public, the organisers have 12 months to collect one million signatures. There was some disagreement between Commission, Council and Parliament and those contributing to the consultation on the ECI as to the minimum number of Member States from which signatures must be drawn. The final Regulation states that signatures must come from at least one-quarter of EU countries: seven out of 27. But to ensure that the one million is reasonably representative – and not just from one or two Member States – a *minimum* number of signatories from each of the seven Member States has been established. This threshold is degressively proportional to the population of each Member State, following the proportions used for the number of MEPs (and multiplied by 750). Thus the minimum number of signatories from Malta is 3,750; compared to 74,250 from Germany.

Assuming the organising committee has been able to collect the requisite number of signatures and fulfilled the relevant national thresholds, national authorities then have three months to verify the signatures from their polity. Assuming

[8] For the European Commission's guidance on the ECI, including the relevant Regulation, see http://ec.europa.eu/dgs/secretariat_general/citizens_initiative/index_en.htm.

[9] See Art 4 Reg 211/2011.

that the verification is successful, the organising committee is then in a position to formally present the initiative to the Commission. The Commission has three months to respond, during which time officials are expected to meet with the organisers to ensure the details of the proposal are understood and a public hearing is organised at the European Parliament. Having examined the initiative, the Commission is required to adopt a communication explaining its response to the initiative: reasons for action or otherwise.

IV EMPOWERMENT THROUGH THE ECI?

The institutionalisation of the ECI can be seen as part of the broad movement in advanced industrial democracies towards institutions that offer more direct control over political and constitutional decision-making to citizens.[10] The ECI bears a family resemblance to forms of direct legislation and explicitly – but arguably incorrectly – borrows the name of one particular direct democratic design, the citizens' initiative. As that term is typically understood, the successful collection of signatures is followed by a binding popular vote on the proposition. While the ECI does not include a popular vote in its design – it is simply the petition element – evidence from the theory and practice of direct legislation may still offer insights into its potential effect on empowerment.

A Wording of Regulation 2011/211

For theorists of direct democracy, it is the principle of equality, expressed in both the right to launch a petition and the right to vote on valid propositions, on which the democratic legitimacy of direct legislation rests.[11] Even if the ECI only empowers citizens to put forward propositions for the Commission's consideration, the principle of equality ought still to hold. In practice, with a polity as complex as the EU, political equality is not always easy to realise, and the design of Regulation 211/2011 generates a number of potential inequalities.[12]

Article 3(4) of the Regulation states: 'In order to be eligible to support a proposed citizens' initiative, signatories shall be citizens of the Union and shall be of the age to be entitled to vote in elections to the European Parliament.' This apparently innocuous statement generates potential inequalities of participation. First, who is defined as 'citizen' will vary across national polities. The lack of universal documentation to identify European citizens means that Member States will use

[10] S Scarrow, 'Direct Democracy and Institutional Change: A Comparative Investigation' (2001) 34(6) *Comparative Political Studies* 651; Initiative and Referendum Institute for Europe, *The Initiative for Europe Handbook 2008* (Marburg, IRI Europe, 2008) 11.

[11] M Saward, *The Terms of Democracy* (Cambridge, Polity Press, 1998).

[12] This analysis of Regulation 211/2011 borrows heavily from M Dougan, 'What are we to Make of the Citizens' Initiative?' (2011) 48 *CML Rev* 1807.

different procedures to verify signatories. For the majority of nations, personal identification documentation will limit signatories to nationals. For others that do not require such documentation, the category varies between residents (Ireland, the Netherlands and the UK) or residents and non-resident nationals (Belgium, Denmark, Estonia, Finland, Germany and Slovakia). And because of these differences, it is not clear how national verification processes will deal with citizens who have exercised free movement rights, but do not have the relevant verification documentation for the State in which they are resident when they sign a petition. So, for example, it is possible that French and UK nationals living in Spain will be treated differently because of the national verification system in place. Not only will verification be a confusing task for national authorities, but it introduces significant differences into how the status of citizenship is realised across the European Union, raising challenges related to equal treatment and free movement of citizens. A second differentiation in citizenship status emerging from Article 3(4) relates to voting age. While for most Member States this is 18, in Austria, for example, 16-year-olds are able to participate in European elections.

A further area where inequalities will creep into the process is in relation to the threshold number of signatories required in each Member State. We have already noted that there are major differences, with Germany requiring a minimum of 74,250 signatures compared to only 3,750 in Malta. Degressive proportionality again entails deviation from equal treatment, but a deviation that is manifest throughout the institutional architecture of the EU. Setting the same threshold proportions for each Member State would have been too demanding for the larger polities; setting the same total number for all States would have a significant negative impact on smaller States. It is interesting to speculate what this will mean for the signature collection strategies of organisers: a focus on a small number of medium or larger States where a smaller proportion of the citizenry is needed to achieve the national threshold; or a focus on the smaller States where the threshold number of signatures required is lower. And in terms of geographical spread, the seven out of 27 requirement means that an initiative does not need to achieve geographically representative support from across the Union: the ECI certainly requires transnational mobilisation, but the support for an initiative can be concentrated in a minority of Member States.

Finally, there is some vagueness in the Regulation about the scope of an ECI. There will be much opportunity for contestation about what 'manifestly abusive, frivolous or vexatious' entails and how the 'values of the Union' are to be interpreted. The Regulation does not clearly define what subject matters fall within its remit. Article 2 suggests that an initiative must fall within 'the framework of the Commission's powers to submit a proposal for a legal act of the Union for the purpose of implementing the Treaties'. What this will mean in practice is not entirely clear. It suggests, for example, that constitutional questions are out of bounds: the ECI focuses on the implementation of already existing Treaties and not rewriting elements of the Treaties themselves. Again, it appears that it is the powers of the Commission that are to be considered and not necessarily the powers of other institutions of the Union (for example, the European Parliament). The average citizen is unlikely to be cognisant of the nature of the separation of powers with the Union, nor in fact the differentiation of powers between the institutions of the Union and Member States. At some point the policy areas where ECIs can legitimately be launched will need to be clearly defined, otherwise citizens are likely to be frustrated and disillusioned as popular propositions are deemed inadmissible by the Commission.

B Lessons from the Practice of Direct Legislation

Moving beyond the specification of the Regulation, we may be able to draw lessons about empowerment from the significant programme of research on the impact of direct legislation, particularly in the United States and Switzerland. For theorists of direct democracy, direct legislation delivers what they take to be the primary goal of democratic governance: 'responsive rule'.[13] The initiative (with binding vote), in particular, enables citizens to place issues that have been overlooked or ignored by political elites on the agenda. Evidence is emerging that responsive rule – a substantive relationship between the preferences of citizens and policy outcomes – is better realised in polities with direct legislation. Policies in political systems that have institutionalised direct democratic devices tend to reflect the median voter's preferences.[14] In the US, direct legislation is recognised 'as a "median-reverting" institution that pushes policy back toward the centre of public opinion when legislatures move too far to the right or left'.[15] Bruno Frey offers similar evidence for Swiss communes.[16]

This median-reverting effect is not just a response to the outcome of popular votes: unsuccessful campaigns and the very threat of an initiative can affect the political landscape. Elisabeth Gerber and Simon Hug suggest that there is evidence of such an *indirect* effect of direct legislation in the US. Anticipating the potential for initiatives, public authorities tend towards policy that reflects the median voter's preference and hence majority opinion.[17] The potential indirect effect of initiatives is well understood by a range of actors in US politics. Gerber reports that 'economic groups, professional groups, and businesses . . . attribute high levels of importance to signalling and pressuring the legislature and much lower levels of importance to passing new laws by initiative'.[18]

[13] I Budge, *The New Challenge of Direct Democracy* (Cambridge, Polity Press, 1996) and Saward (n 11).

[14] ER Gerber and S Hug, 'Legislative Responses to Direct Legislation' in M Mendelson and A Parkin (eds), *Referendum Democracy: Citizens, Elites, and Deliberation in Referendum Campaigns* (Basingstoke, Palgrave, 2001) 103–05.

[15] A Lupia and JG Matsusaka, 'Direct Democracy: New Approaches to Old Questions' (2004) 7 *Annual Review of Political Science* 463, 474.

[16] BS Frey, 'Direct Democracy: Politico-Economic Lessons from Swiss Experience' (1994) 84 *The American Economic Review* 338, 341.

[17] Gerber and Hug (n 14).

[18] ER Gerber, *The Populist Paradox: Interest Group Influence and the Promise of Direct Legislation* (Princeton, Princeton University Press, 1999) 83.

Wolf Linder finds similar evidence for the effect of direct legislation in Switzerland: even when initiatives are unsuccessful, they can have an effect on the political process by placing new issues onto the political agenda, accelerating the adoption of policies and expressing discontent with the political establishment.[19] Most commentators on Swiss democracy argue that the indirect effect of direct legislation has been fundamental to the development of the country's 'consensus democracy'. Political elites have integrated different interests into the governing process as a way of anticipating challenges and overcoming the threat of initiatives and popular referendums.[20] The process whereby the federal government and Parliament are given time to consider initiative propositions and offer counterproposals means that there is a great deal of interaction between political elites and the authors of initiatives.[21] Simply counting the number of successful initiatives in particular policy areas does not give us a fair representation of the effect of direct legislation mechanisms: their indirect effect must not be discounted.

While this research indicates the extent of empowerment in the sense that citizens' policy preferences are more likely to be reflected in policy, it tells us nothing of citizens' *perceptions* of empowerment. Here analysis undertaken by Shaun Bowler and Todd Donovan is particularly insightful. They compare the reported sense of political efficacy of citizens across the US where states have institutionalised direct legislation to varying degrees. Their findings indicate that both 'internal efficacy' (individuals' perception that they have the resources and skills to influence government) and 'external efficacy' (their perception of the responsiveness of government) are higher in an institutional context within which direct legislation plays a role. They add that 'the substantive magnitude of the effect, moreover, rivals that of education, which has been demonstrated to be a consistent predictor of efficacy'.[22] Their research suggests that the presence of direct legislation devices has a meaningful impact on citizens' sense of empowerment.

A significant caveat to their findings, however, is that the results for external efficacy do not hold for all citizens. In those states that make frequent use of the initiative, there appears to be a negative impact on the sense of external efficacy – their attitudes about the responsiveness of government – on the part of minority ethnic citizens. As Bowler and Donovan speculate, this impact on empowerment may well have been caused by 'several highly visible ballot initiatives [that] have targeted legislative policies that advanced minority interests and campaigns [that] . . . turn mass opinions against minorities'.[23]

[19] W Linder, *Swiss Democracy* (New York, St Martin's Press, 1994) 105.

[20] A popular referendum challenges legislation proposed by legislators as compared to a citizens' initiative which proposes new legislation.

[21] KW Kobach, *The Referendum: Direct Democracy in Switzerland* (Aldershot, Dartmouth, 1993); KW Kobach, 'Switzerland' in D Butler and A Ranney (eds), *Referendums Around the World* (Washington, AEI Press, 1994) and Linder (n 19).

[22] S Bowler and T Donovan, 'Popular Control of Referendum Agendas: Implications for Democratic Outcomes and Minority Rights' in M Mendelsohn and A Parkin (eds), *Referendum Democracy: Citizens, Elites, and Deliberation in Referendum Campaigns* (Basingstoke, Palgrave, 2001) 390.

[23] Ibid, 380.

We need to treat these various findings on direct legislation with care and not simply suggest that the ECI will have the same impact on empowerment. This is evidence from the practice of direct democratic designs that not only generate proposals from the citizen-body, but which also put these propositions to binding popular votes. As I have already suggested, given that there is no such voting process for the ECI, it is disingenuous to use the term 'initiative' for this new European institution. The ECI is better termed a petition, although doubtless this would lead to confusion with the already existing EPP.

But can we draw some speculative lessons from the direct legislation literature? After all, a verified ECI that has at least one million signatures (and arguably one that does not quite make that level) will have significant normative power and will be difficult for the Commission to reject outright. Issues that European institutions have overlooked will be given a higher status on the political agenda. The evidence from Switzerland and the US is that the collection of signatures itself sends signals to political decision-makers, whether or not the proposition makes it to the ballot or is then supported and passed into legislation. It would be strange to believe that there would not be both a direct and indirect effect of the ECI. The Commission will be under pressure to respond positively to validated initiatives and is likely to act on occasion to forestall public pressure and the registering of a proposal. But the absence of the popular vote arguably means that the ECI will not have the same disciplinary effect as citizens' initiatives which include popular voting. Because citizens lack the power to formally discipline an unresponsive Commission through the ballot box, the median-reverting pressure will no doubt be less.

And arguably the same can be said for the sense of political efficacy. Again, we might expect it to increase on average across the population: the ECI does provide a new avenue for citizen engagement. But to expect it to have the same effect as direct legislation is asking too much. The finding that the external efficacy of citizens from minority ethnic communities is reduced in those polities that make most use of direct legislation certainly requires attention. It is likely that organised interests will launch ECIs that directly challenge what are perceived as liberal European policy agendas on immigration, asylum and the like. Whether these are deemed valid and registered by the Commission may well be irrelevant: the hostile debate that is likely to be generated on occasion in the public sphere may itself be enough to have a negative impact on the efficacy of already politically marginalised groups.

A further body of research on direct legislation generates a final set of questions about the extent to which the ECI will empower citizens. There are two ways in which the ECI formally empowers citizens: launching and supporting an initiative. Most citizens will participate in the latter form of participation. Recognising the caveats related to the specification of citizen and the different national thresholds in Regulation 2011/211 (discussed above), citizens will be broadly equally empowered to *support* an initiative; to add their signature to a proposition. But, evidence on direct legislation suggests that this will not be the case for *launching* a successful initiative. While the ECI will likely have significant agenda-setting power, evidence from studies of direct legislation suggests that this power will be exercised and shaped by organised interests rather than citizens qua citizens. A successful ECI will require organisers to mobilise one million signatures from across at least seven Member States in the 12-month period following registration. A minimum figure of signatures has been put in place to protect political elites and perhaps also citizens from being overwhelmed with proposals.[24] But experience from California, where a similar rate of signatures is required for securing a proposal on an initiative ballot,[25] provides evidence that this is almost impossible to achieve without professional signature drives. And such drives are highly expensive: in excess of $1 million to qualify an initiative in California.[26] The 'substantial political resources (money and manpower)' required to meet signature thresholds means that 'organised interests clearly have an advantage over most individuals'.[27] There is no 'mythical citizen'[28] who initiates initiatives and it will be the best-organised CSOs, political parties and business interests that will be able to make most effective use of the ECI. Recalling the earlier Gerber quote, in the US 'economic groups, professional groups, and businesses . . . attribute high levels of importance to signalling and pressuring the legislature'. In other words, citizen participation will be channelled through the agendas of already powerful organised interests. It is these interests that are most significantly empowered by the ECI.

V MISSED (DELIBERATIVE) OPPORTUNITIES?

The ECI offers a very particular take on democratic design: organisers are required to attract one million like-minded citizens to place an issue on the Commission's agenda. But this potentially leaves decision-makers with a headache. How much weight should be given to the voice of one million citizens from a European adult population of around 400 million (in other words, 0.25 per cent)? The capacity to attract so many signatures is significant; but how significant? Here the lack of a popular vote as part of the ECI means that it is difficult to judge broader public opinion on any particular proposition.

Another stream of democratic theory and institutional design – deliberative democracy – questions whether such public opinion is what should guide policy-making. Most citizens signing petitions or responding to public opinion surveys

[24] The European Parliament Petition Committee (PETI) apparently receives over 1,000 petitions per year to consider.

[25] In California, the number of signatures required for a successful petition is 5% of the turnout for the previous state election (around 400,000 signatures) collected within 150 days.

[26] Lupia and Matsusaka (n 15) 471.

[27] DB Magleby, *Direct Legislation: Voting on Ballot Propositions in the United States* (Baltimore, Johns Hopkins University Press, 1984) 58.

[28] TE Cronin, *Direct Democracy: The Politics of Initiative, Referendum, and Recall* (Harvard, Harvard University Press, 1999) 207.

are not likely to have given the issue much thought. Public opinion tends to be based on raw, rather than reflective, preferences. For deliberative democrats, institutions need to be crafted that allow citizens to engage in free and fair discussion with their fellow citizens with different social perspectives under conditions of mutual respect. Deliberative democrats offer a different take on empowerment, placing a great deal of emphasis on the importance of reasoned deliberation between citizens and the transformation of preferences that can emerge from this process. As Bernard Manin has argued, 'the source of legitimacy is not the predetermined will of individuals, but rather the process of its formation, that is deliberation itself'.[29]

It is striking that 'the period of reflection' that immediately followed the failed Constitution process was characterised by experimentation with a series of transnational deliberative designs for engaging citizens: over 20 separate initiatives according to one estimate.[30] These were sponsored under 'Plan D for Democracy, Dialogue and Debate' adopted by the European Commission in 2005,[31] later superseded by 'Debate Europe', as well as a series of other programmes including Citizenship Programmes, eParticipation Preparatory Action Programme and the 6th and 7th Framework Programmes for Research and Technological Development of the EU.

A variety of different approaches to deliberative design were attempted to deal with the challenges of scale and national and linguistic diversity.[32] For example, the Futurum website, established to enable citizens to contribute to the debate on the European constitutional process, made explicit reference to the need to 'bring the European Union closer to its citizens and reduce the perception of a democratic deficit'.[33] Futurum translated its basic webpages into 10 languages and citizens could post comments, respond to the posts of others and add new threads in any European language. While this still led to domination by English speakers, space was created on the site for deliberation involving other language-users.[34] In contrast, two face-to-face transnational deliberative polls – Tomorrow's Europe (under Plan D) and Europolis (under the 7th Framework programme) – brought a randomly selected sample of citizens from each Member State together in the European Parliament building to debate pressing European policy issues. Both deliberative polls relied on a barrage of translators to ensure that a participant

[29] B Manin, 'On Legitimacy and Political Deliberation' (1987) 15(3) *Political Theory* 351–52.

[30] M Yang, 'Europe's New Communication Policy and the Introduction of Transnational Deliberative Citizens' Involvement Projects' in R Kies and P Nanz (eds), *European Citizens' Deliberation: A Promising Path for EU Governance?* (Farnham, Ashgate, 2013).

[31] See European Commission, 'The Commission's contribution to the period of reflection and beyond: Plan-D for Democracy, Dialogue and Debate' COM (2005) 494. Eurêval/Matrix/Rambøll-Management, *Evaluation of the Plan D/Debate Europe Citizen Consultation Projects Final Report* (Brussels, 2009) provides an evaluation of the programme. Note that although the programme funded deliberative experiments, the majority of funded activities under Plan D are best described as information campaigns

[32] See Kies and Nanz (eds) (n 30) for an evaluation of some of these deliberative experiments.

[33] Futurum website quoted in S Wright, 'A Virtual European Public Sphere? The Futurum Discussion Forum' (2007) 14(8) *Journal of European Public Policy* 1167.

[34] Ibid; R Wodak and S Wright, 'The European Union in Cyberspace: Multilingual Democratic Participation in a Virtual Public Sphere' (2006) 5 *Journal of Language and Politics* 251.

who spoke any of the EU's official languages was not excluded from following and contributing to discussions. As with previous national and local-level deliberative polls, significant changes in participants' policy preferences and knowledge were recorded at the end of the event.[35]

Evaluations of these different experiments provide evidence of the empowering effect of deliberative engagement on participants, a finding that replicates evidence from such democratic innovations across the world.[36] However, there was a failure on the part of organisers and European decision-makers to embed effectively any of the deliberative designs in the political decision-making process. The sense of empowerment felt by participants in this initial wave of experimentation is likely to be tempered or even dissolve as they realise that their contributions are not considered valuable by decision-makers.[37]

There is no clear evidence that any of the EU institutions receiving reports on the judgments and outputs of these deliberative experiments made any use of them – they are rarely if ever mentioned in later official justifications of related decisions. And what is abundantly clear is that there is no sense that officials have drawn together evidence from across the variety of experiments in order to learn lessons for future engagement strategies. Part of the explanation for this is because of the way in which the different innovations were funded from a range of different European programmes – it provides another vivid example of the fragmentation of this complex institution. The collective wisdom that could have been accrued from the different democratic innovations is in danger of being lost.

The emergence of the ECI is likely to crowd out much further experimentation with deliberative design. This is a shame, because one of the weaknesses of the current structure of the ECI could be ameliorated to a certain extent through complementary deliberative design. While direct and deliberative models of democracy are often viewed as competing and antagonistic, their principles and practices can be mutually supportive.[38] As noted above, one of the limitations of the current ECI is the difficulty for European decision-makers (in the first instance the Commission, which must respond formally to a valid initiative) to judge the extent of public support for a proposition. A deliberative response to this problem would be to empower a representative sample of European citizens to consider any proposition that achieved the requisite thresholds. This could be in the form of a transnational deliberative poll, which would generate considered preferences from participants, or more substantially a Citizens' Assembly of the type institutionalised in British Columbia and then Ontario to deliberate on a new electoral

[35] JS Fishkin, *When the People Speak: Deliberative Democracy and Public Consultation* (Oxford, Oxford University Press, 2009); P Isernia, J Fishkin, J Steiner and D Di Mauro, 'Toward a European Public Sphere – The Europolis Project' in Kies and Nanz (eds) (n 30).

[36] G Smith, *Democratic Innovations: Designing Institutions for Citizen Participation* (Cambridge, Cambridge University Press, 2009).

[37] J Talpin and L Monnoyer-Smith, 'Talking with the wind? Discussion on the Quality of Deliberation in the Ideal-EU project' in Kies and Nanz (eds) (n 30).

[38] M Saward, 'Making Democratic Connections: Political Equality, Deliberation and Direct Democracy' (2001) *Acta Politica* 361.

system.[39] While a particular organised interest might be able to mobilise one million signatures in support of a proposition, a transnational mini-public would then offer the Commission – and the wider European public – a considered judgment representing a diversity of perspectives from across the European citizenry. The deliberative experiments that were organised in the aftermath of the aborted Constitution indicate that such a transnational deliberative engagement is possible; and it would certainly offer significant empowering effects for participants and arguably the broader public sphere.

VI CONCLUSION

The introduction of the ECI is likely to lead to a degree of empowerment for the citizens of Europe, simply because it offers a new mechanism for placing issues on the political agenda. But this effect – both in terms of substantive impact on decision-making and citizens' perceptions of efficacy – is likely to be much less than in those polities that have embedded direct legislation. After all, the ECI is not an initiative in the general usage of the term: it does not provide an occasion for citizens to pass a binding judgement on valid propositions. But any general statement on the potential impact on citizens needs to be tempered. First, it is likely that the ECI will disempower particular minority groups if it is used to pursue anti-minority issues. And secondly, it is organised interests that will be most significantly empowered through the process rather than citizens. Organised interests will have the resources and networks necessary to raise the required number of signatures across the necessary number of Member States. Any citizen empowerment will be shaped by the activities of these interests. Thus we can recognise that the ECI embodies the *idea* of an empowered European or transnational citizenship, but *in practice* this will not be realised to the extent that the rhetoric of supporters suggests.[40] I have suggested that lessons could be learnt from the series of deliberative experiments spawned from 'the period of reflection', with space created for transnational deliberation to complement the ECI. But given that European decision-makers have failed to systematically draw lessons from these experiments, more creative democratic innovation is little more than wishful thinking at this point in time.

[39] ME Warren and H Pearse (eds), *Designing Deliberative Democracy: The British Columbia Citizens' Assembly* (Cambridge, Cambridge University Press, 2008); and Smith (n 36) ch 3.

[40] I owe this point to Jo Shaw.

13

The Legislative Initiative: A Comparative Analysis of the Domestic Experiences in EU Countries

MATT QVORTRUP

I INTRODUCTION

THE ARTICLE WAS buried on page 9 in *Le Monde* on a Saturday when the media was dominated by a US-led attack on Libya and the continuing crisis following a massive earthquake in Japan, which had led to nuclear contamination. Still it was there. The French newspaper reported how the German Social Democrats (SPD) and their colleagues in the Austrian Labour Party (SPÖ) were preparing to introduce a Bill through the 'Initiative Procedure' introduced in the Lisbon Treaty. The proposal was to force a moratorium on nuclear energy, which – in the view of the proposers – had shown itself to be unsafe in the wake of the Japanese earthquake. The French Socialist Party (PS) was not amused. The party remained – and remains – a staunch defender of nuclear energy, which is the main source of energy in France.[1] What will come of the proposal remains unknown at the time of writing. Whether we can expect development on this front is an open question. But what is interesting is that the legislative Initiative is used at all – or even contemplated.

The reason that this issue was raised at all is due to the fact that the Lisbon Treaty includes a novel provision for citizen-initiated legislation, known as the European Citizens' Initiative (ECI). According to Article 11(4) TEU, citizens can propose legislation:

> Not less than one million citizens who are nationals of a significant number of Member States may take the initiative of inviting the Commission, within the framework of its powers, to submit any appropriate proposal on matters where citizens consider that a legal act of the Union is required for the purpose of implementing the Treaties.

[1] F Lemaître, 'La gauche allemande et autrichienne veut un referendum en Europe', *Le Monde* (19 March 2011) 9.

There have been great expectations as to the effect of the new mechanism.[2] The question is whether these expectations are justified. To answer this question this chapter proposes that we adopt a comparative approach and analyse how Citizens Initiatives (CI) have worked in individual Member States.

'The ultimate goal of a positive science is the development of a "theory" or, "hypothesis" that yields valid and meaningful (i.e., not truistic) predictions about phenomena not yet observed', observed Milton Friedman.[3] This study takes this approach as its point of departure. The aim is, on the basis of a comparative analysis of EU states, to determine if the ECI is likely to have any effect in EU policy-making. We do this by analysing the experience with CIs in individual Member States.

Of the countries in the EU, there are 11 that allow citizens to propose legislation. In four of these (France, since 2008;[4] Lithuania; Latvia; Hungary) the citizens can propose a referendum on a proposed Bill. In Austria, Italy, the Netherlands, Poland and Spain, citizens can but propose legislation, which has to be enacted by the respective Parliaments. The latter system also exists in 12 of the 16 German *Länder*.[5]

In many cases these institutions of semi-direct democracy were ostensibly inspired by American state constitutions. Yet, it should not be overlooked that many of the countries had themselves discussed the introduction of the CI many years ago. Thus in Poland, in 1930, a constitutional amendment proposing the introduction of the right of legislative Initiative (subject to signatures from 100,000 Polish citizens) was proposed, but was unsuccessful.[6]

Overall, the countries that became democracies after the fall of communism are more likely to make provision for citizen-initiated legislation. Sixty per cent – or six out of the ten – post-communist EU countries have provisions for CIs. Conversely, only 29 per cent – or five out of 17 countries – in Western Europe have provisions for this device. Statistically speaking, there is a .45 Phi Correlation between post-communist democracies and the provisions for citizen-initiated legislation (significant at 0.018), perhaps indicating a distrust in representative institutions at the time of the establishment of democracy after communist rule.

But the norm is that only elected representatives, ie typically members of national or regional parliaments, can initiate legislation. Citizen involvement is foreign to most European countries, and in many ways the role of the citizen is limited to participation in local, parliamentary and presidential elections, and the odd referendum once or twice every decade.

[2] B Kaufman, A Lamassoure and J Meyer, 'Welcome to the Future of European Democracy' in B Kaufman, A Lamassoure and J Meyer (eds), *Transnational Democracy in the Making* (Amsterdam, IRI-Europe, 2004) 11.

[3] M Friedman, 'The Methodology of Positive Economics' in *Essays in Positive Economics* (Chicago, University of Chicago Press, 1966) 5.

[4] P Roger, 'La revision constitutionelle a franchi une première haie', *Le Monde* (5 June 2008) 4.

[5] T Schiller, 'Direkte Demokratie auf Bundesänder- und Kommunalebene' in M Freitag and U Wagschal (eds), *Direkte Demokratie: Bestandaufnahmen und Wirkungen im Internationalen Vergleich* (Berlin, Lit, 2007) 115.

[6] J Litawski, *Bezpo rednie ustawodawstwo ludowe* (Kraków, Drukarnia Ericha Frommera, 1932) 102.

Table 1: Citizens' Initiatives and relevant Articles regulating the right to initiate legislation in the Constitutions of EU Member States (countries with rights to initiatives indicated with 'Y').

Country	Citizen Initiative	Article in Constitution
Austria	Y	Art 41
Belgium	N	Art 61
Bulgaria	N	Art 87
Cyprus	N	Art 80
Czech Rep	N	Art 41
Denmark	N	Art 41
Estonia	N	Art 103
Finland	N	Art 70
France	N	Art 12*
Germany	N	Art 76
Greece	N	Art 73
Hungary	Y	Arts 19, 26*
Ireland	N	Art 20
Italy	Y	Art 71
Latvia	Y	Arts 72, 74*
Lithuania	Y	Art 9*
Luxembourg	N	Art 47
Malta	N	Art 73
NL	Y	Art 82
Poland	Y	Art 118
Portugal	N	Art 167
Romania	Y	Art 70
Spain	Y	Art 87
Slovakia	N	Art 88
Slovenia	Y	Art 87
Sweden	N	Art 7
UK	N	N/A

* A referendum has to be held subsequent to the enactment of the Initiative.

II A CONCEPTUAL UNDERSTANDING OF THE CITIZENS' INITIATIVE

It is useful to consider the role performed by the Initiative device. According to David Easton's much cited model[7] – especially as developed by political scientists like Almond, Dalton, Powell and Strøm[8] – the political system can be seen as an input-output model, in which groups in the surrounding environment *articulate* demands, which are channelled into the *political system* by *aggregators,* and transformed into policies (*outputs).* In the traditional structural-functional model, the role (or function) of *articulators* was performed by civic groups and trade unions.[9] The role of *aggregators* was performed by political parties that 'aggregated'[10] the views 'articulated' by organisations and civic groups.

By performing this function, the political parties ensured that concerns and demands from the environment were translated into policies.[11] Citizens' Initiatives can thus be seen as an alternative aggregator, as well as an alternative articulator, ie an alternative mechanism for channelling demands (*inputs*) into the system, but also as a mechanism for raising (*articulating*) demands.

III THE EFFECT OF THE CITIZENS' INITIATIVE

There has been considerable support for engaging citizens in initiating legislation. The OECD, for example, argued in a policy paper that governments should 'tap [into] new sources of policy-relevant ideas, information and resources when making decisions'.[12] Yet, tellingly, they did not provide a mechanism for doing so. The CI may be seen as a mechanism for increasing the input from citizens. But would it work? Indeed, has a similar mechanism worked elsewhere in Europe, at the level of Member States?

Proponents of direct democracy are prone to outline a number of positive policy benefits of the introduction of mechanisms for direct democracy.[13] Yet, to determine the direct effect of political institutions such as electoral systems, provisions for referendums or, in this case, the CI, is a difficult undertaking. Even James March and Johan P Olsen – the doyens of the new institutionalism – have noted that 'the causal relation between institutional arrangements and substan-

[7] D Easton, *A Framework for Political Analysis* (Eaglewood Cliffs, NJ, Prentice Hall, 1965) 3.

[8] GA Almond, RJ Dalton, GB Powell and K Strøm, *Comparative Politics Today: A World View* (New York, Pearson Longman, 2006) 67.

[9] Ibid, 67.

[10] Ibid, 81.

[11] Ibid, 67.

[12] OECD, 'Engaging Citizens in Policy-Making: Information, Consultation and Public Participation', *PUMA Policy Brief No 10* (2001) 1.

[13] See, generally, J Matsusaka, *For the Many or the Few: The Initiative, Public Policy and American Democracy* (Chicago, University of Chicago Press, 2004).

tive policy is complex'.[14] Perhaps it is for this reason that there are very few studies that directly look at the relationship between institutions and policy outputs.[15]

Given that political science is struggling to find a direct causal connection between institutions and policies, it would be optimistic to expect direct revolutionary changes as the result of the introduction of the CI. What we can do, however, is to look at the individual countries that provide the citizens with opportunities for petitioning legislation through CIs.

Surveying the limited literature on the effects of the CI, we find that observers have been rather sceptical, and – as I shall suggest – perhaps a bit too pessimistic as regards their efficiency. Before reaching a verdict it is useful to look at single-country studies, though it must be noted that this list is selective as linguistic difficulties make it difficult to access the information in this case.

Table 2: Signatures required for CIs in EU Member States at national level

Country	Population (millions)	Signatures required	Type of Initiative
Austria	8.1	100,000	A
France*	59.6	4,100,000	B
Hungary	10.2	50,000	B
Italy	57.6	50,000	A
Latvia	2.3	230,000	B
Lithuania	3.5	50,000	A
Netherlands	16.3	40,000	A
Poland	38.6	100,000	A
Romania	22.3	250,000	A
Slovakia	5.3	350,000	B
Slovenia	1.9	5,000	B
Spain	39.4	500,000	A

Types of Initiative: A: Citizens' Initiative. B: popular Citizens' Initiative with subsequent referendum.

* According to Art 11 of the French Constitution, a citizen-initiated referendum must be held if supported by *both* one-tenth of the voters *and* one-fifth of the members of the legislature.

Sources: National Constitutions and IRI Europe. I am grateful to Carsten Berg for information and advice when compiling this data.

[14] J March and JP Olsen, 'Elaborating the "New Institutionalism"' in RAW Rhodes, S Binder and B Rockman (eds), *The Oxford Handbook of Political Institutions* (Oxford, Oxford University Press, 2006) 8.

[15] R Taagepera and M Qvortrup, 'Who Gets What, When, How and Through Which Electoral System?' (2011) 10 *European Political Science* Issue 4.

It might be useful to go through each country's experience with CIs.

Austria is the 'godfather' of CIs in Europe. Experts in Austrian politics suggest that CIs have been used with 'diminishing effects', since 'increasingly, opposition parties have been (ab)using them [*Volksbegehren*] for their own purposes'.[16] Still, 33 of the 213 petitions put before the *Nationalrat* (Parliament) have been enacted, and six of these have been enacted in the form in which they were presented by the initiators.[17]

The situation is somewhat different in the Netherlands. There was a long debate about the introduction of mechanisms of direct democracy in the Netherlands.[18] Since its introduction in 2006, 40,000 Dutch citizens have had a right to initiate legislation (*Burgerinitiatief*). There have been 11 attempts for such an Initiative, of which six were declared inadmissible, as the *Tweede Kamer* (the lower house of the Dutch Parliament) had discussed the issue two years prior to the Initiative. Five Initiatives were successful in the sense that they resulted in a parliamentary debate. These include an Initiative in February 2007 by *Milieudefensie* (an environmentalist organisation) fighting for sustainable cattle breeding.[19] In 2010 the group 'Free Will' was successful in addressing the issue of the legalisation of hospice provision (active euthanasia); in 2011 an action group 'Platform Raise Old Age Pensions' had enough signatures to get a debate in the Second Chamber on this issue. In 2011 an interest group for people suffering from Lyme disease asked for the establishment of an expertise centre for this disease; and in July 2001,[20] a CI sponsored by the activist Henk Bres sought the banning of the controversial *Martijn* organisation (which has been accused of promoting paedophilia). The Initiative succeeded in gathering the required 40,000 signatures within 15 days and a debate was scheduled for August 2011.[21] None of these Initiatives has – as at the time of writing – resulted in legislation.

In a way, the situation in Spain is very much like that in the Netherlands: there are provisions for CIs but they are used very rarely. In Spain there are provisions for CIs at both the central and at the regional level. At the regional (*auonomias*) level there have been 172 popular Initiatives registered up to 30 April 2007.[22] At the national level there have been nine Initiatives that have been formally debated in the Plenary Session of Congress. To date, the only popular Initiative approved by the national Parliament was related to the 'claim of community debts',

[16] A Pelinka and S Greiderer, 'Austria: The Referendum as an Instrument of Internationalisation' in M Gallagher and P V Uleri (eds), *The Referendum Experience in Europe* (London, Macmillan, 1996) 21.

[17] F Rehmet, 'Volkspetitionen. Praxis und Wirkungen. Das Beispiel der unverbindlichen Volksbegehren in Österreich', Mehr Demokratie e.V., Diskussionspapiere und Untersuchungen, No 16 (14 November 2003).

[18] J Van Holsteyn, 'The Netherlands: National Debates and Local Experience' in Gallagher and Uleri (n 16).

[19] See, generally, J McCarthy-Groen, *Het burgerinitiatief: een verkennend onderzoek naar een 8-tal burgerinitiatieven in enkele Nederlandse gemeenten* (Heerlen, Open Universiteit Nederland, 2006).

[20] J van Holsteyn, University of Leiden, personal communication (14 May 2011).

[21] J van Holsteyn, University of Leiden, personal communication (13 July 2011).

[22] See, generally, V Cuesta Lopez, *Participación directa e iniciativa legislativa del ciudadano en democracia constitucional* (Madrid, Civitas, 2008).

promoted by the Federation of Professional Land Agents.[23] Conversely, the autonomous legislative assemblies have taken into consideration fifteen out of the thirty-nine propositions voted on.[24]

The Spanish provisions for CIs grew out of the process of democratisation that started after the fall of the dictatorship. The provision for CIs in Poland is a result of a similar process of democratisation, though the mechanism has been slightly more successful in Poland than in Spain. As of 2005, the procedure had been used 55 times. The 'legislative procedures initiated by people have resulted in adopting statutes in seven cases',[25] and resulted in six instances of primary legislation, mainly in the areas of occupational health and the environment. In Poland the CI has mostly been used to enact legislation that none of the parties, for different reasons, were willing to sponsor. Thus a law on the regulation of pharmaceutical products in 2003 would have been unlikely to be enacted had it not been for the pressure generated by the Initiative process.[26]

Italy is not unlike Poland. A total of 213 *iniziative di legge* were proposed from 1948 to 2005, of which 29 (13 per cent) resulted in legislation.[27] It is not, therefore, entirely accurate to conclude, as Uleri did in a study from 1996, that 'there has been very limited use of this institution, which has had little significance'.[28] The signature requirement is 50,000 voters. In neighbouring Slovenia – a country that has otherwise used mechanisms of direct democracy extensively – CIs have not taken off. Here a mere 5,000 people can propose a law (Article 58 of the Slovenian Constitution) provided they can gather the signatures within 60 days. Yet, they have done so rarely.[29] According to the search tool of the Slovenian National Assembly, out of the 6,245 adopted laws and proposed laws in *Parlament Slovenije*, only three cases were CIs.[30]

In addition to these countries, the CI is used extensively at the *Land* level in Germany. As all of the *Länder* have populations that exceed the smallest States in the EU, it makes sense to include this experience in our overview. All the States have provisions for CIs. Of 103 valid *Volksinitiativen* that have been proposed, 31 have been (at least partly) accepted by parliaments.[31] Most of the enactments until

[23] F Astarloa-Villena, 'La iniciativa legislativa popular en España' (2009) *Teoría y Realidad Constitucional*, No 10–11, 2º semestre 2002 – 1er semestre, 273.

[24] I am grateful for comments by Luis Bouza García (Robert Gordon University) on this section.

[25] A Rytel-Warzocha, 'Popular Initiatives in Poland: Citizens' Empowerment or Keeping up Appearances?' in T Schiller and M Setälä (eds), *Citizens' Initiatives in Europe: Procedures and Consequences of Agenda-Setting by Citizens* (Basingstoke, Palgrave, 2011) 9.

[26] Ibid, 6.

[27] www.democracy-international.org/italian-initiative.html.

[28] PV Uleri, 'Italy: Referendums and Initiatives from the Origins to the Crisis of a Democratic Regime' in Gallagher and Uleri (n 16) 107.

[29] I am grateful to Dr Tomaž Deželan from the University of Ljubljana for this information and other insights into Slovenian politics.

[30] T Deželan, M Sever and A Jakulin, 'Analiza kohezijskih vzorcev Državnega zbora Republike Slovenije v obdobju od leta 1994 do leta 2008. dinamika s potencialom krepitve parlamentarne dimenzije Evropske unije?' *Teor. praksa*, Jan–Apr 2009, letn 46, št 1/2, str 161–78.

[31] T Schiller, 'Direkte Demokratie auf Bundesänder- und Kommunalebene' in Freitag and Wagschal (eds) (n 5) 112.

2006 (34 per cent) concerned education and culture; the second highest number (28 per cent) concerned democratic reforms.[32] There are some indications that the use of the mechanism has led to more political engagement at the *Land* level, but most of the evidence is anecdotal.[33] The signature requirement ranges between 2 per cent of the voters in Bremen, to signatures from 50,000 voters in Rhineland-Palatine.[34]

IV ASSESSMENT OF THE CITIZENS' INITIATIVE

In many ways, the CI is – at least on paper – a weak weapon. The problem with the device is that parliaments are in no way legally obliged to take action, and the political pressure is often not strong enough for a group to apply pressure on the elected representatives. If a parliament – or even just a majority thereof – has a stated interest in a project, even an unpopular one, the CI is of little use. This was obvious in Austria in 1982, when the *Nationalrat* 'ignored a petition signed by over 1.3 million electors against construction of an additional United Nations Conference Centre, and so took no heed of the demand not to construct it'.[35] Yet, other proposals have arguably had an impact: 'the 353,906 signatures to a 1985 petition opposing the construction of a hydro-power dam on the Danube certainly played a part in persuading the government to scrap the plan'.[36]

Another example of the use of CIs to get an issue on the agenda is the debate about female parliamentary representation in Poland. Women currently make up 20 per cent of Polish members of parliament and just 8 per cent of Polish senators. The idea of parity is supported, not only by women or feminist activists. Among those who spoke in its favour were Oscar-winning director Andrzej Wajda, the government's economic advisor Michal Boni and the President of the European Parliament Jerzy Buzek. President Lech Kaczynski announced he would sign the Bill if it passes through both chambers of Parliament.

Proponents of the Initiative collected 150,000 signatures in support. Opponents of the Bill, including the government's plenipotentiary for equal status, claimed that imposing a gender quota in such an artificial way is offensive to women and ineffective (while others claimed that women should not be given power they are not ready to handle yet). The proposal came to nothing. Yet it raised an issue that would probably not otherwise have been discussed.[37]

But talk is cheap. It would seem to be a fatal limitation that voters cannot force parliaments to act. Surely, or so one would think, it would be better to have the

[32] Ibid, 115.

[33] I am grateful to Carsten Berg for information and advice on this section.

[34] www.mehr-demokratie.de.

[35] A Pelinka and S Greiderer, 'Austria: The Referendum as an Instrument of Internationalisation' in Gallagher and Uleri (n 16) 21.

[36] www.bbc.co.uk/news/world-europe-11791272.

[37] *Polskie Radio*: www.thenews.pl/national/artykul125873_citizens-initiative-on-female-representation.html.

actual Initiative, as in Hungary, Latvia, Lithuania and (although in more limited circumstances) France.[38] Yet the evidence seems to suggest otherwise.

If we measure success by statutes enacted – not an unreasonable requirement! – we find that there are many more examples of CIs resulting in primary legislation than there are citizen-initiated referendums resulting in the same. Hungary, Latvia and Lithuania are the only European countries in which the citizen-initiated referendums have been successfully employed. But the record is modest at best. Indeed only three laws have been enacted through Initiatives and referendums, and of these only one (namely in the referendum on direct election to the presidency in 1989 in Hungary) was fully implemented. To be sure, the citizen-initiated referendum can send a strong signal to the powers-that-be, as was the case with the *Fidesz*-(then opposition party's) sponsored referendum on the abolition of tuition fees and fees for primary health care in 2008. The referendum passed by 80 per cent – but the government said that it was unable to find funds to pay for the services.

The same is true for Lithuania and Latvia. Although there have been, respectively, three and two citizen-initiated referendums since 1990, none of these have passed. This, admittedly, is partly due to the stipulation that turnout must be at least 50 per cent for the result to stand. The referendum on 'funds from privatization' (in Lithuania in 1996) thus gained the support of 52 per cent of the voters, but failed as the turnout was only 38 per cent. Yet turnout was not to blame in the other two referendums in this country, on 'illegal privatization' (1994) and on the Ignalina Power Plant (2008), which failed to win majority support despite dire warnings from politicians.[39]

The record is equally unimpressive in Latvia. Consider the experience of the referendum on the Security Law (2007) – a referendum sponsored by President Vaira Vike-Frieberga to block Parliament's security law, which would have given the law-makers controversial access to otherwise classified security information. Citizens gathered signatures for a referendum, and succeeded in getting the support of the required 230,000 citizens. Although the referendum was won, the outcome was nullified as it did not meet the 50 per cent turnout requirement. However, despite the referendum legally failing, Parliament withdrew the law.

In Lithuania and Latvia, as in Hungary – and as in citizen-initiated referendums in Uruguay[40] and New Zealand[41] – the provision has been used to propose populist measures, such as the proposal that a certain percentage of the social security spending should constitute at least half of the national budget in both Uruguay and Lithuania and a freezing of pensions in Latvia. Such proposals –

[38] R Roger, 'La revision constitutionelle a franchi une première haie', *Le Monde* (5 June 2008) 4.

[39] See, generally, http://diepresse.com/home/wirtschaft/international/421400/Litauen_Gehen-ohne-Atom-die-Lichter-aus?_vl_backlink=/home/index.do.

[40] M Qvortrup, 'Uruguay's Constitutional Referendum' (1997) 16 *Electoral Studies* 549.

[41] M Qvortrup, 'Citizen Initiated Referendums (CIR) in New Zealand: A Comparative Appraisal' (2008) 44 *Representation* 69–78.

especially when they have not received a ringing endorsement – are comparatively easy to ignore, and governments have frequently done so, as indeed they did in Hungary on the issue of the law on double citizenship in 2004.

The situation is generally rather different with CIs. Given that they have actually led to legislation in all the countries that allow citizens to propose legislation it is difficult to argue that the more extensive and (on paper) more radical provision of citizen-initiated referendums would be more effective. The CI, perhaps precisely *because* it needs to be ratified by parliament, is less likely to be used to propose outlandish and unrealistic proposals. Generally speaking, CIs have been used to introduce – and in some cases enact – legislation that political parties did not wish to propose.

This was certainly true in Poland, where the Bills adopted have included a law about retaining national control over strategic resources in 1999.[42] Further, a committee created by the Trade Union of Polish Teachers (ZNP) prepared a draft law which aimed at changing rules for determining salaries for teachers by introducing a centralised wage system. The Initiative was successful as the citizens' proposal was adopted by the Parliament only four months after the first reading of the Bill.[43]

The same types of mundane issues have been the subject of the CIs in Italy. Here an *iniziative di legge populare* on the strengthening of children's rights (1983), the retirement age (1988) and regulation of organ transplants (1999) are but some of the examples of successful CIs.[44]

In general, it seems that laws which have resulted from the process have frequently concerned mundane and relatively uncontroversial issues, as in the Austrian CI on smaller class sizes (*Volksbegehren zur Senkung der Klassenschülerzahl*) in 1989[45] – though it should be noted that legislation to introduce the 40-hour working week was introduced not through the initiative of Parliament but as a result of a CI in 1969, namely, the *Schrittweise Einführung der 40-Stunden-Woche* (literally: 'the gradual introduction of the 40-hour week'). The word 'gradual' (*Schrittweise*) is not, it seems, accidental!

The Spanish experience points towards a greater use of CIs in issues concerning environmental issues and industrial relations. This is particularly true at the regional level. Thus, almost half of the Initiatives adopted (seven out of 15) were related to environmental protection. The Parliament of the Canary Islands approved three laws originating from CIs, which all concerned different aspects of the protection of different natural areas of the islands. The remaining Initiatives related to environmental protection were approved by the legislative assemblies of Aragón, Catalonia, Galicia and the Balearic Islands.[46] We might hypothesise

[42] A Rytel, 'The Popular Initiative in Poland', Institute of Constitutional Law and Political Institutions, University of Gdansk (8 May 2006).

[43] A Rytel-Warzocha (n 25) 10.

[44] www.c2d.ch.

[45] See www.bmi.gv.at/cms/BMI_wahlen/volksbegehren/Alle_Volksbegehren.aspx.

[46] Cuesta Lopez (n 22) 1.

Table 3: Initiatives and treatment in the Polish Parliament (1999–2009).

Year	Initiatives launched	Proposal formally correct or successfully reformulated*	Signatures submitted	Handed to the parliament**	Rejected in the 1st reading	Procedure finished due to delaying***	Enacted by the parliament	**Initiatives still in the committees Dec 2010**
1999	1	1	1	1			1	
2000	10	7	3	1		2	1	
2001	4	3	3	3		1		
2002	12	11	3	3		2	1	
2003	11	9	4	3		1	2	
2004	12	9	5	5		4	1	
2005	5	4						
2006	5	5	1	1				1
2007	–							
2008	10	6	4	4	1		1	2
2009	9	6	3	3	2			1
total	**79**	**61**	**27**	**24**	**3**	**10**	**7**	**4**

* 18 Initiatives were rejected because the proposal was formally incorrect and the required changes were not made.

** In 3 cases the signatures were submitted but they were declared as non-valid.

*** End of the following parliamentary terms of office.

Source: A Rytel-Warzocha, 'Popular Initiatives in Poland: Citizens Empowerment or Keeping Up Appearances?' in T Schiller and M Setälä (eds), *Citizens' Initiatives in Europe: Procedures and Consequences of Agenda-Setting by Citizens* (Basingstoke, Palgrave, 2011).

that the lack a genuine Green Party in both Spain and Austria, meant that demand for environmental legislation did not go through the party-political channels and that the CI performed the function of an alternative aggregator that swept up demands articulated by the citizens. The same pattern might explain why industrial relations legislation was demanded and passed.[47]

Slovenia is the only country where the CI has been used to enact more substantial legislation. Thus in 2005 the Student Association of Slovenia, *Študentska organizacija Slovenije*, was able to ensure an amendment of the Personal Income Tax Act. The amendment that was successfully adopted was about the taxation of the student (and for secondary school pupils) incomes from student work, in other words, a technical and ideologically uncontroversial change, which fits the general picture that the CI is used to enact uncontroversial legislation.

Does this mean that we should endorse the CI? There have been a fair number of warnings against the introduction of such measures. Stephen Loe Strachey, one of the proponents of direct democracy in the United Kingdom, criticised the Initiative proper:

> Under the initiative, you do not get the committee stage for legislation. The stage under which trained advocates, critics and lawyers debate the clauses of the Bill and render it workable in practice as well as sound in theory. The initiative is an encouragement to crude legislative schemes . . . The fact is the initiative, though it may very well suit a small community . . . does not suit a great and complicated modern community with a vast number of laws already on the statute book.[48]

This objection to citizen-initiated referendums – which perhaps paints too rosy a picture of the power and wisdom of parliamentary committees[49] – does not, however, cut a lot of proverbial ice with CIs. For this device – as opposed to citizen-initiated referendums – does indeed allow parliamentary committees to scrutinise the proposals and thus make them 'workable in practice'. The CI, while not a revolutionary mechanism, has thus been instrumental in providing an outlet for pent-up grievances, as well as providing a mechanism that has allowed citizens to get legislation on the statute book that parliament would not otherwise have enacted. All this could, as I have suggested elsewhere, be analysed using a 'setter' model.[50] The CI is successful if the proposals fall within the 'win-set' of both parliament and initiators. The reason why citizen-initiated referendums fail is because they result in outcomes that fall outside the win-set of the legislature. But a more formal analysis of this type is beyond the scope of this chapter.

[47] Astarloa-Villena (n 23).

[48] J St Loe Strachey, *The Referendum: A Handbook on the Poll of the People, the Referendum and the Democratic Right to Veto* (London, Fischer, 1924) 29.

[49] N Polsby, 'Legislatures' in F Greenstein and N Polsby (eds), *Handbook of Political Science Vol 5: Government Institutions and Processes* (Reading MA, Addison-Wesley, 1975) 257.

[50] M Qvortrup 'United Kingdom: Extreme Institutional Dominance by the Executive . . . Most of the Time', in G Tsebelis and BE Rasch (eds), *The Role of Governments in Legislative Agenda Setting* (London, Routledge, 2011) 78.

Of course, it is methodologically unsound to simply extrapolate from these experiences at the national level to the qualitatively different set of circumstances at the EU level. The lack of a genuine EU-wide political debate, the linguistic barriers and – at least for the time being – different political cultures mean that the factors that have generated CIs in single countries are unlikely – under the present circumstances – to be replicated at the pan-European level. Indeed, the fact that the aforementioned attempt by the Austrian and German Social Democrats originated in two countries using the same language, and was uncoordinated with like-minded parties in other EU countries, might be an indication that the ECI may fare less well when introduced at the supranational level.[51] But the fact that CIs – contrary to expectations – have been successful in getting legislation enacted perhaps suggests that we should refrain from dismissing the device too quickly.

V CONCLUSION

This chapter has found evidence to suggest that the CI – though on paper a weak mechanism – has had direct effect and has led to the enactment of primary legislation. Somewhat counter-intuitively, the CI has, in fact, been more successful than citizen-initiated referendums such as those in Hungary, Latvia and Lithuania.

There are many examples (dozens, in fact) of CIs that have resulted in primary legislation in Poland, Italy, Austria and Spain, as well as at the *Land* level in Germany. More than 40 measures have been enacted as a result of CIs. Conversely, there are only a couple of citizen-initiated referendums that have resulted in primary legislation (both in Hungary). The fact that citizens have proposed realistic and constructive – as well as popular – proposals means that the CI has arguably had more success than more radical provisions.

Whether the same pattern can be expected at the EU level will depend upon the regulation of the device, yet there is nothing that suggests that the ECI will be ineffectual. Sceptics might still question the usefulness of this device. The CI is clearly not a panacea, however nor has it had negative consequences. It has worked in its own little way in giving citizens a voice where otherwise they would have had none. Sometimes good things come in small packages.

Appendix: In Which Countries are there Provisions for Citizens' Initiatives?

The question arises whether there is a pattern of where the CI occurs. Based on so-called logistic regression analysis, there is statistical evidence to suggest that provisions for CIs are more common in countries with fewer parties. Measuring the number of political parties can be a relatively subjective endeavour and there

[51] I owe this insight to Dr Charlotte O'Brien (University of York).

has been a considerable debate over which parties to count. Following standard convention, we can use the Laakso-Taagepera Index[52] and then correlate this figure with a dichotomous variable (1=provisions for CIs; 0=no provisions for CIs). The hypothesis is that the lower the effective number of (parliamentary) parties, the lower the probability that the country will have – statistically speaking – provisions for the CI. Of course, it is equally possible to hypothesise that the device is mainly a characteristic of newly democratised countries, ie that the CI was introduced during the time of the fall of communism as a part of the enthusiasm for more democratic involvement, which characterised the 1989 Revolutions. Both these hypotheses can be tested using logistic regression analysis, using the data set out in Table 1.

A logistic regression analysis allows us to measure the probability of a relationship between the existence of a phenomenon, in this case the CI, and a number of other factors. Based on the figures contained in Table 1, we can conclude that there is a statistically significant relationship between the number of parties and the provisions for CIs. Table 4 outlines the results of the logistic regression.

Table 4: Logistic Regression Model: Factors contributing to provisions for Citizens' Initiatives

		B	S.E.	Wald	Df	Sig.	Exp(B)
Step 1*	ENP	–1.584	.683	5.376	1	.020	.205
	PostCom	2.697	1.535	3.087	1	.079	14.836
	Constant	3.512	1.898	3.423	1	.064	33.503

* Variable(s) entered on step 1: ENP, PostCom.

While this model is not the final word on the matter – statistical models never are – we can conclude that the model is significant Chi-square (6, N=29) = 64.32), p<.002. This indicates that the model was able to distinguish between countries that have provisions for CIs and countries that do not. The model as a whole explained between .67 per cent (*Cox and Snell R Square*) and 100 per cent (*Nagelkerte R-Squared*) of the variance in the results. The model correctly classified 71.1 per cent of cases. However, of the two variables tested only the effective number of parties made a unique statistical contribution to the model (ie p<.02). There is no strong indication that CIs are more prevalent in countries that have enacted constitutions after the fall of communism, as the Post-Communist Dummy was not statistically significant at the 95 per cent level normally required in quantitative analyses. Why CIs are more prevalent in polities with fewer parties is another question that requires further research.

[52] M Laakso and R Taagepera, '"Effective" Number of Parties: A Measure with Application to West Europe' (1979) 12 *Comparative Political Studies* 3.

Index